The Gift of Freedom

NEXT WAVE: NEW DIRECTIONS IN WOMEN'S STUDIES

A series edited by Inderpal Grewal, Caren Kaplan, and Robyn Wiegman

MIMI THI NGUYEN

The Gift
of Freedom

WAR, DEBT, AND
OTHER REFUGEE
PASSAGES

Duke University Press   Durham and London   2012

© 2012 Duke University Press
All rights reserved
Printed in the United States of America
on acid-free paper ♾
Designed by C. H. Westmoreland
Typeset in Minion with Stone Sans display
by Keystone Typesetting, Inc.
Library of Congress Cataloging-in-
Publication Data appear on the last printed
page of this book.

FOR MY PARENTS, HIEP AND LIEN,
AND MY BROTHER, GEORGE

CONTENTS

PREFACE

Rebuilding Iraq will require a sustained commitment from many nations, including our own: we will remain in Iraq as long as necessary, and not a day more.
America has made and kept this kind of commitment before — in the peace that
followed a world war. After defeating enemies, we did not leave behind occupying armies, we left constitutions and parliaments. We established an atmosphere
of safety, in which responsible, reform-minded local leaders could build lasting
institutions of freedom. In societies that once bred fascism and militarism, liberty
found a permanent home.
                              —GEORGE W. BUSH, February 26, 2003

And there we are, ready to run the great Yankee risk.
So, once again, be careful!
American domination — the only domination from which one never recovers.
I mean from which one never recovers unscarred.
                              —AIMÉ CÉSAIRE, *Discourse on Colonialism*

In a televised address from the Oval Office on August 31, 2010, President
Barack Obama declared the U.S. combat mission in Iraq ended, over seven
years after it began: "Operation Iraqi Freedom is over, and the Iraqi people
now have lead responsibility for the security of their country." Outlining
an accelerated timetable for complete troop withdrawal by the end of the
following year, and the subsequent transfer of security functions to Iraqi
forces, Obama continued solemnly:

Ending this war is not only in Iraq's interest—it is in our own. The United
States has paid a huge price to put the future of Iraq in the hands of its
people. We have sent our young men and women to make enormous sacrifices in Iraq, and spent vast resources abroad at a time of tight budgets at
home. We have persevered because of a belief we share with the Iraqi people
—a belief that out of the ashes of war, a new beginning could be born in this

cradle of civilization. Through this remarkable chapter in the history of the United States and Iraq, we have met our responsibility. Now, it is time to turn the page.[1]

The preoccupations at the heart of this statement (and those statements that have come before and after), including responsibility, history, and sacrifice, also capture for us something crucial about the force of time, war, and freedom, and a feeling for them—and so, the observance through these terms of the gifts that pass between an *us* and a *them*, and the debt that follows. The prerequisites for "Iraqi freedom" are now secured at an incalculable cost to the United States, here the steward of human perfectibility and progress, and its consequent achievement is the obligation of racial, colonial others. On the following day, September 1, the operational name for the U.S. presence in Iraq was changed to "Operation New Dawn," to name the Iraqi peoples' hard-won return to the continuous history of the world.

What, to borrow from Judith Butler, is the frame for this war?[2] On the one hand, the transition from one operation to another appears to occasion not much at all. Despite so-called endings, 50,000 remaining U.S. troops once classified as combat units are designated anew as "advise and assist brigades," though the practicum that determines each set of duties is not wholly distinguishable, as troops continue to engage in combat and counterterrorism operations. Even with complete withdrawal in December 2011, the U.S. presence in Iraq is transferred from the military to the State Department, which aims to maintain a 18,000-strong contingent in the country, including thousands of armed private contractors (or mercenaries) to man "enduring presence posts." Occupation, we see, is not ended. On the other hand, that liberal peace is not distinct from liberal war is indeed an urgent predicament. Since September 2001, when Congress passed the Authorization for Use of Military Force against Terrorists Act, the United States has pursued ever-expansive state powers to underwrite the aggressive prosecution of a permanent war. Indeed, withdrawal from Iraq underwrote the intensification of the U.S. military presence in Afghanistan, Pakistan, and Yemen, including airstrikes and targeted assassinations. (We might set side by side the practices of Iraqification with Vietnamization, disavowing the final future of freedom, as well as the conclusion of war, while maintaining or even escalating violence in targeted zones.) As of this writing, the United States is embroiled in scores of martial adventures; in 2010 alone, U.S. Special Operations forces were reportedly deployed for preemptive or retaliatory strikes in seventy-five countries—including the Philippines, Columbia, Yemen, Somalia, and elsewhere in Africa and Central Asia—in what one counterinsurgency advisor has called "an almost industrial-scale counterterrorism killing machine."[3] War further annexes "homeland security"; the domestic front is now contiguous with the battlefield and recruited to a state of permanent potential paramilitarization. The 2012 National Defense Authorization Act codified into law those powers the Bush and Obama administrations had until now claimed as emergency actions for the conduct and intensification of a global war on terror (including indefinite detention, among other programs). Toward this end, the United States as the uncontested superpower on the world stage today instrumentalizes an idea of human freedom as a universal value, and intensifies an administrative and bureaucratic legality as its rational order to reinforce a politics of war, terror, and occupation. We therefore find in the passage between liberal peace and liberal war a "zone of indistinction," to borrow Giorgio Agamben's phrase.[4] Because war is no longer finite—no more a violent event "out there," but instead a vital presence permeating our everyday—we might say that the transition between war and peace is rule by multiple and mutable means. Nor can we yet know this project in its totality (though we know that there are more refugees, and more deaths, being created through both war and peace making), especially because we are still caught in the terrible engines of modernity—perfectibility and progress.

Edward Said observed in the preface to the twenty-fifth anniversary edition of *Orientalism*: "Every single empire in its official discourse has said that it is not like all the others, that its circumstances are special, that it has a mission to enlighten, civilize, bring order and democracy, and that it uses force only as a last resort."[5] The task before us is to theorize the significant ways in which liberal war and liberal peace as conjoined operations proceed under the *signs* of exception and emergency, and which are neither. Especially with never-ending war on the horizon, it is more crucial than ever to understand how the exception is foundational to liberal empire, while tropes of *transition* and *timetable* in fact prolong the duration of war, terror, and occupation. How then do we parse the seeming paradox in which U.S. military interventions are described through beneficence and defense, and at the same time demand occupations and dislocations of racial, colonial others in the name of the human, through invocations of peace, protection, rights, democracy, freedom, and security? I describe the premise of a global power that perceives that its self-interest is secured by granting to an other the advantage of human freedom as the gift of freedom, and it is the purpose of this book not only to explore some part of the historical emergence of the gift of freedom as a story about the emergence of U.S. global hegemony from the Cold War in general, and the hot war in Viet Nam in particular, but also to rethink the significant collocations of war and peace, bondage and freedom, that organize contemporary structures of liberalism in an age of empire. Thus, *The Gift of Freedom* endeavors to provide a diagnostic of our present in order to retheorize the terrible press of freedom and its histories unfolding asymmetrically across the globe through the structures and sensibilities of modern racial governmentality and liberalism's empire.[6]

In this attempt to engage the past and near future of empire, I argue the gift of freedom is not simply a ruse for liberal war but its core proposition, and a particularly apt name for its operations of violence and power. It is for this reason that this book brings together in the preface's epigraphs President George W. Bush's declaration that "America" leaves not occupying armies, but constitutions and parliaments, with Aimé Césaire's observation that from "American" domination, one never recovers unscarred. (Half of the world's refugees today are fleeing from the U.S. wars of freedom in Iraq and Afghanistan.[7]) In and against the spirit of a "new dawn," *The Gift of Freedom* follows from the ashes of war to understand the cumulative repercussions of enduring freedom (the name, of course, of the U.S. war in Afghanistan), a phrasing that suggests both freedom's duration and also duress. From these ashes rises the afterlife of empire as the promise that presses the moving target into the shape of "finally" human, and as the debt that demands and defers repayment from those subjects of freedom who are even now emerging from the ruins. This book is thus addressed to those crisscrossing histories of our presents in order to reckon with ghosts among us, life after death, the future of life, and more deaths to come.

ACKNOWLEDGMENTS

It is perhaps obvious to say that the present work is also a refugee passage, though the route it follows is long and winding, and has no single origin. That said, I cannot begin to acknowledge enough the enduring imprint of my first and most influential interlocutor, Caren Kaplan, whose unfailing friendship and insight have been crucial for me in forms traceable, and as yet unfathomable. To her I also owe my greatest debt as a scholar, a debt I gladly bear into the future. For nearly as long, Inderpal Grewal has been an encouraging and critical commentator, whose brilliant scholarship and deep commitment to the field formation of women and gender studies I hope to honor on my own path. As well, Elaine Kim has been unstinting with her warm and wise counsel, and her intellectual perspicuity and professional generosity are an inspiration. I thank Caren, Inderpal, and Elaine for their ongoing commitment to engage both ethical obligation and critical inquiry in necessary collaboration with others. What good I do as a scholar, a colleague, and a teacher, I owe to their examples.

This book's first incarnations were generously encouraged by May Joseph and George Yudice during my brief time in the American studies doctoral program at New York University. Among my cohort there, I recall with particular fondness Kimberly Johnson, Kristen Elliot Hood, Jerry Philogene, Alondra Nelson, and especially Thuy Linh Nguyen Tu, who is both a good friend and a sympathetic collaborator. In the ethnic studies graduate program at the University of California, Berkeley, I am thankful for Sau-Ling Wong, whose kindness as a graduate advisor I remember well; Michael Omi, who greeted my sometimes wild-eyed discourse with good humor; and Patricia Penn Hilden, whose rigor and conviction that theory must be made to matter so informed this project. For demonstrating collegiality and commitment (as well as sharing antics), I thank David Hernandez, Harriet Skye, Karina Cespedes, Steven Lee, Irene Nexica, Kathy Yep, Mercy Romero, Robert Soza, Matt Richardson, and Oliver Wang.

Vernadette Vicuña Gonzalez in particular is a comrade in arms, and to her I am beholden not only for her enduring friendship and her insights into empire, but also the good timing that brought forth at once our completed dissertations and my beautiful, brilliant goddaughter Inez.

I consider myself lucky to have as my colleagues in the Asian American Studies Program and the Gender and Women's Studies Department at the University of Illinois, Urbana-Champaign, Nancy Abelmann, Teresa Barnes, C. L. Cole, Augusto Espiritu, Karen Flynn, Stephanie Foote, Samantha Frost, Pat Gill, Moon-Kie Jung, Susan Koshy, Esther Lee, Vicki Mahaffey, Martin F. Manalansan IV, Cris Mayo, Erik McDuffie, Chantal Nadeau, Lisa Nakamura, Kent Ono, Yoon Pak, Sarah Projansky, Junaid Rana, Siohban Somerville, Sharra Vostral, and Caroline Yang. Among other colleagues across the colleges, I am also glad for Susan Becker, Jodi Byrd, Isabel Molina-Guzman, Edna Viruell-Fuentes, and Deke Weaver. Without the dedicated staff, I would be much poorer at this labor. My thanks to Jennifer Chung, Mary Ellerbe, Viveka Kudaligama, and Piavanh Sengsavanh in Asian American Studies, and Jacque Kahn, Virginia Swisher, and April Thomas in Gender and Women's Studies. I received generous support as an Andrew Mellon Postdoctoral Fellow at the Rackham School of Graduate Studies and Women's Studies at the University of Michigan, Ann Arbor. There, my office mate, Melanie Boyd, offered both good humor and lively conversation during this initial foray into the Midwest. Other support for this project was generously provided by multiple grants from the Research Board at the University of Illinois and the Asian American Studies Consortium of the Committee for Institutional Cooperation, which funded a manuscript workshop at the University of Illinois. Kandice Chuh and Laura Hyun Yi Kang generously read drafts and provided both scrupulously attentive comments and much-needed encouragement at a critical juncture.

As academics we cast wide nets, and though I am separated from some friends and colleagues by long distances, I appreciate those things—times, meals, ideas—we share. Many of the Asian American studies postdoctoral fellows at the University of Illinois have kept company with me during the years, and I often wish I could gather them closer now, including Naomi Paik and Bianca Isaki, who both spent time with parts of this manuscript, and the backyard grill; and Kimberly Alidio, Victor Mendoza, Cynthia Marasigan, and Elda Tsou, who all provided glad fellowship and occasional chocolates on the second floor. Kirstie Dorr and Sara Clark Kaplan brought Berkeley to Champaign for a brief time, and Minh-Ha Pham, with whom I coauthor *Threadbared*, is my partner in new feminist publics. I thank as well Vivek Bald, Toby Beauchamp, Cynthia Degnan, Christina Hanhardt, Yumi Lee, Nhi Lieu, L. J. Martin, Mike Masatsugu, Golnar Nikpour, Erica Rand, Beth Stinson, and Craig Willse for cerebral and subcultural camaraderie. Lauren Berlant, David Eng, Minoo Moallem, Louisa Schein, and Jennifer Terry offer kind words and encouragement whenever our paths cross one another's. Among my former undergraduate students, Stephanie Murphy and Elizabeth Verklan together broke the mold. Far-flung friend and collaborator Mariam Beevi Lam never fails to impress me with her agile mind, and to her I am thankful for unstinting support and buoyant good humor.

Many others shared with me their love and friendship during the years of writing this book. During graduate school, the *Maximumrocknroll* compound was a second home, and I am grateful for the crucial reminder that we can do it ourselves. Whether green-taping records, hauling bulk mail bundles, or just hanging out at the house or show, Arwen Curry has ever been an incisive and imaginative interlocutor on matters intellectual, political, fantastical, musical. Mark Murrmann has been a stalwart friend for road trips, pinball marathons, and rock 'n' roll. Jennifer Allen, a fellow traveler, taught me invaluable lessons in generous self-care and graceful movement through a sometimes-wearying world. And, to the countless friends whose fierce passions and politics continue to inspire me, I say, "Up the punks!"

Among my colleagues I also found good friends whose generosity and goodwill sustain me. While this list of their virtues is necessarily partial, nonetheless I wish to thank Stephen Hocker for devastating desserts and sly jokes; Dustin Allred for an impeccable aesthetic and wry disposition; Mireya Loza for thrifting adventures and bumping it freestyle; Ian Sprandel for glad fellowship in nerddom; Ruth Nicole Brown for her strength of spirit and commitment to girl genius; David Coyoca for late-night ruminations on human natures and postcolonial fictions; Isabel Molina-Guzman for her openhanded counsel as well as her boundless compassion; Lisa Marie Cacho for her ethical compass and horticultural aptitude; and Soo Ah Kwon for an even-keeled outlook and unwavering solidarity. I must also thank the small people, including Max for sharing so generously with me chocolate cake and butter chicken, Blake for bookending our workdays with his sly smile and mischief making, and Luciano for brightening the last days of copyedits with his elemental presence. Last, but not at all least, I am grateful to Yutian Wong, who is a paragon for her buoyant, savvy intelligence in all things.

Ken Wissoker has been a tireless champion of this manuscript from its earliest incarnations, even when I was not. To him I extend heartfelt gratitude for editorial guidance and support. At various stages, Anitra Grisales, Mandy Earley, Jade Brooks, and Mark Mastromarino provided cheerful, calming navigation through the labyrinthine publishing process. Beth Stinson and Rachel Lauren Storm rescued me during panicked moments and completed the bibliography and endnotes with good cheer. Hong-An Truong generously provided me with stills from *Explosions in the Sky* and permission to reproduce them, while Hellen Jo illustrated so well the beautiful, but oh-so sinister, presence on this book's paperback cover. I also thank the two anonymous readers at Duke University Press for their insightful reviews and concomitant belief in this manuscript, and the Next Wave series editors, Inderpal Grewal, Caren Kaplan, and Robyn Wiegman, for accepting me to their roster.

From my parents, Hiep and Lien Nguyen, I received unwavering love and unconditional, if sometimes worried, support for their wayward daughter. From their example, I learned at a young age to push for more than what is given, and to protect that which is truly important. The consequences at times caused them concern, but these gifts are how I understand what I am to do each day. To them, I will always be indebted, which is no doubt just what they intended. The generous and steadfast friendship of my brother and oldest ally, George, has sustained me through every stage of my journey, and this project. Gina Fan is the kindest sister-in-law I could hope for, welcoming me whenever my wandering heart brings me home. Though we share no blood, Iraya Robles is the soul sister of my heart, and our almost twenty-year-old friendship is a source of constant renewal and pleasure. Smallest but hardly least among those closest to me, Morton always knows my need for an enormous cat to sit on my hands or chest, or to accompany me when I take a turn around the room.

Fiona I. B. Ngô is my heart. The passage that brought me through the final writing of the book and beyond would not have been possible without her love, her luminous insight. There are not enough songs for her, but I will sing them all.

INTRODUCTION

The Empire of Freedom

EX-REFUGEE WILL THANK AMERICA WITH
A PERSONAL ROSE PARADE FLOAT

Los Angeles—Madalenna Lai arrived on U.S. soil in May 1975 after fleeing the Communist takeover of Vietnam in a boat and staying in a Guam refugee camp.

She was 34, penniless and the sole provider for four children, all younger than 10.

Lai quickly created a career for herself, starting beauty shops in El Monte and then in Pomona before opening a cosmetology school in Pomona. She raised her children by herself, although she jokes that at some point some of her children began raising her.

The Vietnamese refugee sees the life she has cultivated in the United States as a gift from the people and country that adopted her, she said. In 1993, she decided to thank as many of them as she could and let the world know how grateful she is.

On New Year's Day she will do just that to a worldwide television audience estimated at 350 million people and an audience along the parade route of 1.5 million. Amid the floral pomp of the Tournament of Roses will come Lai's version of a thank-you card: a fully bedecked parade float that suggests the story of the boat people like her who left Vietnam by sea.

In a year in which the Rose Parade is expected to be awash with red, white and blue patriotism—plus University of Nebraska red—Lai's Vietnam-themed float will carry a simple message from an immigrant: "Thank you America and the world."

—**TIPTON BLISH,** *Los Angeles Times*

This is not an analytics of truth; it will concern what might be called an ontology of the present, an ontology of ourselves.

—**MICHEL FOUCAULT,** "The Art of Telling the Truth"

On a clear January morning in Pasadena, a fishing boat in the form of a golden bird made of a hundred thousand flowers washed ashore. Floating along a boulevard lined with celebrants, the boat carried refugees to the new world, bearing with them a message of love: "Thank You America and the World." Two tales surface alongside this particular boat—the chronicle of a refugee grandmother and her profuse gratitude, and the more uncanny story about its making. Fleeing the war-torn country on a small fishing boat; raising her four young children alone in a new world, while her husband remained behind, and missing, for an interminable decade—throughout the long years, the first story goes, Madalenna Lai not only endures but triumphs. Now a prosperous entrepreneur operating beauty salons and a cosmetology school, she wishes to show her appreciation to "America" (and, as an afterthought, "the world") for the gift of her life, her freedom.[1] For years, Lai had solicited donations in front of local Vietnamese supermarkets and in door-to-door encounters, even going so far as to sacrifice her hard-earned wealth in order to convey her gratitude with the sumptuous, spectacular beauty that America made possible. In interviews she enthuses: "I think this country looks like heaven. I have peace of mind. I didn't have to worry about the people being unfair."[2] "The more I see of this country the more I feel I have to say thank you. This is a country of freedom and human rights."[3] "The United States opened her arms to me and my children. We no longer went hungry and my kids received a good education. I told myself after my children finished school and I reunited with my husband, I would give my life to thank America."[4]

Her gratefulness invites us to consider a second tale, about the powers through which a benevolent empire bestows on an other freedom. In Lai's words, we find all the good and beautiful things the gift claims as its consequence—the right to have rights, the choice of life direction, the improvement of body and mind, the opportunity to prosper—against a spectral future of their nonexistence, under communism, under terror. That she is rescued from such psychic death through the gift of freedom as a promise of care encodes a benign, rational story about the United States as the uncontested superpower on the world stage today. But the gift of freedom also discloses for us liberalism's innovations of empire, the frisson of freedom and violence that decisively collude for same purposes—not just because the gift of freedom opens with war and death, but also because it may obscure those other powers that, through its giving, conceive and shape life. So I begin with a story in which we are invited to know the refugee's sorrow, and her indebtedness for its cure, in order to tell us something meaningful about the genealogies of liberal powers that undergird the twinned concerns of this scene: the gift of freedom and the debt that follows. The present work considers this twofold nature by posing these questions: How is this act of thankfulness, and all that it implies about the gift and its giving, a problem of imperial remains? What special significance does this act carry from a refugee, especially *this* refugee from *that* tarnished war of American ambition? Why are we—those of us who have received this precious, poisonous gift of freedom—obliged to thank? What powers oblige us?

One significant challenge to theorizing the powers of liberal empire is the elasticity of its terms. The coupling of *empire* with the assumed scenes of liberalism—human self-possession as the property and precondition for freedom, especially as the consciousness to act, to enter into contract with others—has led to triumphant claims to an exceptional power, through which the tolerant collectivity of the well governed bears a grave duty to ease the suffering and unhappiness of others. The contemporary political life of this empire often goes by the name *the gift of freedom*, a world-shaping concept describing struggles aimed at freeing peoples from unenlightened forms of social organization through fields of power and violence. This altruistic self-concept has long been under siege, of course. (As we well know, the crucible of the United States, christened by Thomas Jefferson as an "empire of liberty,"[5] is conquest and captivity.) Noam Chomsky, a rigorous critic of the U.S. wars in Southeast Asia, scoffs, "When precisely did the United States try to help the South Vietnamese choose their own form of government and social order? As soon as such questions are posed, the absurdity becomes evident."[6] So critics of our present moment, wrought through the exception to encompass indefinite detention, brutal torture, and incalculable death, regard with incredulity and outrage the gift of freedom that purports to refute the lethal nature of empire. But the now-familiar "disclosure" that the gift of freedom is an insubstantial ruse for what might be called a liberal way of war, both then and especially now, has scarcely attenuated invocations of freedom as an intuition, and an at-times blunt instrument, for the disposition of hope and despair, life and death.[7] The idea of the gift of freedom therefore may capture something more than bad faith and falsehood, but indeed, an ever-expanding crisis of confusions and conflicts around the ethics and assemblages of liberal knowledge and power. This book is an attempt to consider freedom as a force, one that can indeed humiliate and exclude but also embrace and inspire—arousing such startling spectacles as refugee thanks spelled out in a kaleidoscopic cascade of blossoms. Because empires thrive on conceptual pluralities, it seems so too must our critiques of empire.[8]

The Gift of Freedom forwards a partial genealogy of liberalism's tactile and intangible consequences as empire, including the densely tangled assemblages of power and violence that undergird the promise of freedom, and the subject of freedom, whose humanity is the moving target of this promise. The gift of freedom is not a universal value or a formal structure, but is instead the frequent name for the both familiar and strange ways in which liberal empire marshals its forces for and against others and elsewheres. Rather than challenge the gift of freedom through refutation or inconsistency (which would presume that freedom is something other than a force, and that the ideal presence of freedom is calculable in truth), this concept inhabits the book as an analytic, a lever of sorts, for a historical investigation into the forms and events that constitute us as subjects of its imperial powers. These powers constellate allocations and appropriations of violence with a view toward injury and death, but also with a horizon for the preservation of life—with dispositions and structures of feeling, to invoke Raymond Williams,[9] within and between empire's subjects that rouse and animate love and gratitude, guilt and forgiveness, and other obligations of care levied on the human heart; with political and also phenomenological forms of graduated sovereignty and differential humanity that endure beyond the formal exercise of military operations or occupation.[10] In short, the present moment, such that we find liberal war regarding the whole world as target (to borrow from Rey Chow[11]), in fact warns us that to dismiss the gift of freedom as a trick, a ploy, would be to deny that freedom is precisely the idiom through which liberal empire acts as an arbiter for *all* humanity.

This idiom festoons the parade float that launches this query, three months after the commencement of another war to free more distant peoples from violence, from terror. (In a prior time, the enemy was named communism and postcolonial immaturity; in this time, fundamentalism and global terrorism.) With the fall of Saigon to communist forces in April 1975, and the abrupt close of U.S. operations in South Viet Nam (years after Vietnamization and the Paris Peace Accords proposed such endings), hundreds of thousands of Vietnamese sought haven, or hospitality, elsewhere, fearful of the regime to come. Multitudes fled over land or by sea, and of these many fell to brigands or starvation or despair; those who chanced the perilous voyage on the open water were colloquially dubbed *boat people*. This harrowing tale takes a fantastical turn decades later, as a humble fishing boat is transformed into a mythical bird, ferrying her passengers to an Eden of abundance and awesome beauty. As refugee-cum-happy-citizen, Madalenna Lai is similarly converted in the encounter with America, but because the gift of freedom secures her life in multiple dimensions—its preservation, convenience, and pleasure—her debt comes through as literally monumental. Particularly meaningful, then, in these accounts is their economy of arguably impossible equivalence. On the one hand, all that Lai gains through her freedom is coupled with all that she waives in recompense: she sells her home, she invests all her "free" time, and still (she confesses) she cannot hope to acquit her debt. On the other hand, this nonequivalence is "proper," since the philosophical and political truth of freedom is paradoxically beyond value. Such impossible calculations (enduring debt for all that is given) haunt the reception of this refugee's homage: "You're welcome!"[12]

I begin with the particular optimism of this figure of the Vietnamese refugee, not to recoup a different story about her arrival, but to inquire about the powers that promise her freedom and demand an enduring consciousness of her debt. In doing so, I focus on the subject of freedom as an object of knowledge and a critical methodology that discloses for us the assemblages and powers through which liberal empire orders the world.[13] Each chapter addresses those refugee figurations that do not just indict imperial powers as premised on devastating violence, but that also emanate through beauty, through love, through hope—in short, the promise to life—as equally world-making powers, thus allowing us critical purchase on the protracted nature of liberal imperial formations found in both "minor" and major events and encounters.[14] Especially because structures of race and coloniality, as well as organizing forms of gender and sexuality, are at the center of this simultaneous promise and duress—granting access to some intensities of happiness and virtue while impeding others—the gift of freedom emerges as a site at which modern governmentality and its politics of life (and death) unfolds as a universal history of the human, and the figuration of debt surfaces as those imperial remains that preclude the subject of freedom from being able to escape a colonial order of things.

The Gift of Freedom queries just how an empire of liberty, and the contemporary United States as an exemplar of this beautiful, sinister regime, brings into being the world as a target across the twentieth and twenty-first centuries. If the gift of freedom is no untruth, but instead coexists with violence, or because of violence that appears as something else, then the concept of the gift of freedom must encompass all those forces that promise new subjects as well as new forms of action, new events, a new order—such as a grateful refugee or enduring war.

The Gifts of Freedom

In what follows, I give a brief overview of the political and theoretical problems the gift of freedom raises for consideration. I draw on multiple critical genealogies of those powers that claim to care for or protect life and liberty to argue this concept. First, in observing that both terms named by the gift of freedom are complexly wrought through asymmetry and calculation, I look to the works of Jacques Derrida, who argues that the gift (especially the gift that announces itself as gift) incriminates an economy of exchange and obligation between giver and recipient, and Michel Foucault, who suggests that liberal government proposes to manufacture freedom, and in turn, that freedom is never anything more than a "relation between governors and governed."[15] Second, I consider how structures of race and coloniality underpin modern concepts of human freedom and progress, and the government the human deserves. Postcolonial and other critics aptly observe that though imperial expansion promises enlightenment and civilization, these are themselves violences— and that through such a cluster of promises, we encounter at least one violence as an ontology of time (through its measure, organization, limit). If, as Derrida argued, "a promise must promise to be kept, that is, not to remain 'spiritual' or 'abstract,' but to produce events, new effective forms of action, practice, organization, and so forth,"[16] postcolonial and other critics query just what *events, new effective forms of action, practice, organization, and so forth*, the gift of freedom, as an object of desire and dominance, holds out—or circumscribes—as possible futures. These critical genealogies inform this book's naming the gift of freedom as the workings of liberalism in its imperial form and as a metaphor and a medium for grasping continuities and innovations between operations of power and violence. Enfolding Derrida and Foucault with postcolonial and other critiques, then, I observe that the dual character of freedom as the development of capacities and the intensification of power, to draw from Foucault once again,[17] has ever operated as a global-historical project of modernity hinged upon structures of race and coloniality, and through which liberalism's empire unfolds across the globe through promises to secure it for others.

The Gift and Freedom As so many others have understood before, the gift is a great and terrible thing. The counterintuitive continuities between gift and appropriation, giving and taking, have long preoccupied anthropologists, linguists, and philosophers.[18] For the purposes of this book, I am drawn to, and depart from, the concept of the gift as articulated by Derrida (in response to Marcel Mauss) as the impossible. The aporia of giving can be condensed as follows: the gift as the transfer of a possession from one to another shapes a relation between giver and recipient that engenders a debt, which is to say that the gift belongs to an economy that voids its openhanded nature. "For there to be [genuine] gift," Derrida acidly observes, "there must be no reciprocity, return, exchange, counter-gift, or debt."[19] For there to be gift, the giver cannot recognize that he or she is giving, because to do so would subsume the gift as testimonial to the self who gives so generously, and the recipient cannot know who is giving, lest he or she be obliged to reciprocate in equal or greater measure.[20] The gift thus is annulled by consciousness of the gift as being or appearing a gift, by anything that proposes equivalence or recompense, because pure gift must not demand commensurability or otherwise calculative reasoning. This gift that is not an entirely gratuitous gesture is instead an aporia, through which the gift conveys these conditions of possibility and impossibility, and that is also the issuance of its power. Derrida notes of the gift's capacities, "one may say as readily 'to give a gift' as 'to give a blow' [*donner un coup*], 'to give life' [*donner la vie*] as 'to give death' [*donner la mort*]."[21] He elaborates further:

> To overtake the other with surprise, be it by one's generosity and by giving too much, is to have a hold on him, as soon as he accepts the gift. The other is taken, caught in the trap: Unable to anticipate, he is delivered over to the mercy, to the *merci* of the giver; he is taken in, by the trap, overtaken, imprisoned, indeed poisoned by the very fact that something happens to him in the face of which he remains—having not been able to foresee any-

thing—defenseless, open, exposed. He is the other's catch or take, he has given the other a hold. Such violence may be considered the very condition of the gift, its constitutive impurity once the gift is engaged in a process of *circulation,* once it is promised to recognition, keeping, indebtedness, credit, but also once it *must be, owes itself to be* excessive and thereby surprising. *The violence appears irreducible, within the circle or outside it, whether it repeats the circle or interrupts it.*[22]

To give a blow, to give life, to give death—the gift is itself a surface on which power operates as a form of subjection, and its magnitude might indeed be profound. As Judith Butler notes of Foucault's concept of subjection, it is, "literally, the making of a subject, the principle of regulation according to which a subject is formulated or produced. This notion of subjection is a kind of power that not only unilaterally *acts on* a given individual as a form of domination, but also *activates* or forms the subject."[23] To accept a gift is to be compromised by the one who gives (*to overtake the other with surprise, the other is taken in, caught in the trap, imprisoned, indeed poisoned, the violence appears irreducible, within the circle or outside of it*), to enter into an economy of indebtedness that is the concession or negation of his or her desires or directions. The gift is freighted further with asymmetry and nonequivalence, with the dispensation of power *over time,* because the gift cannot be returned straightaway lest its significance be undone. Describing this "given time" during which the consciousness of the debt must be sustained, Derrida notes, "There must be time, it must last, there must be waiting—without forgetting."[24] Even more, countergift or recompense may well fail to equal the gesture of giving and relieve the debt; it may instead prolong its duration. For these reasons, Derrida comments that what is given is always in excess of the gift.

This critical purchase on the gift as a *power over,* and its duration *over time,* underscores this book's critique of liberalism's benevolence, posited through both abundance and altruism (put another way, things enough to bestow surplus on another). My concerns here draw upon the awesome power of the gift's subjection, first through the want or absence of those things of which the gift consists and second through the debt that holds the giftee fast, as these powers produce his or her possible desires, movements, and futures. (These powers also engage multiple temporalities, both as an event perpetrated on an other and as the debt that commits an other to continuous subjection.) We can observe here that in the first mode through which the gift of freedom functions, the gift stages the circulation of persons and things (in the case of war, troops and armaments) to bind a relation of giver and recipient across the globe. In the second, duration and deferral take on deep resonance as concepts of time in which what is given here—that is, sovereignty, freedom, virtue—is always "to come" because the debt extends endlessly. It is on these grounds that the gift is not just an alibi of power but the first conceptual wedge that pries open the arguments of this book.

The second is freedom, one of the most common multitudinous concepts with which critics have long labored because freedom is so complexly bound to notions of human nature and questions of justice. For example, Hegel writes, "No idea is so generally recognized as indefinite, ambiguous, and open to the greatest misconceptions (to which therefore it actually falls victim) as the idea of Freedom: none in common currency with so little appreciation of its meaning."[25] Kant presents freedom as nothing less than the "keystone of the whole architecture of the system of pure reason," while Jean-Luc Nancy observes that freedom might be experienced as "thing, force, and gaze."[26] These remarks, proliferating ever-widening questions rather than answers, are nonetheless useful for reckoning with freedom as a radical plurality, or at least seemingly limitless in its workings. Indeed, we might propose that with freedom, presumably *all is given*.

Though freedom is often surmised to be the end of a universal evolution of consciousness, and all human life believed to harbor a desire for freedom, freedom is not already everywhere. For these reasons, liberalism as a practice, a principle, and a method for the rationalization of the exercise of government claims at its heart freedom as the reference for its politics, as power's problem. In the lectures collected as *The Birth of Biopolitics*, Foucault suggests that liberalism is a consumer of freedom, "inasmuch as it can only function as a number of freedoms actually exist: freedom of the market, freedom to buy and sell, the free exercise of property rights, freedom of discussion, possible freedom of expression, and so on. The new governmental reason needs freedom therefore, the new art of government consumes freedom. It consumes freedom, which means that it must produce it. It must produce it, it must organize it."[27] Accordingly, Foucault observes, "So, freedom in the regime of liberalism is not a given, it is not a ready-made region which has to be respected, or if it is, it is so only partially, regionally, in this or that case, et cetera. Freedom is something which is constantly produced. Liberalism is not acceptable of freedom; it proposes to manufacture it constantly, to arouse it and produce it, with, of course, [the system] of constraints and the problems of cost raised for this production."[28] In other words, liberalism not only produces freedom as a property of its modern art of government, but it also ceaselessly subjects it to review, to regulation. Foucault further cautions, "Freedom is never anything other —but this is already a great deal—than an actual relation between governors and governed, a relation in which the measure of the 'too little' existing freedom is given by the 'even more' freedom demanded."[29]

Foucault stops just short of addressing at least one problem of freedom as a force, when he insists that "we should not think of freedom of as a universal gradually realized over time, or which undergoes quantitative variations, greater or lesser drastic reductions, or more or less important periods of eclipse,"[30] or, we might suppose, as a universal that can be *given* or even *earned* (what Foucault might call *the problems of cost*). Foucault means to unseat liberalism's manufacture and consumption of freedom— which calculates, and conceives of, freedom as a property—but we might also usefully linger here to consider just how freedom is thought in these terms. Indeed, an attachment to freedom is foundational to liberalism's claim to a heightened attention to its presence or lapse, an attention that thereby continually commits free peoples to sustain or manufacture it in all directions, across the globe. I argue, both with and against Foucault, that freedom as never anything other than an actual relation between governors and governed, and as that which functions as an object of calculable, quantifiable exchange between them, is precisely the story of liberalism as empire.[31]

Calculations of freedom include criteria for organizing, assessing, and manufacturing its ideal presence. Such criteria require liberal government as the consolidation of apparatuses that underwrite political freedom through state citizenship, economic liberty as wage labor and market exchange, and civilization as the education of desire, among other things, and also a self-conscious subject as the rationale, and the target, of their governance. Under modern humanism, this individual is understood to be "free" on the condition that he or she act autonomously, that his or her actions reference—and be the result of—his or her own will and self-direction rather than external force, whether this be custom or other coercion. The consciousness of the modern subject thus proceeds through self-referential enclosure as a precondition for rational action and contract with like others, including wage labor, marriage, and family deemed the most natural of such forms, through which *possessive ownership* is perceived as a historical necessity for human freedom. As Lisa Lowe succinctly observes, drawing on Hegel's original formulations: "Through property the condition of possibility of human self-possession—of one's body, interiority, and life direction—is established."[32] But in this and other accounts, liberal theories measure and manufacture freedom for the human person and society in terms that also presuppose the alienability of the self—or *dispossession*. Thus, we might grasp the abstraction of human freedom as a property—both as capacity and capital—as the necessary ground for ethical interactions with others and its profound consequences. Ideas of gender, race, and coloniality are central to these assumed scenes of liberalism, and to the global empires that found liberalism's emergence.

This productive encounter between these critical genealogies helps us not to dismiss the experience of the gift of freedom as a ruse, or revert to the very terms that are under scrutiny, in the hope that an ideal presence might lie elsewhere. (As Chandan Reddy observes, "the unevenness in the meaning of freedom"—an unevenness that nevertheless establishes features in common, alongside failures in application—fueled so many twentieth-century struggles and revolutionary movements.[33]) Bringing together Derrida and Foucault now, we chance on an uncanny, semantic plurality between "to give" and "to govern." Foucault further registers "to govern" multiply, as "to conduct someone," in the spiritual sense of the government of souls; "to impose a regimen," in the form of command or control that one might exercise over oneself or another, "body, soul and behavior"; or "to an intercourse, to a circular process or process of exchange between one individual or another." We might well consider that "to give" holds these same powers and properties in hand, through obligation and recompense.[34] Indeed, and as I elaborate throughout the book, it is precisely in their crisscrossing compulsions we find the measures of the "'too little' existing freedom," "'even more' freedom demanded," and "all is given," setting liberalism's empire in motion.

We also learn from this unfaithful passage through Derrida and Foucault, bringing us to the work of postcolonial and other critics, that the gift of freedom does not merely replicate liberal subjectivization, even if we are to understand freedom as a rationale of government, and as the development of capacities and the intensification of powers, for all persons. These forces produced by the intersection of gift and freedom are not additive, but exponentially, distinctly new. The gift of freedom as a cluster of promises therefore produces *events, new effective forms of action, practice, organization, and so forth,* far beyond what the gift of freedom claims to do. In this manner, the ethical and moral force of the gift of freedom, as a means of connecting individuals to the world and to each other through a mutual if uneven attachment to freedom as a universal end, can become a medium through which ever more comprehensive forms of power connect these affective intensities to geopolitical interventions. As to that which I now turn, the gift of freedom that "discovers" an absence to next graciously confer presence is fraught with volatile questions of power, inclusion, exchange, and imperial reason.

The Subjects of Freedom What, then, is the gift of freedom? For our purposes of this book, we can begin to understand it as an assemblage of liberal political philosophies, regimes of representation, and structures of enforcement that measure and manufacture freedom and its others. To elaborate further: where the attachment to freedom appears an intuitive, universal issue, the implementation of its measure as such (as an absolute value) conceives, and consolidates, fields of knowledge and power whose function lies in the idea that freedom's presence cannot manifest in the present of some peoples and spaces for whom it is currently absent, and that produces a regime of control and interference that provides *and* defers its substantiation for an indefinite time. In the terms of our discussion, the attachment to freedom and its implementation through gift giving are therefore precisely the forms through which the encounter with the racial, colonial other can be appropriated, through an existing continuity with imperial discourse, into liberal empire.

Consider the example of President Harry Truman's 1949 inaugural address that proposed a four-point program for ensuring the liberty and prosperity of the United States and the world. Revisiting some of the tenets from his 1947 address that set forth the so-called Truman Doctrine (including the stratagem of containment, discussed in the first chapter), Truman unequivocally places the United States against coloniality, and "that false philosophy of Communism." He grieves that so many of the world's peoples suffer, often "in conditions approaching misery. Their food is inadequate. They are victims of disease. Their economic life is primitive and stagnant. Their poverty is a handicap and a threat both to them and to more prosperous areas."[35] As the final point in his four-point program, Truman pledged to share technical knowledge and skills with such miserable peoples in so-called primitive places to aid and assist in their development:

The old imperialism—exploitation for foreign profit—has no place in our plans. What we envisage is a program of development based on the concepts of democratic fair-dealing. . . . Only by helping the least fortunate of its members to help themselves can the human family achieve the decent, satisfying life that is the right of all people. Democracy alone can supply the vitalizing force to stir the peoples of the world in triumphant action, not only against their human oppressors, but also against their ancient enemies —hunger, misery, and despair. . . . Slowly but surely we are weaving a world fabric of international and growing prosperity. We are aided by all who wish to live in freedom from fear—even by those who live today in fear under their own governments. We are aided by all who want relief from the lies of propaganda—who desire truth and sincerity. We are aided by all who desire self-government and a voice in their own affairs. We are aided by all who long for economic security—for the security and abundance that men in free societies enjoy. We are aided by all who desire freedom of speech, freedom of religion, and freedom to live their lives for useful ends.[36]

This historic speech is less an origin story than an immensely useful clustering of the concepts and targets that underwrite the gift of freedom. Such that the hope to unite all the world's peoples under the signs of universal virtue are at the heart of liberalism's empire, the gift of freedom calls for the realignment of heterogeneous social forms of organization with abstract categories and properties, rendered natural, ineffable, and inalienable, but also *objectified*, *calculable*, and *exchangeable*—in one form, as an example, we know them as human rights. Freedom therefore replicates other commitments, other investments—in American imperium or liberal capital, for instance, which also goes by the names of democracy and development —rendered analogous to liberty and prosperity for all. But especially clear because this speech preceded imminent war in Korea and what was then Indochina, such ambitions to sovereignty and virtue—truth, social health, compassion, freedom, abundance, beauty—are realized through the alibi of the wanting other, the negative image. Truman's speech is concerned with this other's desire and its education for freedom, "implanted within (underdeveloped) subjectivity," as María Josefina Saldaña-Portillo notes, and "evinced by 'wishes,' 'desires,' 'voice,' 'longing,' and ultimately choice."[37] These ambitions and alibis are thereby epistemological, inasmuch as they shape a politics of knowledge about those persons or social formations through calculations of an ideal presence, and they are also ontological, because these constitute categories of human life for sorting, saving, or, in Foucault's well-chosen words, "letting die."[38] These coordinates name a politics of life that finds Truman declaring, on the eve of empire, a civilizational divide between humanity and those who wait: "For the first time in history, *humanity* possesses the knowledge and the skill to relieve the suffering of *these people*."[39]

In the following chapters, I outline some of the continuities and innovations that toggle between colonial schema and liberalist alibi, through the gift of freedom. First, an annotation: this book is not necessarily about abandonment and social death and human ruin, though the devalued, the dead to others or marked as dead, populate this book as spectral.[40] But it is also not *not* about these persons, those who are targeted, who are the terrible cost or condition—for gift, for empire—as either the reason for its delivery or the awful result. Whether its primary focus or collateral damage (and the distinction is indeed blurred), such racial deaths found liberalism's empire, and they certainly secure what Denise Ferreira da Silva calls the "globality of race," and what Lisa Marie Cacho calls the "violence of value," causing death and commiting the dead as a life necessity for others.[41] That is, a biopolitical regime may transfigure a human person into what Giorgio Agamben calls "bare life," devoid of rights or history, or what Hortense Spillers refers to as "mere flesh," a body that is killable or trafficable with impunity, in the name of the human.[42] As Derrida observed so aptly: "The just measure of 'restoring' or 'rendering' is impossible—or infinite. Restoring or rendering is the cause of the dead, the cause of deaths, the cause of a death given or requested."[43] The gift of freedom bears such racial deaths as its macabre overture, rendering real not just the divisions between those who possess full humanity and those who are the constitutive outside, but also those whose partial or possible realization of freedom as a universal consciousness arbitrates and advances liberalist powers and politics of life, and unlife.

In other words, liberal empire claims an interest in improving, and prolonging, the life of a subject of freedom as a rationale and a target for governance, even while the lethal circumstances that make this claim possible (that is, those schema of race and coloniality that relegate some peoples to the outside) remain foundational to its project. In this sense, the gift of freedom introduces a vexing problem both as judgment and solution. In the carving out and delimiting of areas of social existence and belonging, the gift of freedom is normative, as a means of making other ways of being in the world appear to be insecure, illegible, inadequate, illegal, and illiberal, and it is also instrumental as a means of partitioning the world into spaces commensurate or incommensurate, comparable and incomparable, with the rule of liberalism, which thus require certain forms of action, or force, to manufacture freedom. In doing so, the gift of freedom inevitably calculates and coheres an ordered taxonomy of what is deemed necessary for human being, a movement that stretches from the loss or absence of certain properties, such as reason and rights, into the often brutal achievement of the conditions for their possibilities in the future.[44] As a promise to freedom-loving peoples that refits structures of race and coloniality, even as this promise registers these structures as a political affront, the gift of freedom gives imperial reason new life, and more time. The postcolonial or anticolonial unease with such dreams of sovereignty and virtue thus derives from both the coordinates of such a promise and their practicable implementation. As Lila Abu-Lughod warns of another war engaged for the gift's delivery: "When you save someone, you imply that you are saving her *from* something. You are also saving her *to* something. What violences are entailed in this transformation, and what presumptions are being made about the superiority of that to which you are saving her?"[45]

The injurious properties of freedom are well documented in the complicity between philosophical discourses of human consciousness and metaphysics of racial and sexual difference since the Enlightenment. Intruding here is the brutal history of violence operating—insidiously and insistently—through the instrumentalization of colonial cartographies and racial classifications that sort and grade stages of human being. These cartographies and classification schemata are central to the genealogy of human freedom, not exceptional to it. Liberalism hypostatizes areas in which we find freedom and unfreedom, and it shapes a politics of knowledge about those persons or places with differentiated access or acclimation to freedom that are symptomatic of other measures—of cultural difference, technical competence, or a nonbiological, but nonetheless evolutionary, sociology of race—that mark out anew the racial, colonial other. If we think again of Truman's atlas of enlightened obligation, naming those "underdeveloped areas" where half the world's peoples are plagued with hunger, disease, primitive economies, and other "conditions approaching misery," we see these distinctions map tidily onto the colonial globe.[46]

Nor is the picture of unfree peoples—captive to misery, atavism, primitivism, poverty—complete without imperialist ontologies of time. Humanism's ideal presence does not just conceive freedom as autonomous self-enclosure but also as persistence or passage through historical time.[47] Imperialist discourse framed cotemporaneous territories and peoples as primitive and anachronistic, or in other words, intransigent, or impassive, to forward movement or progress; such discourse encloses racial, colonial others as *on the outside* through instrumental uses of time. Thus do postcolonial critics reveal these temporal modes as worlding processes that fire the crucible of empire, of modernity. On the outside is what Anne McClintock calls "anachronistic space": "According to this trope, colonized people . . . do not inhabit history proper but exist in a permanently anterior time within the geographic space of the modern empire as anachronistic humans, atavistic, irrational, bereft of human agency—the living embodiment of the archaic 'primitive.'"[48] In what Johannes Fabian calls a "denial of coevalness," humanist knowledges such as anthropology thereby engage "a persistent and systematic tendency" to contain the racial, colonial other to a time other than the present of the modern observer.[49] Imperial discourse further establishes a linear, evolutionary view of history that is deterministic and teleological. Bliss Cua Lim, drawing on the work of Henri Bergson and Dipesh Chakrabarty, comments: "The colonial trope of time-as-space, of *the globe as a kind of clock*—with the metropolitan center marking the path to progress, while the colonized other remains primitive and superseded—is a version of what Bergson exposes as the 'all is given' logic of homogenous time."[50]

The gift of freedom is both a continuation and an innovation in imperial time consciousness. Where freedom's absence appears as an empirical issue—for example, perceived through anachronism, underdevelopment, or failure—the assessment of subjects, practices, and geographies as such may coincide or become complicit with the temporal logic of colonialism. Because the measure of freedom underscores the distancing of some peoples from, in Walter Benjamin's phrasing, the secular, empty, and homogeneous time of history, the gift of freedom hinges upon a historicist consciousness through which the future of the anachronistic human is already known. But though dependent on structures of race and coloniality, liberalism's empire is also distinctly new. While wrought through concepts of historicism and teleology that comprehend history as the actualization of an ideal presence, which here goes by the name of human freedom, *the gift of freedom presumes to knowingly anticipate and manufacture this present and presence* through liberalism as the rational course of human progress and historical and political transformation. Putting it another way, one in which a colonialist sharing of time is "not given but must be accomplished [and can be denied]," as Rey Chow cites and builds on Fabian, suggestively hints to us that the liberalist distinction *is* this given time, which of course brings us again to Derrida, who notes of the gift that what it gives is time.[51] The provocations of given time as liberalist alibi are therefore multiple. If we return to the linear, evolutionary view of colonialism, given time might refer to a deterministic understanding of time that forecloses the future. But given time also names the liberalist power *to set and speed up the timetable*—the timetable for progress through known processes or discrete stages toward freedom as the achievement of modernity. In other words, the gift is among other things a gift of time: time for the subject of freedom to resemble or "catch up to" the modern observer, to accomplish what can be anticipated in a preordained future, whether technological progress, productive capacity, or rational government. But the invitation to coeval-ity also imposes violence—including a politics of comparison, homoge-nous time, and other commensurabilities—through the intervention (a war, or development) that rescues history for those peoples stalled or suspended in time. We could say that the gift of freedom aims to perfect the civilizing mission.

But the gift of freedom also eclipses the scope of colonialism inasmuch as its claims to universality (through which liberty and prosperity are the due and desire of all) are precisely the mandate of liberal empire to address its powers to *all* peoples. The liberalist alibi of given freedom thus revolu-tionizes imperial discourse and opens up histories of racial, colonial pow-ers for regimes of subjection but also subjectivization, through which persons are actuated as free—to contract their labor, to educate their desire, for instance. What then does it mean for a racial, colonial other to "finally" possess freedom? How can it be that the possibility of "owning" freedom is worth everything and nothing? These questions return us to Derrida and Foucault, who configure for us the gift of freedom in terms of a differential (found in "'too little' existing freedom" and "'even more' freedom demanded"); a differential, furthermore, that administers the gift through its cost and calculation and incorporates freedom's others (misery, hunger, poverty, communism, terror) into a chain of appropriations to secure its authority, and then to order elimination, if necessary. Where misery and hunger are forged out of contrast with ideal freedom, for instance, this equally shows that an abject people's access to freedom is also a social construction forged from the same contrast. Therefore, because the suspect genealogy of human consciousness is wrought through ideas of dispossession and dependency as its constitutive outside, the gift of freedom is not an escape from these chains of signification but is instead *their extension*.

There is another history of the promise of freedom that we might well remember. In *Slavery and Social Death*, Orlando Patterson traces the concept of manumission, the master's act of granting freedom to a property, a slave. This gift replaces the property of the slave-turned-freedman with something else—not self-possession, but the duration of the freedman's devotion, which includes continuing labor as well as his indebtedness. *This property passes to the master and not the slave.* It is in this way that manumission, that act of granting freedom, comprises a will to subjectivity (what Saidiya Hartman, in her brilliant study of "scenes of subjection," calls "a burdened individuality"[52]) that is also the perpetuation of domination and subjection in another, perhaps more pernicious, form. Patterson resumes, "Everywhere the freedman was expected to be grateful for the master's generosity in freeing him, however much he may have paid."[53] For Patterson and Hartman, manumission does not replace captivity with freedom, but translates a state of alienable life into a stage of anachronistic human.[54] Under liberalism's purview, the transmutation from possession to personhood (at least to "full" personhood) is impossible, because there is no gift without debt—which is to say, no gift without claim on the other's existence. For the anachronistic human targeted for transmutation, freedom is not generated from his or her own interiority but is manufactured, in the sense that this freedom bears the provenance of another's hand. It is at once an incomplete possession and a permanent relation of bondage, securing his or her government ceaselessly, exhaustively (in the senses Foucault lists: "to conduct someone," "to impose a regimen" or "an intercourse, . . . a circular process or process of exchange between one individual or another"). *To be given freedom is a process of becoming without being.* Thus does the gift of freedom carry a stubborn remainder of its absence—this trace may be called race or gender, among other names, and does not subside with the passage of time.

Another name for this trace is debt, first as those properties that are provisionally held and in constant danger of suspension, and second as the duration of the past as continuous subjection. For Derrida, "there where there is gift, there is time. What it gives, the gift, is time, but this gift is also a demand of time. The thing must not be restituted immediately and right away."[55] Especially because the gift of freedom is the promise of human being in time, and is hence *the gift that keeps on giving*, the debt it imposes (both *power over* and *power over time*) troubles the recipient far into the foreseeable future. To be freed, as Hartman remarks, is to be a debtor forever. The nature of this duration is also twofold. The debt first requires the perseverance of anachronism, the trace of what was once absent, and second imposes the onus to recompense the spirit of the gift to the one who gives.[56] (Of the former, we might further observe that debt is the echo of what Lim lyrically calls "immiscible times"—"multiple times that never quite dissolve into the code of modern time consciousness, discrete temporalities incapable of attaining homogeneity with or full incorporation into a uniform chronological present."[57]) In this way, the gift sits alongside debt as the subject of freedom's absolute condition of existence. Made to desire a presumably complex personhood that circumscribes agency and consciousness as autonomous and self-governing, while bound indefinitely to those particularities of race or gender that are traces of his or her debt, the subject of freedom is obliged persistently, without possessing fully, a liberal ideal. Turning once again to Derrida's given time, what is given is time to diminish—but never to close—the distance between the anachronism and the modern, and time to linger under the lengthening shadow of debt. This dilemma might also be phrased: *They will never be like us; they can never catch up.* If duration is the condition of subjectivity—or, as Lim observes, "an ever accumulating ontological memory that is wholly, automatically, and ceaselessly preserved"[58]—debt requires an open register on which anachronism or absence is inscribed forever.

On the one hand, then, a truth of the gift of freedom lies in value as exchange. Although freedom has so often claimed an exemption from crass political maneuvering, freedom defined as a universal virtue regularizes an equivalency between its constituent parts (bourgeois interiority, constitutional democracy, human rights) for social and political exchange.[59] We know this in freedom's longtime consignment to a function of the market economy, for example, or in the contemporary wartime adage "freedom isn't free." On the other hand, another truth of the gift of freedom is value as debt. Also voiced in this adage, the obligation to remember and return the value of the gift means that freedom is imperfect, and alarmingly provisional. As it turns out, the gift of freedom is not the end but another beginning, another bondage.

Unfolding with the codification of a universal right to national self-determination precisely timed with decolonization movements across the globe, the gift of freedom thus renews and innovates imperial reason. For us, this historical moment unfailingly returns us once again to liberal war. Though liberalism names war as excessive and external to sociality, a violent event believed to happen "out there," liberal war avows an exception. War perpetrates deliberate violence to injure the bodies and properties of a named enemy; liberal war perpetrates violence that it claims is incidental to its exercise of power to free others from a named enemy who is in their midst (giving rise to the computational concept of *collateral damage*). Such violence is vital to the genealogy of human freedom in which freedom, as liberalism's impetus for the preservation of life, conceives of war and violence as calculative functions for a biopolitics. Such are the calculations that require us to fathom liberal war not just as militaries and machines (as I argue in the third chapter), but also as the continuous government of freedom. This seeming contradiction—that liberalism's empire purports to free others from violence and captivity through more violence and captivity—instead points us as critics toward a radical plurality to which our analyses must be addressed. We need not neglect war as the will to injury in order to also observe through the gift of freedom the normalization of liberal war as a productive force. What else might be made of the claims that to grant freedom is to be at once observant to the aliveness or the need of other persons, and cognizant that our self-interest and security are enriched by unfree peoples having the advantage of freedom?[60] (Or, as President Lyndon B. Johnson once stated, "if freedom is to survive in any American hometown it must be preserved in such places as South Viet Nam."[61]) That is, democratic ideals can themselves be the scenes of violence. We might understand this ominous pledge again through Foucault, who observes: "Liberalism formulates simply the following: I am going to produce what you need to be free. I am going to see to it that you are free to be free."[62]

For these reasons, the other side of the coin—that the gift of freedom is incidental to the exercise of power to kill others—is equally not true. The gift of freedom is no mere excuse or authorizing ruse, and even if it were, recall Derrida's prescient caution: "Even if the gift were never anything but a simulacrum, one must still render an account of the possibility of this simulacrum and of the desire that impels toward this simulacrum."[63] Moreover, war is only the most spectacular form through which empire grants freedom. Once again, the semantic plurality of the concepts that present themselves as either gift or freedom (and the multiple apparatuses that secure them, including but not restricted to state forms) are here precisely the origin of their power, their politics of life.[64] No comparison may seem possible between the expenditure of lives and resources in combat operations; nation building in the form of contractual economies and democratic polities; displacement and encampment in the name of sanctuary; economic development by international aid and agencies as the capitalization of resources and productive capacity; the dissemination and discipline of expert knowledges about hygiene, health, and "right living"; and even witness to evil, as kinds of exchange, but these are in fact collocated in the calculations of freedom all the time.[65] Nor are these distinct from the gift of being, which is both a philosophical statement about an experience of the world and also a social practice for the development of capacities and structures of feeling (such as chosen sociality or lavish beauty) comprising a will to subjectivity by another's power. While distinguishing between these political, ethical, and economic forms is crucial, nonetheless it is this conceptual multitude, with its confusion of categories and crises of referentiality, that invests the gift of freedom with its tremendous power. For all these reasons, the gift of freedom compels us to think in terms other than calculation, contradiction, or comparison in order to see beyond ideal presence. This requires holding a multitudinous concept of the gift of freedom as a property presumed to bear a particular shape or dimension, nevertheless unfolding through time and space as the diffuse transmission of power from empire to other that can suddenly, violently— but also slowly, lovingly—seize control over life and death.

The Gift of Freedom thus haunts empire, not just with mournful ghosts but also with beautiful visions.[66] The task of this book is not to peer beneath or behind the gift but to understand the concept of the gift as a medium and a metaphor for grasping continuities between operations of liberalism's powers. Observing the emergence of the gift of freedom (and with it, a politics of life and a concept of the human) as conceived and shaped by murderous structures of race and coloniality, this book reads the gift of freedom as relating to a set of compelling, connected, but not commensurate discourses about the signals, sensations, and mandates that freedom is believed to emit and the uses for which these promises—to make alive, to make live, as well as to make dead—are pressed into service. Bringing together critiques of liberalism and its continuous government of human freedom with postcolonial approaches to the modern cartography of freedom and progress, I propose the gift of freedom as the name for liberalism's difference from coloniality, but also its linkage to it—through which freedom as "thing, force, and gaze" re-creates modern racial governmentality for a new age.

Refugee Passages

To create the new American out of the pipe dream of "We, the People," or out of the bogus concept of the world's policeman, or to give democratic ideals a kind of moral luck is to forget the violence at the origin.
—GAYATRI CHAKRAVORTY SPIVAK, "Acting Bits / Identity Talk"

It is with these concerns in mind that *The Gift of Freedom* identifies the war in Viet Nam—and Southeast Asia more generally—as a particularly pressing and durable event to query what messages of power are transmitted through the gift of freedom. As the Cold War United States christened Viet Nam (though of course the war trespassed throughout Southeast Asia) the key theater for the Asian conflict with communism (a proxy, as it were, for the Soviet Union), we find the simultaneous emergence of modern forms of state power and biopolitics that inherit colonial and imperial schema, including those historicisms that order human life and freedom through stratum and asymmetry but that also mediate between liberal imaginaries of the good and the true, those things that enliven compassion and beauty, and liberal structures of government, including contractual economies, democratic politics, and chosen sociality. That is, in this historical moment a modern paradigm for liberal government and empire emerges, codified in the 1948 UN Universal Declaration of Human Rights preamble (which begins: "whereas recognition of the inherent dignity and of the equal and inalienable rights of all members of the human family is the foundation of freedom, justice and peace in the world"[67]), through which freedom is calculable, and hence subject to maximization and securitization by freedom-loving peoples that they may promise and produce, according to need and want, new configurations of the global order of things. Underwriting this declaration, which is also a directive, are arrangements of intuitive and institutional knowledges establishing that no one is free unless all are free. We might abridge these knowledges as *all peoples wish to be free* and *one is free under liberal government*. As the defender of the "free" capitalist world, then, the United States during the Cold War justified its campaigns throughout Asia in response to anticolonial struggles and decolonization movements where those struggles and movements rendered those places deficient in proper governance and disqualified from the rights of sovereignty, and hence susceptible to occupation and control by other powers.[68] As I elaborate in the first chapter, the war in Viet Nam and its aftermath illumine for us the conditions of possibility that structurally link new forms of action with emerging configurations of violence and power, in which managing the "crisis" of the human requires the mobilization of both armies and aid.

The refugee figure from this war is subject to the gift twice over. In the first instance as an object of intervention in the Cold War, and in the second as an object of deliverance in the aftermath of military defeat, the gift of freedom suspends the distinctions between those processes that play out in former colonies and those that appear at the imperial centers. Throughout April 1975, the United States marshaled its battered forces to protect and preserve what could be from a disastrous war. The Defense and State Departments evacuated hundreds of thousands of Saigonese denizens and displaced persons from around the country and encamped these refugees at military bases throughout the Pacific archipelago, where foregoing wars had established imperial outposts, and the U.S. mainland. On May 23, 1975, the U.S. Congress, at the urging of President Gerald Ford, passed the Indochina Migration and Refugee Assistance Act, granting refugees from South Viet Nam and Cambodia unprecedented large-scale entry to, and residence in, the United States. Coordinating both state and civilian institutions, these operations were auspiciously dubbed New Life and New Arrivals, presumably that which is given to the subject of freedom. In the decades that followed, the United States granted asylum to tens of thousands more refugees, the enduring echo of what President Ronald Reagan called a "noble cause."[69]

This book's task is to engage with the refugee figure as a target and also an instrument for the gift of freedom, as an object marked for rescue and refuge, and as a subject emerging from these claims to care. Toward this end, the fantastical tale that opens this book, the flowering fishing boat that recalls earlier and more desperate voyages, is a stunning illustration of the labor that the gift of freedom performs on behalf of liberal empire. In this scene we find the metamorphosis of the boat people, those unmoored persons who fled in the war's aftermath, forced onto small boats to share unsafe space and time on the open water. In *Slander*, the Francophone novelist Linda Le satirizes the spectacularization of the boat people within this story of life in suspension: "Remember when your people began to leave the Country. The fugitives piled by the hundreds into little boats as fragile as giant matchboxes. They crossed the ocean on these boats. Back here, people rubbed their hands together. *They had found the ideal victims, they called them freedom fighters*. Why, the frivolous people were just about ready to run to their yachts and go rescue the victims. They piled into boats in their turn, overloaded with cameras and photographic equipment, fighting to get the first shots of those victims with such sweet, sad eyes."[70] In this brief passage, Le underlines a compulsory visibility that operates through the commonplace convergence of photographic media with modern humanitarianisms. The coupling of subjection and subjectivity also slips into the frame, here in the names *ideal victims* and *freedom fighters*.[71] Both names, cited simultaneously, christen the subject of freedom for whom the West might imagine itself a benefactor.[72] This conjoined figuration, and certainly its pathetic spectacularization, precedes the parade float as its historical referent (its "before" snapshot) in order to irrefutably revise this image once the gift is given. The flowering boat with its happy passengers draws attention to this lamentable past in order to attest to a thriving present (in multiple senses of the word *present*, as contemporaneity, against absence). A common trope in refugee figurations, the wretched collectivity of boat people is at once denied and embraced as the othered past of ourselves.[73] This transmutation of object into subject precisely conceives the doubled temporal consciousness of the gift of freedom and the debt as an enduring trace of liberal empire.[74] Toward this end, *The Gift of Freedom* examines that gift, composed of pipe dreams, bogus concepts, and moral luck as well as violence at its origin, through its spectacularizations in other such refugee figurations and imperial remains.

This book focuses not on objects that are lost and must be recovered, such as subjectivity or sovereignty, though these objects might be otherwise understood in these terms. Instead, in pursuing what Yen Le Espiritu has dubbed a "critical refugee studies,"[75] each chapter focuses on a figuration of this refugee's reception of these objects, those properties of freedom, to get at something significant about the imperial forms and forces that endure beyond the cessation of military intervention and occupation.[76] It is without a doubt an understatement to observe at this stage that the refugee is no simple figure. A historical event, a legal classification, an existential condition of suspension or surrender (Agamben understands the refugee as "nothing less than a limit concept"[77]), and a focal point for rescue or rehabilitation, the refugee figure is mired in complicated and ever emerging matrices and crises of referentiality within political as well as ontological processes of signification and subjectivization.[78] This book focuses on the impact of some of these figurations of crisis, connecting a series of specific events and conditions in a time and a place to implicate the Enlightenment project of modern liberal humanism, now mobilizing the gift of freedom as a system for reordering the world. As I demonstrate in what follows, the gift of freedom helps us to map those other forms and forces that include mutable measures of a human person and his or her self-possession; greater or lesser calculations of partial sovereignty and ambiguous rights; and certainly the manufacture of sentiments and structures of feeling within and between empire's subjects as part of imperial statecraft, including gratefulness for the gift, and forgiveness for those trespasses that are the sometimes unfortunate "error" in its giving. Thus, even as declarations of reciprocity obscure the violence of liberalism's powers (for example, the letter from a minor government functionary at the U.S. State Department's Bureau of Population, Refugees, and Migration to Madalenna Lai that praises her due diligence in honoring her debt in the spirit of the gift, through which being free also denotes forms of right living), they also aim to affirm the desire for freedom and the course of its development, under liberalism's empire. Each chapter considers some part of this refugee's passages—or, more precisely, the uncanny story of those passages as a movement from subjection to subjectivity, and the poisonous promise of this movement. In doing so, as Fiona Ngô puts so well, I hope to discern the troubling "continuities between the remains of war and the rehabilitations of peace."[79]

In theorizing the gift of freedom throughout these chapters as collocating liberalism, colonialism, and modernity, I locate this book at the interface of transnational feminist studies and postcolonial cultural studies, especially scholarship on questions of race and war that interarticulate fields of inquiry that have each exerted considerable influence, but whose mutual implicatedness as knowledge formations has only recently been theorized. (The often-troubled encounter of ethnic studies and area studies, for example, has long looked away from their shared connections as postwar U.S. academic phenomena that can and do follow from the dangerous premise of a national order of things.[80]) This work thereby follows from Kandice Chuh's proposal that we pursue studies in "comparative racialization and intersectional projects that deliberately unravel seemingly stable distinctions among identificatory categories and disciplinary divisions,"[81] and Lisa Lowe's motion that our queries address the "economy of affirmation and forgetting" that structures the intimacies of four continents (such as refugee thanksgiving, for instance).[82] Furthermore, as Caren Kaplan and Inderpal Grewal press us toward transnational feminist cultural studies as a methodological guide, informing this book's genealogies in particular are theories that pay particular attention to the materiality of signification, and in doing so query the politics of knowledge, referentiality, and normativity.[83] From such scholarship, as well as its uses and challenges to poststructuralist claims, it follows that the ideas in which we traffic—for instance, freedom and security, humanity and sovereignty—must be interrogated not as unambiguous values but as transactional categories that are necessarily implicated and negotiated in relation to contests of power, their colonial histories and imperial futures. My work builds on all these analytic insights about the theoretical and structural antagonisms between liberal and neoliberal political philosophies and institutional exercises and transnational and postcolonial feminist theories, as programs of rescue or rehabilitation are increasingly understood as inseparable from deployments of structural and other forms of dominance.

The first chapter looks closely at the occasions of war and refuge to outline the dual character of freedom as the development of capacities and the intensification of power as these are bound to the passage of time as a historical necessity. This crucial dimension of the first chapter follows from Derrida's given time to consider the achievement of freedom over time, alerting us to the confluence of colonial schema with liberalist innovation in those disciplining intents and powers that target the new friend in wartime and the refugee in the aftermath, to induct him or her to the truth of freedom. In doing so, this chapter considers multiple analytical concerns, first through the temporalizing concept of transition as liberalism's difference from brutish coloniality, and second through the traumatic diagnostic of the refugee condition as difference from crude racialization. In elaborating further on these passages from war to refuge, I turn to Timothy Linh Bui's *Green Dragon*, a refugee camp melodrama set at a Marine Corps base in Southern California, and in particular to the two incidents of violence it portrays—the first being the aerial bombing that begins the film, and the second being the midnight removal of a willfully anachronistic refugee from the camp. In reconciling us to these incidents, the story about a benevolent hospitality that this film tells collocates the operations of power and violence that usher the refugee from anomalous time and space into a universal, modern consciousness—or, as the filmmakers insist, "from purgatory to a newfound freedom."[84]

It should be clear by now that one of this book's imperatives is to challenge the wish for a founding presence, as well as a guarantee of recovery. As Foucault would put it, I am less interested in an analytics of truth than in an ontology of ourselves. In this regard, it is the willing of subjectivity and sovereignty (such as that which occurs in the refugee camp) that is precisely the seduction of the gift of freedom, premised on a transparent subject of universal consciousness and, in all its insidious implications, self-possession. We might even say that this willing of subjectivity is the surprising form through which decades-old imperial ambition returns, as the overdue achievement of President Johnson's wartime counsel—which we might read as an imperative in retrospect—that "the ultimate victory will depend on the hearts and minds of the people who actually live out there."[85] This premise should serve as a caution against the resurgence—even or especially in this instance, in which I query the particular resonance of this refugee figure as well as her losses and gains—of a compulsive interiorization, a wish for a metaphysics of voice or a kind of nature, whether attached to a condition (being a refugee) or other presence (a self).[86]

To be sure, the refugee figures I consider in this study might awaken just such a wish or a will, inasmuch as these might otherwise appear inscrutable or inassimilable to a political project critical of empire. Certainly, the figure at the heart of the second chapter, Phan Thi Kim Phúc, illumines this "problem." Because the image-event of napalm burning her child's body is so often cited as an indictment of *something terrible*—sometimes empire, sometimes the nature of war—her forgiveness might appear unfathomable. But though we need not understand Madalenna Lai and Phan Thi Kim Phúc as identical to their public selves—devoted partisan or angel of mercy —neither can we divine their true feelings through modes of difference or depth ("Does she really feel grateful? Does she really forgive?"). This book refuses to conjecture that these figures might, or should, disclose to us *something else* simmering beneath the surface, perhaps an interiority, am-bivalence, or some other sign that would seem more theoretically tenable as resistant, or disruptive. I am mindful that Caren Kaplan cautions against appointing critical insight as a consequence of distance or estrangement; Sianne Ngai questions the long-established belief that true feelings (includ-ing the more politically efficacious ones) await release in internal spaces; Saba Mahmood warns that the category of resistance as a progressivist ontology (another map for the troubling historicist consciousness that per-sons desire, or can be made to desire, to be free) may obstruct our analytics of power; and Rey Chow worries that in search of a resistant figure, our critical labors in fact lose their specificity.[87] Likewise, I focus on these refu-gee passages to grasp something vital, and vivifying, about the liberal impe-rial structures that actuate and shape subjects without my own wish for transparency, or a will to subjectivity. Instead, my chapters elaborate the need for a reading that is attuned to the political traffic that glimpses into the heart perform, and to constructions of the *freed* subject, in order to trace the phantoms of colonial classifications and imperial remains that might be found there. To do so is necessarily to push against metaphysical fantasies of otherness as authentic resistance, *or* of sameness as common humanity—both of which presume transparency as well as the truth of interiority. For these reasons, the specter of the gift of freedom here haunts the overdetermination of our political hopes.

The second chapter elaborates on the iconic photograph of the na-palmed girl to consider both the failures of empire and the humanist critique that profoundly undermines an analytic of it. In liberal theories of freedom that trope failure as the dissolution or denial of personhood, "*the presumption that if a body is found, then a subject can be recovered*" (to borrow Anjali Arondekar's neat turn of phrase[88]) is one course that liber-alism's empire might take to atone for its violence. In a counterreading of the humanist critique, I trace the arc of the subjectivization of the girl in the photograph through the rhetorical formation of her as an autonomous subject across a series of flashpoints—her longing for beauty and chosen love, which also inform her capacity for forgiveness. In doing so, my second chapter wrestles with multiple concerns, through which relations of seeing in particular animate the force of liberal war. Both bomb and picture interpolate a feeling observer who, shuddering before the scene of the precarious other and desirous of diminishing her misery and misfortune, may himself or herself suffer harm in doing so. To put another way, the vexing issues presented by the girl in the photograph as a consequence of imperial violence allegorize precisely the "problem" of liberal empire—both as a model for subjectivization through war, through the gift of freedom, and as an analytic of it.

Furthermore, the imperial archive that had once fixed this photograph as forensic evidence of the horror of this war is transmuted when the girl in the photograph recompenses our gaze with her grace. The scene of communion between victim and perpetrator—the girl in the photograph grieves at a monument to the warrior dead, beside a seven-year prisoner of war—further conceives of the war as a shared, traumatic ordeal. Here a profound, affective investment in a humanist covenant, in which empathy, compassion, and grace negotiate the painful distance between self and other, informs the bind wherein liberal discourse, in rehabilitating the victim, also redeems her violator. In the juxtaposition of these scenes (the photograph, her pardon), I hope to shed light on a significant trope of the gift of freedom, to theorize the place of *feeling* subjectivity in the order of liberal empire as a reason for pursuing war—to want to give of itself, its surplus—and the rationale for pardoning its crimes.

In the final chapter, I return to liberal war making and the normalizing of race war on behalf of freedom as life necessity in the present moment. In an age of empire ascendant, the United States pursues what could be considered supersovereign powers, contravening international and domestic law in the name of exception—which here coincides with the gift of freedom. Untimely comparisons between the wars in Afghanistan and Iraq with the wars in Southeast Asia of the previous century become enveloped in the continuous history of liberalism's empire as an empire of humanity, and the Vietnamese refugee is recruited to testify to the gift of freedom and to recompense the debt through its extension to others. This is purported to be a loving gesture, inasmuch as it proclaims gratefulness to the empire, which gives so well, and a sense of empathy and obligation to those others bereft of freedom (as the refugee once was). But it is also a violent gesture, which returns the gift in the same spirit. Pledging unceasing war, authoring radical new powers to police and imprison, and devising more devastating weapons to destroy and kill, as the patriot acts in this chapter do, the refugee patriot as a imperial figuration allows us to connect and comment upon the refugee and his *other other*, the terrorist, as limit figures through which all human life becomes a rationale and a target for global governance, and continuous histories of liberal war claim to produce the rule of freedom in a neoliberal age. Through his or her receipt of the gift of freedom, which I here name *transnational multiculturalism*, the operations of sovereign violence via a Foucauldian concept of race war are established through the biopolitical imperative to prolong life—through asylum, through preemption—and to allow some death as a necessary expense. And, inasmuch as the refugee patriot manifests a living memory of *what has already come to pass*, and *what has not yet come*, he or she lends this memory as prosthetic to liberal empire, enabling permanent vigilance, and continuous intervention into life itself, in the name of acquitting his or her debt for freedom.

It bears noting here that the crux for this book surfaced with, but also *against*, the wish for historical continuation, and the seduction of retrieval, in the aftermath of war. That is, this book's crucible might be said to start with another origin story, told at Operation Homecoming, a twenty-year commemoration of the refugee camps at Camp Pendleton, north of San Diego, California. Held in 1995, and attended by a thousand Vietnamese from all over the United States, Operation Homecoming bespoke a hunger for objects and voices assumed lost or at the least neglected in the sweep of the war's history, and their recovery as the sanction and celebration of a surviving present.[89] On the campground, dotted with decommissioned helicopters and other arsenal from past conflicts, former refugees wandered through the small-scale reenactment of the tent city, overseen by a uniformed marine; before a cleared field where vendors hawked food and souvenirs; a sweat-drenched musician plunked on his electric keyboard; dignitaries and celebrities orated about American benevolence and refugee success. Issuing a "THANK YOU, AMERICA" (as the stage's banner trumpeted), the event intimates that affirmation and presence are not exceptional to empire's violence. Also troubling, what appears to be gratefulness for the gift of freedom is also the normalization of war, not simply as a cornerstone to the U.S. self-image of enlightenment and altruism but also as a *refugee* feeling for state sovereignty.[90] Yet the commemoration's disquieting palimpsest (of war, through refuge) echoed most for me in a vivid encounter with the gift's principle of danger and shadow of death as concomitant with its promise of life. Under the bright lights of a barrack converted for the event into an impromptu display room for historical artifacts, glamour photographs, and abstract paintings, a young white man in a buzz cut fingered a photograph of Vietnamese dead tucked into a pile of other loose materials before pushing it across the table in my direction, with a smile. (He enthused, "Viet Cong, man!") Struck dumb with horror, I could not know if he pushed the photograph toward me to say, "We saved you, and you are now one of us," "We saved you, but you owe us," or "We saved you, but you can still be undone," as each promise seemed to flex the particular power of a liberal politics of life, as the complex history of modern racial governmentality. Rather than understand this uncanny chance encounter with a brash marine as distinct or apart from the celebratory tenor of the larger event, which located the camp as a *home*, I propose that it is in fact the event's menacing backstory. The questions that struck me then are still the same: What sequence of subjection and subjectivity brought "us" here, not just to "America," but to this particular story of restoration and renewal? How do we grasp the violence of value (to again borrow a phrase from Cacho), or the imposition of indebtedness?[91] And how do we parse the partial sovereignty and ambiguous endowment that underscores the gift of freedom with the threat that freedom can also be revoked from those to whom *it had to be given*?

This "minor" event set the scene and the tone for this book, which could be described as a collection of other jarring, unsettling encounters with both the tactile and intangible powers of U.S. dominion. To understand this event, as well as the other events it references (the commemoration, the exodus, the war), at which the history of modern racial governmentality haunted me so, this book brings together other figures, other stories, that fold empire into debt—a grandmother sells her house to enter a parade to thank her benefactors, a film director stages a frightening midnight removal as a rescue, a scarred woman offers her forgiveness on global television, a patriot acts to bestow the gift of war he has been given on others. Caught up in the narrative possibilities of the gift of freedom, the scenes collected in this book may tell us something terrible about the will to subjectivity when this will is also the affirmative assignation of a person or devastating event to the limbo of a progressive history.[92] Likewise, this book counsels against the seduction of access and reclamation that so often accompanies the citation of the archive.[93] Against the impossibility of comprehensive retrieval, *The Gift of Freedom* is instead a provisional account, pieced together from fragments of evidence, of the conditions that permit a particular discourse or discipline to arise and order worlds, which give the gift of freedom a particular form in ways that speak to its simultaneous making of life and death. As such, this skirmish also marks the point at which I wish to end, not with an answer that can illuminate for me the young marine's "real" meaning, but with an understanding that the liberal promise folds all potential meanings (value, debt, threat) into the lineages of freedom's empire. With this, we might reconceive debt not as the duration of gratitude, or the demand for repayment, but instead as a troubling reminder of unfinished histories that continue to cross us.

It may be freedom's task to banish the specter of misery or captivity, but it accomplishes this only by enforcing equivalences impossible to recompense because all is given, and foreclosing upon a presence invariably compromised through its giving. But the gift of freedom need not be true (whatever this might mean) to nonetheless hold sway as a structuring principle of liberalism's empire. We need not deny the violence and destruction that undergirds the gift of freedom to also take seriously its promise to reverence beauty, or respect aliveness, because these are part of its power. That the cause of death and the life necessity that calls for more are not after all distinct, requires of us an analytical and political alertness to their collusions and complicities within histories that target the subject of freedom for its force. As unending war and enduring freedom traverse the globe to produce more stateless nonpersons, more refugees, and more dead, the ways in which a onetime refugee might compose a beautiful scene from her life's debt may prove to be a minor worry, but they may also confirm the frightening mutability of liberalism's imperial pretensions. This book is one effort to understand how these pretensions might metamorphose into the form of a beguiling gift, the promise of freedom.

1

The Refugee Condition

At the present moment in world history nearly every nation must choose between alternative ways of life. The choice is too often not a free one. One way of life is based upon the will of the majority and is distinguished by free institutions, representative government, free elections, guarantees of individual liberty, freedom of speech and religion, and freedom from political oppression. The second way of life is based upon the will of a minority forcibly imposed upon the majority. It relies upon terror and oppression, a controlled press and radio, fixed elections, and the suppression of personal freedoms. I believe that it must be the policy of the United States to support free peoples who are resisting attempted subjugation by armed minorities or by outside pressures. I believe that we must assist free peoples to work out their own destinies in their own way.

—HARRY TRUMAN, "Special Message to the Congress on Greece and Turkey: The Truman Doctrine"

Liberalism formulates simply the following: I am going to produce what you need to be free. I am going to see to it that you are free to be free.

—MICHEL FOUCAULT, *The Birth of Biopolitics*

This book begins its inquiry into the genealogies of the gift of freedom with the continuities of powers between war and refuge. I foreground the refugee passage to look closely at the dual character of freedom—the development of capacities and the intensification of power—as it is bound to the passage of time. In particular, I wish to consider further and somewhat unfaithfully Derrida's provocation that "what it gives, the gift, is time, but this gift is also a demand of time,"[1] to fathom the time consciousness of the gift of freedom. What have time and freedom to do with the other, and what is the significance in their giving? Most obviously, perhaps, the liberal conception of freedom is constitutive of both the narration and the notion of linear, evolutionary time wrought through indices of race and coloniality. In this familiar strategy, the temporal distancing of some peoples as anachronistic, irrational, captive to super-stitious or atavistic faith, and otherwise outside—in Walter Benjamin's words—the secular, empty, and homogeneous time of history counter-poses the autonomous individual as the end of "natural" human con-sciousness, endowed with those capabilities to inhabit and act within modernity's now.[2] But inasmuch as world-historical homogeneous time and its core concept of progress emerge from the crucible of empire, these stories of human ontology are bound anew to liberalist alibi for the inten-sification of global power. That is, the gift of freedom also names those forms of liberal government that produce the measures and means by which the racial, colonial other be given to diminish—but never to close—the distance between anachronism and history proper. Brought together to narrate the refugee passage, these modes of given time speak to the conceptual commitments and structural investments that reconcile war and refuge as they meet over the figure of the benighted other, which becomes the troubling story of the subjection to freedom.

Timothy Linh Bui's *Green Dragon*, an independent film thematizing such refugee passage, tells one story of this movement and supplies a schematic map of this chapter's concerns about these conjoined scenes of power. The film opens with a complex sequence of image, sound, memory, and event, rapid-fire cuts syncopating cause and effect, chaos and command. *Green Dragon* begins as so many films about this war do, with historical footage of warplanes releasing their fatal cargo over dense jungle. In the next set of frames, stitched together by sounds of exploding munitions and indistinct cries over an instrumental track, Saigon's would-be evacuees flood airfields and collapse fences with the bludgeon of their desperation, hoping to es-cape the coming regime. These archival sequences are succeeded by choreo-graphed scenes of marines digging trenches and erecting tents under the Californian sun. Purposeful and efficient, these soldiers brace for the thou-sands of refugees to come.[3] The screen goes black before it abruptly is illuminated by an intense flashbulb, throwing into sharp relief the fatigue and sorrow creasing an aged refugee's face. The scene shifts inside a non-descript building filled with desks and stations where soldiers and social workers shoot photographs, ink fingers, and administer oaths to new arri-vals. From this well-organized chaos, the film plunges us once more into silence and shadow, as a young boy wakes amid other sleepers in a seemingly windowless barrack. Choosing a cautious path to the far side, the boy opens a door onto a blinding light. It is "April 1975," and the young boy is the promise of a new life, seeded in sorrow.

With these opening scenes of the film as a guide, this chapter is divided into several sections. I begin with war, not just as a necessary starting point for refugee passage but also to outline an initial schematic for the rhetorics and pragmatics of liberal war as a gift of freedom. How might we begin to understand the gift of freedom as liberal war? How might we imagine war as continuous with refuge? What are the intuitive and institutional structures that constellate imminent freedom with occupation, strategic hamlets with hospitality? While the conduct of this war, the war in Southeast Asia, has come under scrutiny for its terrible violence (we know that in those warplanes were devastating weapons that would continuously commit ruinous harm into the present[4]), I am interested in war as the calculation of freedom's continuation, the futural projection that goes by the name *security*, and of the capacities of the *new friend of freedom*—in this instance, to overcome anachronism or alien dominion.[5] Here I linger on the tropes of transition and timetable, naming those powers that sequence the before and after of the gift of freedom, and that animate the characteristic claims of liberalism's empire. The argument of the first part of this chapter is therefore more than an attempt to think the contexts for the gift of freedom as fictive—because the extent of violence is both dehumanizing and devastating—and constantly changing. Instead, this brief history considers the empirical claims that measure and manufacture freedom as making and unmaking the subject of this freedom in relation to these claims.

The second section of this chapter returns to the passage between war and refuge and to the conception of the particular pessimism of the refugee figure—stuck, stalled, and otherwise detained (by law but also in heart, in mind) for an unforeseeable duration. In doing so, I look closely at how the racialized story of anachronism reenters through the diagnosis of abnormality, in which the refugee condition, described as a state of arrested development or traumatic compulsion, is a target of disciplinary knowledge and power. These layered histories of transition and condition coalesce in the case study that closes this chapter, Timothy Linh Bui's refugee melodrama *Green Dragon* (for which he shares story credit with his filmmaker brother Tony Bui), a work that both envisages the refugee condition as held captive to an interior, idiosyncratic tempo and lauds the freedom granted through the external, regularized time of liberal capital. To consider refugee encampment, I turn to another of Derrida's aporias, hospitality, to grasp something of the structures of feeling and social forms through which encampment, appearing precisely at a moment of emergency, receives and rescues the ontologically destitute other with violence and power. As borne out in the opening montage, and indeed in its very making, the film commemorates the freedoms found in acceding to the demand of time, both in the plot's unfolding and the story of its creation, which avows the achievement of new life (to call to mind the military operation) as a historical reality.

By orchestrating a conversation between these ways of giving freedom to others—war and refuge—which is also giving the demand of time, this chapter interweaves brute force, epistemic violence, stories of development, pro tem hospitality, and conditional freedom to elaborate on some of the powers of liberalism's empire for the rest of this book.

Transitional Times

In the first half of the twentieth century, the freedom-loving peoples of the world determined that their own self-interest and security were best served by distant others' having the benefit of freedom. Calling for the United States to aid these others against the danger of communist dominion, in March 1947 President Harry Truman, addressing a joint session of Congress, set the stage for the ensuing Cold War and its theaters of operation: "I believe that it must be the policy of the United States to support free peoples who are resisting attempted subjugation by armed minorities or by outside pressures. *I believe that we must assist free peoples to work out their own destinies in their own way.*"[6] This request for aid to Greece and Turkey to prosecute insurgency was no departure from U.S. foreign policy. What was "radically new" (as Walter LeFeber puts it) in Truman's address was the argument that civil unrest in those countries indicated that a global war between the forces of freedom and captivity had been joined.[7] The United States—as the global guardian of freedom, especially as world wars and anticolonial struggles collapsed European claims to the same— bore a singular obligation to give what it could of itself.[8] This stratagem, through which Greece and Turkey were subsequently delivered from communism—as was Korea, in part—forecast the open U.S. intercession in Indochina, especially after the so-called loss of China in 1949. In 1954, with the Geneva Accords recognizing the territoriality and sovereignty of Indochina and drawing a provisional military demarcation line between North and South Viet Nam, the French accepted defeat as colonists, and the Americans (who, with the new South Vietnamese, refused to sign the accords) assumed their place as nation builders.

Conceived in the mid-twentieth century, the gift of freedom hypothesized a departure from the colonial order of things. After the Second World War, the United States christened Asia—first Korea and then Viet Nam (with, as we know, Cambodia and Laos, too)—as the key theater for the global conflict with communism, a conflict that also presumed the mantle of anti-imperialism, and vowed its policies be understood as begetting not a people's wretched dependency, but instead enlightened self-government. An early U.S. advisor to the new Republic of Vietnam, in particular to Prime Minister Ngo Dinh Diem, and a Central Intelligence Agency operative, Edward G. Lansdale stressed the importance of the so-called South Vietnamese experiment in a 1955 memo to a U.S. Army general: "Certainly the responsible Americans here would like to see the Vietnamese capably assuming an increasing share of their own burdens in all fields of national life. Thus, I would like to see our efforts here geared as completely as possible to the operating philosophy of helping the Vietnamese to help themselves."[9] And, inaugurating his new presidency in 1961 with pronouncements of U.S. ideals in a time of escalating war, John F. Kennedy declared, "Let every nation know, whether it wishes us well or ill, that we shall pay any price, bear any burden, meet any hardship, support any friend, oppose any foe to assure the survival and the success of liberty." Recalling the American Revolution, Kennedy continued his pledge to the decolonizing world: "To those new states whom we welcome to the ranks of the free, we pledge our word that one form of colonial control shall not have passed away merely to be replaced by a far more iron tyranny. We shall not always expect to find them supporting our view. But we shall always hope to find them strongly supporting their own freedom."[10]

These pledges of support both repeat and renounce the expectations of empire. Because this historical moment found colonialism under fire, the gift of freedom presumed to distinguish between forms of encounter and obligation—esteeming those born of generosity and friendship, rather than dependency and fealty—which subjectivize others, and ourselves. Thus liberalism proclaimed its antagonism to colonialism, naming colonialism a tyranny, a violation of the universal nature of human freedom.

Of course, there are hugely serious continuities between liberalism and colonialism as global forms, including the persistence of reason as the central feature of self-government, or, to put this in terms of freedom's dual character, what we might call the historical consciousness capable of apprehending and acting on the world, and liberal government as its means of exterior existence, with all the colonial cartographies and racial classifications these capacities and powers imply.[11] But even as the gift of freedom is in many ways contiguous with colonialism, and may exist with it simultaneously, it is not just as a consequence of the delegitimation of colonialism that the gift of freedom is distinct as a liberal narration for human enlightenment.[12] Liberalism's regime not only proposes to produce freedom continuously, but it also importantly resolves that distant others' having the benefit of such freedom is to "our" advantage; "freedom is never anything other—but this is already a great deal—than an actual relation between governors and governed,"[13] to recall Foucault's caution. I suggest that a figuration of freedom especially as a relation, doubling as a property, that can be produced continuously and gifted provisionally grants us critical purchase on the protracted nature of liberal imperial formations as well as their assemblages of knowledge and power.

I begin with a brief review of the conduct of war so that we might come to recognize the details through which the measure and the manufacture of human freedom become the promise of both liberal war and liberal peace. In this book's introduction, I described the gift of freedom as existentially established through the links between evolutionary time, in its temporal *and* spatial dimensions, and a given time. In this double movement, to be gifted freedom, which is also the demand of time, is to be beholden to an unfolding of human sovereignty *that has already happened elsewhere*, that has yet to happen here, and, crucially, *that may yet fail to do so*. Helping us attend to these distinctive conceptual commitments and political investments, the trope of *transition* as the occasional name for the knowledges and capacities that help others to help themselves is key to the innovations of power that underwrite liberal empire. Though every empire, as Edward Said observed so well, claims exception to enlighten and civilize, I suggest that liberalism privileges transition as an accelerated timetable for the directional advance of distant peoples and, in doing so, anticipates and proposes to hasten the termination of its mandate.[14] Foucault suggests something of the trouble with transition, however, in outlining the passage of life into the regime of biopower: "The fact of living was no longer an inaccessible substrate that only emerged from time to time, amid the randomness of death and its fatality; part of it passed into knowledge's field of control and power's sphere of intervention."[15] Where human history is determined to unfold in ostensibly universal and successive stages, then, the concept of transition demonstrates the premise of given time as a force, one that governs over the capabilities of the subject of freedom and constructs a liberalist alibi for the intensification of imperial powers.

In this historical moment, freedom emerges as a a paradigm for liberal government and empire, codified in the 1948 UN Universal Declaration of Human Rights preamble. Throughout this declaration, we find the human defined through sovereignty and self-determination, and freedom determined as abstract, objectified, calculable, and exchangeable—or, to use Foucault's phrasing, "as a universal gradually realized over time," one undergoing "quantitative variations, greater or lesser drastic reductions, or more or less important periods of eclipse."[16] By defining freedom as a relation and as a property that is converted into measurable and comparable articles, the declaration—although an object of contestation and controversy—elides its creation story to universalize the asymmetry of liberal political and economic thought in relation to illiberal others.[17] Writing about the global preserve of modern liberalism, Vivienne Jabri observes thusly: "Of crucial significance here is that 'peace' is at once rendered political, is, in other words, a product of distinctly political arrangements and not simply a produce of moral judgment."[18] Especially via *perpetual peace*, following Immanuel Kant, this state of being is conditional on a constitution based on such articles as the "civil right of individuals within a nation," the "international right of states," and "cosmopolitan right" applicable to both individuals and states "regarded as citizens of a universal state of mankind."[19] The declaration also proclaims these rights and freedoms regularized in its articles to be subject to maximization and securitization by free peoples. We discover here that questions of peace and freedom center not just the conditions for human self-possession and the governance that the human deserves, but also the calculation of possible or probable danger that threatens their actualization in the here and now, and in the future. That is, the document assumes universal value but also imperfect presence. Hence it refers, if somewhat obliquely, to structures of enforcement directed at the protection and production of human freedom: "Every individual and every organ of society, keeping this Decla-

ration constantly in mind, shall strive by teaching and education to promote respect for these rights and freedoms and by progressive measures,
national and international, to *secure their universal and effective recognition and observance*, both among the peoples of Member States themselves
and among the peoples of territories under their jurisdiction."[20] Thus did
Truman pose his case before Congress. The attachment to freedom, he
claimed, must continually recommit free peoples to support the recognition and observance of rights and freedoms in an increasingly unstable
global order. From such concerns, the category of totalitarianism—and
most of all communism—became known as freedom's opposite (occlud-
ing individual rights as well as constitutional and contractual forms of
collectivity), which is to say totalitarianism incarnates the premise of a
mounting danger to humanity, subsuming complicated social and political forms under its lengthening shadow. Here we discern two sides of the
same coin: the infamous domino theory, based on the speculation that
contiguous intimacies between subjugated peoples might smooth the passage of virulent misery to communism, also proposed that such peril be
countered by its antithesis, the dissemination of freedom and democracy
through *other* intimacies.[21]

Of primary significance here is the declared necessity of the global
aspirations of liberal government to counter the imperial pretensions of
communist tyranny. To conjure the language of the Cold War, this modern dynamic of freedom and its antinomy, captivity, thus called for a
strategy of not just containment but conquest. This dynamic of freedom
and captivity is made clear in the National Security Council report widely
known as NSC 68, called "United States Objectives and Programs for
National Security," and issued by the council on April 14, 1950, under
Truman's directive. This document shaped the contours of U.S. policy
throughout the Cold War.[22] Following a study of the superpowers and
each one's feasible or extant acquisition of thermonuclear weapons, NSC
68 reviewed U.S. strategic and military policy programs in the lengthening shadow of China's "fall" to communism and the Soviet Union's deto-
nation of an atom bomb. From this document emerged a tale of an
ensuing contest for life and death: "There is a basic conflict between the
idea of freedom under a government of laws, and the idea of slavery under
the grim oligarchy of the Kremlin, which has come to a crisis with the
polarization of power. . . . The idea of freedom, moreover, is peculiarly and

intolerably subversive of the idea of slavery. But the converse is not true. The implacable purpose of the slave state to eliminate the challenge of freedom has placed the two great powers at opposite ends. It is this fact which gives the present polarization of power the quality of crisis."[23] As Jodi Kim describes, this report framed the conflict between the United States and the Soviet Union as "a revised Hegelian lordship and bondage schema in which the slave does not aspire to transcendence and freedom but aspires to destroy freedom itself."[24] To avert disaster, a global humanity must act on the side of contract against captivity. Liberal empire comes to a self-image that has no limits, even as it is itself the author of limits, through recourse to such universality. As we shall see, this responsibility for preserving and proliferating human freedom and other vital properties is how liberal empire becomes an empire of humanity.

Found in the characterization of a tumultuous moment or series of moments—particularly in the picture of freedom's promulgation over time and space, simultaneous with swelling insecurity in newly postcolonial states—is the echo of those colonial conjectures through which empire encountered racial others in terms of the anachronistic and alien or, more precisely, in terms of strategies of civilizational distancing. In his brilliant *Provincializing Europe*, Dipesh Chakrabarty observes the dimensions of the story of human development unfolding over a single, evolutionary world-historical time, referring to this hegemony as historicism: "Historicism is what made modernity or capitalism look not simply global but rather as something that became global over time, by originating in one place (Europe) and then spreading outside it. This 'first in Europe, then elsewhere' structure of global historical time was historicist; different non-Western nationalisms would later produce local versions of the same narrative, replacing 'Europe' by some locally constructed center. It was historicism that allowed Marx to say that the 'country that is more developed industrially only shows, to the less developed, the image of its own future.'"[25] The development of Western modernity and liberal capitalism over time, and their expansion across space, thus underwrites the premise of empire as the universalizing story of human historical consciousness. Chakrabarty continues, observing John Stuart Mill's arguments, that colonial others are thereby consigned to "an imaginary waiting room of history." "In doing so, it converted history itself into a version of this waiting room. We are all headed for the same destination, Mill averred, but some people were to arrive earlier than others. That was what historicist consciousness was: a recommendation to the colonized to wait. Acquiring historical consciousness, acquiring the public spirit that Mill thought absolutely necessary for the art of self-government, was also to learn this art of waiting. This waiting was the realization of the 'not yet' of historicism."[26]

Historicism, as the name for those philosophical and political mandates enabling European domination of the world in the nineteenth century through a particular logic of time and space, is changed in the twentieth century—the so-called American century—with the gift of freedom. While still dictating the unfolding of modernity and capitalism across the globe over time, as "an image of its own future," liberalist historicist consciousness is less "a recommendation to the colonized to wait" than the guidance of the (formerly) colonial other through the opened door into history proper. That is, liberalism's empire hangs on the "not yet" that is both a denial of coevalness, in Johannes Fabian's well-known phrase, but also the conferral of catching up, or the hastened arrival of enlightenment—as Kennedy saluted would-be contemporaries, "welcome to the ranks of the free." Once again, colonial schema are not on the outside of liberalist structures of knowledge and power, which name certain forms of racial, civilizational difference as anachronistic and alien to universal enlightenment. Akhil Gupta writes of the regularized timetable for newly "modern" states: "In the Third World, the utopian time of the nation is profoundly shaped by a sense of belated arrival, of being born into a world of nations competing against each other, but in which the new arrivals are positioned in the starting blocks of a race already underway."[27] But we might also recall here Pierre Bourdieu's astute observation that strategies of power consist of "playing on the time, or rather the tempo, of the action,"[28] such that liberalism as an imperial discourse invariably refers to the near future and to a hastened tempo that anticipates, and labors for, the moment in which the formerly colonial other is "finally" capable of self-government. In other words, the historical and conceptual interface between racial distance and human development together narrate a people not yet consequential to human history, but capable of becoming so. Or, as Denise Ferreira da Silva aptly observes, in this war—and we could say in liberal war on the whole—"the defining political decision is not the naming of the enemy but the identification of a particular kind of friend, the 'new friend' of freedom."[29] It is in this way that liberalism—wrought through temporal concepts of historicism and teleology that comprehend history as the actualization of an ideal presence, which here goes by the name *human freedom*—presumes to knowingly realize and manufacture this present and presence, through the gift of freedom as its rational dissemination across the globe for human progress and historical and political transformation.

What social forms emerge here, addressed to a transitional being as a target of knowledge, power, and action, precisely when the future of human life and freedom is caught in a state of emergency? Here the concept of transition invites further reflection about given time as a liberalist innovation of power, inasmuch as transition synthesizes two kinds of temporalization, encompassing the "imaginary waiting room"—that historicist chronology ordering racialized, colonial populations—and also the release or reprieve from a regularized timetable to hasten the arrival and achievement of human freedom and sovereignty. On the one hand, the concept of transition is defined precisely by a temporal distancing of distant peoples across the colonial globe. On the other hand, transition professes an optimism about the elasticity of the subject-in-becoming, given time and proper guidance. In this regard, in the cant of records like NSC 68 and presidential statements, we discern that liberalism not only assumes that the desire for freedom should look the same everywhere, but that this desire nonetheless unfolds in progressive chapters or stages, and that this achievement, as the story of the universal human, lies with a liberal government to speed its necessary end. Put another way, the gift of freedom first diagnoses some peoples as anomalous and anachronistic and then intervenes to mediate and guide "their natural developments" toward the world historical project of modernity.[30]

Here the gift of freedom vows a radical rethinking of human sovereignty as a planetary phenomenon, unfolding from a particular understanding of the United States as the center of an emergent world order. Of this temporalizing figuration of the "new friend," Denise da Silva offers:

> A people who have just been welcomed in the territory of freedom find themselves infiltrated by enemies of freedom—or their agents. Because they are unable to help themselves, the US sends troops to liberate and/or protect the new friends of freedom, who would otherwise fall prey of the enemies of freedom. While the story has three characters—the enemies of freedom, the friends of freedom, and the new friends of freedom—only the last two are necessary for its meaning to come about. As a modern narrative, this story

reproduces the ethical program as it narrates the trajectory of a mind toward self-determination. But the story it tells is different. Because it is not a self-regulated and self-developing subject, without military and economic aid from the friends of freedom, the 'new friend of freedom,' the subject-in-becoming, would not be able to sustain itself as a self-determined polity.[31]

In light of such political and moral indeterminacy, the forces of freedom must compensate for native delinquency. Impeded in his or her maturation by colonial dependency, primitive culture, or abject poverty, the new friend for want of reason is rendered unusually susceptible to alien compulsion. NSC 68, for instance, surmised that insidious Soviet powers found a "particularly receptive audience in Asia," where still immature peoples might yet be responsive to a spectacular scene of dominion.[32] National Security Council Report 48/1, "The Position of the United States with Respect to Asia," authored in the aftermath of China's totalitarian turn, determined that Asia, due to "traditional social patterns antithetical to democracy" and a lack of "leaders practiced in the exercise of responsible power," to be a "fertile field" for "communist control and Soviet influence."[33] This vocabulary of immaturity and guided development also borrowed from the evolutionary figuration of the other as child that cohered the translation of colonial knowledge into liberalist alibi.[34] Famously, then-Senator John F. Kennedy proffered commitment as a moral—and paternal—imperative at the 1956 American Friends of Vietnam conference: "If we are not the parents of little Vietnam, then surely we are the godparents. We presided at its birth, we gave assistance to its life, we have helped to shape its future. . . . This is our offspring. We cannot abandon it."[35] Thus, the new friend cannot wage this war (the taking of life) against the enemy on his own, not least because the right to do so is reserved for sovereign states. (As Achille Mbembe notes, "colonies are similar to the frontiers" because the colony is "not organized in a state form" and has "not created a human world."[36]) To these vulnerable peoples, so newly awakened to futurity (not least of all the futurity secured by the right to war), the United States must commit to produce what others require to be free. Kennedy again: "To those people in the huts and villages of half the globe struggling to break the bonds of mass misery, we pledge our best efforts to help them help themselves, for whatever period is required—not because the communists may be doing it, not because we seek their votes, but because it is right."[37]

Importantly, the concept of transition does not refer only to what is chronologically sequential on a continuum of linear, teleological time. Just as transition integrates two contrasting temporalities, transition also divides development into the normal and pathological, and orders peoples across the colonial globe according to these measures of presence and potential. Put another way, transition also locates the subject of freedom at a juncture before the present of liberal modernity, poised precariously between horizons of possible, antithetical times. This historical antagonism underwrites (as one example) NSC 68, which ominously framed these incompatible futures as freedom against slavery, nature against pathology. Transition supposes the subject of freedom may yet close in on modernity's now, but at the same time, as an object of intervention, it may also disrupt the continuity of progressive time, veering away from one horizon into its other, communism, a political and also existential enslavement. In this schema, enlightenment as a rule of common chronological succession open to all peoples is less an inevitability than an ideal—a rule and an ideal under constant threat of decline or destruction. Consequently, inherent in the concept of transition is a paradoxical plasticity. Historicism does not assure the so-called natural developments of distant peoples; transition requires the continuous review and regulation of necessary political and psychic structures, occasioning what Ann Laura Stoler usefully describes as "*states of deferral* that mete out promissory notes that are not exceptions to their operation but constitutive of them."[38]

Thus did the Cold War United States defend its intercessions throughout Asia as necessary policing actions to secure peoples and places where anticolonial struggles and decolonization movements rendered them deficient in proper governance, defined as constitutional structures or civilized arrangements, and disqualified them from the rights of sovereignty, and hence susceptible to occupation and control by alien powers. In this schema, these reviled powers are insidious in their totalitarian will to smash the clock of human progress, to hold human beings in captivity. In contradistinction to these terrible powers, liberalism is conceived as a gift of quickened time to those who are waiting and wanting, through which freedom must come from a place other than the one to which it must come. Calculating freedom's continuation, transition disciplines the time and space of the racial, colonial other into the political and economic logics of the known future, modernity's now. In doing so, liberalism's empire claims to desire an end to itself.

Through the concept of transition, then, we find the simultaneous emergence of modern forms of state power and biopolitics that inherit colonial and imperial schemata, including those historicisms that order human life and freedom through stratum and asymmetry but that also mediate between liberal imaginaries of the good and the true, "freedom, justice, and peace in the world,"[39] and liberal structures of government, including contractual economies, democratic politics, and chosen sociality.[40] In other words, the manufacture of freedom as the culture and art of government of the liberal center converts the colonialist underpinnings of modernity's manifest destiny through the generous gesture ("to produce what you need to be free") into a technology for managing and establishing the United States as the empire that claims not to be one, granting other peoples a boon. In 1948, one year after Truman targeted some peoples in insecure elsewheres as freedom's problem, the U.S. State Department released a statement of U.S. policy toward Indochina, in which we might discern what would become a practical system of world remaking:

> Our long-term objectives are: (1) to eliminate so far as possible Communist influence in Indochina and to see installed a self-governing nationalist state which will be friendly to the US and which, commensurate with the capacity of the peoples involved, will be patterned upon our conception of a democratic state as opposed to the totalitarian state which would evolve inevitably from Communist domination; (2) to foster the association of the peoples of Indochina with the western powers, . . . to the end that those peoples will prefer freely to cooperate with the western powers culturally, economically and politically; (3) to raise the standard of living so that the peoples of Indochina will have an incentive to work productively and thus contribute to a better balanced world economy; and (4) to prevent undue Chinese [Communist] penetration and subsequent influence in Indochina so that the peoples of Indochina will not be hampered in their natural developments by the pressure of an alien people and alien interests.[41]

Read against the grain of staged generosity, these statements of policy emerge as a dense textual accounting of an imperial regime's underwriting of freedom's invocation and, in the terms of this book, the gift's subjection. We can easily observe in these documents the language of evaluation and assessment of a people's competencies and their potential—*commensurate with the capacity of the peoples involved, the peoples of Indochina will not be hampered in their natural developments by the pressure of an alien people and alien interests, to see the Vietnamese capably assuming an increasing share of their own burdens,* et cetera—language that inscribes onto the bodies of the Vietnamese, those foreign to freedom, a chronopolitics of development.

But we might also discern from these same materials that the gift of freedom derives from a particular conceptualization of liberal power, or governmentality. Foucault describes governmentality as a mode and a mandate of power concerned with the maintenance and control of bodies, persons, and populations, and with the production and regulation of the life that falls under its purview. Beyond sovereignty or territory, governmentality aims to arrange "the complex of men and things."[42] And indeed, the manufacture of freedom and self-government—"helping the Vietnamese to help themselves"—is pronounced over and against (according to the 1948 statement of policy) undue and alien influence, as the substance of what the United States has to give. NSC 68, in outlining four courses of action, names war (with the Soviet Union) as one course of action, but war is not the final recommendation. Instead, the report forwards a much more labyrinthine course, "a rapid build-up of political, economic, and military strength in the free world." Of course, wars did happen, and were in no way "cold"— more than ten million people died in the wars in Asia alone.[43] We know that atrocities and unlawful measures unfolded in the course of a liberal way of war, including civilian massacres, political assassinations, and the continuing afterlife of biochemical and herbicidal devastation. The conduct of these wars as military actions and intelligence operations are discussed at length, and with more close attention, elsewhere (though I do argue in the following chapter that attention to military excesses do not necessarily counteract liberal claims to exception about war making). Nonetheless, these wars occurred under the auspices of what NSC 68 named "an affirmative program" (echoed in the statement of policy toward Indochina): "a strengthening of central institutions, an improvement in administration, and generally a development of an economic and social structure within which the peoples of Asia can make more effective use of their great human and material resources."[44] Passages such as this point to a fundamental shift in the conceptualizations of power captured in the gift of freedom as a narration but also a program for the manufacture of freedom in ostensibly insecure elsewheres. The gift of freedom names an ensemble of powers exercised not over a finite territory, but as an intermediary toward arranging a "complex of men and things" into a modern administrative state, or a liberal empire.

Into this complex, liberal war is described as a *tactic*. Liberal war may well be the motor of history, and perhaps also its measure, but it is not its rationale. Such undertakings as those that found the gift of freedom, seeking to usher a new friend toward becoming recognizably human to a global hegemon that promises the conditions for freedom and all that follows from it, are therefore distinct from sovereign power. Sovereignty traditionally is concerned above all with preserving territory. The exercise of sovereign power might be discerned in empire's objections to the 1954 Geneva Agreements, which the United States refused to sign so as not to be bound by their provisos, or the 1973 Paris Peace Accords (calling for U.S. military withdrawal from Viet Nam, among other stipulations), which President Richard Nixon sought to sabotage and later to contravene. But we cannot conceive of the conduct of the war, or liberal statecraft, solely through sovereignty. Governmentality instead has become the main way such state power is vitalized, Foucault suggests, and into which war (defined as apparatuses of security) is thoroughly absorbed. Consider in this case the Strategic Hamlet Program, an early joint operation between the United States and South Viet Nam whereby rural populations were forcibly removed from their homes and exposed to strict discipline and control within so-called fortified villages. Ostensibly to protect them, the program in fact seized and detained them as likely conscripts to the Viet Cong.[45] But these actions, radically redrafting space as the "raw material"[46] of sovereignty, are also part of a set of tactics characteristic of governmentality that, as Judith Butler put so well in her work on our contemporary wars, "operate[s] diffusely, to dispose and order populations, and to produce and reproduce subjects, their practices and beliefs, in relation to specific policy aims."[47] Thus the U.S. policy aims lay in the final, "security phrase" of the Strategic Hamlet program, in which, according to the Department of Defense, "the populace was to be 'reoriented,' political control was to pass to civilian hands, and economic and social programs were to be initiated to consolidate government control."[48] Brought together under the charge of transition, sovereign powers that include dislocations and encampments of racial, colonial others become enfolded into the governmentality of liberal empire.

The logic of this "reorienting" characterizes the labor of transition, marshaling sovereign and governmental powers together to discipline the wayward other according to liberalism's dictates of time and space, and in the image of empire's now.[49] Unambiguously on the horizon of liberal modernity, then, is the establishment and (presumably) interim supervision of the necessary structures that would gradually enable self-government in the fullness of given time. These necessary structures, as enumerated in the statement of U.S. policy toward Indochina, include a sound state able to guarantee to an abstract juridical subject his or her individual rights and a historical person endowed with the necessary properties of self-possession equal to these rights. Pursuing a wartime strategem that we now know as nation building, the United States sought to foster an anticommunist, quasi-democratic regime, sending millions of dollars in aid and hundreds of advisors to the newly formed government of Ngo Dinh Diem, who sustained little support in South Viet Nam (though much in the United States, initially), and his multiple successors after his assassination (which the United States also supported). It is in this way that the logic of "distinctly political arrangements" characterizing Jabri's analysis of perpetual peace, in which "the external peace between states is made possible through certain arrangements within the state," applies also to the measure and manufacture of human freedom.[50] Recall that the 1948 statement of policy on Indochina numbers among its objectives the imposition of a debt in the form of "freely" chosen dependency: "(2) to foster the association of the peoples of Indochina with the western powers, . . . to the end that those peoples will prefer freely to cooperate with the western powers culturally, economically and politically." As well we must name the debt to capital, banishing compulsory labor under colonial administrations for waged labor as choice and the market as freedom in its stead, through which security in this liberal schema was guaranteed: "(3) to raise the standard of living so that the peoples of Indochina will have an incentive to work productively and thus contribute to a better balanced world economy." We cannot dismiss as disingenuous these claims to wish for the subject of freedom the achievement of self-government, or otherwise disguising more ignobly mundane, material ambitions—because both liberal political modernity (understood as citizenship and rights, including the right to contract with others) and liberal capitalism are of one piece as referents for human peace and freedom. Through intuitive and institutional structures that dictate the want or absence of these things of which the gift consists, and that ensure their continuity, the gift of freedom hence levies a twofold obligation to accept and then to acquit the debt—that is to say, compliance with those liberal forms of sociality and organization presented as the gifts of freedom. Such compliance thus foregrounds a dynamic of liberal supplementarity rather than one of symmetry: the one who receives is also the supplement to (or the surplus of) liberalism's empire.

Clustered together in the figuration of the new friend to freedom, the characterization of "not yet" consciousness as credible promise is also its plausible failure.[51] We find this historicist sensibility, through which the sped-up timetable of transition might have the unfortunate consequence of a stumbling progress, in the contemporaneous words of the political scientist, state advisor, and erstwhile friend to the ill-fated Diem, Wesley Fishel: "The peoples of Southeast Asia are not sufficiently sophisticated to understand what we mean by democracy and how they can exercise and protect their own political rights . . . That individual human rights may often be neglected or sacrificed in this period of national infancy should not be surprising."[52] Homi Bhaba put so well this postcolonial's predicament, whom historicist discourse interpellates as "a reformed, recognizable Other, *as a subject of difference that is almost the same, but not quite.*"[53] As a narrative of generosity then, the gift of freedom secures its alibi in the event that the new friend does not hold fast. Such that the noncontemporaneity of the new friend supplies justification for intervention, the postulate of freedom as given time positions him as responsible for his own fate, in the fullness of that time. In a 1963 televised interview, President Kennedy thus equivocated on whether the United States would continue to control the war: "In the final analysis, it's their war, and they are the ones who will either win or lose it."[54]

Transition is marshaled as a defense against empire's defeat. In this instance, its name was "Vietnamization." On November 3, 1969, President Nixon in a televised speech debuted Vietnamization, "a plan in which we will withdraw all our forces from Vietnam on a schedule in accordance with our program, as the South Vietnamese become *strong enough to defend their own freedom.*"[55] With no trigger for dramatic reversals, under Vietnamization the war's conduct coupled troop withdrawals and the accelerated training and strengthening of the South Vietnamese army with semi-clandestine military escalation, including the U.S. invasions of Cambodia in 1970 and Laos in 1971 and two massive bombing and mining operations against North Viet Nam in 1972. As a name for transition and timetable, however, Vietnamization laid the onus of failure upon the new friend. Nixon again: "The defense of freedom is everybody's business—not just

America's business. *And it is particularly the responsibility of the people whose freedom is threatened.* In the previous administration, we Americanized the war in Vietnam. In this administration, *we are Vietnamizing the search for peace.*"[56] With the defeat of the U.S. mission in Southeast Asia, the capacities of the new friend were judged anew through anachronism and its remainders, such as despotism, tribal schism, and an unreasonable predisposition to alien subjugation, as the dereliction to comply with, or indeed to merit, the gift of freedom.[57] On the eve of the communist capture of Saigon, the South Vietnamese capital, the *Washington Post* published an editorial titled "Deliverance," which indeed sought to rescue America from culpability for this war: "For if much of the actual conduct of Vietnam policy over the years was wrong and misguided—even tragic— it cannot be denied that some part of the purpose of that policy was right and defensible. Specifically, *it was right to hope that the people of South Vietnam would be able to decide on their own form of government and social order.* The American public is entitled, indeed obligated, to explore how good impulses came to be transmuted into bad policy, but we cannot afford to cast out all remembrance of that earlier impulse."[58] In a more damning postwar evaluation of empire's collapse, the historian Brian Van-DeMark censures the Vietnamese people repeatedly through pathologies of underdevelopment, bereft of the "political will necessary to create an effective and enduring government," afflicted with a "fundamental debility" and "a chronic and fatal political disorder." Deeming these poor friends unfit for the rigors of democracy, VanDeMark concludes, ominously: "South Vietnam's shortcomings taught a proud and mighty nation that it could not save a people in spite of themselves."[59] And, decades later, President George W. Bush, in an interview with Fox cable show host Bill O'Reilly about U.S. efforts for regime change via Operation Iraqi Freedom, agreed that "the South Vietnamese didn't fight for their freedom," whereas the Iraqis surely would.[60]

In this respect, the gift of freedom as a historicist discourse is the renovation and revitalization of structures of race and coloniality.[61] Liberal empire targets the subject of freedom as an incomplete person who lacks the properties necessary for self-government and who balances on the knife's edge between antithetical futures. It is as such that the gift of freedom unfolds before us as a historicist, hierarchical differential, thoroughly imbued with histories of racial governmentality and—because the biopolitics of liberal peace shares the same premises as liberal war—as a circuit that renders the object of intervention, the subject of freedom, a moving target. Thus, the transition, the "not yet," is both the principle that exhibits the gift of freedom to its best advantage and the foil that denies blame for its failure. Anachronism or other-possession presumes to name the alterity of the other, the not-same, the heterogeneous—what remains recalcitrant to transition to modern, homogeneous time. It is precisely this trace of race and coloniality that are "the continuities between the remains of war and the rehabilitations of peace" underwriting liberal empire.[62]

The Refugee Condition

CAVANAUGH: Now how do you set up that kind of housing almost overnight?

JONASON: Oh, my gosh, you know, they had Marines and sailors and civilians and everybody just chipping in 24/7 building the tent cities, using—cleaning out Quonsets, the Quonsets at Talega, excuse me, at San Onofre were not really ready for people to move in so they had to be prepared, cots brought in, trenches made, you know, all kinds of wash situations created, food brought in. Clothing, a lot of these people didn't have clothing. Some of them didn't have shoes. . . .

CAVANAUGH: Right, that's—so when you receive the refugees, were—describe to us the way they came to Camp Pendleton.

JONASON: Well, they landed at El Toro, as I understand, and then they were bused down from El Toro, sometimes in the middle of the night, depending on what group they came in. And then they were housed in the various camps that were set up for them, and they were crowded in. I mean, you could barely, you know, step over all these people that were sleeping all over the place trying to find a place to stay.

CAVANAUGH: What kind of condition were they in when they arrived?

JONASON: It's my understanding that they were, some of them, in pretty bad condition as far as, you know, they'd been traveling, they were frightened, they were displaced totally. These were people not knowing what the next day was going to bring, and so they were happy to be here.

—"Camp Pendleton's Tent City Housed 50,000 Vietnamese
Refugees," the KPBS *These Days* host Maureen Cavanaugh's
interview with the Camp Pendleton Museum historian
Faye Jonason, April 29, 2010

In April 1975, after training thousands of military personnel who would secure the foreign policy aims of the United States in Korea and Viet Nam, Marine Base Camp Pendleton in Southern California began preparing for another part in the Cold War—this time, as a city of refuge. (It bears noting here that the camp bears the name of Major General Joseph Henry Pendleton, a career officer whose imperial adventuring sent him to Nicaragua, Santo Domingo, Cuba, and the Philippines at the dawning of the twentieth century.) With reports of North Vietnamese forces marching toward Saigon triggering panic and plans for withdrawal, President Gerald Ford established the Special Interagency Task Force for Indochina on April 18, charged with coordinating eighteen federal agencies, including the Department of Defense, for the evacuation of "high risk" Vietnamese with ties to the U.S. occupation infrastructure, and the Senate Judiciary Committee approved emergency asylum for more than 150,000 "Indochinese."[63] Continuous with the war's waging, a concept of transition is reintroduced in the name of Operation New Life.[64] In a matter of days, Camp Pendleton became the first of four military installations, reorganized into centers of care and control, to receive Vietnamese evacuees as once again subjects of freedom.[65]

With this passage between war and refuge, I point to the crossing of racial anachronism from its being a sign of subject status for the new friend of freedom, to its making as a symptom of the refugee diagnosed through arrested affect or potentiality, a discursive, medico-juridical disposition I am calling the *refugee condition*. In doing so, I veer away from the refugees' "hearts of sorrow," so familiar to us from official papers, literary archives, academic writing, and individual testimonies, and I turn instead toward the schema and stakes underlying this figuration.[66] A more critical reading of the refugee condition as an object of biomedical study, without denying or dismissing profound psychical disturbance, may demonstrate how a racialized rhetoric of anachronism reenters through the diagnosis of abnormality. Whereas the transition targeted the absence of necessary institutional structures for self-government, with more or less elliptical reference to psychical structures, the condition specifically diagnoses the dearth of psychical structures, with more or less oblique reference to institutional structures for the same. That is, the compulsive interiorization of a refugee consciousness may also be complicit in liberal schema for distributed life capacities: first, in the form of the condition described as a state of arrested development or traumatic compulsion with its assumption of an empirical normalcy; second, in the causal background the refugee condition in particular names; and third, in the refugee condition as a target of disciplinary action. To note that the condition is underpinned by liberal epistemes is to insist on the genealogical character of scientific-technical and affective knowledges about the space and time of the refugee. I argue that in naming the condition (after the manner of transition), the cluster of references that establish abnormality dramatizes for us more their usages for liberal governmentality than as empirical evidence of the psychical failures the condition purports to categorize and codify. For these reasons, I consider the refugee condition less a record of psychic disorder and more an embedded sign whose evidentiary status decisively connects deprivation, development, and discipline.[67]

In the lectures collected as *Abnormal*, Foucault concludes his genealogy of the abnormal individual with an outline of the condition as that which targets, and focuses, disciplinary systems through powers brought to bear on the thing called the psyche (what he dubs the "Psy-function"—or, elsewhere, "the psychiatric, psychopathological, psycho-sociological, psycho-criminological, and psychoanalytic function"[68]). Not an illness, but also not not-an-illness, according to Foucault, "the condition is a sort of *permanent causal background* on the basis of which illness may develop in a number of processes and episodes. In other words, the condition is the abnormal basis upon which illness become possible."[69] In a "normal" state, human consciousness is aimed toward possible action and probable consequence, in a universe that is knowable through empirical measures. This capacity for human freedom and intercourse with others rests in discriminating by moral reasoning between that which belongs to the interior, and to the exterior, of the subject. The condition therefore names the absence of an underlying structure, or the underdevelopment of such a structure, that would otherwise commit the faculties of human consciousness to their proper place and proportion.

It is not difficult to find statements imputing to the refugee the underdevelopment, or arrested development, of apperception, understanding, and reason. Indeed, out of the refugee camps emerged a disciplinary specialization that, as Aihwa Ong observes, sought the "systematic naming and ordering of refugee illnesses."[70] Thus did anthropologists, sociologists, psychiatrists, and other "experts" perceive that "Anxiety, fear, frustration, and emotional disturbance appear, and often the refugee regresses to a more infantile state, loses his willpower, and becomes apathetic, helpless, or manic and aggressive."[71] "The refugee loses structure, the ability to coordinate, predict and expect, and his basic feelings of competence."[72] Consider also the following statements from camp ethnographers, in which we find a refugee consciousness absent of interest or calculation: "The Vietnamese role was passive: things were done to them; they did very little. And, like much of the camp life that followed, they stood in interminable lines waiting for something to happen."[73] Or, in this fanciful description, refugee passivity and powerlessness: "This mental state [of helplessness] resembles that of a billiard ball which, devoid of inner self-propelling force, allows its path and movement to be governed by outside forces beyond its control."[74] Such reports from camp ethnographers and biomedical personnel, echoed in refugee testimonials, reinforce that the condition, to borrow from Foucault, "is precisely the characteristic structure or structural whole of an individual who has either been arrested in his development or who has regressed from a later to an earlier state of development."[75] He is profoundly, painfully, stuck in time.

In these reports and studies, we confront once again the measure of capacities as an empirical concern, through which notions of the viable human are acted out in the global arena, and through which the condition of being a refugee is construed as a generalizable state of abnormality, shorthand for deprivation, deindividuation, and deficiency. It is also important to note that the refugee's arrested time consciousness, in this telling, forecloses the hope that time in its forward progress and plentitude might soothe his or her pain. Consider this 2001 supplemental report from the U.S. Department of Health and Human Services: "Studies document high rates of mental disorders among these refugees. A large community sample of Southeast Asian refugees in the United States found that premigration trauma events and refugee camp experiences were significant predictors of psychological distress even five years or more after migration."[76] Or, as one reporter muses, "How long does a refugee remain a refugee? Perhaps forever. Even after settling in a new land, a refugee may find that being rootless and adrift is not a transient condition but a permanent, sometimes debilitating state of mind."[77]

In this way, the refugee condition also acts as an explanation for the fervent response—understood as an interpretative gap, a jarring noncoincidence between event and meaning—to any undistorted figuration of Ho Chi Minh.[78] Consider this complicated chain of causally disparate, but discursively linked, image-events behind the shuttering of the English-language, youth-produced television show *Vietnamese American eXposure* (VAX), formerly broadcast on Saigon TV—based in Westminster, California—in response to hostile denunciations of the show's screening of a brief clip from the 2004 documentary *Saigon, USA*. The documentary, which aired on PBS nationally, is loosely organized around the 1999 Hi-Tek incident in Little Saigon—in which a Vietnamese video store owner dared to hang a poster of Ho Chi Minh, alongside the Vietnamese flag, in public view—and the fifty-two days of massive protests and rallies that followed. Following the national news coverage that spotlighted the Hi-Tek incident, the documentary includes a seconds-long clip from a CNN news report featuring a camera close-up of the poster hanging in the store, gaily decorated with Christmas lights. This brief moment, appearing as part of a five-year retrospective about the months-long controversy by VAX, inspired enough outcry and accusation of communist sympathy for Saigon TV's chief executive officer to cancel the show. Even this highly mediated sight of Ho Chi Minh, trauma tells us, destroys the refugee's precarious peace of mind. In which feelings are also subject to a rational, and rationing, governance, the condition operates as a gauge for them, in their proportion and duration.[79] Here are multiple layers of what might easily be characterized as the derealization of reality. Such confusion, so systemic that it might be understood as a symptom, appears "secondarily, as a sort of epiphenomena, with regard to this condition that is fundamentally a condition of abnormality."[80] With the dissolution of those structures that perceive causality and continuity, the refugee cannot distinguish between subconscious ghosts and external stimuli, between forms and genres of image making or storytelling, or between two temporally distant moments —as in the near-instantaneous response to the five seconds of a documentary image of a poster of Ho Chi Minh, five years after the Hi-Tek incident and the months-long protests that followed, three decades after the revolutionary leader died and the war ended in defeat.[81] The condition thereby is a prison house, in more ways than one. Allowing for both the diagnostic imposition of illness, as well as the discovery of a comprehensive cause, the condition has an absolute power that structures all signification. Foucault writes: "It allows any physical element or deviant behavior whatever, however disparate and distant they may be, to be connected with a sort of unified background that accounts for it—a background that differs from the state of health but nevertheless is not an illness. Consequently, this notion of condition has a formidable capacity for integration: It refers to nonhealth, but it can also bring into its field any conduct whatsoever as soon as it is physiologically, psychologically, sociologically, morally, and even legally deviant."[82]

Such disturbance also goes by the familiar name *trauma*. What comes through so clearly in innumerable narrations of protest (sympathetic or condemnatory) or other perturbation is the rhetoric of noncontemporaneity and captive consciousness, for which the principal cause seems obvious.[83] War is a catastrophic event, and, as Marilyn Ivy observes, "provide[s] the occasion for the most sustained theorizing of the traumatic."[84] The traumatic consciousness finds that one is not at one with oneself, that one is divorced from and dispossessed of self-knowledge. Drawing on Freud, the literary critic Cathy Caruth names trauma a "wound of the mind—the breach in the mind's experience of time, self, and world."[85] Because those internal structures that preside over the faculties of human consciousness are missing or maimed, the sufferer cannot integrate those faculties for a rational, and timely, calculation of interest or consequence. Trauma, as the concept tells us, instead imposes itself again and again on his or her consciousness, as nightmare or repetitive compulsion. The force of grief is so disturbing that he or she cannot perceive reality as fixed and knowable, and thereby subject to will or intervention. It is in these terms that war in general, and the war in Southeast Asia in particular, triggers the nomination of such illnesses as post-traumatic stress disorder, in which nightmares and revenants plague individuals who are damaged by the catastrophic, and as the so-called Vietnam syndrome, in which pathological doubt arrested the capability and willingness of a nation or state to conduct further war.

Because the refugee seems so incontrovertibly traumatized, the condition as a description of ontological destitution importantly constellates knowledge about that which is presumably compulsory for complex personhood. Though the stranger who claims a right to asylum or sanctuary is an archaic figure, in its modern legal classification the refugee is a historical effect of liberal governance and statecraft, a global category of care. In the mid-twentieth century, the emerging international system regularized the state as the self-evident referent for political being, in which the stateless person—including the refugee—is an abnormality. The 1951 UN Convention Relating to the Status of Refugees more narrowly defines the refugee as "any person who, owing to a well-founded fear of being persecuted for reasons of race, religion, nationality, membership in a particular social group or political opinion, is outside the country of his nationality and is unable or unwilling to avail himself of the protection of that country" or is unable or unwilling to return.[86] Later protocols specific to Africa and Latin America expanded these parameters to include persons fleeing from war or violence in their home country. Most laws governing refugee asylum in European and North American countries, including the contemporary United States, follow from this formula to establish the refugee condition as radically anomalous to what Liisa Malkki calls the "national order of things."[87] As a political noncitizen, the refugee is outside the law, devoid of rights, the effect of a terrible exception through which his or her life is forsaken. The refugee at the same time is an object of imperative concern for the arbiters of law and sovereignty. The refugee is therefore suspended in time and in space, a figure of humanity on the outside. Writing in *The Refugee in the Post-War World*, Jacques Vernant encapsulates such a view:

> The refugee is, in the first place, a symbol of instability. . . . The refugee symbolizes, in the second place, isolation. Social groups react almost with an instinctive mistrust of those who have been cut off or who voluntarily cut themselves off from the community to which they belong by origin or adoption. Lastly, the refugee is the unknown. . . . He is no longer on his land, he has fled his country, he has been cast out by his group, or by those who speak in the name of the national group of which he was a member. The refugee is therefore one whose ties have been doubly cut, both his territorial ties and those with the national group, or, rather, with the state which is its legal expression. What stamps the refugee as a man apart, justifying his classification in a specific social category, is his inferiority; he is inferior both to the citizens of the country which gives him shelter and all the other foreigners, not refugees, living in that country.[88]

Others have thoroughly documented the epistemological and ontological coordinates of the "refugee problem" (expressed so thoroughly by Vernant), through which changing and ever-conditional criteria for asylum demonstrate the instrumental nature of refugee classification, and the damning conviction of refugee pathology as an existential threat.[89] Of these damning thoughts, Nevzat Soguk writes: "Although an object of compassion and pity at times, in the final analysis she [the refugee] is truly 'unwanted' or 'undesirable,' representing, 'like the plague,' disruptions in the conditions of normality in life. *She stands accused.*"[90]

This phenomenon is indeed well observed, but here we ought to consider again how refugee abnormality incarnates a long and enduring history of liberal humanist ontology. Soguk summarizes the refugee "problem" as follows: "Refugees are seen as incapable of participating as effective, knowledgeable actors in the tasks essential to the efficient and orderly organization of the community—obtaining security, stability, welfare, and self-governance."[91] What is the substance of this incapacity? What is missing, impairing the refugee's humanity, inhibiting his or her actions and passions as untimely? Here the concept of dispossession as a telic and ontic description is telling. Looking once again at the narration of the modern individual who possesses interiority of person, as well as a private household, in the liberal political tradition (with particular attention to Hegel), Lisa Lowe elaborates:

> Property in oneself and in the objects one makes through will, labor, contract—all are levels in Hegel's dialectical development that resolve in the unity of the particular will of the individual with the collective universality of the whole, or the state. "Property" is the way that Hegel explained the individual initially investing will and work into nature, making the nature objective, transforming world and self. Through property the condition of possibility of human self-possession—of one's body, interiority, and life direction—is established. Indeed, Hegel argued that property is an essential condition for the possibility of moral action because without property, without a locus of independence of the individual will, the person cannot be independent, thoughtful, or self-conscious; without property he will be dominated by others, by needs, and by nature.[92]

Given these epistemological and ontological coordinates, the refugee figure is patently bereft of property—possessing neither interior faculties for the rational and moral calculation of interest and consequence, nor external properties for their "right" exercise in intercourse with others, including legitimate citizenship, proprietary rights, or simply things ("Clothing, a lot of these people didn't have clothing. Some of them didn't have shoes."). Profoundly dispossessed, from this perspective the refugee has lost *every thing.*[93]

Giving a name to such violence but also the damage that ensues is a challenge because naming bears far-reaching political stakes. For these reasons, I understand psychoanalytic concepts such as trauma as a form of biomedicine implicated in liberal structures of power, especially those delineating between freedom and captivity, ownership and dispossession.[94] Such a diagnostic vocabulary is why a critique of analogy is crucial to the deconstruction of the refugee condition, especially where trauma and political disenfranchisement act as analogies for each other, which assumes that *one or the other condition might be read through or doubled by the other*. Allowing us to perceive connections between objects through the selection and emphasis of features taken for "the real," and as signs signaling presence, analogies work to make each object known. In this way, my critique of this analogy continues from Susan Sontag's warning that "illness is *not* a metaphor."[95] Consider this early description—by Freud, in a collaborative work with Josef Breuer—of trauma as an external or alien encroachment: "The psychical trauma—or more precisely the memory of the trauma—acts like a *foreign body* which long after its entry must continue to be regarded as *an agent that is still operative*."[96] Such analogies of incursion, occupation, and warfare are plentifully available in trauma theory.[97] I make note of their presence because trauma theory too often reproduces a relationship of psychic to political dispossession that is ubiquitous and presumptive.[98] This sequence of figurations allows the circumstances of bankruptcy or disenfranchisement to be viewed as necessarily manifesting abnormality, or something missing. To cite just one example, Hannah Arendt famously draws attention to what she identifies as "an ever-growing new people comprised of stateless persons, the *most symptomatic group* in contemporary politics."[99] In this intriguing phrase, Arendt resorts to a figurative vocabulary of illness to represent the stateless peoples cast adrift in the aftermath of Europe's world-shattering wars. Functioning metonymically, even tautologically, the stateless person is like the mentally ill because his or her mind-set is disturbed; because he or she is outside of reason, outside of civilization; because he or she has no property, if we understand these conditions to be bound to a sense of freedom and human history. (Such statements also warrant refugee encampment and corrective ministrations, as we shall see, in which the refugee—like the ostensibly mentally ill—is involuntarily isolated because he or she is not considered able to judge and act according to norms of acceptable reasoning or volition.) Thus does traumatic consciousness mirror back to political expulsion a shared negativity of reference, and present reason for pause.

The analogy itself thus constitutes a complex historical event, which problematically presumes the increased rationality, comprehensiveness, or logic of each object or term in the comparison. That is to say, such analogies produce not only an ensemble of subjects but also a set of empirical criteria for competency and capacity, which also establish the bounds for a global order of things taken to be necessary and natural conditions of their existence. (These analogies also regularize troubling schema presuming citizens and refugees to be irreconcilable travelers. As Caren Kaplan observes, "many modern subjects may participate in any number of . . . versions of displacement over a lifetime—never embodying any one version singly or simplistically."[100] The refugee is no exception.[101]) In doing so, the terms of these analogies are complicit in the co-construction of categories of normal and abnormal, presence and absence, action and passivity, futurity and anachronism, property and deprivation, freedom and captivity, balance and danger.

It is important to note that the condition has never been aimed solely at the cultural or racial, colonial other, but that it does often bear the weight of colonialist underpinnings. (A civilizational discourse, for instance, was consistently deployed against refugee arrival.[102]) In which the refugee is the bearer of antecedent failure—or what we might call a recalcitrance to transition—the condition that pertains to this abnormal individual is the consolidation of the diffuse structures of liberal humanism as the substance of a global order of things. Thus, the refugee condition as a medico-juridical structure may be read less as a diagnostic of underdevelopment (in multiple senses) than as a sign or symptom testifying to the entanglement of race and temporal distancing with the subtle, insidious forces of liberal governance. As a functional imbalance, the condition names the *alienability* of these faculties, and therefore anything pathological in the body or mind that might be understood to arise from this absence, with especially racializing consequence.

In other words, whereas the condition acts as an absolute value structuring all signification, conceptualizations of the proper and proportionate reason and tempo for feelings, and for actions, coincide at the suspect scene of modern racial governmentality. That is, inasmuch as trauma discourse individuates the subject, it can also strategically collectivize the condition. In this way, the refugee condition does not only diagnose the psychic-political subject whose capacities are stuck or stalled, but also diagnoses as a technical-political object a population statistically organized and managed via its features and characteristics, including these medico-biological "problems." Or, as Lisa Marie Cacho offers: "When culture, race, and space appear sutured to 'abnormality,' 'criminality,' and/or 'disability,' through the concept of the 'condition' as its underlying psychological causality, they are acting as interchangeable signifiers for 'affectability.' This fictive condition that renders afflicted people of color vulnerable to irreversible spatial disablement can be traced to what Denise Ferreira da Silva has named 'affectability.' Silva defines 'affectability' as 'the condition of being subjected to both natural (in the scientific and lay sense) conditions and to others' power.'"[103]

It is through affectability that the refugee experiences interruption twice over, first as target and second as origin. Malkki wryly observes: "It is striking how often the abundant literature claiming refugees as its object of study locates 'the problem' not first in the political oppression or violence that produces massive territorial displacements of people, but within the bodies and minds of people classified as refugees."[104] The repercussions (which echo the allegations that the wayward other failed to secure his or her own freedom) ring out through the long years since the end of the war. The seemingly rational observation that such passion as that inspired by the merest glimpse of Ho Chi Minh is out of proportion coincides with a principle of liberal commensurability that, as Sianne Ngai points out, performs a symbolic violence "when there is an underlying assumption that an appropriate emotional response to . . . violence exists, and that the burden lies on the racialized subject to produce that appropriate response legibly, unambiguously, and immediately."[105] Given that condemnation and disappointment exist on a continuum, through which moral action depends on resemblance and rationality (including temporal causality), these events and feelings manifest a disturbed condition: "I felt the community was on this slippery slope, that we were not progressing toward having open dialogue and being more tolerant of different political viewpoints." "The war and what happened afterward, of being refugees and having to restart their lives, left scars that have never been dealt with. None of us know if the community is ready for [open dialogue] now, or if it will take another 10 years."[106] "Our families came here because they sought those freedoms denied in Vietnam. They didn't come here to be denied them, once again, in their own community."[107] Such consignment of refugee protests against communism's seemingly spectral affront to memory and grievance to un-reasonable and therefore undemocratic compulsion circumscribes their claims as groundless and dislocates these protests from the surviving pres-ent.[108] (To acknowledge some others as persons with legitimate grievances would be to acknowledge capitalism's catastrophic content, or democratic states' terror.[109]) The traumatic tempo of repetition and return increases ugly feelings (to borrow a felicitous phrase from Ngai), such that the refu-gee, having been contravened and herself contravening against others, be-comes the *source* of illiberal violence.

Certain conditions, in this instance unfolding and compounding each the other (the refugee condition that includes welfare dependency thus furnishes the causal background for urban poverty), thus operate as signs of latent criminality. We know, for example, that the refugee is seen to pose a threat to public security because he has lost his rational, and thus moral, bearings. It is in those terms through which the condition renders refugees both disabled and disabling,[110] that legal and political discourses of South-east Asian "gang violence" understand gang members as especially incapa-ble of moral action, allowing their indefinite detention and, after 2002, eventual deportation as criminal aliens in the wake of new memorandums of understanding between the United States and Southeast Asian countries, in pursuit of new wars elsewhere.[111] The adoption of trauma theory also informs even those compassionate accounts of the 1991 Good Guys "crisis," instantiating the refugee condition and a judgment of abnormality. It seems obvious perhaps that the young Vietnamese men who held forty-one people hostage at a Sacramento, California, electronics superstore in the hope that they might extort arms to return to the scene of the war to *win this time* inherited an overwhelming, alien compulsion. For instance, the so-ciologists Michael Peter Smith and Bernadette Tarallo, in reviewing the "construction of the 'Vietnamese' other" by news reports and police state-ments during and after the crisis, describe these youth as alienated from self-knowledge and thus from "meaningful identity,"[112] resulting in "deep confusion" and untimely allegiance "to a precommunist Vietnam where the father, now on welfare, held a position of authority."[113] These youths' violence, according to this diagnosis, occurs in the false hope that the past is indeterminate enough to be changed in the present. (We also know this as the trope of *the cycle of violence*.) In a meditation on the hostage takers titled "Love, Money, Prison, Sin, Revenge," Andrew Lam, son of a former South Vietnamese general, claims profound insight into their distress: "They tried to bring dignity to their fathers by fighting their war. They coveted being good Vietnamese sons: To assuage the old man's grief, the young man must defeat his old man's enemy."[114] But where temporal disjunction appears as an empirical "fact," the traumatic problematic of incoherent causality may coincide with the denial of coevalness, in which the West's colonial or racial others are persistently classified as anachronistic and discontinuous. To demarcate these youths' actions as primitivism and parochialism, as "outdated passions" and "Old World gestures of self-sacrifice and revenge,"[115] is the expression of a politics of comparison through which the encounter with a persistent or perverse heterogeneity can be appropriated into the symptomology of the condition as a scientific system of knowledge and discipline.

The refugee condition as a problem of unfreedom becomes a target of action, whether "indefinite intervention" or provisional transition, once again.[116] Such that war may well be the foremost crucible for trauma theory, it is also the grounds for an ideology of rehabilitation, a system of supervision and procedures for normalization based on notions of the present and presence as necessary properties for normal personhood. In his history of disability, Henri-Jacques Stiker notes that the concept of rehabilitation arose from the scene of modern war as the restoration to the person violently made partial a sense of wholeness: "Mutilation applied to all alteration of integrity, of integralness. It amounted to a degradation, but one by removal—or deterioration—which has the effect of suppression. The maimed person is *someone missing something precise, an organ or function.* Thus, the first image presented by this change in terminology is that of damage. *The war has taken away, we must replace.*"[117] Rehabilitation, Stiker continues, "implies returning to a point, to a prior situation, the situation that existed for the able but one only postulated for the others. In any case, reference to a norm."[118]

Neither the metaphor nor the medium of rehabilitation are benign, especially when integrity, integralness, or normalcy is yet to be achieved for the person sutured, as Cacho observes, to "culture, race, or space."[119] Indeed, whether the epistemic and evidential structures that register scales of harm regard an offense as calamitous or routine may enact more harm. It is for these reasons that Fiona Ngô argues disability theory must be brought to bear on critical refugee and war studies to challenge the narrative overdetermination of the forcible inscriptions of trauma and disability on racial, colonial others.[120] Where statelessness is conceived through medical or psychopathological analogies, such analogies sanction intervention as an authoritative form of social action that bolsters its legitimacy with scientific, biomedical rationality, anchored once again in liberal schema for the autonomous individual and for human intercourse. Importantly, then, rehabilitation is absolutely continuous with liberal war in their disciplining intents and powers. Corresponding once again with a historicist consciousness, such disciplinary actions that might accompany this practical system refer to a "final or optimum state," either as the return to the normal or its achievement in the future.[121] This discourse of normalization can be observed, for example, in UN High Commissioner for Refugees Sadako Ogata's diagnosis for the refugee "problem": "Lack of national protection is an aberration of the normal in which the state accepts the responsibility for its own citizens. The objective must be to return to the *status ante*."[122] In this regard, the rehabilitative objective first concurs with the condition as a narration of refugee abnormality that covers over its epistemic violence (in which state and capital collude to produce dispossessed peoples) and then conceals the political stakes for intervention, which present disciplinary actions as technical solutions to social pathologies perceived as *on the outside*. It becomes quite clear that the refugee, because he or she is the aberration, is less the ideal subject of rehabilitation than the sovereign state and the global order of things.[123] These diagnostic conditions and their disciplinary consequences we may say, after Ngô, "[make] visible what is simultaneously apparent—bodies indelibly marked by war, race, gender, disability, and immigration status for particular surveillance—and yet rendered only tenuously visible [the] biopolitical processes engaged through and by states, militaries, media, and the medical-industrial complex."[124] Thus, one potentially devastating consequence for the refugee diagnosed as malingering is the eclipse of other harm that the diagnosis or cure might itself enact. Let me now return to that story.

Green Dragon and Lost Birds

Rather than leading us to some authentic origin or giving us verifiable access to the real, memory, even and especially in its belatedness, is itself based on representation. The past is not simply there in memory, but it must be articulated to become memory. The fissure that opens up between experiencing an event and remembering it in representation is unavoidable.

—ANDREAS HUYSSEN, *Twilight Memories*

As a child my mother would tell me stories of her first days in America. Of how she feared the moonlight because it only brought her sorrow. I wanted to understand that sorrow. Thus is the genesis of GREEN DRAGON. . . . In 1975, four refugee camps were set up across the United States to assist in relocating Vietnamese refugees to their new homes. Though this film is set at Camp Pendleton Marine Base, Ca., the movie represents the compilations of all such camps and how they were our purgatory to a newfound freedom.

—TIMOTHY LINH BUI AND TONY BUI, "Note from the Filmmakers,"
Green Dragon DVD insert

Green Dragon holds documentary realness and fictional license in precarious balance. In a note from the filmmakers included with the DVD release, Timothy Linh Bui and Tony Bui point to their mother's stories of her *first days in America* as the genesis of the film. While claiming fealty to their mother's biography, the filmmakers also assign great importance to the collective experience that is inseparable from her passed-on personal impressions: "It was at the open calls where we began to hear other comments from hopeful thespians of how touched they were for us to tell 'their' story. Their stories carried the same loss that our mother felt, and *their stories were identical to the ones in the script*. Such stories were truly universal."[125] The film's referential claims thus insist that what we see on screen emanates from social and historical knowledge about the real world. Many of the set pieces were filmed in the same Quonset huts, the DVD's bonus commentary informs us, that had housed the camp's inhabitants ("It's the real environment," the filmmaker and cinematographer insist). The film also operates on the premise that the feeling is true too, as the director Timothy Linh Bui and his cinematographer describe their decision to use a particular camera lens to evoke the mother's memory of a cold, blue moon. The fact that many of the film's extras were themselves refugees is another reminder, according to the Bui brothers, that behind the dramatic narrative lies a deeper truth about a collective response to a catastrophic loss—heart and body, life and country, those things we reputedly require to be right with the world. As these real refugees reenact their documentation upon entrance to the camps (flashbulbs illuminating their faces) and relive the moment they heard that Saigon had fallen, in their blank stares and real tears we are meant to discern the long-settled traces of despair and sorrow.

Green Dragon aims to render the authentic meaning of memory, piecing together a refugee archive of feeling—and the achievement of freedom, at least for some.[126] The first clue for the film's concerns about the refugee condition lies in its depiction of time's passage. The camera's flash, arresting the image of the refugee on his or her arrival (and whose documentary purpose might also be understood to indict a politics of knowledge through which we know the refugee in his or her generality), imagines the interruption of world-historical, homogeneous time in unmistakably visual terms. After we wake with the young boy in the dark, the film slows, and our sense of the passage of time in the refugee camp begins to move at a tempo apart from the rest of the world. In the haunting echo of an old man beating on a Buddhist drum according to a now otherwordly measure, such asynchronicity is made perceptible. For most of the film, the camp is filtered through cold blues and muted earth tones, with the color red reserved for those moments and details—a bicycle, a pepper —that stand in for movement and the assurance of a brighter future. The film's affective stance literally colors the film with this dichotomy between anachronism and futurity.

As a film about that passage between war and peace, *Green Dragon* occasions a twofold query. First, the film presents the refugee condition as a state of extreme dispossession, and through references to reality (the nonprofessional actors, the Quonset huts, the living persons on whom the film's characters are patterned), the film is asserted to be a truthful, even mimetic, portrait of this condition. To be encamped is to be caught outside of reality and normal time; thus, the camp is achingly felt as an unbearable suspension—suggestively dubbed by camp ethnographers a "transition to nowhere," and described by the filmmaker as well as film critics as a limbo, a purgatory.[127] Second, in positing once again the refugee as an aberration, an anachronistic human, whose tempo must be aligned with liberalism's meter, this portrait allows us to inquire into the powers directing the refugee toward certain real objects and ideal values, from which freedom is presumed to follow. Here we find that refugee encampment, as the paradoxical obligation to receive and to rescue the dispossessed other, produces a biopolitical space for discipline and sovereign power to function once again as part of the general tactics of governmentality.[128] In doing so, *Green Dragon* illuminates those conventions of the story of freedom—including its interpretation of unfreedom not just as a political state but also as a psychic phenomenon—that solicit more narrative acts and regulatory forms. That is, the film asks that we grasp the subjectivizing force of the gift of freedom as a promise to the future. Furthermore, to attend to the story of *Green Dragon*, especially through its petition to realness, is to understand the film as a hermeneutic device for the gift of freedom. The presence and facticity of such a film, as a mirror of the story it narrates, presume to act as the substantiation of freed subjectivity and, for our purposes, as the seduction of historical recovery.

The refugee's dispossession of "body, interiority, and life direction" appears to us in this film as an unlivable interval, removed from history and at an impassable distance from the rest of the world, for whom life goes on. Loosely organized as a moody sequence of vignettes in which very little appears to happen, the film catalogs such unfreedom in the impressionistic details. *Green Dragon* thus focuses our attention through brief glimpses into unhappy refugee life, shot in muted, desaturated tones: Little Minh and his littler sister Anh, cared for by their uncle Tai Tran (the unofficial camp manager), search faces for their missing mother and check the bulletin boards and buses bringing new arrivals daily. Awarded three precious seats on a plane evacuating Saigon, Tai's decision to keep one and bestow the other two to the young children of his sister haunts him as an unforgivable betrayal (left behind, his sister, their mother, dies from sorrow and starvation). The second wife to a once-rich man meets the husband under the night sky for perfunctory (and, for her, joyless) sex, and his pregnant first wife treats her as she would a despised servant. The beautiful and spirited Thuy Hoa harasses the mess hall attendants for milk for another woman's infant, but cannot help her own nearly mute father, a former general who sinks deeper into despair with every passing day. Men in the camp while away the time playing cards, trading rumors, and listening to the radio for news about decisive actions elsewhere. Dragging the refugee deeper into the stultifying rhythms of daily rituals conducted without a future tense, the film's fragmentation of time provides a sense of the asynchronicity of the refugee condition, of time out of joint.

For our purposes, I focus on a sequence of scenes connected through the mournful lament, "Saigon Oi Vinh Biet," now a standard in the exilic musical repertoire and composed by Nam Loc, a refugee composer on whom Tai Tran (the film's center) is loosely molded.[129] Under a night sky, Tai strums an acoustic guitar before a small gathering of refugees, crooning an elegy he penned for the lost country: "Oh Saigon, I have lost you in my life. Oh Saigon, my best time is far away. What is left is some sad memory, the dead smile on my lips, bitter tears in my eyes. Oh Saigon, on the street, is the sun still shining? On our path, is the rain still falling? In the park, is my lover still there, passing under the trees, smiling or crying alone?"[130] Such lyrics trace the correspondences between the refugee interior and his or her inability to act upon a world made strange and unfamiliar. Employed as a cinematic mode of captioning, this single song on the soundtrack (except for the credits sequence, all the other tracks are instrumental) supplies the emotional truth of a collective experience with terrible trauma, whose symptoms include the recurring intrusion of the traumatic experience into the consciousness of the present.

"Saigon Oi Vinh Biet" continues its sorrowful lament ("Here I am the bird losing her way, day by day my time just passes by") as the film cuts to the dim, nighttime interior of a Quonset hut, and four uniformed marines enter. As a flashlight's halo bounces across the bowed head of an older woman praying over her clenched fists, a courteous voice murmurs, "Excuse me, ma'am, it's time for you to go now." Other refugees wake from their uneasy slumber to stare in shock as the bewildered woman is forcibly escorted from the building, screaming in Vietnamese all the while, "My sons! Why are you taking me away from them?" The marines take no heed of her unintelligible (to them) cries; there seem to be no children, no sons, in the hut. Knocked to the ground after his attempt to pry the woman from her captors' grip, Tai stumbles to her camp bed. He breaks into frustrated tears as he observes, and the camera lingers on, two small black-and-white head shots of her sons in military uniforms, taped to the otherwise bare wall above her canvas cot.

Her home destroyed and her children gone, it is clear that the song is meant to mark the mother's dispossession—this refugee is a bird who has lost her way. The song thus becomes a now-nondiegetic commentary, the articulation of knowledge that exceeds the unhappy subject who cannot fathom what is happening to her, because *this terrible thing has happened to her*. Here we might recall Peter Brooks's classic argument about melodrama as a "text of muteness," in which inner conflict and ineloquent emotion are expressed through the "inarticulate cry and gesture," the composition of a mise-en-scène, the swells and ebbs of a musical interlude.[131] As a text of muteness that mirrors the mother's loss of voice, the song sutures the loss of country to the rift in her own self-government. Irregular and insubordinate, this mother is unable to act with reason or within reality; in a liberal humanist arrangement, she is not free because she does not possess her self, nor can she engage intercourse with others. While she is not literally mute, her cries are nonetheless inarticulate. She cannot make herself understood to the marines, who cannot see the ghosts of her sons hovering above her cot, drawing her close in the incomprehensibility of their battlefield deaths; her dispossession is such that she has lost even her grasp on the texture of reality, the truth of her condition.

In this film, the dead do not impart to us secrets about how to cohabit the past and the future.[132] They are instead placeholders for the dead end of anachronism, the disorder of an asynchronous consciousness. Because she will not yield to the inassimilable truth of her sons' deaths, the mother refuses to quit the camp, which would be the same as allowing them to die alone. And because she insists on lingering in an illusory interval in which they might still live (there are no bodies, and she has no proof otherwise of their deaths), the camp's guardians regard her as an anachronism and more—as a disciplinary problem. In the spectacularization of the mother's despair as emotional excess, the film compels us to foreclose the question of the fraught conditions of its staging and to focus instead on the disclosure of the refugee's delusion as disorder and degradation. Her unwillingness to depart from the scene of suspension or to allow the irreversible arrow of time to move forward becomes "a problem that is at once scientific and political, as a biological problem and as power's problem."[133] Thus, the discourse of the condition produces her degradation as an empirical issue and then receives her as an object of discipline, which goes by the names refuge and rehabilitation. That is, even as the camp diagnosed the refugee condition as a wretched dependency, it is precisely through this dependency that the camp becomes operational as a biopolitical technology.

Reflecting on refugee encampment, I wish to linger for a moment on the "problem" of hospitality, as that which the generous state grants the stranger in a moment of danger. (Or as one postwar editorial put it: "The effort made to assist those Vietnamese was an admirable demonstration of loyalty to a group of human beings otherwise bereft of hope."[134]) The aporia of hospitality, as Derrida traces, helps to name those structures of feeling and social forms that welcome the ontologically destitute other with violence *and* power. The "impossible" logic of hospitality characterizing Derrida's analysis of this altruistic concept is particularly useful here: "At bottom, before even beginning, we could end our reflections here in the formalization of a law of hospitality which violently imposes a contradiction on the very concept of hospitality in fixing a limit to it, in de-termining it: hospitality is certainly, necessarily, a right, a duty, an obligation, the greeting of the foreign other as a friend but on the condition that the host . . . the one who receives, lodges or gives asylum remains the patron, the master of the household, on the condition that he maintains his own authority in his own home, that he looks after himself and sees to and considers all that concerns him as thereby affirms the law of hospitality as the law of the household."[135] To be hospitable, Derrida writes, it is first necessary that one possess the power to host, a power contingent on property as an essential condition for the possibility of moral action, and continuous with a self-concept as a self-possessed individual, "the master of the household." Of a piece with his concerns about the gift and forgiveness (which are also the concerns of this book), genuine hospitality as an ethical obligation to others must be unconditional, but this unconditional gesture is impossible. As is, hospitality necessarily hinges on the host's *control* over the stranger who comes from another place and brings with him nothing, lest the stranger subvert the concept of property ownership itself. For these reasons, Derrida writes, "hospitality is a self-contradictory concept and experience which can only self-destruct."[136] We can begin to say of this encampment then that what it claims as "a right, a duty, an obligation, the greeting of the foreign other as a friend" is also the imperative disciplining of the other, especially where the refugee and his or her capacities are judged to be disordered and disorderly.

In turning to these scenes in the film, and the ones that follow from it, I consider the interpenetration of forms of power to ask the following questions: How does the analytic of hospitality, as one part of the gift of freedom, make sense of these powers operating as the context for this scene of a grieving mother's detention in and subsequent forcible expulsion from the camp? How is the tent city, also the spectacular scene for sovereign power in the fences, barracks, and soldiers all directed at the control of the refugee population, recruited to the governmentality of giving? In many ways, the removal scene captures specific concerns about the potential of the refugee body, where understandings of not just sovereign law (and here we come face to face with not only "ordinary" law, but martial law bound to colonial wars[137]), but also reason and reality as presumably universal laws, structure who and what we understand to be subjects of freedom. Here is a story about the refugee condition in which the mother's incoherence, her disorder, must be subjected to discipline not as undue punishment, we are told, but as the necessary fullness of liberal promise. That is, the gift of freedom requires her subjection, even pursues her further abasement in those same terms that are targeted as her problem (or her condition) in the course of willing her to subjectivity.[138] In regarding the scene of her removal, then, I follow Veena Das, who also departs from a constellation of trauma concepts to attend otherwise to the story of violence: "I am not saying that there is nothing to be gained from such an understanding of history, but it seems to me that notions of ghostly repetitions, spectral presences, and all those tropes that have become sedimented into our ordinary language from trauma theory are often evoked too soon—as if the processes that constitute the way everyday life is engaged in the present have little to say on how violence is produced and lived with."[139]

For Foucault, biopower brings life into political calculation—through biopolitics, and through discipline. We might readily observe the refugee camp and confinement as biopolitical technologies or the regulation of the productive economic and biological capacities of populations. Because of the extremity of their dispossession, the refugee populations detained in this and other camps are targeted at the level of their generality, which is to say their shared condition, for inoculation against all the dangers to society that may arise from this condition (whether foreign customs, bizarre compulsions, or economic and social burdens). (It should be noted here that the grieving mother is never truly an individual character in the film; she is given no name, because she is the generic bearer of the limits of livable being.) Such encampment first concurred with the premise that the refugees are "the most symptomatic," and then established this population pathology as an operational principle for their biopolitical management. Here the refugee population is a mass object in a technical-administrative field of power operating through governmental policies and state laws and managerial and bureaucratic institutions, including charities and other agencies of civil society. This assemblage of interdependent institutions together sought to monitor, measure, evaluate, and develop the refugees' life capacities, as well as contain their potential danger to public health and human security, through tactics encompassing health screenings, immunizations, and the guidance of public but also private conduct (including directives about bathing and using deodorant), as well as employment placement and vocational training programs. Addressed to widespread anxieties and preoccupations about scarce resources and biological contagion, these tactics proposed to ensure the necessary social and economic order for the refugees' reintegration into the external world.

But the ordered space of the camp is also the delivery system for disciplinary powers, targeting the refugee for a whole array of tactics and technologies that produce the subject as a historical reality and that aim to develop his or her capacities. Such an anatomopolitics seizes the life of the individual in terms of "infinitesimal surveillances, permanent controls, extremely meticulous orderings of space, indeterminate medical or psychological examinations, an entire micro-power concerned with the body."[140] Put another way, such tactics and technologies might be understood to be the gift through which liberalism creates the conditions under which one is free to be free. Into this schema, the narrative of the camp is scripted both as the scene of the refugee's profound deprivation (in the tautological logic of the condition, at the camp she has no rights because she has no rights) and the scene of her rehabilitation through discipline, regularity, and occupation. Obliging the refugee to submit to the camp's management and use of time, to the regularity of certain actions and habits, including work, the camp regime also holds the inchoate promise of her freedom. A sign at the Philippine Refugee Processing Center in the province of Bataan proclaimed: "Refugee transformation, the primary goal of the [center's] operations, is achieved through a psycho-social recuperative process involving the 'critical phases of adaptation, capability building, and disengagement' which results in changing a 'displaced person' into an 'Individual Well Equipped for Life in His Country of final destination.'"[141]

Thus did the camp's diffuse, though hardly disconnected, programs seek to "instruct refugees to 'speak good English, be employable, be unwilling to accept welfare, and be happy' in America."[142] On its face, this might seem an odd jumble. However, the will to subjectivity informs the connective tissue between "speak good English, be employable, be unwilling to accept welfare" and "be happy." (These directives to reduce refugee and immigrant dependency, which continue long after resettlement and inform such legislation as the 1996 Personal Responsibility and Work Opportunity Reconciliation Act, are entangled in domestic histories of racialized cultures of poverty.[143]) That these directives together produce the properties that define the individual as a liberal human person is made clear in the detailed and exacting psychometric measures and biopsychosocial assessments that comprised the then-emerging subfield of Southeast Asian refugee mental health, such as the Vietnamese Depression Scale (VDS) and Indochinese Hopkins Symptom Checklist Depression Subscale (IHSCDS). A brief 1995 report on the usefulness of the VDS as a diagnostic measure cites another study finding that Southeast Asian refugees at the highest risk for "clinically important psychological distress" tended to be "the least educated and English-proficient, the most dependent on welfare, the poorest and most frequently unemployed, older and widowed, and those with the most traumatic migration histories."[144] Report after report overwhelmingly focuses psychological health through the script of self-possession (and, as we shall see, self-possession through contract labor and economic exchange), bypassing the more difficult questions about the underlying violence of those structures of capitalism and other subjection found in discipline and compliance. James Tollefson's detailed account of these programs is illuminating. One publication from the International Catholic Migration Commission instructs the refugee to "get along with everybody" and warns: "If you are a bad worker, the company can fire you. Then it might be hard for you to get another job."[145] Reading Tollefson, David Palumbo-Liu elaborates: "Pamphlets are circulated describing how refugees are regarded by employers as a means to suggest proper behavior, reward, and punishment. One State Department publication explicitly notes, 'Instruction must be directed toward meeting refugees' employment needs. Such needs are best determined by an employer needs assessment.'"[146] Games such as the "Free Money Game" aimed to stigmatize welfare dependency as a personal or population failure to learn necessary lessons.[147] "'Success,'" as Palumbo-Liu writes, "is carefully delineated within a complacent, depoliticized subjectivity," defined as a voluntary and rational submission to capital.[148] (Even as this understanding disciplines the particular pessimism of the refugee condition, an identificatory relationship with these liberal knowledge structures can also capture the refugee in its scope. For instance, referencing subsequent enrollment into federal public assistance programs as a temporary and "adaptive" measure under the 1975 Refugee Assistance Act, Andrew Lam laments such an emasculating dependency, which captures an individual's body as well as his sense of worth: "The Vietnamese refugee's first self-assessment in America is, inevitably, of his own helplessness. It is characterized by blushing, by looking down at one's feet, by avoiding eye contact and by waiting: for welfare and food stamps, for the free clinic exam, for free jackets donated by charity, for green cards."[149]) In the disciplining of the refugee through such structures of becoming orderly and timely, the refugee is promised that his or her compliance with, and right relation to, norms and institutions will also be rewarded with the restoration of autonomy, and from this happiness.[150]

Reviewing the authority of these structures of power, couched in references to reality, allows us to situate acts of physical force, carried out by state agents, within the larger project of refugee rehabilitation. The grieving mother who refuses to leave the camp and its paradoxical pleasures—because at the camp she might linger in a fictitious limbo in which her sons might still survive the war—must be dragged forward to freedom. The depiction of violence in *Green Dragon* is not what it appears to be, stark and distressing; nor is it directed at so-called legitimate military targets. It does not occur as part of the brutality of war, which is amply illustrated, we are meant to understand, in the psychic devastation etched so indelibly on the faces we see. Instead, under the emergency conditions of the refugee camp, sovereign power is discharged as a managerial tactic of governmentality. Consider this list from the 1976 Department of the Army After Action Report on United States Army support to the Indochinese Refugee Program, which describes the military functions for Task Force New Arrivals (TFNA) as follows: "coordinate the frequency of refugee arrivals; transport refugees from the arrival airfield to the reception center and to within the center processing stations; provide refugee orientation briefing; ascertain the initial personal information for the refugee data base; provide billeting, subsistence, health care, and security; conduct coordinated civil affairs operations; conduct medical screening as prescribed by TFNA; provide logistic support to TFNA as required."[151] From this vantage point, because the story of *Green Dragon* ultimately calls for us to leave our dead behind (the director describes the earlier scene of a young boy walking over the sleeping bodies of other refugees as a necessary passage away from the war's devastation to the light of a life beyond), to allow ourselves to be reborn in the new world, we are told that *the marines had a good reason.*

To demonstrate this, *Green Dragon* stages a scene in which the refugee is made to recognize that his reduced status in the camp, and the alienability of his rights, is the necessary consequence of his refusal to accept reality. In an angry confrontation between Tai and his immediate superior—Marine

Sergeant Jim Lance, the camp supervisor—about the mother's removal, Tai accuses Lance of betraying a trust. (This is also an implicit accusation about the American withdrawal from the war.) However, Jim refuses him the perverse comfort of the trauma's temporary interval. Instead, he establishes the camp as transitional, in all the senses earlier described: "The moment you stepped foot in this camp, you were on your way out!" In frustration, Tai argues that the war's devastation still looms: "You know why they don't want to go? Is one of the reasons because they are scared? Afraid of what their lives will be like tomorrow?" It may seem as if this skirmish allows Tai to defend the mother and her desperate hopes that her sons might still live, but as a narrative device, what this scene actually does is allow Tai to give an account of the refugee condition in such a way that Jim might employ Tai's answers (as the affirmation of a problem) to strengthen his hold on the disturbed, disturbing other as an object of knowledge and as the subject of discipline. As Foucault observes of the function of the patient confession within the asylum as an instrument of psychiatric power, any answer that Tai supplies is already construed as a symptom in a given field of knowledge about the refugee condition.[152] When Jim charges the mother with an unreasonable refusal to cohabit the present, to become other than a burden, he champions a rehabilitation that denies an awareness of it as acute cruelty.

In this way, the gift of freedom not only presumes a human desire for freedom, as well as a normative schema for knowing and taking one's bearing in the world, but it also presumes that such desire is a natural consequence of the universal truths of reason and reality. As the mother's sympathetic proxy, Tai is made to confront the truth to which her attention, distracted by her insubordinate will, must submit: she cannot stay behind in the camp to shelter her fantasies, but instead must face the fact of her condition. Committed by courteous marines, this disciplinary action does not signify as another terrible trespass or the echo of an earlier one (as Tai charges), *but as the solution to it.* At issue in the mother's removal is the marines' corporal power as an adjunct of the disciplinary state, but also the historicist reach of modern racial governmentality via the manufacture and measure of liberal personhood. Jim promises that such submission to the camp regime, as the foundation for the law of reality, will give rise to the refugee's rehabilitation into the universal story of human freedom. Thus is obedience to the liberal regime presented as the only rational choice for subjects of freedom. To belabor this point, refugee time, as asynchronous time, passes in the film as a blur, barring one significant date—the Fourth of July. Celebrated with fireworks and a dancing, spangled Uncle Sam, there is no more apt moment, we are meant to grasp, for the refugee to embrace his or her becoming a "new American."

The camp's one optimist, the grinning Duc, is a black market fence who understands that *property* is the secret to success. He grasps better than the others what life on the outside will require. Smuggling goods into the camp with the aid of an American mess hall cook and trading them to camp inhabitants, Duc is constantly on the move, crisscrossing the camp on a red bicycle, one of the film's few bright details. His heart is broken too (his childhood love is the unhappy second wife to the rich man), but he knows better than to linger in the bitter past. Unlike other refugees, who are directionless and perhaps delusional about what their lives will be, Duc looks forward to what he might do (and own) once he leaves the camp, dreaming of developing a business district for his people. (This dream is a reference, of course, to the now-bustling residential and commercial neighborhoods of Little Saigon in Southern California.[153]) In the model of a good American, an entrepreneur, and a go-getter, Duc is unlike his fellow refugees: his directional advance toward capital and property proves him mobile, adaptable, and unstuck. Thus, it is no coincidence that further demonstration of the rightness of the mother's midnight removal occurs via an ecstatic encounter with capitalism, as the motor of modern historical, homogeneous time. To assure Tai that the refugees have nothing to fear in departing from the camp's asynchronous interval, Jim takes Tai outside, beyond the camp, to see America—an adventure we importantly do not see. Instead, we see a smiling Tai return to the camp in the passenger seat of a convertible (that Hollywood avatar of a specifically Californian mobility) closely holding a paper bag full of groceries. Tai later relates the wonders of the world beyond barbed wire to the refugees, who gather around him as he tells his tale of America's riches, just as they had during his song of lament. Tai paints a paradisiacal picture: the houses are large and uniform; the streets wide and clean; and the stores generously full of goods. In America, he enthuses, even a carwash attendant earns a good living on minimum wage, the oft-repeated magical number "two dollars and ten cents an hour."

It turns out that even as the refugee despairs, the world is not ended. The world's historical, homogeneous time marches on most obviously in the ecstatic utterance "two dollars and ten cents an hour," measuring out newfound access to the good life and the intentional self who, it is suggested, might earn a good living at this wage. This equation is uttered throughout the film as the mysterious property of a future deferred in this world out of time: once during a card game among refugees swapping fanciful rumors about the outside, and again during Tai's tale of American prosperity. It is for this reason that, in the midst of Tai's recitation, it is Jim we hear utter "two dollars and ten cents an hour." This insertion of Jim's body, of his omniscient voice as the passage through which reality asserts its power, in the midst of Tai's storytelling underscores the film's reification of both the necessary imbalance of power in the camp regime as a regime of discipline, and the reality of modern, homogeneous time—which is, as Marxist critique emphasizes, a labor relationship. Thus is liberalism as a temporal regime subservient to capital, and the voluntary contract of labor (and the promise of property) a sign of the eventual achievement of self-governance. In *Green Dragon*, this abstraction, *two dollars and ten cents an hour*, stands for the gift of freedom, which is the gift of independence or, under liberalism, the right to contract one's labor. The coupling of the promise of minimum wage with Tai's paper bag full with groceries (and his assertion that "everyone" has a car) operates as a narrative device, in contrast to the camp's world of deprivation and dependency, and as a sign for the self-possession recovered through voluntary labor and for the absence of want found in capital's exchange. (That the minimum wage is still an unlivable wage, even or perhaps especially in 1975, goes unremarked here. We would do well to note, as Rosalind Morris does, that "there may be a reason to distinguish between the trauma that arises in war and the injury that is the function of insertion into new and painful economic structures."[154]) Freedom, this scene promises, is achieved through a developmental process in which the individual first possesses his or her own interiority, and then applies his or her will to the acquisition of certain objects that make up the good life (family and home, for instance), dependent on the rational calculation of interest and consequence and also the temporal consciousness these require. (By film's end, Tai is married to the beautiful Thuy Hoa. Together with his sister's children, they board a bus departing from the camp, moving them forward to a future.) Thus, Jim's utterance—and indeed his actions in removing the mourning mother from her bedside vigil—encourages the refugee to modulate her inner time not to the achronological tempo of her deep memory or intense grief, but to the durational categories that measure time in real and rational terms, such as those of capital and contract labor, epitomized again in the chain that links "be employable, be unwilling to accept welfare," and "be happy." That the film does not follow Tai and Jim outside the camp is an especially subtle device. Viewers are encouraged to experience anew this utopia of big cars and clean houses, and to esteem the refugees' fortitude and achievement, especially the (allegedly reasonable) trust that what is promised through discipline, regularity, and occupation is real. It is no accident that, at the end of his recitation of the wonders of the world, Tai exults: "We no longer need to be afraid of what's out there. Stop being afraid. We can make it."

Green Dragon is useful inasmuch as the film is a site from which multiple systems of representation, both diegetic and nondiegetic, produce as necessary the relation of the development of capacities to the intensification of power. This concern returns us to this book's seed, the twenty-year commemoration of the refugee camps—called Operation Homecoming in clear reference to military maneuvers and orchestrated by both state and nonstate groups—and to those acts of thanksgiving through which we find that violence and refuge are not separate but the same. At the scene of this commemoration and those that follow, a particular composition of space, time, and power marks barbed wire and barracks as central to the refugee passage. Once upon a time, I focused on the commemoration's claim to "America" as a home or new life; the camp, especially as a military garrison, conceived explicitly as an instrument in the service of security and the protection of territory. In doing so, I sought to grasp the nature of this thanksgiving as a haunted attachment to the apparatus of statecraft, especially war making as the assurance of a nation's perpetuity. But it now appears to me that this commemoration merely recruits these instruments of sovereign power to governmentality, both as the subjection of freedom as well as the subjectivity obliged to honor the debt, as these are extended into the foreseeable future. (There are new commemorative events every few years.) Through these simultaneous alignments uncoiling at the scene of refugee encampment, I would now suggest that transition as the difference of liberal war, and rehabilitation as the demand of liberal peace, are distinct names for adjoining arrangements of liberal powers.

Itself a sort of commemoration, *Green Dragon*'s stagings of subjection and subjectivity are insidious not because they are sentimental (the most common complaint of film critics), but because they render routine and rational the forces that demand compliance for freedom. Not least among these forces is historical, homogeneous time, which is also the ladder of *over time*, as the development of capacities, as the tempo of political action, and as the clock of liberal capital—all describing the government of freedom. For the grieving mother who refuses to leave behind her ghostly sons, there can be no absolute sense of time and place in these ways. For her the camp is a palimpsest, in which time does not move forward but is multiply copresent. Her time is subject to repetition and return, exercising a determining force on her life; she speaks to ghosts, she is a ghost, she cannot turn away from the ruin of the past. But to the heroes of this film, including Tai, Duc, and Jim, all these other times and places that threaten to conquer the senses must be put in their proper order. Belonging is further fostered, then, as an effect of mediating, and modulating, feeling states. (Lost in this film's telling are all those whose stories do not fit neatly into this dichotomy of grief-stricken, noncoincidental time and well-adjusted, progressive time. The card players, the gamblers who pass time thusly, could be considered doing something other than be stuck *or* productive.[155]) Although *Green Dragon* appears nostalgic, especially in its claim to documentary realness, it instead curbs the place of the past, its power, and its repressive relation to the present. (This too is the press of the camp commemoration that marks time as forward movement, and as a relation of debt.) In this regard, we might say that the film itself presumes to function as a testimonial to the subjectivity and self-possession earned in the confrontation with the existence of one's anachronism, "our" refugee condition. The achievement of liberal personhood begins here (and in the other scenes of this chapter) with the rational decision to submit to the government of the state, to the rhythm of capital, and to durableness of the debt, in exchange for some share of human freedom.

Coda: Giving Up the Ghost

Among the happy stories of fresh starts in *Green Dragon*, a former South Vietnamese general commits suicide. For much of the film he appears to be waiting. (Thus suspended, he is provocatively unnamed.) He beats a Buddhist drum in an unaccompanied cadence, out of place in the camp; he plants the seeds of a chili pepper in the soil outside his Quonset hut, while others doubt that it might root in unfamiliar soil. And although the plant does flower for others—the young boy who walks into the light, and the general's daughter who marries the camp manager—it never bears fruit for him.[156] As the camp tunes into Radio Free America's broadcasts about the war's collapse, and the news of the fall of Saigon spreads across the camp like blood from a fresh wound, the general slits his wrists off-screen and dies, collapsed on his camp cot.[157]

Although this book, as I have mentioned, is not about the dead, the dead do haunt. The nature of their haunting, however, is not clear. The general's despair is a subplot to the forward momentum of an otherwise hopeful story. His death could be read against the film's resolution: his pain finding an authentic historical consciousness. We might say, for instance, that he refused to exchange grief for gladness, to accommodate himself to a new life in America because the optimism it offered was for him too cruel.[158] Such cruel optimism (to borrow from Lauren Berlant) is poised precariously between the knowledge, and the disavowal, of the failures of liberalism to give what it promises. But this possibility is not precisely my aim in calling attention to the general's death. I am less interested in what is forgotten and what is remembered, than in a narrower sense how some mournful attachments are narrated through a desire for freedom that is underpinned by those structures that are vested as the conditions for its possibility. That is, what does the general mourn, give his life in remembrance? Even as we acknowledge that this refugee soldier is the bearer of much of empire's brutality and the instrumentalization of a modern racial governmentality, to recover him in death as resistive, an outsider, loses the specificity of this figure in the larger structures of knowledge and power that produce his difference. His alienability does not reside outside this chain of signification; indeed, it is from this system of already circulating signs that the refugee condition unfolds. That is, at least some part of his tragedy is captured in the tensions that inform his figuration as both the refugee who *cannot* act on his own behalf because the war had wrecked his powers to do so, and as the agent of the state who *must* act because states necessarily subsist through war's seriality. (The short-lived Republic of Vietnam, established in 1956 and ended in 1975, haunts the diaspora.[159]) Such tensions produce a particular paradox that may well inform this characterization. To be a refugee soldier is to be defined by the presence of the last war, but also by the absence of war to come. Faced with this denial, which is for him the end of future being, the general gives his life for the state that has ceased to exist. In this way, his suicide does not controvert the expectation that certain things are the necessary and natural conditions for the achievement of human freedom. His suicide may speak of his loss but also his refusal to meet the future without the murderous structures that shaped this loss as meaningful. If indeed his heart broke, because the nation he loved ceased to be a structure of power and became instead a state of feeling, we might usefully bear in mind Cacho's call for further meditation: "Perhaps, figuring out the collective story of 'how we die' runs the risk of silencing the story of how we live."[160]

2

Grace, the Gift of the Girl
in the Photograph

Photographs state the innocence, the vulnerability of lives heading toward their
own destruction, and this link between photography and death haunts all photographs of people.

— SUSAN SONTAG, *On Photography*

And the person or thing photographed is the target, the referent . . . which I
should like to call the Spectrum of the Photograph, because this word retains
through its root, a relation to "spectacle" and adds to it that rather terrible thing
which is there in every photograph: the return of the dead.

— ROLAND BARTHES, *Camera Lucida: Reflections on Photography*

You're like an angel that's come to talk to us and to let everyone know.

— Anonymous woman addressing Phan Thi Kim Phúc, *Kim's Story*

The wartime photograph of her near-tangible terror is iconic, not least
because the shadow of her death looms so near. When the U.S. military
ordered South Vietnamese air forces to attack the village of Trang Bang, villagers sought shelter in a nearby temple. The temple was hit with incendi-
aries, and children burning and sometimes dying from napalm streamed
onto the highway, where the South Vietnamese combat photographer
Huynh Cong "Nick" Ut stood with other cameramen and soldiers, guns
slung low. Her clothes are torn away, and she holds her arms away from her
body like broken wings as napalm sears her naked flesh. The photograph,
and its depiction of the ruin wrought by war, inspired shock, horror, outrage, and grief. War, even liberal war, delivers to her not freedom but death;

not the future, but an ending. It is a commonplace to say that this photograph irrevocably changed the course of history, disclosed the ruse of promised freedom—the U.S. war machine unleashed here against an innocent child, no enemy. Hence the prospect of pain in the photograph imparts to observers long after the event a terrible sense of what Judith Butler calls the "precarious life of the other."[1] This perception is credited as precipitating the end of the war, and cited as a caution against more.[2]

And yet—more than twenty years later, the girl in the photo goes to Washington City as a political refugee, and also as a solicitous mourner to the 1996 Veterans Day commemoration, at the polished, jet-black granite wall that is that war's memorial to the American dead.[3] The event, centering reconciliation, featured a former prisoner of war, who cited the soldier's trauma in a bid for peace, and the most famous victim of that war. Addressing herself to "dear friends" from the stage, Phan Thi Kim Phúc turned away from the scene of the photograph—"I do not want to talk about the war because I cannot change history"—to forgive past transgressions. "Even if I could talk face to face with the pilot who dropped the bombs, I would tell him we cannot change history but we should try to do good things for the present and for the future to promote peace."[4] Her words reported widely, the story of the photograph came to a serendipitous ending, in which a betrayed past confronts its future, our present. One writer traced this route traveled together by the girl in the photograph and a collectivity of "us," those observers who first encountered her at the scene of her wounding, as a communion with precarious life: "A little girl, naked and in pain and with burned arms outstretched, staggers toward us down the middle of a highway. A quarter-century later, she reaches us. Who would have expected that when she finally covered that last patch of pocked road, she would offer her hand in grace?"[5]

These two scenes at the heart of this chapter deepen this book's elaboration on the gift of freedom, in which even the vision of heinous force may not be the undoing of empire. Both scenes bear the hallmarks of decisive eventfulness, whose conditions of production and critical reception secure them a place in the making and remaking of liberalism's arrangements. The first is regarded as an emblematic photograph of the war, in which liberal war as the calculation for freedom's continuity is troubled by the return of the dead, splintering the horizon of empty, world-historical time. Picturing for us the spectacular disaster of freedom's bestowal, the photograph exhibits the temporality of hauntology—*she is always dying before us.* But though we might understand the photograph as a trace of empire's unremitting violence, this trace might yet be undone by the presence of the referent—the refugee, the recovered body. Thus does Kim Phúc's visitation bear the effect of restoring our progressive time consciousness, with each survivor affirming the aliveness of the other. What are the spatial and temporal logics that here compel the return of the dead? What sort of archive does such a resurrectionary hermeneutics assemble? How is this photograph, remembered for being a record of an imperial history, reencountered in the subsequent recovery of the body pictured there?

The first part of this chapter looks closely at the scene of the photograph to ask how liberal war making is made visible within an imperial history, and how this process incongruously discloses the limits of that visibility. In thinking this paradox, I consider (unfaithfully, to be sure) the consonance of Achille Mbembe's concern about "the place . . . given to life, death, and the human body (in particular the wounded and slain body)"[6] with Theodor Adorno's conception of "the shudder," in this instance coming out from the confrontation of horror, as "a kind of premonition of subjectivity, a sense of being touched by the other."[7] How are each of these, the wounded and slain body and the shudder, inscribed in a liberal order of power? I hold them together to grasp the photograph as a reckoning with the forces and obligations understood to rest in both the bomb to target a racial enemy and in the picture to shudder before the outcome—the wounded and slain body. These relations of seeing animate the force of liberal war particularly, through which bomb and picture together interpolate an observer (who may also be an operator, a plane, or a camera) alert to the precariousness of the other and, desirous of diminishing her misery and misfortune, who may himself or herself suffer in so doing. To put it another way, the vexing issues presented by the girl in the photograph as a consequence of imperial violence are precisely the problem of liberal empire.

In between these two scenes, the girl in the photograph is the subject of numerous histories and biographies that approach her as a rescue mission, as the restoration of her presence to our present. The second part of this chapter examines the wish to narrate the story of this wounded body in the imperial archive as a knowable subject in a continuous history. This commitment to subjectivity becomes a narrative one, entailing, as Paul Ricoeur writes, "an indefinite extension of duration both backward and forward,"[8] and thereby promising a linear progression from the traumatic consciousness of the photograph toward the world-historical time of a life. In the magazine feature and literary biography that I treat in this section, the presence of beauty serves to gender and atomize this progression, but also to vilify the anachronistic (that is, the illiberally orthodox) vocabulary of race and coloniality used to censure the imperial war of the photograph's making. In perceiving them in counterpoint, these biographies aim to contextualize the photograph as a *moment* in a continuous history, and they call forth beauty as the means through which the girl's life is furthered.[9] The danger that follows from such contextualization, as I detail here, lies in what is consigned to the irreversible past with the photograph —such as injustices, or violences, that persist in the present.

Accordingly, the third part of this chapter considers the communion of victim and perpetrator at this second scene, in which the girl in the photograph grieves at a monument to the warrior dead, beside a seven-year prisoner of war. In their copresence, the traumatic past of war comes to be experienced as a shared ordeal, especially where the diagnostic concept of post-traumatic stress disorder comes to overdetermine the pathology of liberal war. For her part, Kim Phúc is framed as the personification of beatific grace, whose pardon absolves an empire of the criminality of war. The notion that pardon is a moral but also a historical necessity is perhaps most emphatically proclaimed by Hannah Arendt in *The Human Condition*, inasmuch as human communion, which is to say human history, cannot continue in its absence: "Without being forgiven, released from the consequences of what we have done, our capacity to act would, as it were, be confined to one single deed from which we could never recover; we would remain the victims of its consequences forever, not unlike the sorcerer's apprentice who lacks the magic formula to break the spell."[10] In this regard, forgiveness acknowledges the aliveness of the other and a common humanity of victim and perpetrator, and it lobbies for forward momentum, toward a promise of renewal. But, as the last two sections of this chapter suggest, though the girl in the photograph appears before us to restore a sense of historical responsibility and solidarity, it is not to the dead or damaged who occupy the past's horizons of terrible destruction. Instead, her pardon corroborates the belief that liberal peoples are hurt by their wrongdoing against others and serves to restore social order by redeeming empire from being held hostage to a shameful, irreversible past.

In a liberal order of power, the observer, who shudders in response to perceiving pain in an other, seeks to alleviate suffering and may be successful, or not, in this endeavor. Yet through the succession of these chapter's scenes, the girl in the photograph offers her assurance that the present might yet fulfill the failed expectations of the past. Last, as the fourth section of this chapter details, Kim Phúc becomes a model for a moral obligation to a human collectivity collocated with, and championed by, an empire of freedom. In this genealogy, the wounded and slain body that becomes the object of shudder and shame is obligated to return feeling with like feeling. Her grace becomes that which she recompenses liberal empire for the gift of freedom—*even napalm*. The global circulation of her message of forgiveness addressed to others who endure injustices to pardon such offenses, the question of historical accountability is thus profoundly conceived through historical antagonism. If, from the standpoint of empty, homogeneous time, forgiveness is an agency of human freedom, the victim of imperial violence is caught in a terrible contradiction. Namely, she may once again be named an anachronistic other to freedom and progress, unless she grants forgiveness to those who committed injustices against her in her own name. We may put this another way: if forgiveness as a moral obligation compels the subject of freedom to recompense liberal war makers for the costs of war, that forgiveness may consequentially disappear the wounded and slain body into the universal history of the human, and banish those who experience violence *as* violence to beyond the human altogether. The juxtaposition of these scenes sheds light on the significant power of the gift of freedom: the place of the shudder in the order of liberal empire as a reason for pursuing war, and the rationale for pardoning its crimes.

War Frames

The problem of the photograph is the problem of liberalism's empire—what grace can possibly be found in napalm? First, and most obviously, this photograph is itself a theater of war. That is, the photograph most obviously refers to the scene of sovereign power, to war as violence. It is proof that life is precarious, that life can be lost, destroyed, or neglected to the point of death. There is the devastation of the other's body into mere flesh; the girl in the photograph is the stark figuration of radical unmaking. Thus sustained attention to the wounded and slain body is so often solicited: in hopes of publicizing the racialized violence of liberalism's empire. But the photograph also occasions contests of meaning about that violence, about the conflict in Southeast Asia and the nature of the United States as global hegemon. That is, the photograph that appears to be historical bears an effect of narrativity: for all that the photograph registers a precise moment, it nonetheless refers to an anterior and posterior time through which we presume to know what it is we are seeing. (As Wendy Hesford and Wendy Kozol observe of the more "haunting violations," "visual images do not merely reflect historical conditions but rather mediate those historical forces to shape social understandings of political struggles."[11]) The photograph bears the force of evidence that *something having been there* is in crisis, but what precisely can we say it is? Indeed, the photograph tells of multiple and complicated encounters between the powers that bomb, and which are also the powers that picture, and their targets; or, as Roland Barthes puts it, between "two experiences: that of the observed subject and that of the subject observing."[12] This relation between the observed subject and the subject observing binds together some of this book's concerns about the relation between recipient and giver, governed and governor, especially where something precarious—gift, freedom, bomb, compassion, subjectivity—passes between them to illumine an imperial history of the will to see and to know the other.

Consider the contests of meaning that follow from disputes about the cause and culpability for her pain, unfolding from the concept of *accident*. How does accident, here summoned to narrate the succession of events leading to the photograph as an intelligible whole, reflect on (or deflect) the violence of liberal empire? Originally captioned as "accidental napalm" (by the Associated Press, for whom Ut freelanced), in this reading the image-event of the photograph is deemed inconsistent and incompatible with the promise of the United States to free others from such heedless destruction. Understood as the absence of purpose, bad timing, or a failure of "correct" action, the accident is the experience of the distance between an ideal and an actual outcome. Such an accident as napalm calls for sorrow at inexplicable and arbitrary terror, and perhaps also an appraisal of that which is implicated in accident. However, accident is less ontological than circumstantial—it is perceived as an exception, or an emergency. As Foucault observes, "at the root of what we know and what we are lies neither truth nor being, but the exteriority of accident."[13] Thus, the facticity of napalm is not disputed, but the *intention* is. Accident in this instance is therefore the name for the all-too-ordinary violence that brings about the corporeal and social negation of subjected others, a violence that cannot be admissible as foundational to liberal government. That is, accident occludes the criminality of the ways the United States conducts its wars. Accident, as the saying goes, is only human.

For other observers, some property of the photograph (and the nature of its transmission) strikes a false note.[14] The same image-event was also callously dismissed as a "hibachi accident at a family bar-b-que" by no less a personage than General William Westmoreland, deputy commander of Military Assistance Command, Vietnam.[15] (Westmoreland infamously stated elsewhere that "the Oriental doesn't put the same high price on life as does a Westerner. . . . We value life and human dignity. They don't care about life and human dignity."[16]) *Accident* is more insidious in its usage here. We are not meant to understand Westmoreland's phrase "hibachi accident" as true in fact as much as true in feeling. In this view, as explicated so well by Mbembe's concept of necropower, terror as colonial warfare is not subject to legal and institutional rule in the seeming wilderness that was Viet Nam. (Some named this wilderness "Indian country."[17] As Jodi Byrd argues so well, a paradigmatic Indianness has ever facilitated an imperial United States.[18]) In such spaces outside the purview of civility, "weapons are deployed in the interest of maximum destruction of persons and the creation of *death-worlds*, new and unique forms of social existence in which vast populations are subjected to conditions of life conferring upon them the status of *living dead*."[19] Napalm is one such devastating weapon, dispensing deaths far beyond the *eventness* of bombing.[20] "Hibachi accident" is therefore not a refutation of accidental napalm as much as it is the rhetorical realization of necropower, through which *some deaths do not matter*. For Westmoreland, the story of accident is the nonobservance of "Oriental" fatality (because they are the living dead, because they do not value life and human dignity as "we" do). Some life is not as human, neither is it grievable.[21] That is, we further find in Westmoreland's statements (and other conflations of all Vietnamese with a general racial enemy[22]) the echo of Foucault's economy of biopower, in which racism is the biopolitics of disposability, or "the condition for the acceptability of putting to death."[23] In this context, the photograph is suspect as evidence of terrible wrong because the racial death pictured there is nondeath. The question of fraud and false cause does not dispute the fact of lethality, but it instead annuls the obligation for compensatory feeling.

In a more radical view, the photograph precisely pictures the racial deaths that the United States commits in the course of liberal war.[24] Together, the terrible event and the photograph that seizes *things as they are* measure the distance between what is promised and what is given. In their study of "iconic photographs, public culture, and liberal democracy," Robert Hariman and John Lucaites feelingly observe of event and photograph: "Like the explosion still reverberating in the background, the photograph ruptures established narratives of justified military action, moral constraint, and national purpose. It is a picture that shouldn't be shown of an event that shouldn't have happened."[25] Likewise, Butler ends her consideration of a precarious life with reference to this photograph, which suggests something of its enduring, insistent importance: "These were precisely pictures we were not supposed to see, and they disrupted the visual field and the entire sense of public identity that was built upon that field. The images furnished a reality, but they also showed a reality that disrupted the hegemonic field of representation itself."[26] Here, critics contend that the photograph contains *things as they are* that *we were not supposed to see*, because *this event shouldn't have happened*. Against claims to a tolerant collectivity, and in contrast to a concept of unaccountable accident, in this view the photograph reveals the murderous structures of race and coloniality that consign some life to subterraneity, to death. Or, to paraphrase badly a line from Herman Melville's Civil War poem "Shiloh," *what like napalm can undeceive!* Michael Warner observes in his reading of this poem for our present wars: "What had been sacred justice becomes mere violence, in part because it stands in visible contrast to that which had been violated—namely, a deep subjectivity."[27] For those who are "undeceived" by napalm, this deep subjectivity is found in the damaged body that faces death (a movement of the individual into history, as Mbembe understands Hegel).[28]

Through these controversies, the photograph draws our attention to a politics of seeing as a politics of life. It is as a structure for perception that the photograph discloses for us the so-called intuitive structures of the gift of freedom, through bomb and picture, violence and power, in tremendously significant ways. Such incongruous encounters with the photograph bring together a number of analytic consequences that I wish to consider of the power to observe and of observation as a power over others, and their particular arrangements for liberal empire. First, the dynamic between spectacle and spectator, particularly regarding the pain of others, once again names the knowledge structures, intuitive as well as institutional, that make it possible to bomb and to picture simultaneously. We know—from Paul Virilio, Jennifer Terry, Fiona I. B. Ngô, and Caren Kaplan, among others—that war and vision share an affinity.[29] The confluence of circumstances that led to the scene of the photograph can be attributed to a development in the age of bombing, as Rey Chow argues (supplementing Heidegger's "world picture"), in which the world is conceived of simultaneously as an object of knowledge and as a target for war. Put another way, though the photograph seems to attest to empire's errors, the photograph is continuous with racial and civilizational knowledge about the self and other —what Chow calls "the 'eye' and the 'target.'"[30] Most obviously, military command apprised the cameramen who captured the scene of her bombing in a mutual creation of the conditions of subjection pictured there—a common scenario (even before the practice of embedding journalists in military units) that makes explicit the bonds between these viewing subjects and the objects they encounter in their simultaneous, converging fields of vision. Departing from Roland Barthes, for whom the "Operator" focuses on the scene before him as an emotionally detached machine-eye, while the "Spectator" experiences an emotional attachment to the photograph, or the scene pictured there, operator and spectator are not so distinct in this liberal empire.[31] Both are noninnocent in their viewing, especially with regard to a shared target as other to freedom and progress.

Second, the photograph is not only a reminder of the referent's body, it is also the vessel for this body's passage forward into our presence. That is, to summon Adorno's shudder, the photograph subjectivizes an observer. *What does my body know of this photograph?*[32] *What have I to do with this?*[33] Or as Barthes ponders: "I am the reference of every photograph, and this is what generates my astonishment in addressing myself to the fundamental question: why is it that I am alive *here and now*?"[34] The photograph animates an embodied subjectivity, but the shudder in response to seeing pain is ambiguous. It may prompt a premonition of another's deep subjectivity, but it may also renew self-consciousness on the part of the one who observes. Because the girl appears to be fleeing toward the observer (toward the photographer, toward the outside of the frame), presenting to us her naked terror, the encounter with the other's pain is a confrontation with the boundary between us. To this experience of "the thing of the past . . . [that] has really touched the surface which in its turn my gaze will touch," racial difference or civilizational noncoincidence may be central.[35] The perception of pain interiorizes for the observer an experience of distance and approximation, through which contact with the photograph and *the thing that has been there* elicits recognition of the other's specific relation to oneself, and the revelation of oneself in relation to an ideal. Most heinously, "hibachi accident" names a distance that perceives no obligation to that precarious life, that vents indignation at having to look at all. But this encounter may also mirror Chow's analyses of Julia Kristeva's "discovery" of the limits of Western knowledge in the alien presence of Chinese women, through which the Westerner becomes self-accusatory and confessional when confronted with the other: "If these others have been turned into objects, it is because these objects' gaze makes the Western 'subject' feel alienated from her own familiar . . . humanity."[36] Following Chow, the other's silence occasions the witness's speech. Consider the epilogue to *The Girl in the Picture*, the biography of Kim Phúc, in which Denise Chong opines that the photograph "simultaneously dispatches each of us into our own personal history of darkness. We privately flail at our human limitations, failings and self-indulgence in the face of the chaos and wrongdoing of war."[37]

If it follows that the encounter with boundary becomes a means of self-knowledge, what returns to the observer from the scene observed might be especially troubling here. This question—"why is it that I am alive *here and now*?"—is so much more fraught for the imperial observer. The witness (who is in some cases also the perpetrator) is subjected by the gaze of the other, and is made conscious of himself or herself as having *power over*. Condensing "a mute and frozen accusation,"[38] the photograph exerts pressure on the observer to consider again the moral life of free peoples. But, in a long-standing philosophical tradition, the observer is also *overpowered* by what he or she sees. That is, in perceiving freedom's unevenness, liberalism also claims the vulnerability of the observer before the vulnerable thing or person observed. The increasing helplessness of the observed may also heighten the power of the vulnerable thing or person to command the observer's attention, to seize him or her through sudden tremor or feeling. We may condense this *power over* and *over power* as follows: the moment of perceiving the precarity of the other confers on the other the gift of life, though sometimes this simultaneously confers death; but this is also the moment of conferring on the observer (who is also the operator of bomb, of camera) the gift of life, the premonition of the shudderer's subjectivity—which in turn illumines the precarity of the observer. In just this way, Dipesh Chakrabarty describes the modern subject: "The person who is not an immediate sufferer but who has the capacity to become a secondary sufferer through sympathy for a generalized picture of suffering, and who documents this suffering in the interest of eventual social intervention—such a person occupies the position of the modern subject. In other words, the moment of the modern observation of suffering is a certain moment of self-recognition on the part of an abstract, general human being."[39] Like Adorno's shudder, Susan Sontag dubs this "the pleasure of flinching."[40] With these insights in mind, we may therefore say that, once incorporated into a social exchange (because the shudder, and also the photograph, cannot be frozen in the moment of what we might call the unselving of the observer, as Adorno might wish), the shudder may become a possessive investment in the subjectivity of the one who observes. Put another way, while the shudder names a moral consciousness about the other as the abstraction of a universal collectivity, and as a crucial property of liberal humanism, it is a relation and a property caught up in an asymmetrical exchange. For just this reason Sherene Razack wryly observes of "those who witness the evil" that "we come to know ourselves as a compassionate people."[41] And, as Saidiya Hartman writes about another century's iniquity, the abolitionist's empathy is not apart from possession, inasmuch as the capacity of the liberal person to identify with pain is "both founded upon and enabled by the material relations of chattel slavery"[42] and, we might follow, colonial practices and imperial governments.

Reading the photograph can coalesce for us those assemblages of knowledge and power that bind the subject observed to the subject observing, the recipient to the giver, the governed to the governor. Both instrumental to the U.S. self-concept, the bomb and picture interpolate an observer conscious of the helplessness of others, and an operator capable of interceding to lessen their distress, and who both or at once may endure a concomitant pain (not confined to the shudder, because war is violent) in so doing. That is, the photograph is understood as a traumatic event for U.S. empire, too: "A brutal image from a brutal war, it is imprinted on our national psyche."[43] Or: "The psychological history of the war seems inconceivable without it."[44] In this regard, bomb and picture, to paraphrase

Chow, are a kind of investment whose profits return to the "eye" that targets.[45] This investment, as we shall see, is crucial to the story of the gift of freedom—*even in case of failure*—as a narration of liberal empire.

Such consequences for observing the scene of the photograph most spectacularly incriminate liberal war—the "eye" of the bomb—but also implicate an art of liberal government through which human freedom is settled via the idiom of presence and self-possession. Following from the above, the photograph is perceived as an other means of the girl's abstraction, her arrested development, following but not apart from napalm. Part of the haunting of the photograph (and, indeed, all photographs, if we follow Barthes) is its noncoincidence with presence. As the trace of a body that once was there but is there no longer, the photograph is the alienation of subjectivity. Or as Ngô offers, "being seen creates a tension between being known as an object of study and remaining unknown as a subject."[46] In this vein, what is most terrifying about the photograph, for some witnesses, may be that the girl in the picture wants nothing more of us.

Against this, the photograph also occasions a wish to wrest her away from such repressive objecthood. (As per Chow: " 'Subjectivity' becomes a way to change the defiled image, the stripped image, the image-reduced-to-nakedness, by showing the truth behind/beneath/around it."[47]) The desire for subjectivization springs from the *shock* of recognition, through which her pain, as the seat of her deep subjectivity, might be known to us. In this way, confrontation with the photograph calls forth alternate or supplementary knowledge that would transfigure the denouement, the death, forewarned by bomb and picture. Indeed, this photograph—perhaps more than any other[48]—gave rise to a legion of endeavors to do just these things. The wish to produce her truth outside the frame of the photograph is the hope to restore what has gone missing in the radical unmaking of a self—the body, interiority, a history that is also the sharing of time. This is not the erasure of the photograph, or of her defiled image, because the photograph persists as the pivot on which this movement turns. The girl in the photograph as an archival object comes into existence only through this loss. Indeed, both the historical and ethical gravity of the promise and her presence are produced and sustained through more stories of the loss figured in the photograph. Or, to borrow an apt phrase from Anjali Arondekar, "the archival mode here shifts from savage to salvage."[49]

In the remainder of this chapter, I look to an itinerant archive that compiles texts and images from different histories and fantasies to consider the scenes of subjectivity that revivify the girl in the photograph. Given that these stories do elaborate on her story of terror and harm, what does it mean to otherwise restore the girl in the photograph "in context" to a concept of continuous history? There are two interlaced theoretical and historical provocations here. In the first, the imperative to restore the wounded and absent body pictured at the scene of destruction cannot proceed without an implicit concept of the self-possessed individual, anchored in liberal schema of passivity and action, alienation and ownership, captivity and freedom—through which she (in this photograph, she) becomes simultaneously singular and universal. In the second, something must return to the one who watches and shudders, and from the desire to remake her in our image anew. Or, to put it another way, how does the gift of consciousness and contemporaneity, which is also the promise of freedom, in restoring her presence to our present, return to us as supplement or surplus value? How might salvaging the subject of freedom also salvage liberal empire?

Once again I take my cue from Foucault, this time from his critique of liberal humanism in *Archeology of Knowledge*, to unthread the consequences of her subjectivization for her and for an "us" that is empire. Foucault writes:

> Continuous history is the indispensable correlative of the founding function of the subject: the guarantee that everything that has eluded him may be restored to him; the certainty that time will disperse nothing without restoring it in a reconstituted unity; the promise that one day the subject—in the form of historical consciousness—will once again be able to appropriate, to bring back under his sway, all those things that are kept at a distance by difference, and find in them what might be called his abode. *Making historical analysis the discourse of the continuous, and making human consciousness the original subject of all historical development and all action, are the two sides of the same system of thought.*[50]

With these insights in mind, this chapter deconstructs the recovery of Kim Phúc's continuous history, the girl in the photograph who, engaged in contemplation of herself as a perceptual object, desires the sort of presence that is pledged and at the same time compromised by bomb and picture. The salvaging of these histories, contexts, and specificities become complicit with a continuous history of empire, which secures its hegemony in its capacity to metamorphose—even in their representation and recovery—those experiences that resist it as errors or accidents in the irreversible past. Through such an archive, the overwhelming effect of Kim Phúc's continuous history as a woman is the disappearance of the ghost (the trace, the photograph) and the murderous structures of race and coloniality that both visualized and disappeared her. That is, such habitual violence that follows from these murderous structures is rendered a mere interruption, an extraordinary event: "In this system, time is conceived in terms of totalization and revolutions are never more than moments of consciousness. In various forms, this theme has played a constant role since the nineteenth century: to preserve, against all decenterings, the sovereignty of the subject, and the twin figures of anthropology and humanism."[51] Hence it is not as Walter Benjamin's angel of history that the girl in the photograph appears before us.[52] Benjamin's angel would choose to linger among the ruins, to rouse the dead. Kim Phúc turns away from the devastation amassing behind her to welcome with open arms a restored covenant, a renewable future. These, then, are the signs of her grace, her gift.

Beauty and the Beholder

In a 1989 *Los Angeles Times Magazine* feature story called "The Girl in the Photograph," Kim Phúc is reintroduced to us as a newly fashioned beauty:[53] "It's the magic hour in Havana, when the sky goes iridescent indigo before the light drops. The young woman poses for the photographer on the low wall of the esplanade above the sea, with racing clouds as a backdrop. The young woman loves the camera, and the camera loves her. She's a Vietnamese Marilyn, wrinkling her nose, giggling and tugging at her skirt. She flirts with the photographer, wants to pose rubbing her cheek against his, giggles and tosses hair caught back by an orange and silver flower." The feature continues, "Seventeen years ago, there was a different picture." This photograph—here reporter Judith Coburn echoes so many other observers—"came to symbolize, more than any other photograph taken in Vietnam, the atrocity of war." But Kim Phúc has "outlived" this ugly, "savage" image—on the eve of a six-week trip to the United States, "the country that brought both the napalm that almost killed her and the doctors who saved her," she is found whole. Her laughter, the orange and silver flower behind her ear, bear out her triumph: "The agonizingly wounded child had grown into a beautiful young woman, not a crippled, embittered war victim."[54]

In "The Girl in the Photograph," beauty comes into view as a conceptual wedge in the historiography of the photograph to transform the relation between observer and the scene observed. This displacement of our experience of her as an object of our sustained regard, from *the* photograph to another, and from *that* moment to another, turns on the apparent non-coincidence between pain and beauty.[55] That is, she is *given time* as the present and as presence through the work of beauty, recorporealizing her wounded body. As an example, the *Los Angeles Times Magazine* published the uncropped photograph of her headlong flight down Highway 1 across the centerfold (as well as the frames that came before and after) together with a present-day portrait. In this second photograph, Kim Phúc smiles charmingly, her "Jackie O oversized white sunglasses" tucked into the V-neck of her dolman-sleeved, flower-appliquéd white T-shirt. Enthralled with beauty's unguessed-at presence, Coburn marvels at her resemblance to culturally iconic and quintessentially American figures of girlish innocence: she is "a just-discovered ingénue," a "Vietnamese Marilyn, wrinkling her nose, giggling and tugging at her skirt," and "a small-town beauty queen on the Greyhound to Hollywood," embued with a sense of fledging romance, for her, with others.[56] If the depths of Kim Phúc's abjection are confronted once again in the detailed descriptions of her painful recovery in hospital (one American plastic surgeon, a wartime volunteer who operated on her in 1972, remembers: "Changing the dressing was like being flayed alive [for her]. There's nothing more devastating than third-degree burns. They're not only the most painful wounds to flesh and blood there are; it's a wound to the soul.") and of the burn scars that traverse her body ("back, chest and arm pitted, gouged and ridged like a hillside strip-mined of precious metals"), then these other passages attest to beauty's capacity to radically vivify a human relation to others, and to the world:[57] "Kim Phúc giggles, pirouettes and open her arms, vamping in the international sign language of the star."[58]

These two photographs, from two radically distinct moments, are arresting for their material yet highly metaphoric inscription of the duration between them, exercising a historicist consciousness as a determining force. As we press harder on the narrations that tether these images together, we will see how the seemingly neutral, linear progression between them as a natural development (the girl cannot help but grow up, become a woman) animates these successive scenes through an ideology of continuous history. Thus did Barthes dub the photograph a "clock for seeing," inasmuch as the suspended moment refers to a before and an after.[59] Death haunts the first photograph of her burning; the photograph's paranormal time is haunting. In counterpoint and as postscript, the second photograph is presented as both fantastical and determinedly ordinary because the ghost—the agonizingly maimed child who is, by virtue of having *something missing*, partial and unwhole—is resurrected as a beautiful young woman. Coburn's magazine feature and Chong's biography conjure continuous histories in which the past of the photograph is *passed* in this manner, in which murderous structures of radical unmaking are superseded by an ideal concept of beauty as subjectivization—the sign of an interior life, propelling the photograph farther and farther into the irreversible past.

In which a scene of pain and a scene of beauty are presented to us of the same body in order to make sense of the time and space of her precarious life, questions about the particular circumstances through which we are obliged to others figure importantly in this chapter's focus on righting (which is also, in this instance, rescuing) liberalism's arrangements in the age of the world as target. Whether in flayed and peeling flesh, or in the bright flower in her curled hair, the presence of pain or beauty impresses on us a demand to make it an object of sustained regard. Though these are difficult and unwieldy concepts, I wish to concentrate on the presence of pain or beauty as structures of feelings embodied in the photograph. Though pain and beauty are often conceived of as starkly incompatible, here I consider them as sometimes contrary, sometimes complicitous, arrangements that are inseparable as forms for organizing race and gender, and that produce knowledge about a body. Regarding this intimacy between pain and beauty as both epistemology and ontology, we find commensurabilities: both pain and beauty produce a felt sense of the lacuna between life and death—at times a subjective, individual, and private experience, and at other times a universal, communal one. But conceptions of pain and beauty are often also paradoxical. Regarding the pain of others or an absent or aberrant beauty (which might morph into ugliness) might beget an experience of the distance between the body pictured there, apart from the observer here and now.[60] Indeed, aesthetic judgments that communicated and condoned racial dread or disgust acted as alibis in imperial encounters. For instance, Immanuel Kant's infamous schema of "national characteristics," in which distinctions in aesthetic judgments are commensurate with moral feelings, and with racial and colonial knowledges,[61] or Edmund Burke's infamous moment of racial antipathy and sublime terror ("the first time the boy saw a black object, it gave him great uneasiness; and that some time after, upon accidentally seeing a negro woman, he was struck with great horror at the sight"[62]), aptly illustrates for us the historical complicity between a metaphysics of racial difference and philosophical discourses of aesthetic and moral sensibilities since the Enlightenment. (Antipathy also imputes to the racial other the terrifying power to bodily overwhelm an observer. In this case, the shudder may be a spasm of revulsion, flinching, or cringing from the touch of the other.) For these reasons, beauty has a long and compelling history as a force for wounding.[63]

It is also suggested that consciousness of pain or beauty in others alerts us to precarious life. Through such cognizance, we are encouraged to heed some property of a common humanity through which we will come to experience the other as different than before, and we will want to ease or prolong their presence in the world. In this manner, the shudder in the confrontation in horror may be comparable to the *frisson* of pleasure in the meeting with beauty. Such frisson is also perceived as a premonition of subjectivity, especially as beauty is so often bound to an experience of life. Kant describes beauty as arousing a direct "feeling of life's being furthered."[64] The philosopher and art critic Arthur Danto names beauty a "necessary condition for life as we would want to live it."[65] For Elaine Scarry, beauty calls forth in the beholder a wish to preserve and even to provide to others the benefit of beauty. Our attachment to its presence, she opines, induces in us a heightened attention, "voluntarily extended out to other persons or things. . . . Through its beauty, the world continually recommits us to a rigorous standard of perceptual care."[66] Such a conception of beauty hopes to extend its life in all directions: traversing distances between the viewer and the object of his or her gaze, beauty calls forth a rescue mission, pressing the sustained regard given to the beautiful thing into new forms toward other (even if less beautiful) things. But though beauty is summoned as a salve, it is not precisely the absence of pain; beauty also catalyzes the consciousness that its loss harms us, and thereby renews in us a commitment to foster life. Such imbalances of power that invest in the care and cultivation of beauty, which could also be understood as analogous to the claims of empire, illumine how an attachment to beauty might call for the annihilation of its antithesis—ugliness—as a life necessity.[67] In other words, a politics of beauty establishes a politics of life, and vice versa.

The imprint of this politics of life is perceived in the caesura between the first photograph and the second and in the transition between the scene of her death making and the scene of her life saving. It is as such that the attachment to beauty, especially as antagonism to those wrong arrangements perceived to impart pain or ugliness, also acts to review and regulate those political structures and structures of feeling that stimulate or strangle beauty. What epistemological and affective amendments occur when we see these images together, especially via a historicist consciousness that given time aligns the body in development with an ideology of progress? What might it mean for the girl in the photograph to come to possess beauty, and for the beholder to perceive her as beautiful? Does the second, beautiful photograph cover over or derealize the scene of pain, or does it marshal pain otherwise? What happens, in part, is that a presumably universal, natural femininity covers over, at the same time that it is a site for, racial subjectivization and liberalist consciousness. In a dense and detailed memoir, Chong acquaints the reader with a subjective, individual experience of Kim Phúc's alteration of a damaged self through beauty—an experience that also importantly renders her suffering as singular while connecting her longing for beauty and romantic love to a human universality.

The Girl in the Picture returns the girl in the picture to a continuous history to make sense of her life within a century's colonial and anti-colonial warfare. At the beginning of Chong's biography, Kim Phúc, now a young mother and wife, wakes from a recurring nightmare of the war. Though she is decades removed from the event, and safe in the arms of her doting husband in their Toronto apartment, Kim Phúc still feels the heaviness that has been weighing on her heart all these long years. To exorcise this nighttime terror, Kim Phúc endeavors to put this torment in its place—the past. The resulting re-creation of her life's story is an operatic recitation of dramatic and devastating events, of which the war and the napalm are just one part. Yet, one detail stands out from among the often-unvarying scenarios of deprivation and doubt that fill the biography. Our heroine is repeatedly grateful to accident, and later to God, that despite the burn scars furrowing her upper body, her face is unscarred.[68] (*The Girl in the Picture* reports that her mother prayed, "If Phúc is going to be ugly and deformed, better that she dies than lives."[69]) In this biography, her unblemished face provides her with a disguise—because she can pass as undamaged—and provides others a connection (she is described as almost always smiling). But it is also her face, that presumably real surface that endows particularity and the representation of an individual self, that stages the scene for human interiority as an absolute and autonomous truth of the subject. As the newspaper profile marvels before this second photograph, "Her perfect moon face is carefully and skillfully made up. It's an act of self-transformation that makes a charade of the old putdown that beauty is only skin-deep," we see here the provocative accord, rather than antagonism, between beauty and interiority.[70] For this beholder, beauty confers an immanent presence of depth, what might also be known as grace, but also a means of self-making through which life might be furthered. To observe her unscarred face, her "perfect moon face," is therefore to perceive her desire for beauty and freedom—and with these, romantic love and self-expression—through a deep singularity, and also a globalist conviction that beauty and freedom be extended in all directions. This is, however, no innocent observation.

Throughout *The Girl in the Picture*, Kim Phúc endures multiple alienations, most obviously the alienation from her own body. After napalm, her body—boundaries, organs, vital fluids—is no longer her own: "A big enough mass of burning napalm will consume the full thickness of skin; gone instantly are hair follicles, sweat glands and sensory nerve endings. In such a third-degree burn, the burned area appears red, mushy, and oozing. If the napalm continues to burn downwards, feeding on fat, muscle, and other deep tissue, the injury has the severity of a fourth- or fifth-degree charring."[71] Re-creating for the reader the confrontation with another's pain, Chong describes Kim Phúc's wounds, and her recovery, in grueling detail. "Phúc sustained burns to the severity of third degree or worse to 30 to 35 percent of her body surface. Those burned areas included almost her entire back, reaching around on her left side to her chest, the back of her neck and into her hairline, and her entire right arm. Lesser burns resulted from burning napalm that splashed from her clothes onto her right arm, buttocks, and stomach. The inside of her right hand was also burned from where it touched napalm on her other arm, and she had singeing to her left cheek and both ears."[72] Dead nerves, hardened scars— these burns render her unrecognizable to herself. Something or someone is missing: her body is a stranger to her, and she can no longer control her limbs, her gestures. "At the dinner table, when a porcelain rice bowl clattered to the floor, she looked around in surprise, unaware it had fallen from her left hand."[73]

But Kim Phúc experiences at least two other forms of alienation, through which she comes to know herself as others do. Most obviously, the photograph of the napalmed girl (a shadow beneath which Kim Phúc labors) is transmuted into a commodity object of significant value in what Elizabeth Spelman calls "the economy of attention to suffering."[74] And, inasmuch as *The Girl in the Picture* engages this economy too, as a biography of the girl in the photograph, a metanarrative of an ever-expanding body of images and image making underlines the biography itself. The camera, unseen in the photograph, is a recurring character in this story, and through it the time of the photograph is prolonged. This book also relates the stories of the photograph's operators, and spectators, including Ut, the photographer whose image we first come to know as *accidental napalm*. We are presented with long passages in which photographers and filmmakers navigate state bureaucracy and premodern rurality in their search for the girl in the photograph—whether to commemorate anniversaries or recommence "frozen" histories. The photograph also produces more photographs that circulate within this economy, including those that expose her uncovered body to diagnostic intervention. (Though the biography does not engage these terms, the photograph's economy, as Mieke Bal might suggest, is also monetary, "an exchange where the subject is exposed, even in the most painful and intimate moments, while the photographer cashes the earnings the viewer is willing to give."[75] We might consider in this manner some of the photographs Kretz published in *Stern* after his first visit, in which a naked Kim Phúc showers in a plastic tub to ease the lingering pain of her burns.) These photographs, many of them reprinted in the centerfold, thereby augment the story event of the first. Chong refers constantly to these secondary photographs and other life stories, including *Life* magazine's 1974 issue "The Year in Pictures," which published a two-page story titled "Kim Phúc, Memories Masked by a Smile," featuring a photograph of a smiling, ten-year-old Kim Phúc at home, inset with Ut's photograph; *Stern* magazine's multiple stories about her years-long recovery, posted each time by the German photojournalist Perry Kretz (whom Kim Phúc welcomes and names her "savior"); and the *Los Angeles Times* feature about Kim Phúc's blossoming sexuality as a young woman in Cuba. In this way, the biography underlines the photograph's existence as a fetish, precisely as a structuring absence—that is, not the whole story—that incites substitutions and supplements. In doing so, *The Girl in the Picture* reflects back to us our awareness of the photograph's stature as both representative and exceptional *in* the archive and *as* an archive. Finally, as further evidence of the distance between the girl and the photograph, Chong provides multiple scenes of Kim Phúc's perceptual experiences in encountering her image as an auratic object in an age of mechanical reproduction: "Phúc was mesmerized by the twenty-five-minute film entitled *Kim Phúc*, dubbed in Vietnamese. The narrator began with the Vietnam war and told of the napalm attack that injured her, and how, ten years later, she was a medical student in Vietnam. Never having seen herself on film, Phúc was proud of her performance: she was articulate, her voice was lifting, her smile bright."[76]

Though Kim Phúc at times takes pleasure in her own image, she also confronts the photograph with much more ambivalence. This is yet another scene of her alienation, in which the photograph supersedes war as her life's catastrophe. Because this violence, endured by an individual—Kim Phúc, here—has become public as an injury to a community, as the heinous ruination of a people, Kim Phúc is shadowed by foreign journalists and agents of the communist state. She is not just any victim; because of the photograph, the evidentiary value of which lies in freezing a moment, and seizing its singularity, she is perceived as the victim par excellence. Called on to press her scars into propaganda, in her heart she rebels against the preoccupation with the past held captive in the photograph. Here napalm, and the photograph, leads to another order of pathology, in which the state (in this telling) imposes on her a traumatic consciousness. Kim Phúc is subject to the intrusions of the ruinous past onto her fettered present, her subjectivity held hostage by the state's need to tell again the story of her injury as a collective one: "When speaking to journalists, Phúc stepped into the spotlight and played the part of the happy student, the life she wanted; when they departed, she was left in darkness, with the life that had been forced on her. . . . She railed in silence: *They have destroyed my life. Why do they do this to me?*"[77] Thus did government handlers (in this story) closely supervise, and suppress, Kim Phúc's voice. Denied her wished-for education because schooling interfered with her duties, she is made to play at being a medical student (putting on a nurse's uniform or a lab coat) for reporters from elsewhere. Inasmuch as she is impeded from pursuing her dreams in the present, in order to present over and again a story of her injury by empire alongside a fiction of her flowering under communism, the photograph acts as a visual distantiation between the girl pictured there and the woman surviving here. Kim Phúc is made a party to her own doubling; she represents not herself, but the ghost life of the girl in the photograph: "She could make as much as she liked of her physical suffering from her napalm burn endured in the American war, but she was *not* to portray the people as having suffered under the new regime."[78] In this way, the communist state that claimed to stand for "the people," for the also-wounded community figured by the photograph, sought to convert her damaged body into human labor on this abstraction's behalf. (As Chow usefully observes, "In a 'third world' nation whose history is characterized by a struggle against imperialism as well as internal turmoil, the history that 'ought to be remembered' is the history of the successful collectivization of the people for the establishment of a national community."[79]) It is in these very terms—as an instrument and as a prop, among others—that Kim Phúc comes to doubt the value of the photograph. However, and importantly so, her complaint is not made against the historicity of her body as an object, but against the particular economy of her life's value and exchange.

What emerges from these carefully interlaced stories is an overwhelming sense of the complex ideological intersections of power and violence within the nonsingular scene of the photograph. That Kim Phúc welcomes, sometimes warmly, the Westerners who seek her out to take her picture, but resents the state that trades on her infamy, is no mercurial caprice. (Of course, one class of observers is hardly disassociated from the other, since Kim Phúc addresses the fiction of her successful student life from one to the other.) In narrating this disparity, the biography distinguishes between the rhetorical techniques and social imaginaries that inform these politically specific modes of vision. With regard to the former, the biography ascribes an empathic voyeurism that searches for a human face for universal tragedy; to the latter, an enforced exhibitionism that charges those structures of race and coloniality responsible for tragedy, but at a cruel cost to Kim Phúc herself. Put another way, her singular experience of pain (which, paradoxically, is also the pathway for her universal humanity) is so thoroughly documented here that its annexation for a racial collectivity, for political propaganda, is depicted as another ruinous act. In this telling, Kim Phúc is caught in the bind of a desubjectifying visual apparatus that produces and sustains a historical act of silencing, but this apparatus is not the bomb but the photograph. That is, what is most striking about the biography's stance toward the photograph is the tactical critique of the communist state through the formal quality of the photograph to fix an object against the continuum of history and progress. In this view, the use of the photograph to indict a history of imperial encounter becomes the scene of subjection—and not the structures of race and coloniality themselves. The photograph functions as a sign of evidence, *but not as evidence of itself*. The photograph, in the state's view, is not just a picture of her wounded subjectivity but also a picture of the race discourses that subsume whole populations to nonsignificant death. However, the racialization of this wounded body is visible only through what the biography claims is a distorting lens of display. Although the biography hopes to rescue the subject from the unbearable objecthood of bomb and picture, in doing so it functions to forget the fact of global war as that which engineered both bomb and picture.

It also becomes clear that the operations that desubjectify also ungender.[80] Again, the bomb is the more conspicuous culprit. Its violence is deeply corporeal, and profoundly psychical. Viewing her scars as ugly, Kim Phúc mistrusts romantic interest in her because she believes her body will betray her objecthood: "*Boys see me as normal*, she had told herself, *but once I become close enough to marry one, he will have to see my scars. Once a boy sees me as ugly and weak, how can he still love me?*"[81] But in this telling, the bomb is not indicted as a metric of race and coloniality, though it is one instrument of ungendering bodies into flesh. Kim Phúc's fears of disfigurement as feminine ugliness follow from the bomb, but also from temporal disjuncture. Such disjuncture is located in the scene of the photograph (she cannot escape its iconicity), and it is also in the political rationale of the communist state. That is, the existential crisis precipitated by communism also begets "unnatural" gendered and sexual consequences.[82] It is as such that the biography presents life under communism, again citing Chow, as "the alienation of human life par excellence through what poses as the 'collective' good. The collective is now perceived as that mysterious, objectified Other against which one must struggle for one's life."[83] It is in this narration that Kim Phúc's desires for beauty and romantic love become the stubborn remainders of outlaw feelings that exceed social expectations and state orthodoxy.

Here conceptions about beauty as signaling an interior property of the observed, and as interpolating an enlightened observer capable of judgment, are crucial to what Minoo Moallem calls "civilizational thinking."[84] Such conceptions inform a politics of comparison between structures that abet or assail beauty. Chong's biography devotes long passages to Kretz's perspective on the strangulation of beauty and with it love under the shadow of the state. Returning to a new regime and presented with "revolutionary heroes" to interview, Kretz muses: "*Communists*, he said to himself, noting the severity of the women's clothing and hairstyle, the absence of make-up."[85] This image of grim severity condenses and organizes knowledge for the reader about communist Viet Nam and its forms of gender. In a familiar caricature, the female-bodied worker under communist dictate garbed in utilitarian clothes and unadorned is denied that which affords both singularity but also intimate community: her femininity. On this same trip, Kretz laments the "good old days" on the streets of Saigon, "when pretty bar girls walked arm-in-arm with tall, good-looking American soldiers." He mourns: "Now, girls sat on the backs of motor scooters of their Vietnamese boyfriends, waiting for something that would never happen."[86] Here, "waiting for something that would never happen" marks the indeterminate passing of time; outside of the capitalist systemization that sets the tempo of modernity, there can be no progress for a pretty girl from before to after. In other words, Kretz insists on the non-coincidence of communism with empty, world-historical time. This regime is instead perceived to regiment and reject those emotions and sensations deemed necessary in a liberal chronology of a good life—such as romantic love or grand rescue by a white knight, from the bind of staid or stunted sociality.

But, of course, the anticommunist charge of Kretz's discourse is also complexly tangled with structures of race and coloniality. For him, the problem of temporal immobility as a moral and aesthetic failure is evident not just as a property of communism (despite communism's obvious investments in industrial modernization), but also as the absence of liberal empire. In this schema, the motor of modern history is, borrowing from Gayatri Chakravorty Spivak's sarcastic aside, "brown women saved by white men from brown men."[87] Without war as the intercession of enlightened moderns, the benighted other slows to a standstill. What emerges from these passages is a racial—which is also a civilizational—identification between the photographer and the soldier over the bodies of other women, who become bearers of multiple suspensions. And, like U.S. soldiers, Kretz is capable of making something happen for Vietnamese girls. Kim Phúc calls him as her savior, who returns over and again to rescue her from being held hostage to the machinations of her inferior countrymen, and who presents to her the myriad wonders of modernity's now.[88] At a stopover in cosmopolitan Bangkok, the German photojournalist, escorting Kim Phúc to a Bonn clinic specializing in burns, establishes his "number one" concern thusly: "I'm taking the poorest girl from the poorest country in the world shopping."[89]

Thus, the category of the beautiful comes to counteract the deadening alienation she otherwise experiences due to napalm, photograph, regime.[90] In 1986, Kim Phúc gained admission to the prestigious University of Havana, where she could continue her studies in medicine (under the watchful eye of Cuban functionaries), and there she commenced an alternate education. Though communist Viet Nam is depicted through a stifling androgyny, the grim consequence of a denaturalizing polity, communist Cuban forms for organizing gender and sexuality are read in this text through what Frances R. Aparicio and Susana Chávez-Silverman call "tropicalization."[91] Cuba, even under communism, is translated through racializing tropes of hyperfemininity and unreserved romantic couplings, closeness to which frees Kim Phúc to embrace her "blossoming" sexuality.[92] The sympathetic mother of a schoolmate, Nuria, commits to Kim Phúc's informal schooling in cultivating a commodity femininity as a natural and normal development: "She made it her mission to give Kim the self-confidence to see herself not as a burn victim but rather, *first and foremost, as a woman like any other.*"[93]

> Ultimately, Nuria triumphed. Kim came to use perfume and to curl her hair, often pinning it to one side with an orchid, and she began to brighten her face with rouge, lipstick, and eyeliner. She shed an image of herself as weak and ugly, and started to think in terms of strength and beauty. Years ago, in the dark of the noodle shop, Nu [her mother] had taught the teenage Kim that tragedy had dimmed her prospects for love, if not marriage. Where Nu had seen a normal life for her daughter as something already stolen from her, Nuria showed her it was still within reach.[94]

Anchoring this scene of intersubjective and intrasubjective pedagogy, the practicum of beauty is also a movement of coming to knowledge. In this and other scenes, such as the occasion of her first bathing suit ("a dance leotard in white accented with fuchsia flowers"[95]), beauty offers Kim Phúc a sensual, vital experience of the linkage between herself and the world. Instead of persisting in an alienated relation through the effect of representation (the picture) and the labor of repetition (the propaganda), beauty renders her damaged body through an idiom of pleasure and presence for itself. In this view, we might be conscious of Kim Phúc's insistence on the distinction between her private body and her public face not exclusively as a claim to the liberal entitlement to privacy, but as a protest against the theft of her subjectivity, and the regimentation of her gestures and emotions—that is, the other-production of the war and its afterlife. But it is equally true that beauty as an idiom of pleasure and presence for itself is not outside usage and exchange. Beauty is the miracle that accomplishes exactly what the bomb proposed to do: free her from the arrested time of the noncontemporaneous other. Beauty hence propels, as Sarah Nuttall so elegantly observes, "a politics of hope and anticipation, a surge of feeling beyond the merely given present moment."[96] Via beauty, Kim Phúc is transformed: enlivened and empowered, she comes to discover that she can affect the events and outcomes of her life's direction—the propagative machine of romantic love, for instance, which she finds in Cuba. Romantic love, as an act of self-expression of the subject, is enfolded into an idiom of rights and freedoms.[97] Elizabeth Povinelli theorizes intimate love as a liberalist fantasy of self-actualization and abstraction: "We literally reform the social by believing in and demanding this form of love. Every time we are in this form of love, or wish to be, or are frustrated because we are not, we make social status appear as a form of bondage, mere surface or impasse, perhaps the vital frisson that lets us feel it as resistance."[98] So roused, Kim Phúc seizes freedom during her honeymoon flight—disembarking in Canada during a layover, she and her new husband seek and receive political asylum at the airport.

The story of her life is rerouted away from the violent history of empire, and through the idealist promise of beauty, we encounter the finite circumstances and determinate courses through which liberal observers are charged with responding to others. Through this narration of her personal loss and liberation, the biography "contextualizes" the photograph as evidence of a concept or practice that is in demise. That is, both the structures of race and coloniality indicted in the photograph, and also those critics who would dwell overlong on imperial violation, are things of the past. (And, we shall see, both are narrated as things that "we" did in madness.) She resurfaces as a beautiful young woman, and the cognizance of blossoming beauty licenses to the observed as well as *to the observer* a radical break—not simply with the awful past, but also with the ongoing anachronisms of Vietnamese postcoloniality. Indeed, it is the photograph's afterlife as an anti-imperialist touchstone that is the source of so much socially produced ugliness in the present.

The turn to the authentic self, present in biographical accounts of the girl in the photograph, becomes the generic scene of her emancipation, especially as a narration of her captivity and hard-won freedom from alien powers. Hence instruction on the proper care of the beautiful converts personal revelations into truth statements about self and sociality, substantiated by an asymmetrical politics of comparison. One of the key dimensions of the concept of beauty—and those other properties that attach to beauty, like human interiority and self-expression—is its radical singularity, but another is its desirable replication in all directions, which only certain forms of state governance and capital can secure. That is, Kim Phúc's consciousness of the revolutionary properties of *rouge, lipstick, and eyeliner* are collocated with an acute longing for those structures that allow beauty to flourish. Her subjectivization through her insistent desires for love and beauty thereby redirects the girl in the photograph, the bearer of so much horror, away from other wounded and slain bodies, away from the postcolonial regime that denounces the murderous structures of empire. In other words, when the wounded and absent body is made to appear through the visibility of race and coloniality (as an exemplary war victim), this rendering proves to feel fictional, or at least backward looking. In contrast, the affective intensity of beauty as a psychic and material experience of herself marks a story of development and self-possession that promises to deliver Kim Phúc to an alternate life-world, one in which she might be free to be "first and foremost, a woman like any other."[99]

An Empire of Shame

Never before had Phúc considered what had happened to others caught in the napalm attack in the time elapsed before she emerged from it into the camera's eye. . . . *Now that I see the film*, Phúc told herself, *I understand why the people in the United States feel for my pain. Now I know what I myself suffered through.* She understood why she had emerged alive from the fire of the napalm—to be a living symbol of the horror of war. *The film, the picture made me into a moment of history. It is only me in that moment of history. I know I am not the only victim of war, but others don't have the evidence. I have the film, I have the picture, and I have the body.*

—DENISE CHONG, *The Girl in the Picture*

In the above scene, Kim Phúc comes to apprehend her auratic personhood: "I have the film, I have the picture, and I have the body."[100] These things mark her as unique, not just because these are evidence that it is her subjectivity that has been wounded, but also because these things in their publicity set her apart from a generality (that is, other victims of war whose wounds are unknown, or unknowable, in their unthinkable totality). And it is because of these distinctive things that her understanding of her own precarious life is not achieved in kinship with others whose lives are just as precarious, and to whom more fortuitous accidents did not also happen—such that she had "never before . . . considered what had happened to others caught in the napalm attack," these others who did not register a "moment in history."[101] Even in this brief passage, she does not dwell on these archival absences, the missing bodies; she does not linger on other atrocities in other photographs. (There are other children, children who did die, haunting photographs from that same bombing.) Simply put, she does not regard the photograph as an empathic joint between herself and others targeted for nonsignificant death. Instead, on viewing raw footage of the bombing, Kim Phúc becomes conscious that those spectators and operators for whom the world is target feel her pain.

Because the photograph is perceived as a spectral presence, or a phantom wound, in the consciousness of liberal empire, the resurrection of the dead reanimates the time and place of the girl in the photograph in the present. But the photograph must be appended further, because it has a durable presence as a social figure apart from the girl, in order to renew and reinvest in American empire as a liberal and tolerant collectivity. This chapter's second scene extends our line of inquiry by focusing attention on the time and place of Kim Phúc's communion with strangers who are also, in this scenario, confined to the scene of the photograph. In which the girl in the photograph grieves at a monument to the warrior dead, beside a seven-year prisoner of war who bespeaks the soldiers' trauma, this scene is a disturbing disquisition on the intersubjective exchange through which catastrophic war comes to be experienced as a *shared* ordeal of precarity between other and empire.[102] Introduced as the girl in the photo responsible for "reawakening the conscience of America," Kim Phúc delivers a brief statement to "dear friends":

> As you know, I am the little girl who was running to escape from the napalm fire. I do not want to talk about the war because I cannot change history. I only want you to remember the tragedy of war in order to do things to stop fighting and killing around the world. I have suffered a lot from both physical

and emotional pain. Sometimes I thought I could not live, but God saves me and gave me faith and hope. Even if I could talk face to face with the pilot who dropped the bombs, I would tell him we cannot change history but we should try to do good things for the present and for the future to promote peace.[103]

That this war's ending, as Marita Sturken has aptly observed, is both proclaimed and continually foreclosed by such commemorative events, should give us immediate pause.[104] The questions that concern me about this scene of communion as a performance of closure follow from its cachet as an allegory not just about victims encountering perpetrators, but also perpetrators encountering *themselves* as victims. Both the prisoner of war and the napalmed girl attest to their scars, but only she speaks of those who perpetrated her wounds as hurt, and in need of healing. Accordingly, the most revelatory attribute of the girl in the photograph is her world-renewing return of our regard—in this reading, the photograph no longer is the shattering figuration of her radical unmaking, but the empathic bond through which she bears witness to trauma in the interior of liberal empire. What might be illumined about the relation between victim and perpetrator, scene observed and observer, governed and governor, were we to re-view the "problem" of liberal empire through the photograph as the surface through which the observer touches the other with care, with a gift of life, and through which she recompenses this touch? (Barthes contemplates: "From a real body there, proceed radiations which ultimately touch me, who am here."[105]) If the scar she shares, to paraphrase Barthes,[106] becomes the mode of knowing or being that frames empire as tormented by its own trespasses, how might we refuse this turn of sanctifying the scene of forgiveness, and thus enriching ourselves precisely with the liberalist consciousness that results from exchanging places with the girl in the photograph, in which she names us "dear friends"?

The increasingly common belief that *witnessing* but also *perpetrating* is a traumatic experience, at least for those whose humanity is not in question, acts as a pivotal trope for managing the murderousness of liberal empire.[107] That Kim Phúc is preceded by the seven-year prisoner of war who describes the soldiers' trauma and desires a "time of healing" for "our great nation,"[108] and that both arrive together as pilgrims to the monumental state, bring us again to consider trauma as a story about the normal and the pathological, and in this instance its epistemological and ontological coordinates for conceiving, and recouping, liberal empire as a tolerant collectivity.[109] From this perspective, the universalizing of trauma's symptomology in postwar United States might be characterized as the opening act for salvaging liberal war. Here we might note again Cathy Caruth, who writes that there are two stories involved in any remembrance of traumatic violence: "the story of the unbearable nature of an event and the story of the unbearable nature of its survival."[110] In their incorporation into liberalism's self-concept as a sacrificing collectivity (the prisoner of war begins: "those of us who went in harm's way to serve our nation and to help our friends do not want our sacrifice to be in vain or forgotten"), these stories compulsively *interiorize* the violence of war.[111] As Susan Jeffords argues in her study of the post–Cold War "crisis" of national manhood, "the male Vietnam veteran—primarily the white male— was used as an emblem for a fallen and emasculated male, one who has been falsely scorned by society and unjustly victimized by his own government. . . . No longer the oppressor, men came to be seen, primarily through the imagery of the Vietnam veteran, as themselves oppressed."[112] But it is also the state that braves the unbearable. Rick Berg and John Carlos Rowe wryly note: "We are obsessed with the trauma and injury we have suffered, as if the United States, not Vietnam and Kampuchea [Cambodia], were the country to suffer the bombings, the napalm air strikes, the search-and-destroy mission, the systematic deforestation, the 'hamlet resettlement' programs."[113] This seeming inconsistency is precisely the ontological claim of liberal empire, inasmuch as liberal empire surrenders *what it has to give* in securing freedom for distant peoples. The wall of the Vietnam Veterans Memorial materializes this costly expenditure, and the ensuing traumatic condition, as a catastrophic wound that punctures the flesh in the original surgical sense and the psyche in its metaphorical transposition.[114] (That some veterans denounced the memorial as a further degradation—because it is a "black gash," designed by a "gook bitch" —only rehearses the traumatic story of an unbearable experience.[115]) We might further observe the narration of all the wars that follow, referencing Viet Nam in comparison, and the so-called Vietnam syndrome as a crisis of "something missing" that assumes the normal state must be able and willing to pursue more war.[116] As Marilyn Ivy astutely observes in her study of Japan's postwar disarmament as a traumatic interval, some states are "frozen at the moment of defeat because there is no more war to come. Without the futurity of war, there is no real escape from the past war."[117]

Especially where psychic trauma and political passivity (including martial hesitation) act as analogies for each other, it is important—even at the risk of stating the obvious—to underscore trauma's epistemological and ontological coordinates, as a universal norm for a naturalized interiority, through antinomies of freedom and captivity. Most significant for our purposes is the inclusion in 1980 of the diagnostic category *post-traumatic stress disorder* in the third edition of the American Psychiatric Association's *Diagnostic and Statistical Manual of Mental Disorders*. Like other diagnostic categories, post-traumatic stress disorder emerged in committee with psychiatrists who in their sessions with returning combatants conjectured that perpetrators might present disturbances identical to those of their victims. (I will return to this postulation of "identical" in a moment.) Indeed, public disclosures about cruelties committed by U.S. military forces—including the My Lai massacre, in which U.S. servicemen savagely murdered four hundred Vietnamese (women, children, and elderly)—were hugely influential in the diagnosis's codification. Here Didier Fassin and Richard Rechtman's genealogy of trauma is useful. In the history of modern warfare, the troublesome presence of combat neurosis (once named *shell shock*) was treated with suspicion; such suffering was construed as malingering, a pretense owing to personality defect or moral flaw. The U.S. war in Southeast Asia provided the conditions of possibility for the emergence of trauma as a legitimate illness.[118] As Fassin and Rechtman recount, psychiatrists, in response to revelations of war crimes in Southeast Asia, argued that soldiers were also "victims of the war," "who held the details of the atrocities in their tormented memory, reliving them in nightmares. . . . These men should therefore be considered war victims, broken by what they had witnessed and by what they themselves had done—men traumatized by what war had made of them."[119] Because their symptoms on the strictly psychiatric level are similar, no distinction is made between victims and perpetrators.[120] A diagnosis of trauma, as the classification of a spectral or somatic remnant of unremitting, incomprehensible violence, thus "allowed [perpetrators] the benefit of the doubt with the aim of rehabilitating them, crediting them with a residue of humanity evidenced by the traumatic memory they retained of their actions."[121] This is not to deny that soldiers are the objects of tremendous discipline, nor to disregard that veterans are experienced as disordered and delinquent, but to point to how their pain is narrated in order to rescue liberal empire from the criminality of its wartime conduct.

In this regard, the so-called ordinary soldier, traumatized by his own actions, is demonstrably not a monster, because the presence of pain is proof of his humanity; and because trauma is a condition—that is, a real, and radical, diagnosis that might "produce absolutely anything, at anytime, and in any order"[122]—he is also not wholly responsible, because war is an intolerable, if necessary, event.

The American Psychiatric Association committee's forfeiture of moral judgment, presaging an "end to suspicion," bore hugely significant consequences for the terms through which we know liberal war. Where shell shock once signaled a suspicious failure to comply with the demands of the state, post-traumatic stress disorder now registered a normal response to an extraordinary, incomprehensible event. This event, "outside the range of usual human experience," becomes the sole etiology.[123] Through its classificatory schema, persons who suffer are narrowly understood through characteristic symptoms as an empirical, factual concern, rather than as effects of disciplinary powers. Disparities in pain and suffering that are the effects of historical power are flattened in their articulation as symptoms and their circulation through liberal discourses of therapeutic and administrative government. Fassin and Rechtman argue: "Abandoning suspicion meant that the uncommon nature of the event itself had to be brought to the fore, in order to highlight the very ordinariness of the victim. In terms of social norms, classing perpetrators of atrocities with victims of violence offered new insight, reinforcing the notion that trauma was indeed the locus of incontrovertible fact. In this version, testimony to trauma—independently of any individual narrative, but also of any moral evaluation—holds ethical truth that clinical practice can finally confirm: *trauma is itself the proof of an unbearable experience*."[124] Fassin and Rechtman further observe the political usefulness of post-traumatic stress disorder, both for those who sought to denounce war without censuring soldiers and for the state that hoped "the soldier's trauma offered the undeniable advantage of mitigating some of the horror by showing men now destroyed by what they had done."[125] Post-traumatic stress disorder is constituitive to the decriminalization of state violence—the traumatized soldier does not possess the freedom to *not* commit the crime.

Of course, perpetrator and victim are not actually identical in their pain, even in the evidentiary equivalence of their symptoms. As Allan Young notes in his history of this diagnosis, of the seven categories of events understood to precipitate post-traumatic stress disorder, only one denotes violence undergone at another's hand; the other six categories consist of events in which the traumatized person is the perpetrator.[126] Much, then, could be made of his casual observation that this "self-traumatized perpetrator" is exceptional as a "*regional phenomenon*, limited mainly to the United States."[127] Though Young does not linger long on this speculation, it might indeed follow that the "self-traumatized perpetrator" is a figuration particular to U.S. empire, because this empire's powers claim to act through exception. The perpetrator who is damaged through the same murderous actions that he commits against others, whose sense of being at one with himself is thus devastated, means that what violence this empire commits under such extraordinary circumstances as war might be disclaimed as exceptional—rather than normal—to a liberal order of human freedom.

In this regard, post-traumatic stress disorder is less a record of observable symptoms than a register of the colonial and imperial epistemes that undergird its foundation. The genealogy of post-traumatic stress disorder and, concomitantly, the sidelining of the dead that evinces this disorder buttress an imperial project that declares its own innocence. But, as I argued in the first chapter, the trauma concept as alien or other-possession is often complicit in liberalism, and with its empire. Most obviously, racism as a biopolitical caesura that distinguishes between human and other is lost in the spectacularization of violence as a psychic wounding of the perpetrator through the trauma diagnosis. Post-traumatic stress disorder takes a heinous historical incident, like a massacre, and transfigures its narrative causality through psychic disturbance. (Notably, in this diagnostic schema, servicemen who refused to partake in brutalities with their fellows were the abnormal ones.[128] Nor are racial enemies, who may also commit brutality, diagnosed in the same terms. For some persons, asynchronous symptomology, when aligned with a discourse of trauma, grounds claims to dignity; for others, such properties fuel their racialization, feminization, or sexualization.[129]) In this schema, the state of normalcy for the liberal subject is rational, moral action, which is sometimes disturbed in the extraordinary circumstances of war, such that atrocities committed against racial others are disavowed as indices for empire and dubbed instead *acts of madness*. Thus does post-traumatic stress disorder function as an all-structuring condition, or a radical indeterminacy, enfolding into its diagnostic field any conduct whatsoever that might be grasped as deviant as its consequence. It follows from this understanding that the derealization of the racial other is a secondary symptom following from the paramount dehumanization of the perpetrator. That is, racism becomes merely an expression of a disordered condition, aberrational rather than foundational to his apperception.

Post-traumatic stress disorder thus underscores the ways in which historical events of imperial violation, especially those brutal acts continually recommitted against racial, colonial others, are transfigured into unimaginable pain for their perpetrators. This diagnosis, which at once reduces and reifies an unbearable experience for some persons, is also determinedly focused on their rehabilitation.[130] As I already suggested, rehabilitation as a system of disciplinary intents and powers is based on the present and presence as categorically required for normal—which is also to say, liberal —subjectivity. Here we might note the work of Robert McRuer, who observes that rehabilitation restores rank, honor, "true function," and desirability, and also these properties that make human action and passion possible, and indeed timely: "Finally, rehabilitation restored complexity; if the degradation, in Stiker's words, 'of integrity, of integralness' seemed to simplify the *mutilés de guerre* . . . the complex mechanisms of rehabilitation resisted such a reduction and (re)produced complex modern men."[131] Where the subject of rehabilitation is the proxy figure for a liberal way of war, the self-traumatized perpetrator becomes the bearer of its limits but also the object of its redemption. From this point of view, the originary trauma of defeat must be remedied, and the perpetrator must be restored to humanity and history proper, so that he and the empire he stands for may be released to act anew.

Returning to the wall, we may now reiterate the point that Kim Phúc's story, its singularity notwithstanding, here manifests itself specifically through the scar she shares with the perpetrator, resulting in an act of grace that takes the form of a permission to *substitute his suffering for hers*. That is, in recasting atrocity as uniquely traumatic for perpetrators, we are invited not to turn away from the facticity of her injury, *but instead to turn toward her injury's claims on the interior life of liberal empire*. The pain of "the people in the United States who feel [her] pain,"[132] the pain of "the pilot who dropped the bombs," becomes the focus of her feeling. In the months following Kim Phúc's appearance at the memorial, the story of Reverend John Plummer unfolded on a global stage. Claiming to be the U.S. commander who ordered the offensive against rumored infiltrators in Trang Bang, his story is that of a perpetrator whose guilt and grief weighs on him unbearably. Through all these long years, the girl in the photograph haunts him: "It seemed to be everywhere he turned—newspapers, magazines, films on television, even in books on his own book-shelves. Each time Plummer saw it, he was stricken with remorse. It got so that her screams haunted his nightmares of war."[133] Because of these ugly feelings, he loses himself in drink and divorce before turning to the bed-rock of his Christian faith. Told that the girl in the photograph would be in attendance at the commemoration, Plummer undertakes a quasi-religious pilgrimage to the wall. As recounted in *The Girl in the Picture*, upon Kim Phúc's utterance "if I could talk face to face with the pilot who dropped the bombs," Plummer is moved to pen and pass a note to a guard: "Kim, I am THAT man." Through machinations he entrusts to divine intervention, Plummer finds himself before the woman whose wounding he believed himself responsible for:[134] "She turned around and looked into a face of pain. She held her arms out."[135] Plummer confesses to his crimes, and then—a miracle: "'She just opened her arms to me. I fell into her arms sobbing,' he testified. 'All I could say is, I'm so sorry. I'm just so sorry.' She patted Plummer's back. 'It's all right,' she told him. 'I forgive, I forgive.'"[136]

This brief exchange presents a provocatively familiar way of grasping both the diagnosis of trauma and the question of forgiveness. In this way a perpetrator is enslaved to "one single deed" and is in danger of being detained by its "consequences forever" (to recall Arendt's formula); Plummer's story follows this formula closely. First, his confession establishes the fracturing of Western subjectivity and consciousness, of which his post-traumatic stress disorder is a paradigmatic example, as a damaging, de-subjectifying experience. Because of war and what he feels he did, he is a person who has become, in an ontological sense, destitute: drunk, de-pressed, and directionless, he is divested of those faculties of consciousness that guarantee a concept of human freedom. The demonstrative act of his confession—performed in public, for a public—communicates to us his captivity and torment and also necessary release from this fracturing, grief-stricken state. Here lies what Foucault calls the "internal ruse of confession": "Confession frees, but power reduces one to silence; truth does not belong to the order of power, but shares an original affinity to freedom."[137] But Plummer's freedom, as that which he comes into posses-sion of with peace of mind (or, in the language of rehabilitation, in the normal state of autonomous individuality), cannot be redeemed without the grace of the girl in the photograph. Second, then, another must ab-solve him so that he might be delivered from this traumatic past. In a religious routine, this higher power might be God, and indeed Plummer turns to the divine for release from shame. But such a spiritual rebirth is perhaps less compelling than one in which his victim grants her pardon.[138] So Plummer prays that he might one day make his apology ("*If she could look into my eyes*, Plummer thought, *she would see my pain and remorse for what I did to her*"), and he credits her appearance at the commemoration as the sign that God has answered his prayers.[139] As a divine envoy, an angel of history, Kim Phúc is empowered as a moral arbiter; having suffered so singularly, she has nonetheless forgiven her perpetrator, even without knowing his repentance. Her pardon thus accomplishes his return to a truer self—he is saved.

That Plummer may not have been in the chain of command that ordered the air strike, as soon became clear, does not detract from this plot.[140] As Fassin and Rechtman observe, "trauma is itself the proof of an unbearable experience." And as Kim Phúc commented in an interview about this second confession, "whether or not he played a major role or minor role, the point is I forgive him."[141] It is as such that the salvage act focuses on acknowledging the pain of others, telling personal truths, and pursuing reconciliation, rather than on facticity and knowledge. The causal, referential event disappears in favor of an intersubjective exchange between *two* victims; the "point" is that liberal empire suffers from its trespasses against others. We might suppose that to suffer so well means that you are not without virtue. (Sara Ahmed might more succinctly say, feeling bad means being good.[142]) Reportedly crying, Plummer told one writer, "I realized I did not have to bear the guilt of my sins—all the hurt I caused other people."[143]

For these reasons, the path of forgiveness is perilous. Once again I invoke Derrida, whose insights about the aporia of forgiveness add further dimension to this reading. For Derrida, writing in the historical context of forgiveness as an ever-expanding idiom in law and diplomacy (especially after atrocity), genuine forgiving must denote the impossible—the unforgivable, the "crime against humanity." This juridical concept, first formulated in 1907 at the Second Hague Peace Conference and subsequently institutionalized in the UN Charter and Universal Declaration of Human Rights, "remains at the horizon of the whole geopolitics of the pardon . . . furnishing it with a discourse and legitimating it."[144] For Derrida, it is the geopolitics of the pardon that is contaminated by calculative reasoning; once notions of commensurate punishment or measures of repentance become conditional to the pardon, it becomes politics rather than ethics. Against the proliferation of scenes staged for the mediation of horrors such as state racism, Derrida explicitly states that "genuine forgiveness must engage two singularities: the guilty and the victim," who remain wholly other:[145] "As soon as the victim 'understands' the criminal, as soon as she exchanges, speaks, agrees with him, the scene of reconciliation has commenced, and with it this ordinary forgiveness which is anything but forgiveness."[146] Indeed, Derrida insists that a rigorously ethical forgiveness must be heterogeneous to the order of politics and against historical finality, lest it become mere calculation, or worse still, normalization.[147]

Given these conditions, what occurs at the wall is the introduction of forgiveness into a circuit of social exchange. This is clearest in that Kim Phúc deliberately performs her forgiveness to America, and before the world, at the monument to the warrior dead, with a former prisoner of war at her side, while Plummer admits that his public disclosure was evangelical in nature. *The Girl in the Picture* also hints that their fortuitous encounter was staged for a global audience, helpfully mediated by a documentary film crew.[148] While Shelley Saywell's documentary, *Kim's Story: The Road from Vietnam* (1996), proposes to record the sadness and indomitable spirit of the girl in the photograph, it also narrates the war as a traumatic experience for both victims and perpetrators.[149] In fact, the diegetic structure of the documentary builds toward this meeting, this allegory.[150] Even as the documentary begins with generic, ground-level footage of planes dropping bombs across Highway 1, as well as film of *her* escape, the somber narrator states the photograph's ever-expanding power to wound observers too: "This is the story behind the picture that touched the world." Framed loosely in the genre of the road trip, the documentary stages her encounter with self-knowledge, which comes circuitously with understanding others' experience of her.[151] In one decisive transition, which sutures for the viewer the scar she shares, the documentarians' camera sweeps across Kim's puckered scars as her bare back and shoulders are massaged by a pair of hands, revealed in a slow pan to belong to her husband, and into a doctor's office in Chicago, where she clasps a white sheet to her chest and submits to an examination by one of the surgeons who operated on her burns as a volunteer in Viet Nam. She thanks him for his labors, and he modestly demurs, observing that she more than compensates for his care on a monumental scale: "Now she's attempting to heal the Vietnam wounds of our nation."[152] This move to re-place the unbearable experience to the interior of liberal empire, a move that is appropriative since its pivotal operation is a matter of reversing and repossessing what had been established as traumatic (the napalm bomb that haunts her still to the act of witnessing and perpetrating atrocity), is the documentary's understated change of direction. Though Kim Phúc begins her travels with the photographer and doctors who sought to capture, and to relieve, her suffering, this reversal repeats with increasing frequency as she meets with those who are touched (disturbed, agitated, made helpless) before the materiality of the photograph. Though the documentary names Kim Phúc's story, it ends with an American one—at the memorial to the warrior dead, Kim Phúc cements her signification in an allegory of postimperial rapprochement.

As empire's spectral other or its so-called condition of possibility (because this empire presumably acts on behalf of this other), and as the subject of freedom whose self-actualization is the mirror of the good and the true that liberalism promises (she escapes alien command, she chooses beauty, family), she is endowed with an exceptional moral power.[153] Her capacity for love, to which the documentary ascribes her desire to tell her story, extends in all directions, and in a peace studies classroom, a student wonderingly observes: "You're like an angel that's come to talk to us and to let everyone know," while the camera lingers for a long moment on Kim Phúc's face.[154] Given such thematics, Kim Phúc's grace is central to this plot: in exchange for her moral power, she must submit to a teleological movement from a traumatic past to a future of freedom and progress. I am reminded here of Paul Ricoeur, who writes of the demands of "narrative time" (which we might here ally with Derrida's "determined finalities"): "Looking back from the conclusion to the episodes leading up to it, we have to be able to say that this ending required these sorts of events and this chain of actions. But this backward look is made possible by the teleological movement directed by our expectations when we follow the story."[155] In *Kim's Story*, her self-transformation comes together with the interposition of a feminine "voice" into the history of war in the world, but what results from this documentary is not a dismantling of the desubjectifying apparatus of empire—rather, it is a correspondence between the imperialist and the feminist gaze, meeting over not only the image of the wounded and absent body but also the found and forgiving subject of freedom.[156]

At the documentary's conclusion, Kim Phúc and John Plummer adopt chaste postures of intimacy, his arm around her shoulder, holding both her hands in one of his, as she accepts his confession, and he her pardon.

(He wears, in an odd note, some sort of Civil War soldier's hat.) We are told that both victim and perpetrator have undergone a major conversion —in effect, trading their separate grief and pain into the currency of confession and forgiveness.[157] Viewing this scene, with the tufted couch and tearful smiles, recalls for us Amy Kaplan's insights on "manifest domesticity," through which liberal representations of the domestic, as figured in this instance in a heteronormative embrace, are "inextricable from the political, economic and cultural movements of empire, movements that both erect and unsettle the ever-shifting boundaries between the domestic and the foreign, between 'at home' and 'abroad.'"[158] Hence we come to witness an act of compassion of great consequence, in which a second, gentler touch reorders our sense of history in corporeal and symbolic ways. The encounter between victim and perpetrator and its propagation as an allegory that both erases *and* rehearses specific forms of power between soldier and civilian, empire and colony—that is, portrayed both as two hurt people finding healing in each other, and also as mythic figures signifying the scars shared between those who tried and failed to deliver to an other freedom—bring to the fore the uses of forgiveness in this circuit of social exchange. Chow astutely observes that "forgiveness is a *rescue mission*,"[159] a neat turn of phrase that directs our attention once again to the necessary question—who, or what, is being rescued?

Confession allies the wretched sinner with truth and freedom, and forgiveness releases him from bondage so that he might once again be capable of action—thus do sorrowful states and enlightened empires hope to redeem themselves in translating, and rendering transparent, their past misdeeds within a continuous history of human development. The acknowledgment of pain and suffering perpetrated in the ever-receding past, the consequence of the failed translation of an ideal, becomes the occasion for demonstrating a liberal present through the confession of feelings of shame and grief.[160] Such occasions are increasingly staged in colonial settler states and postcolonial states after wartime atrocities, civilian massacres, or racial violence, including apartheid and other forms of deliberative social death. But scholars such as Vanessa Pupavac, Allan Feldman, and Guiliana Lund query the moral and therapeutic imperatives of truth and reconciliation commissions in Argentina, Guatemala, Sierra Leone, Bosnia, East Timor, and post-apartheid South Africa; and Lisa Yoneyama and Ma Vang parse the issuance of apologies to Japanese Americans and to Hmong refugees (Hmong were recruited as proxy soldiers by the Central

Intelligence Agency during the war in Southeast Asia) for long neglect of their service and sacrifice by the United States.[161] Though these performances of confession and remorse do admit to committing injury to others, nonetheless these acts also transform the nature (if not the fact) of subjection as outside of a continuous history, and a condition of possibility, of state power. These performances, then, are pursued under specific circumstances and with certain sought-after consequences. Writing about "Sorry Books," compilations of statements and signatures that perform a collectivity of shame for the genocidal history of Australian governments toward indigenous populations, Sara Ahmed observes of their confessional nature: "Those who witness the past injustice through feeling 'national shame' are aligned with each other as 'well-meaning individuals'; if you feel shame, you mean well. . . . But this exposure is temporary, and becomes the ground for a narrative of national recovery. By witnessing what is shameful about the past, the nation can 'live up to' the ideals that secure its identity or being in the present. In other words, our shame means that we mean well, and can work to reproduce the nation as an ideal."[162] Confessions and expressions of remorse from liberal states and empires therefore enact claims to the legitimacy of their existence, conceding but also curbing an observable history of abnormal cruelty, and as well the restoration of a tolerant collectivity that submits once again to their government.

The conundrum that the victim faces in the wake of liberal war may be described as follows. Whereupon states and empires confess to spectacular crimes against their subjects, just as victims of state violence are made visible, they are also compelled to forgive. In forgiving, the empire that expresses shame for its wrongdoings is released to the future, to commit more war.[163] (Consider this *Washington Post* editorial from April 30, 1975, published as the South Vietnamese capital was captured and titled "Deliverance"—not for the Vietnamese, but for the Americans who fought this "right and defensible" war: "For the fundamental 'lesson' of Vietnam surely is not that we as a people are intrinsically bad, but rather that we are capable of error—and on a gigantic scale. That is the spirit in which the postmortems on Vietnam ought to go forward."[164]) The confession thus brings us to two suspicious movements. First, the confession grants to victims that which was violently wrested away—that is, their status as sovereign human persons with the capacity to reason and to act. Second, as sovereign persons who bear the moral power to confer forgiveness and futurity, they shoulder an ethical obligation: to pardon the act of aggression and redeem the aggressor without imposing a further debt or, indeed, without dwelling on continuing harm.[165] Those confessional acts that appear to acknowledge an effaced racial, colonial past—of accidental napalm, apartheid, encampment, and so on—instead (or simultaneously) enjoin a politics of renewal, one that compels through moral reasoning the necessary march from *before* to *after* terrible events. This understanding that forgiveness, as an ethical obligation to advance freedom, may involve the troubling equation that the victim is a potential adversary to the renewable future, the possibility that he or she might withhold pardon and in doing so deny to others their humanity, thus informs the theoretical and historical antagonism of the redemption of liberal empire as the necessary crucible for human development and freedom.

A Universe of Love

When I came to Canada I just wanted to build a normal life with my husband. I wanted to escape the picture that had cost my private life so much. I didn't want anyone to know that little girl is me. But now, when I see that little girl, naked and running, I think, "let people learn about war." That's the reason I came back to work with that picture. I want people to see that picture in a new war, and when they see that little girl crying out, see it not as a cry of pain, but a cry for peace. It is important for her life, that people learn the value of healing, freedom and forgiveness.
—KIM PHÚC, "Beyond the Bomb"

It was the fire of bombs that burned my body. It was the skill of doctors that mended my skin. But it took the power of God's love to heal my heart.
—KIM PHÚC, *The Oprah Winfrey Show*

These successive scenes mark a critical epistemic turn in the understanding of the photograph, and the war—one propagated by Kim Phúc herself. Rather than expose the racial particularity of the world as target, Kim Phúc hopes that witnesses to the picture of her suffering perceive themselves in a war for the human heart and "learn the value of healing, freedom and forgiveness." Indeed, her forgiveness is performed not just for Plummer (is there even a question that it was just for him?); it is also addressed to "dear friends" as a feeling collectivity in which the photograph becomes the pivot on which the plot turns to "our" story; this turn creates the conditions for its subsequent circulation in a number of other contexts for healing.

Here I turn to other gendering machines through which a politics of sentimentality, demonstrably key to the episode above, instrumentalizes the further extraction of supplement and surplus from this violated body. When the exchange between Kim Phúc and Plummer, or Kim Phúc and "America," is circulated as allegory, grace (whether religious or secular) becomes the argument and the apparatus for an imagined new history of human communion after war or other reprehensible violence. Through such an exchange, the idealist principles of the United States as a tolerant collectivity founded on human freedom and contract are repossessed from the traumatic errors of history. ("We are good people; we are the ones most hurt by our own mistakes.") In this way, forgiveness as a moral but also a historical compulsion is on a continuum with the gift of freedom, inasmuch as obligation troubles the subject of freedom with the responsibility for such communion, though she may bear the force of the accidental or "mad" mistranslation of an ideal. From this provocation, I follow from scholars such as Sianne Ngai, Elizabeth Povinelli, and Sara Ahmed about the charge of intimacy, and Lauren Berlant about the traffic in pain, through which a culture of true feeling hangs on suffering as a human commonality, and organizes ethical sociality accordingly. If Kim Phúc's touching story as a champion of "healing, freedom and forgiveness" can be understood as a lesson for fostering a tolerant collectivity, the consequences bring home, as it were, an empire of intimacy—requiring that we reflect on, as Berlant urges, the ways in which

> this mode of sentimentality takes up the Enlightenment project of cultivating the soul of the subject toward a visceral capacity to embody, recognize, and sanction virtue, and it expands it into the collective activity of compassionate cosmopolitanism, which places affective recognition at the center of what binds strangers to each other. Yet sentimentality's universalist rhetoric gains its authority not in the political domain, but near it, against it, and above it: sentimental culture entails a proximate alternative community of individuals sanctified by recognizing the authority of true feeling—authentic, virtuous, compassionate—at the core of a just world.[166]

Let me elaborate here with a telling example. On the March 8, 2000, episode of *The Oprah Winfrey Show*, "Celebrated Photos of Our Time," the girl in the photograph is among the handful of images credited with the power to exert or extract a global feeling.[167] In Kim Phúc's segment, the image of her burning looms behind Oprah on an enormous television screen. Oprah's introduction includes horrific film footage (we see other villagers fleeing, Kim Phúc's aunt with her three-year-old son in her arms, his skin peeling away from his flesh in ragged black strips) and these familiar articles of faith: "This photograph touched hearts worldwide and led to a change of public opinion about the war. . . . It is burned into our memory." Kim Phúc is met with an embrace and a standing ovation. During her brief interview (staged on a living room set), Kim Phúc ascribes her survival and peaceful heart to God, responding to Oprah's wondering, admiring question, "You can forgive the war?," with this rehearsed sentiment: "It was the fire of bombs that burned my body. It was the skill of doctors that mended my skin. But it took the power of God's love to heal my heart." Kim Phúc's carefully chosen words trace a satisfying teleology. Smiling, she promises that though she has suffered so singularly, she has nonetheless attained peace of mind. Thus inspired, Oprah wipes away a tear and declares, to thunderous applause, "You are a blessing unto us all."

Kim Phúc's grace resonates in at least two directions. First, she brings to the audience her now signature presence *as a little girl crying out for peace* to demonstrate the workings of inner peace, a state of being in the world secured through her hard labor. Both intimate and communal in its address to a feeling collectivity, *Oprah* is a superlative set piece for this inspirational message, through which Kim Phúc's return organizes for us a scene of empowerment, through which a fractured self might yet achieve freedom. During its twenty-five years on air, the show (and Winfrey's media empire) favored the therapeutic for the signification of human contact and interaction.[168] As Eva Illouz observes, *Oprah* exemplifies the narrative standardization of pain, one embedded in the therapeutic mandates of neoliberal entrepreneurialism, in everyday "work" on the conscious and competent self. "In the quintessential Oprah story," Illouz writes, "closure is reached when the self is able to transcend itself either through will, determination, and self-knowledge or through display of altruistic dispositions. Such self-overcoming is accomplished sometimes through the implementation of moral virtues like altruism, love, and self-sacrifice; sometimes through therapeutic techniques of self-examination, confession, and dialogue; and sometimes through a combination of these. Both the spiritual and the therapeutic discourse insist on transformation and on making the self 'work' toward an improved and pain-free state."[169]

In her pursuit of beauty and freedom, Kim Phúc has undertaken a self-transformation continuous with these also-outward properties. Likewise, without her capacity for forgiveness, it is implied that she would be held hostage to the past of the photograph. In the parlance of the genre, such a capacity is evidence of "perspective," as a temporal and spatial distantiation that periodizes and divides, and of "inner strength"—another name for the autonomous individual and her capacity for directing her own interiority and life direction. (Reviewing *The Girl in the Picture*, the *Washington Post* comments on her buoyant cheer: "As a girl, returning home after more than a year of hospitalization, she 'had the same happy and uncomplaining personality as before she was wounded,' which Chong properly interprets as 'testimony to her strength of character.' "[170]) Kim Phúc's willingness to pardon others for their transgressions both fulfills this condition and then acts as proof of her self-possession. Through moral and emotional labor on her self, she becomes the agent of happiness, secures inner peace—is free.

Second, in this by now familiar scene of the public economy of such beautiful suffering, Kim Phúc stages a further, explicitly ethical, level of instruction, foremost in which is forgiveness as a covenant to embrace futurity. In an interview for National Public Radio that was broadcast in a popular program called *This I Believe*, Kim Phúc's faith serves as a lesson to us all: "Napalm is very powerful, but faith, forgiveness, and love are much more powerful. We would not have war at all if everyone could learn how to live with true love, hope, and forgiveness. *If that little girl in the picture can do it, ask yourself: Can you?*"[171] There are several things I want to note here in this first-person story, typical of both her media appearances and this triumphalist genre, to ponder the query, "Can you?" The first is the passage of time as a progressive, chronological narrative, moving from cause and effect, history's beginning and resolution. In this teleology, Kim Phúc travels, in the title of this particular radio piece and echoed in many other stories, "The Long Road to Forgiveness." Time in its passage and its plentitude advances a moral imperative to establish the unalterable past as *passed* in its commensurate place and proportion. The second is the compression of successive discourses that establish her as a victim through her enunciation as an object of a heinous violence literally carved on her body ("napalm is very powerful"), and then establish her as a not-victim through her enunciation as a subject of truth because she forgives, *even napalm*.

The third point I wish to note is the address here—"Can you?"—which is unspecific and all encompassing. This address is common to profiles about Kim Phúc. The community of fellow feeling presumed to have been drawn into being through outrage and horror at the photograph, through vulnerability before the suffering of another, is called on once again through the different, but still direct, address of the girl in the photograph to turn the lens inward—do you bear pain that obstructs, damages, drags? While the religious aspect here is not unimportant—as other scholars have shown, the imbricated rhetorics of self-help, consumerism, and Christian ethos have a long history[172]—what I want to highlight here is a logic of equivalence. This logic of equivalence operates through analogy, articulating a proliferating series of (hoped for) comparable phenomena or social formations. In this instance, the analogy is not located in visible, or substantial, similarities but, as Foucault argues, in a "more subtle resemblance of relations. Disencumbered, it can extend, from a single given point, to an endless number of relationships."[173] In doing so, analogy extracts each element as independent of historical processes and also interactions with each other, such that complicity and complexity disappear or fade into white noise. In the proliferation of stories of pain, we therefore find the recognition of both great particularity and universal similarity. In the February 2001 issue of O, The Oprah Magazine, the psychologist Robert Karen opens his musings on the necessities to forgive, and to be forgiven, with the reconciliation of Kim Phúc and Plummer: "The story of the pilot and the girl moves us because the need to be forgiven lives so strongly in us, and it is rare that we see it played out in such direct and dramatic form. And yet in our everyday lives we are touched by forgiveness and haunted by its lack in a myriad of ways. Can we be forgiven our insensitivity? Our cruelties? Our betrayals? Can we be forgiven the things in us that feel so terrible we dare not speak them?"[174] In another instance, an online women's magazine published an inspirational profile about Kim Phúc in a section called "Life Stories." Under multiple subheadings further subdividing these stories ("suicide," "spirituality," "eating disorders," and "relationships"), Kim Phúc was once found under "abuse," then later under "relationships."[175] The earlier equivocation between Kim Phúc and Plummer, as well as something of the resonance of "relationships" as a descriptor, is found in the name of one feature, "Two Who Created an Image of War Share Their Pain."[176] In this regard, disparities of power no longer matter, even if these do signify murderous structures or institutional inequities. From the imperial history of post-traumatic stress disorder, we know that analogy names such resemblances in order to attach each incident of suffering to a chain of traumatic symptomology. Furthermore, the etiology named by post-traumatic stress disorder—an intolerable event—fuels this abstraction. Concepts of pain and suffering eschew any valuation of the catastrophic event (consider again the diagnostic end of suspicion with regard to the soldier's atrocity), the unbearable character of the event becomes the scene of our shared vulnerability.[177]

These sentimental stories radically alter the resonance and referentiality of historical violence and our responses to it.[178] The phenomenology of violence, estranged from history into abstraction, even napalm—a devastating biochemical weapon—might be reordered through this reading of Kim Phúc's injuries not as geopolitical or historical, but as intimate and personal. That is, if the U.S. war in Southeast Asia is evacuated of its imperial history, the girl in the photograph indicts no murderous structures in particular. Instead the category of banal, human failure or accident—amorphous, overwhelming, and ahistorical—supersedes the necropolitical, or Foucault's race war, through which some life is consigned to death, excluded from history. Those murderous structures that banish some bodies from the order of the moral and the human are rendered both unthinkable (though they are thought all the time in the most ordinary and destructive ways) and unavailable for apprehending either causality or casualty. Citing Berlant's interrogation of pain as political subjectivity, Sherene Razack points to its serious repercussions: "One important consequence is that we can no longer talk about injustice and how it is organized. When 'feeling bad becomes evidence of a structural condition of injustice' and 'feeling good becomes evidence of justice's triumph' then both the problem and the solution are removed from their material and historical contexts."[179] It is not that war disappears from view. Instead, war too might be characterized as a personal crisis, a moment of psychic upheaval. One Christian magazine insists that Kim Phúc's story is more than a story about the United States in Southeast Asia: "We all go through 'wars'—life is sometimes a difficult journey, battling 'enemies.' Like Kim, we may be left with pain and scars to bear. . . . What will we do? We, like Kim, have a choice—to forgive, extend grace and become better rather than bitter!"[180]

Kim Phúc's story is no simple spiritual rebirth. Despite her gentle touch, the imperative tenor of her comments, and of comments about her, impresses on us the ethical obligations and investments that secure the conditions of possibility for human self-possession and liberal collectivity. One commentator marvels: "What is perhaps most stunning about Kim Phúc is the peace that radiates from her in person. *She is not angry. She is not bitter against her government or anyone else involved in the war.* In fact, Kim's greatest passion is healing."[181] (Here I defer to Ahmed to distill these sentiments in her characteristically astute manner: "To become well adjusted is to be adjusted to colonial history."[182]) In further addressing herself to an enlightened collectivity, Kim Phúc proposes that the choice to "live with true love, hope, and forgiveness" is an ethical one. Her capacity to pardon others is represented as care for human communion, for futurity. Aligned with freedom as that which the autonomous individual possesses and presents to alleviate the suffering of others, forgiveness thus has meaning as a politics of life, as a condition of life's continuity anchored in familiar dichotomies of passivity and action, alienation and ownership, captivity and emancipation. In choosing otherwise, Kim Phúc implies, war—as a metonym for *any* violence—continues.

In such a prescription, the end of violence is an existential crisis (not just the cessation of military operations) whose resolution becomes the paramount responsibility of those others so long marked for injury and death.[183] The denial that the irrevocable past has in fact *passed* is to hold onto ugly feelings incommensurate to the duration between the unbearable event and the here and now. (Such feelings plague the prayerful mother in *Green Dragon*, who refuses to leave the interlude in which her soldier sons might yet draw breath.) In other words, an insistence on speaking as if the trespasses of the past are *still present*, which may include a desire for political agitation or retributive justice, precludes the victim and others whom he or she touches—those who shudder—from inhabiting history proper. Inassimilable and self-destructive, feelings such as anger or bitterness hence are equated with captivity, anachronism, and bondage. Or, as Ngai argues so well, ugly feelings are unproductive and noncarthartic in this psychic network, offering "no satisfactions of virtue, therapeutic or purifying release."[184] These feelings are perceived as generating other social and psychic negativity and even aggressivity—a self-destructive, other-destructive cycle of violence, return of the repressed, or a traumatic stress disorder, through which violence is misrecognized as an abstract or anachronistic category of suspicion.[185] Thus might forgiveness "also work to conceal the causes of hurt or to make others the cause of their own hurt."[186] The failure or refusal to forgive becomes an injury to our own capacity for freedom, an other-possession, but also the freedom of others, who are also otherwise held captive to past actions (which may have been accidents, or acts of madness). We may put this another way: if the effect of forgiveness as an imperative to overcome conflict in the service of communion, to secure the violent event as a moment in an aberrant continuous history, is that of negating murderous structures of race and coloniality as the present of liberal violence, it may have the more terrible outcome of annulling and banishing those who experience violence *as* violence to an outside of the human altogether.

For all that the girl in the photograph is much fetishized, mourned, resurrected, and commemorated, her archive is antimemorial. The photograph is most empty precisely when its presence is most full. It is for these reasons that I argue in this chapter against pinning our hopes on the archive—or, more precisely, on the recovery of presence there. Moreover, we cannot depend on revealed contradiction, or even disastrous failure, to carry our critical longings. The girl in the photograph is less a lost object whose return would correct an absence, or a contradiction and failure of liberal promise, than a sign of more questions whose forms bespeak the entanglement of empire with affirmation, presence, and freedom. Perilously, what Kim Phúc has to teach us are the virtues of love and forgiveness, and from these a historical consciousness through which we might inaugurate and impose a new story of ourselves, and of our collectivity. As Chong tells us at the close of her biography: "None of us is without flaws, but our hope is that we can be flawed yet still have a worthiness of character. We feel that when we are forgiven. Yet the power of forgiveness is realized only if it is sought. This was what the most famous victim of the Vietnam war, Kim Phúc, had to give. . . . In paying homage to her as a living symbol of wartime horror and suffering, others, religious or not, feel a hopeful sense of being able to mitigate the darkness together."[187]

If the story of the girl in the photograph can be understood as an allegory for wrongdoing and forgiveness, these remarks from *The Girl in the Picture* bespeak a troubling proposition. In such an address—to a collectivity in which "none of us is without flaws," though we might share a "hope that we can be flawed yet still have a worthiness of character"—a once-accused liberal empire is figured as *only human*. But in overcoming (and transcending) the boundaries and conflicts that impede a global humanity, it is not the U.S. self-concept as a guardian of human freedom and progress (a metanarrative genealogically traceable to liberalist indices of race and coloniality) that originates those boundaries and conflicts, but the history-halting prospect that empire might be held hostage to past accidents. Or as Ahmed observes, "So the West takes, then gives, and in the moment of giving repeats as well as conceals the taking."[188] Inasmuch as liberal empire claims to be the heart of a caring collectivity—that is, it is as both the center and executor of the free world that Kim Phúc can say to "us" "we should work together to build peace and happiness for all people in all nations"[189]—it is an exchange that brings about a new beginning, that is also no beginning at all. Her gift of grace transforms, and those objects and practices *with which we continue to live* are consigned to other times.

Coda: The Other Girl in the Other Photograph

Before I turn to new wars, I wish to add one last disquieting footnote—another wounded and slain body from this terrible conflict. In his public confession, Plummer admits to his failure to champion the principle of a generous, loving power. But, as recounted (with perhaps deliberate dispassion) in *The Girl in the Picture*, Plummer also carries a personal photograph—a souvenir—of the corpse of a young Vietnamese woman whom he murdered while on guard duty. She may have been a Viet Cong recruit, or an unwilling conscript—that appears to be of no particular concern. She has no story; she is anonymous. She is neither visualized nor articulated in Chong's biography, which is the story of *a* girl, and not *all* girls who are targeted (even accidentally) for death in the course of liberal war. Remarkably, whereas Plummer's secret torment regarding one girl in one photograph is presented in excruciating detail, he does not speculate about this other woman's existence, or confess to guilt or grief at her death at his hands. We are given no clue to how he feels about *her* death, or why he carries the photograph of her wounded and slain body in his wallet.

But we might observe, in light of this chapter's allegory, that because she cannot pardon him, she is rendered ontologically useless to his spiritual awakening. Or perhaps he hopes to retain the pleasure of flinching, that shudder that ensures over and again his own too-human subjectivity. Still, the fact that this photograph's presence does not dispatch him into guilt or grief, or their public performance, might disclose to us something sinister about the singularity of Kim Phúc's photograph, and about the ways in which some of us are granted passage into a common humanity and a continuous history and some others remain outside its bounds.

3

Race Wars, Patriot Acts

The safety of the American people depends on ending this direct and growing threat. Acting against the danger will also contribute greatly to the long-term safety and stability of our world. The current Iraqi regime has shown the power of tyranny to spread discord and violence in the Middle East. A liberated Iraq can show the power of freedom to transform that vital region, by bringing hope and progress into the lives of millions. America's interests in security, and America's belief in liberty, both lead in the same direction: to a free and peaceful Iraq. . . .

I've listened carefully, as people and leaders around the world have made known their desire for peace. All of us want peace. The threat to peace does not come from those who seek to enforce the just demands of the civilized world; the threat to peace comes from those who flout those demands. If we have to act, we will act to restrain the violent, and defend the cause of peace. And by acting, we will signal to outlaw regimes that in this new century, the boundaries of civilized behavior will be respected.

— GEORGE W. BUSH, "The Future of Iraq"

How can a power such as this kill, if it is true that its basic function is to improve life, to prolong its duration, to improve its chances, to avoid accidents, and to compensate for failings? How, under these conditions, is it possible for a political power to kill, to call for deaths, to demand deaths, to give the order to kill, and to expose not only its enemies but its own citizens to the risk of death? Given that this power's objective is essentially to make live, how can it let die? How can the power of death, the function of death, be exercised in a political system centered upon biopower?

It is, I think, at this point that racism intervenes.

— MICHEL FOUCAULT, *"Society Must Be Defended"*

In October 2001, the USA PATRIOT Act dramatically expanded the police powers of U.S. law enforcement agencies to enact sweeping measures of surveillance and incarceration targeting the racial stranger, the possible terrorist.[1] With its passage, Assistant Attorney General Viet D. Dinh was publicly hailed as the chief architect of these new powers and an avatar of freedom and security. Profiles, interviews, and news reports rehearse his flight from communism with alarming details. His mother pummeling with an ax the fifteen-foot fishing boat that carried them from a beach in Viet Nam to a Malaysian port so that she and her children could not be forced onto the open waters once again. The ten-year-old with his mother and siblings remaining in a Malaysian refugee camp for six months, until they were granted parole in 1978 to America, and a eerie, wintry Oregon. After toiling in strawberry fields for some years, his family migrating south, to piecework and fast food counters in Orange County, California. From such wretched beginnings, Dinh labors tirelessly to secure his rise from fields and fast food to editor of the law journal at Harvard Law School, to professor at the prestigious Georgetown University Law Center, and to a prominent post in the Department of Justice under the second Bush administration.[2] But the legacy of the Cold War continues to haunt the genealogy of human freedom, and the sensation of imminent danger, in the present. One profile explained, "His experience in Communist Vietnam, where people were denied freedoms, is the driving force behind Dinh's work."[3] Patriotic and paranoid, this refugee from a previous war returns precisely when the liberal mandate lays claim to a state of emergency.

This book has insisted that through the gift of freedom, liberal empire claims an exception to wage war, and to pardon its own crimes. Whereas the first chapter sought to grasp liberal war as it targeted the so-called new friend, and the second chapter the shortfall and subsequent recuperation of war's violence, I turn now to the refugee who, given time, is made anew as an agent of global race war. In this chapter, the concept of the refugee patriot not only focuses attention on the epistemological and ontological coordinates of the gift of freedom as subjectivization, carving out and delimiting areas of social existence and belonging, but also as these are especially given to ever-expanding empire and violence. I begin with Viet Dinh, and a statement that narrates a continuous history of war as a passage toward freedom, because I am struck by the political and ideological grounds on which refugee subjectivization is made newly relevant in the present moment, in which the liberal mandate to produce what others need to be free is under fire, especially as U.S. empire suspends the law in both national and international forms to prosecute a global war on terror. How might we untangle the knots tying this refugee patriot and his traumatic flight from "Communist Vietnam, where people were denied freedoms," to authorship of the Patriot Act, which inaugurated new measures of unfreedom against the stranger, a fungible biopolitical category defined by dangerous racisms? How do comparisons between this refugee who loves America and the terrorist he hopes to apprehend with his patriot acts help us to theorize modern racial governmentality, through which preemption, encampment, and thermobaric weaponry constitute the now *neoliberal* way of war continuous with peace?

To the extent that his memory, and his speech, is invoked to account for new powers to control more closely the racial, colonial other, the refugee patriot is an imperial figure who is rescued from an outside to incarnate the continuous histories of liberal war that claim to produce (for *this* other at least) the structures and sensibilities of freedom. First, and most obviously, this refugee patriot is grateful for the gift of freedom and returns it in the same spirit. Such reciprocity usefully illumines the analogies and what Ann Laura Stoler and David Bond call the "untimely comparisons" collocating past wars with our contemporary wars.[4] In the context of these wars, the refugee patriot furthermore renders war seemingly benevolent through recourse to interlocking discourses about race and life necessity. Here I situate campaigns to reverence the flag of the Republic of Viet Nam, the old new friend, in the evolving politics of transnational multiculturalism and global race war. In complicated petitions to a "transnational America" (to borrow a phrase from Inderpal Grewal)[5] to honor the gift of freedom and target an enemy that threatens it, race appears as both life necessity and legitimate reason to kill—that is, the refugee patriot both reconfigures race safely through asylum, through multicultural gesture, and through incorporation into an existing interior of freedom's empire, but also conceives race through a biological threat (a pathology) and through existential exclusion. Next, through an analysis of the Patriot Act that detains and encamps the possible racial enemy among us, the refugee patriot illumines for us an imperial hospitality, as that obligation to welcome but also to *discipline* the stranger, lest he subvert the hospitable power. Viet Dinh, especially in the narration of his refugee subjectivization as acutely cognizant of dangers ever present, thus himself argues that increased freedom is commensurate and concomitant with intensified security and amplified spheres for control and interference. In doing so, because he or she has been so radically dispossessed, the refugee patriot and his or her presence in the heart of empire further brings home that war is in the warp of everyday life under neoliberalism. Finally, the refugee patriot as the former stranger turned friend authorizes liberal empire's claim to grant freedom from constraint or violence through its deployment of violence against racial others perceived as threat. As seemingly transparent feelings such as gratitude and love are entangled in transnational flows of troops and weaponry, the refugee patriot consolidates conventional images of the good and true, including family and country, with the murderous structures of race and coloniality. Therefore, freedom is continuous with security, regulation is contiguous with war, and life is contingent on death, and the refugee patriot in his or her receipt and return on the gift of freedom usefully configures for us a contemporary culture of liberal empire.

Untimely Comparisons

Because it is an astonishing coincidence that the author of the Patriot Act should be a refugee from the last unwieldy war of liberal empire against a global evil, I begin with what Ann Laura Stoler and David Bond eloquently call "untimely comparisons in harsh times."[6] In 2001 and 2003, U.S. armed forces invaded Afghanistan and Iraq with the avowed purpose of overthrowing the authoritarian governments of the Islamic fundamentalist Taliban and the Ba'athist secular Saddam Hussein. Both anachronistic peoples were perceived as unruly agents of terror and also unable to govern themselves properly (these failures are necessarily coextensive in the historicist mapping of the globe). Invasion therefore realized both the urgency to "make America safer" in ousting primitive, despotic forces and the urgency to grant those helpless to these forces the necessary structures for securing freedom, such as liberal political enfranchisement, rights of citizenship, and the proliferation of markets for global capital (what detractors called "blood for oil"). In the month before U.S. operations in Iraq began, President George W. Bush (echoing earlier speeches and presidents) stated the necessity of war to help the Iraqi people to help themselves:

The first to benefit from a free Iraq would be the Iraqi people, themselves. Today they live in scarcity and fear, under a dictator who has brought them nothing but war, and misery, and torture. Their lives and their freedom matter little to Saddam Hussein—but Iraqi lives and freedom matter greatly to us.

Bringing stability and unity to a free Iraq will not be easy. Yet that is no excuse to leave the Iraqi regime's torture chambers and poison labs in operation. Any future the Iraqi people choose for themselves will be better than the nightmare world that Saddam Hussein has chosen for them.

The United States has no intention of determining the precise form of Iraq's new government. That choice belongs to the Iraqi people. Yet, we will ensure that one brutal dictator is not replaced by another. All Iraqis must have a voice in the new government, and all citizens must have their rights protected.[7]

The principles of freedom and progress, he declared, invariably recommit free peoples to support rights and freedoms in an increasingly tumultuous global order. Bush administration officials predicted that the scene in Baghdad as U.S. troops arrived would be epically cinematic; ordinary citizens would greet the American liberators with flowers and cheers. Instead, the United States was once again ensnared in a protracted guerilla war, shot through with troubled elections, civilian massacres, and horrific atrocities.

In this chapter, I consider untimely comparisons between the wars in Southeast Asia and the wars in Afghanistan and Iraq, especially where the gift of freedom sutures a continuous history between times. While Cold War legacies also shadow Afghanistan and Iraq (also once proxies for war with the USSR), there are of course distinct coordinates of race and coloniality that render these wars ultimately incommensurate.[8] The political adversaries and geostrategic contests are changed, and the orientalisms of the war on terror operate under dissimilar circumstances and through distinct ideologies than those of the wars in Southeast Asia. And indeed, the contemporary moment is strewn with new claims to supersovereign powers, and to states of emergency for their exercise, in the name of *all* humanity. Indeed, President Bill Clinton in a 1993 address to the United Nations declared that the United States be a "fulcrum" for a new world order: "During the cold war we sought to contain a threat to the survival of free institutions. Now we seek to enlarge the circle of nations that live under those free institutions."[9] Clinton furthermore intimated that the United States would thereafter shoulder the initiative to wage war or policing—so-called peacekeeping—operations against rogue states, in language that Noam Chomsky paraphrases as "multilaterally when possible, but unilaterally when necessary."[10] (Clinton had some semi-legitimate grounds to do so; as Derrida observes of Article 51 in the UN's founding charter, it is an "article of exception."[11] Article 51 reads: "Nothing in the present Charter shall impair the inherent right of individual or collective self-defense if an armed attack occurs against a Member of the United Nations, until the Security Council has taken measures necessary to maintain international peace and security."[12]) Nonetheless, these wars permeate each other as reference, and as pathology. Indeed, the familiar language of *lessons learned* after one experience and applied to another subsequently frames those coordinates of comparison and equivalence.[13] Thus does Jodi Kim refer to the "protracted afterlife" of the Cold War as a structure of feeling and a hermeneutics of power,[14] and Tobin Siebers describe the history of the Cold War as "a history of false endings."[15] Most infamously among such false endings, perhaps, President George H. W. Bush proclaimed that the 1991 Gulf War ended the traumatic temporization that had for so long curbed liberal warcraft: "The specter of Vietnam has been buried forever in the desert sands of the Arabian Peninsula. It's a proud day for America—and, by God, we've kicked the Vietnam syndrome once and for all."[16] More than ten years later, coverage and commentary about the invasions and continuing occupations made ubiquitous reference to quagmires, entrenched guerrilla forces, and battles for the hearts and minds of the native populations, as well as the manufacture of threat (consider the Gulf of Tonkin and weapons of mass destruction) and congressional sanctions short of declarations of war. Vice President Dick Cheney argued that premature withdrawal from Iraq would instigate a domino effect, triggering a catastrophic loss of American power and influence among contiguous countries in the region, while the headline of a critical editorial penned by the former U.S. senator Max Cleland, republished in a one-page advertisement in the *New York Times*, shouted (in implicit reference to George W. Bush's failure to serve "the first time"), "Welcome to Vietnam, Mr. President."[17] And, in one of the more disturbing allusions to the foregoing war, the target's pose in perhaps the most widely disseminated photograph of the brutal torture of Iraqi civilians by American soldiers at Abu Ghraib—in which a hooded man stands on a box with wires attached to his arms, legs, and penis—is known to modern interrogators as "the Vietnam."[18] Such untimely comparisons and false endings are indeed innumerable. From this perspective, as Stoler and Bond remark, the critical task "is, in other words, to attend to what we have and have not recognized about the changing content of these formations, their structures of knowledge production, haunted sites, and unexpected and intimate forms."[19]

At the same time, looping through these wars we also find the narration of a continuous history of liberal empire through the gift of freedom, central to the militarization of humanitarianisms in the last half-century.[20] We ought to consider carefully the refugees of the last war in advance of those who are being made refugees now. And it is especially crucial to investigate the political and psychic economy through which the Vietnamese refugee brings to bear war and indebtedness as his or her agent, and no longer a target of liberal war. Several months after George W. Bush rashly declared the end of major combat operations in Iraq and empire's "mission accomplished,"[21] the nonprofit media service Pacific News Service, in association with the ethnic media–oriented New California Media, published an opinion piece titled "Time to Add Vietnam to Bush's Axis of Evil."[22] In it, Thi Q. Lam, a former South Vietnamese general, commended the Iraqi invasion and proposed another in Viet Nam, which might finally oust the communist regime.[23] (The benefits, he wrote, would be multiple: "To preserve his soaring popularity and to divert the attention of the American people from economic problems at home, President Bush, in fact, may decide to expand his axis of evil. Vietnam, a former foe now allied to China, the new Asian threat, may be a good choice. A regime change in Vietnam under a threat of military intervention or economic sanctions, may eradicate the lingering 'Vietnam syndrome' and remove a dark spot in U.S. history."[24]) The American Vietnamese Republican Assembly of Orange County also addressed an open letter to Bush, requesting that Viet Nam be numbered among rogue states and citing Viet Nam's opposition to U.S. military unilateralism as evidence of terrorist complicity.[25] These concatenating gestures bind together dissimilar enemies from historically distinct times through the narration of a common characteristic, a pathological will to captivity and terror. (I return to this racial enemy shortly.) It is equally important, however, to explore the dimensions through which the refugee patriot submits an empathic call for war: "Vietnamese Americans—who risked their lives to seek freedom in this country or who suffered communist persecution after the Vietnam War—understand the humiliation and sufferings of the Iraqi people under Saddam Hussein."[26]

How do we parse those continuities being drawn between the war across Southeast Asia and the war on terror, as enunciated by and through the patriotic refugee whose escape from the former (in this story) informs his participation in the latter? Against the diagnostic of the condition, how might this refugee patriot's multiple-time consciousness in this instance not be diminished as pathology but lauded as purposeful resolve to fight the future? This is what is new or made new about these wars—*what the comparison itself creates.* These analogies between the Cold War and the war on terror forge, rather than merely point to, these correspondences, determining new explanations, generating new political rationalities, calculating new equivalencies, and disseminating new moral vocabularies. It is useful to observe once again that analogies are often less about the objects being compared and more about the relations or components shared between them, assimilating differences into forms of resemblance for epistemic or taxonomic purposes. That is, in shifting our frames of reference, the analogy calls attention "to details hitherto unnoticed, to emphasize aspects of human experience treated as unimportant, to make new features into 'signs' signifying interiority."[27] The analogy thus transforms how we might understand the history of the present: the pathological hesitation of the not-yet faded Vietnam syndrome, for example, as a warning about the necessity of forceful warcraft, and the refugee as an alarm against too few security measures, too few deployments.

In this chapter, I argue that the refugee patriot as a representational device existentially establishes the continuous history of the gift of freedom, and as an analytic figuration brings together its operations of violence via war with the revelation of power in the imperative to be free. In this calculus, empire emerges as the central locus and guarantor through which the refugees it rescued, encamped, and disciplined are now protected, transformed, and activated as subjects of freedom. Put another way, the refugee patriot is the rightful consequence of given time, through which the refugee becomes a man or woman of action through the intensification of power. As such, the refugee patriot justifies military action precisely in the name of a threatened humanity that he or she embodies. (Notably, this refugee does not necessarily welcome the refugees of new wars.[28]) And, importantly, it is as a comparable stranger to the terrorist that the refugee meaningfully counterposes the new friend whose destitution and defenselessness obliges us to secure his or her freedom and life, and the racial enemy whose monstrous and inhuman nature strives to enslave humanity. In bringing these strangers together in such a freighted antagonism—the refugee who is grateful for the gift of freedom, which the terrorist so hatefully seeks to destroy—liberalism's empire reorganizes the structures of race and coloniality that inform its disciplining intents and powers. While Foucault's biopower and Achille Mbembe's necropolitics are separable and distinct analytics, the former regulating life as the deployment and manifestation of control and the latter distributing death as the ultimate expression of sovereignty, the Vietnamese refugee here highlights their entanglements. Jasbir Puar writes of holding together biopower and necropolitics as analytics of the long contemporary moment: "The latter makes its presence known at the limits and through the excess of the former; the former masks the multiplicity of its relationships to death and killing in order to enable the proliferation of the latter."[29] For us, the refugee who brings to the new world the spectral presence of a death world that lies elsewhere, and elsewhen, might yet become an agent for biopower's mandate to make live, and to create death in the near future.

Through such analogies and comparisons, this chapter now turns to a sustained critique of the mandate of liberal imperium and the emergence of what I call a *transnational multiculturalism*, as an ensemble of biopolitics, culture wars, and security apparatuses through which the refugee patriot recoups the racial liberalism of U.S. empire. In doing so, this chapter does not elide what is specific to either previous or present wars, but rather seeks to make obvious the ways that these wars might be engaged, or reengaged, through those refugee invocations of the gift of freedom that so complexly founds—and extends—the violences of an empire of liberty.

Transnational Multiculturalism and Race War

The refugee soldier who honors his debt to the American sacrifice in a previous war might especially claim the righteousness of the liberal way of war. In January 2005, Army Specialist Bui Thanh Thao's commanding officers granted him permission for a second time to raise the flag of the former Republic of Viet Nam over Baghdad, on the auspicious day of new Iraqi elections under U.S. occupation. Six months earlier, on Labor Day, the first flag raising was "dedicated in remembrance and in honor of the men and women who fought for a free South Viet Nam against communist invasion," and that flag was subsequently sent as a warfront souvenir to the Vietnamese American newspaper *Nguoi Viet Daily News*, in Southern California.[30] The second flag was sent to the Vietnam Freedom March Organizing Committee, for an April 30, 2005, march on Washington, D.C., to commemorate the thirtieth anniversary of the fall of Saigon, and presented there to the Vietnam Veterans Association. In a letter to the committee, Thao proclaimed that refugee soldiers were especially proud to engage the global fight against terror, in homage to the U.S. intercessions in Southeast Asia: "Today the Republic of Vietnam flag is a symbol of the free Vietnamese people against any enemy that harms or threats [*sic*] the national security in the United States of America."[31]

What I am naming *transnational multiculturalism* focuses our attention on the conjoined forms of race discourse that underwrite liberal empire, through which the U.S. volunteer army is depicted as a multiracial, multicultural force for freedom, and the not-yet vanquished "free Vietnamese" flag (as the flag was called in press releases) might supplement the Stars and Stripes in its symbolic promise to new friends in new wars.[32] Transnational multiculturalism brings together the assumed scenes of liberalism—again, self-possession as the condition for freedom, especially to act, to contract with others—to name the racial accord of a tolerant collectivity that is particular (in this instance) to the United States, but that is global, as well as governmental, in scope. After this manner, the geopolitical genealogies of transnational multiculturalism are traceable to Cold War biopolitics and transformed under neoliberalism. Critics have deftly demonstrated that a nominally pluralist stance, or what Nikhil Pal Singh identifies as a reputation for "the harmonious cooperation of different groups within the vast national body, and the broad toleration of cultural, religious, ethnic and racial differences within America," bolstered liberalism's claims to freedom and progress and the United States as their exemplar.[33] Or as Jodi Melamed elaborates, racial liberalism and American aspirations on the world stage were mutually constitutive during the twentieth century. Its racisms (specifically its antiblack violences) condemned by anticolonial and antiracist movements as moral failures and targeted by the Soviet bloc as liberalism's hypocrisy, the Cold War United States sought to manage its race problem through provisional inclusion within a liberal frame of rights and recognition.[34] Developing from this wartime juncture, liberal multiculturalism interlocks domestic and geopolitical coordinates for the government of capacities and the intensification of power, thereby encompassing both civic rhetorics and initiatives about diversity, enrichment, and enfranchisement as well as state measures including population assessments, antidiscrimination laws, provisions governing the protection of minorities, and programs incorporating immigrants into the civic and capital order. In the late twentieth century, multiculturalisms have proliferated alongside global consumer markets and humanitarianisms. While the Cold War state sought to claim an imperial mandate through at least the appearance of formal inclusion of racial, colonial others into the national body politic, the rise of what Inderpal Grewal calls "transnational America" also activates and shapes imperial subjects from citizens as well as immigrants and refugees, even those with other belongings.[35] Through the contemporary emergence of transnational multiculturalism, concurrent with a state of emergency, we can recognize the refugee patriot as one of the more significant forms of neoliberal subjectivization in an era of the world as target.

In querying how loyalty to a vanquished flag might not impede but rather inform an allegiance to an idea of the United States as an exemplar of a global nation, and a liberal empire, I detour now through other campaigns raising this particular flag for America's glory. In the example below, how do we parse a crusade to grant state recognition to the conquered flag of "free Vietnamese" during a state of emergency when the racial, colonial other is suspect? Which other allegiances are deemed anachronistic, if not outright treasonous, and which function to enhance (importantly, provisionally) a U.S. exceptionalism?[36] In what follows, I argue that the campaign to honor the flag of the former republic not only binds a social formation of "Vietnamese America" with a liberal frame of multiculturalism, but it also corroborates the gift of freedom as the logic of liberal empire. Put another way, the flag presumably commemorates what the refugee has lost at the same time that it honors what is given in its place— including the capacity to act on his own behalf, and for a universal humanity. But the recognition of this vanquished flag in a moment of crisis, during which other strangers must present the U.S. flag on their persons, their properties, requires a more comprehensive analysis of the structures of race and coloniality that subjectivize refugees and *other* others. Indeed, in carving out zones through which the world becomes knowable as a target, liberal empire recalibrates those racial and colonial indices that discern which peoples require freeing—and killing. Especially because the new friend and the enemy are deemed at times indistinguishable—resulting in civilian massacres and false body counts as an example in Southeast Asia—the remains of that war can illumine for us the complicated ways that these indices function, and are felt, in the present. Liberal war therefore demonstrates for us the necessary changeability of race discourse, perhaps especially its contrariness, as a force rather than a frailty. Ultimately, transnational multiculturalism here indexes for us that structures of race and coloniality that operate simultaneously, inseparably, are also creatively tiered, shifting moral vocabularies and conceptual pluralities to continuously reframe what counts as race and racism, and what goes by other names.[37] To consider these shifting, sliding operations further, I next turn to recent maneuvering around the wartime epithet *gook* to demonstrate the processes through which race war parses enemies and friends (especially those who "all look the same") via an affinity with freedom's empire. Crystallized as transnational multiculturalism, such affinity affords race war its cover. If social pacification and regulation began as a military project, as Foucault claims, then transnational multiculturalism is a weapon—through which the refugee patriot concomitantly honors a vanquished flag, recompenses the debt for his life, and wars on others to secure human freedom.

Controversies about the not-yet-dead flag focus our attention on the collocation of multicultural gestures with geopolitical structures. In 2003 the Vietnamese American Public Affairs Committee, a now-dissolved political advocacy group based in San Jose, California, launched a national campaign directed at state legislatures and municipal authorities to recognize the pre-1975 South Vietnamese national flag, referred to in notes and press releases as the "Vietnamese heritage and freedom flag," as the official flag of "the Vietnamese American community." Flag resolutions in various forms have been considered—and in most cases passed—in at least ten states, including Texas, Virginia, and California, and at least a hundred cities and other municipalities, including Westminster, Milpitas, San Jose, San Francisco, and Garden Grove, all in California; Fairfax, Virginia; Houston; and Boston. College Vietnamese student associations also participated, requesting that university administrations sanction the use of the heritage and freedom flag in public buildings or at graduation ceremonies, where other national flags might envisage a global order of things. The passage and eventual undoing of one resolution in particular demonstrates both its affective coordinates and material complications. On July

15, 2003, the San Francisco Board of Supervisors passed a resolution to recognize the South Vietnamese national flag as the standard of the "Vietnamese American community," and urged that the state legislature adopt a similar measure. But these resolutions tread dangerous waters because the United States reestablished diplomatic relations with Viet Nam in 1995. According to news reports, most of the supervisors, including the resolution's sponsor, Fiona Ma, were unaware that this flag stood for the defunct state. The consulate of the Democratic Socialist Republic of Vietnam objected, the San Francisco–Ho Chi Minh Sister City Committee disapproved, and San Francisco Mayor Willie Brown vetoed the resolution several days after the controversy erupted.[38] (Other proposals elsewhere were met with similar objections, and varied results.) And even as some members of the board were drafting a new resolution to rescind the first (which was passed), Ma had begun drafting a second resolution also recognizing the flag of the current Vietnamese government to appease critics (which was never brought to the table) even as she claimed that the first was not meant to be "political."[39] Vietnamese American supporters of the heritage and freedom flag celebrated the passage of the resolution and protested the mayoral veto. Citing democratic process, an online petition addressed to the Board of Supervisors requested reinstatement of the flag resolution "on behalf of the 25,000 Vietnamese-Americans residing in San Francisco." Arguing that the flag resolution was a "local" issue, the petition stated: "The resolution's content merely reflects and recognizes an obvious fact: The Vietnamese-American community in San Francisco prefers the original banner as a true representation of our personal sentiments for our race and our proud ethnic identity."[40]

These resolutions interpellate liberalism both as democratic process and as gracious hospitality. On one hand, advocates argued that the flag's revitalization is a simple matter of multicultural multiplicity and chosen sociality—put another way, constitutional forms of self-expression and assembly. Resolutions often included clauses similar to those in the Boston resolution: "WHEREAS: There are a significant number of Vietnamese-Americans who have chosen to make the City of Boston their home; AND WHEREAS: Boston's Vietnamese-American community have made substantial contributions to the cultural, religious, political and business life of the City of Boston; AND WHEREAS: The vast majority of Boston's Vietnamese-Americans embrace the yellow and red–striped Heritage and Freedom flag as the symbol of the Vietnamese-American community."[41] One Vietnamese supporter of the flag resolutions made a canny comparison (via a commodity logic): "It's like the symbol of the gay and lesbian community—the multi-colored flag—something like that."[42] As Minoo Moallem and Iain Boal argue, such a multicultural nationalism "operates on the fault line between a universalism based on the notion of an abstract citizenship that at the same time systematically produces sexualized, gendered, and racialized bodies, and particularistic claims for recognition and justice by minoritized groups."[43] On the other hand, this petition to multicultural representativeness permits us to ascertain a crucial disparity. (I return to some of its other provocations below.) That is, the comparison between the so-called heritage and freedom flag and the rainbow flag allows us to observe that there is no easier equivalence. The heritage and freedom flag is unique; there are no other concerted campaigns to request state and municipal legislatures to recognize the flag of a defunct state as the standard of a resident population. It is precisely because this vanquished flag does not and *cannot* avow loyalty to a sovereignty that its recognition here proclaims liberalism's investment in global enfranchisement and other freedoms, and also points to their eclipse in other quarters of the globe. Thus the resolution approved by the City of San Jose states that the South Vietnamese flag represents "*free* Vietnamese people"; the resolution passed by Garden Grove, California, contains strong language condemning the Vietnamese state for human rights violations of religious freedoms; and Boston's resolution identifies the flag with a "long history as a symbol of resilience, freedom and democracy both in Vietnam itself and Vietnamese-American communities throughout Boston and elsewhere."[44] Defiant of diplomatic repercussions, the resolution's sponsor in Boston refused to meet with Vietnamese officials to discuss their objections: "I felt no need to meet with the communist representatives. . . . We're talking about Vietnamese-Americans, who have come to this country and do not want their flag to be the flag of the regime that drove them out of their country."[45] These resolutions tell us *heritage and freedom are protected here.*

The resolutions also reorganize the disciplining intents and powers that form the basis for liberal subjection and subjectivization, carving out areas of social existence through which multiple flags or belongings might yet connote a continuous history of freedom, and a transnational America. Viet Dinh describes such subjectivization as a wondrous alchemy in the 2002 half-hour documentary called *In America: The Vietnamese Story,* which is one installment in a series on immigration produced by the now-defunct cable network International Channel: "I feel a sense of awe, that this magical place, these wonderful values and institutions . . . can take the ordinary people of the world, the Vietnamese, the Koreans, the Indians, and give them a special magic potion and make us Americans." Echoing Dinh, Colin Powell, in his opening statement before the Senate Foreign Relations Committee as then President-Elect George W. Bush's choice for secretary of state, described the United States as "a country of countries, with a citizen in our ranks from every land, attached by a thousand cords to the world at large—to its teeming cities, to its remotest regions, to its oldest civilizations." He continues that the United States, "a country of countries," inevitably harbors "an interest in every place on this Earth," "that we need to lead, to guide, to help in every country that has a desire to be free, open and prosperous."[46] The provocative image of a thousand cords tethering the globe to a single lead renders once again a liberal historicist consciousness, which presumes to knowingly anticipate and manufacture this present and presence, through the gift of freedom as its dissemination across the globe for human progress and historical and political transformation. Thus does transnational multiculturalism easily subsume the vanquished flag into a self-concept of the United States as the guarantor of futurity (implicit in the directional advance of heritage and freedom) for peoples who share common ground.

Through this, the encounter with the stranger who can be incorporated into an existing interior—a transnational America, an asylum—it absolutely matters here that both Dinh and Powell are multicultural Americans and also architects of the war on terror, against imagined enemies within and those on the outside. While transnational multiculturalism references race in the obvious sense of numerical or cultural heterogeneity, as a weapon of war it also promises self-possession and chosen sociality, which must be secured through either the biopolitical management of life (magic potion, transition, encampment) or more lethal methods—or, in the case of the two personages as welcomed *and* warrior, their coupling. It is in these terms, through which an antagonism haunts the prolongation of life, that the vanquished flag and all it is perceived to stand for (heritage, freedom, free Vietnamese) are imperiled. As microscenes for what Inderpal Grewal calls "transnational connectivities," the flag resolutions stage a multicultural diversity but also name an adversary whose very being injures the refugee. The communist flag (also called the "blood flag" by opponents, as if to reinforce a presumably fundamental pathology, a monstrous propensity to kill[47]) is ousted in these resolutions by the former republican flag, as a blow. Put another way, the life of this dispossessed people as a consequence depends on the elimination of their racial enemy from the global order. Thusly addressed to the world's populations as *America's problem*, we find in the shadow of transnational multiculturalism the Foucauldian formula for total war.

In the lectures collected in "*Society Must Be Defended,*" Foucault suggests that racism "is primarily a way of introducing a break into the domain of life that is under power's control: the break between what must live and what must die."[48]

> By this, I mean the idea . . . that the other race is basically not the race that came from elsewhere or that was, for a time, triumphant or dominant, but that it is a race that is permanently, ceaselessly infiltrating the social body, or which is, rather, constantly being re-created in and by the social fabric. In other words, what we see as a polarity, as a binary rift within society, is not a clash between two distinct races. It is the splitting of a single race into a superrace and a subrace. To put it a different way, it is the reappearance, within a single race, of the past of that race. In a word, the obverse and the underside of the race reappear within it.[49]

Foucault's sense of racism is not quite the same as, if not completely dissimilar from, its conventional structures; racism, he argues, is a technology of biopower that distills and distinguishes threats to the human race. This distinction complicates race discourse, usefully. Conceiving and reshaping schema of capacity and culture, race discourses emerge at the intersection of philosophies, regimes of representation, and structures of enforcement that work in concert to define human beings as racial types.[50] As taxonomies that also split a single race into a super race and a subrace, a race and the past of that race, race discourses are created with and against reference to the race of humanity. Foucault avers, "The discourse of race struggle is not a battle between races, but by a race that is portrayed as the one true race, the race that holds power and is entitled to define the norm, and against those who deviate from the norm, against those who pose a threat to the biological heritage."[51] Furthermore, racism for Foucault is no cover for other taxonomies; it is fundamental, "not simply a way of transcribing a political discourse into biological terms, and not simply a way of dressing up a political discourse in scientific clothing, but a real way of thinking about the relations between colonization, the necessity for wars, criminality, the phenomena of madness and mental illness, the history of societies with their different classes, and so on."[52] Thus the discourse of race, which becomes a discourse of life under modernity, further allows the deaths of some to ensure that life and its foreseeable future remain possible for others.[53] Therefore, Foucault argues that "racism does make the relationship to war—'If you want to live, the other must die'—function in a way that is completely new and that is quite compatible with the exercise of biopower."[54]

In the terms of our ongoing discussion, race as life necessity (as heritage, as tolerance, as diversity) is precisely the affective symptom of a politics of liberal empire that permits the further differentiation of race as a threat to such life, and as a legitimate reason to kill. It is in this regard that race is doubled in transnational multiculturalism, referring both to race as the subdivision of the human into categories (according to changing registers of comportment, genetics, moral sensibilities, beauty, national character, and so forth) and also to race as the mapping of these distinctions onto humanity as the whole ensemble of populations and *its outside*. Rey Chow observes in her study of the ascendance of whiteness in the modern world that this multidimensionality of race requires deconstructing culture together with biopower, with violence. She writes, citing Foucault: "To the extreme acts of violence, this liberalist alibi will mount a morally self-righteous opposition with its many discourses of rights: 'the "right" to life, to one's body, to health, to happiness, to the satisfaction of needs, and beyond all the oppressions or "alienations," the "right" to rediscover what one is and all that one can be'—which have become the issue of political struggles in modernity."[55] That is, in establishing a necessary reciprocity between the optimization of the life of the individual and the liberal government that secures rights and freedoms in the name of that life, transnational multiculturalism generates those distinctions that the gift of freedom operationalizes to celebrate together self-expression and racial harmony, even as it declares war on racial others who disturb or endanger this accord.

As a relevant example, and for the purposes of comparison between wars and their afterlives, the recent history of the term *gook* illumines those complexly drawn categories of race. Although the incident I describe below occurred before renewed war, it is precisely in the interstices of race as diversity and race as death (which the twists and turns of *gook* illustrate) that we find the operations that produce and police distinctions between racial bodies, disciplining some for freedom and disavowing others as monstrous. That is, we find in this example the techniques that at once divide and blur race as mere phenotype and race as heinous pathology, and the echo of war resonating long after ruin. When, in 1999, Republican Senator John McCain referred to his North Vietnamese captors as "gooks," anticommunist Vietnamese Americans rallied in support of the former prisoner of war against his detractors. Both McCain (in his public apology, in which he claimed to stand against bigotry and with diversity) and anticommunists insisted that *gook*, an epithet that has its origins in over a century's worth of American invasions in the Philippines and Asia, and also in *other* colonial locales, was not a racial slur but an ideological one.[56] To demonstrate his ties to the South Vietnamese as a staunchly conservative constituency but also as an old new friend, a former wartime ally, McCain subsequently brought his campaign to Little Saigon where, the *Los Angeles Times* noted, he received a "hero's welcome."[57] At a pro-McCain rally, a small group of protesters wearing handmade "American Gook" shirts decried his casual use of the racial epithet, only to be set upon by a hostile crowd, kicking, spitting, and according to some reports, urinating on the protesters, having identified them as probable communists or at the very least hurtful provocateurs.[58] This skirmish, and one supporter's poster reading "Gook = Communist Only," supplies for us a historical and theoretical provocation that performs the multiple operations of race found here. In its usage, the racialization of *gook* is racial in the sense that it is decidedly an Asian referent—since it was never and is not now being used to describe Soviet agents—and in the sense that it circumscribes the category of the human to expel the North Vietnamese from it. In the case of McCain's—or the anticommunist refugee's—use of the epithet, semantic acrobatics shift the onus of racialization away from liberal notions of visual or somatic markers onto a psychological disposition (fanatical, insensate, cruel, sadistic, "reducible to the desire to kill"[59]) that divides the gook fundamentally from the human race.

This is an ambiguous, and certainly unstable, operation that must be reinforced by the simultaneous inclusion—through something like a transnational multiculturalism, through a symbolic gesture toward new friends from previous wars—of those persons who might share some of those somatic or phenotypical features but who are recognized as on the side of humanity. It is in such a manner, because racism is still understood as an optical ideology or biological disgust, that *some* racisms can be disavowed. The Vietnamese refugee who asserts that "Gook = Communist Only" performs this operation as a slide, and a slipped knot, from a descriptor of race to an ideological fervor but more, to an ontological trait of an absolute alien nature. This use of the racial epithet *gook* epitomizes the malleability of race, through which the encounter with what is understood as irreducibly foreign about the Asian other can be appropriated into another series of racial distinctions (racial at the level of the human against the inhuman) without necessarily erasing nor resolving its Asianness (racial at the level of the somatic, the phenotype).

Again, this is a complicated operation. It is because race is understood to reside in the body that its materiality is taken as a continuous surface of data and information. As Stuart Hall writes, in considering Frantz Fanon, "exclusion and abjection are imprinted on the body through the functioning of these signifiers as an objective taxonomy—a 'taxidermy'—of radicalized difference; a specular matrix of intelligibility."[60] But the cognition of race is never an exclusively visual process. Judith Butler has suggested that the visual is "itself a racial formation, an episteme, hegemonic and forceful."[61] The referentiality of the visual sign of race is thus creatively tiered. In the aftermath of the McCain incident, at other Vietnamese anticommunist protests, signs reading "Gook Ho [Chi Minh]" appeared alongside caricatures that grossly exaggerated the slant of Ho's eyes— colored a bloodthirsty red—and vinyl banners that proclaimed his inhuman appetites, such as "Ho Chi Minh Murdered Girls after Sex." What might be striking at first as the phenotypical citation of popular racial caricature—the extreme tilt to the eyes—references a racial body as an Asian body, *but more a racial body as a monstrous one.* Against a progressive teleology of race (through which race discourse becomes gradually less biological and otherwise more "sophisticated"), this is hardly the replacement of white supremacy as an optic or somatic schema with a liberal paradigm that parses race as cultural form. Indeed, the somatic continues to operate as a pointer to an interior pathology, visual evidence that reads *here be monsters.* As Stoler explains, "the ambiguity of those sets of relationships between the somatic and the inner self, the phenotype and the genotype, pigment shade and psychological sensibility are not slips in, or obstacles to, racial thinking but rather conditions for its proliferation and possibility."[62] Such caricatures and refashioned epithets allow us to remark further on Foucault's argument that race war is the splitting of a single race; thus does race war involve paranoia and purification, what Foucault identifies as "one of the basic dimensions of social normalization," from within society and without.[63] Consider the vitriol that met the protesters who wore "American Gook" shirts and sought to assert the violence of liberalism's promise in naming the Asian body as *gook*; the exposé of this sobering fact instead cathets the epithet as an apt descriptor of their betrayal. *They become gooks twice over.* Certainly, this appropriation is not an easy one, but this is not the failure of such racial thinking but its more frightening flexibility.

The flip side of this racial reference is the displacement but also the postponement of the Asian other as a bearer of racial pathology, an earlier rupture that the name *gook* objectifies and externalizes and that might yet materialize in the future, once again.[64] In a fascinating genealogy of the Vietnam Center and Archive, the most-comprehensive archive related to the war in Viet Nam in the United States (held at Texas Tech University in Lubbock), Long Bui demonstrates for us that where race appears as an empirical issue, racial distinction is conceived in terms of a chain of signification that can loop back to a series of appropriations—and eliminations—between others. After performing futile database searches for *Vietnamese* and *Vietnamese American*, hoping to find documents and oral histories from refugees, the reference archivist suggests Bui use *gook* as a search keyword instead. He then observes,

> The racial terminology of war is linked to the continued use of such terminology in the archive and provides a guiding tool for my search for Vietnamese materials in the archive. Instead of oral interviews where I could hear actual voices and stories, the "gook" marks the epistemological limits through which I locate and trace the material presence of Vietnamese presence within the oral history project. The term "gook" as an understood term of identification for the enemy reveals so much about the phantasmal place of Vietnamese Americans in the archive, since Vietnamese American stories don't have to be physically present in the archive or the oral history program since they are *always* present in *any* discussion of the Vietnam War by American veterans whose perspectives about "gooks" are represented.[65]

The gook as continuous with but also separable from the refugee patriot who denounces this monstrous enemy illuminates a complexly racial schema. A biopolitics of asylum and security, operationalized through transnational multiculturalism, aims to unhinge these figures just enough to guarantee its gestures of inclusion, but also to hold out the necessity for more terminal acts, as well as the continuous processes of distinction and regularization that inform these actions. This concatenation of forms of racial thinking—race as diversity, race as culture, race as character, race as enemy—mirrors the operation of such categories and their modular qualities in the contemporary moment, during which race is both disavowed and sanctioned as the grounds for war.

The race discourses operating in a refugee's adoption of another era's epithet for himself or herself as a racial, colonial other to describe an inhuman enemy allow us some insight into those operations of power through which war invokes life as its reason for being. First, we might note the splitting of race into multiple forms that create and carry those distinctions being made between being "merely" diverse or "totally" other. These multiple forms of race pervade the operations of power and violence that produce radically distinct subject positions—freedom fighter or communist gook, grateful refugee or murderous terrorist. (Once again, these distinctions between strangers may be traced through a longer history, in the wartime necessity to produce "good" Asian subjects—a model minority, as it were— and thereby underwrite the racial liberalism of the United States throughout the twentieth century.[66]) Transnational multiculturalism, as Chow might observe, hence acts as a liberalist alibi, "generating endless discourses of further differentiation and discrimination even as it serves as enlightened correction/civilized prohibition against physical and brutal violence,"[67] or, in this instance, against violence committed by irrational civilians. Thus do some praise the United States for its liberal commitments to multiculturalism and tolerance, in the name of protecting "all citizens": "[In the aftermath of September 11, 2001,] not a single official asked Muslims to become invisible and remove their headscarves. The official policy was to protect the freedom to be visibly Muslim."[68] We can also discern just this precarious operation in Melamed's reading of the Patriot Act's preamble, called "Sense of Congress Condemning Discrimination Against ARAB and MUSLIM Americans": "It rhetorically privileges Arab Americans in order to discriminate against—and to obscure discrimination of—Arabs, Muslims, or South Asians in the United States who cannot or do not claim to be American in a nationalist or idealist sense."[69] Through such liberalist claims to protect and prolong some human life, this empire monopolizes violence and pursues war on its behalf. Although these efforts are meant to defuse the specter of racial animus, imagined here as an irrational hatred of another, they also function to reconcile us to the fact of global race war, identified as the necessary pursuit of peace through annihilation.

Second, as deployed by Bush, McCain (in his apology), and their defenders, transnational multiculturalism is pragmatically established as vital to the government of human freedom as a security measure, distinguishing between forms of proper feeling and belonging to the order of humanity. That is, transnational multiculturalism as the racialization of liberalism's powers incorporates strangers and their multiplicities but also demands their highest allegiance to a transnational America as an empire of humanity. To this stranger, the question is put: *Is your flag showing?* When Bush called for tolerance for Arab Americans in the immediate aftermath of 9/11, during which many ordinary Americans violently lashed out at "Muslim-looking" persons,[70] he did so by distinguishing "good Arabs" by their patriotic acts: "Our nation must be mindful that there are thousands of Arab Americans . . . who love their flag just as much as . . . [we] do."[71] Mosques, temples, taxies, ethnic groceries, and the racialized bodies that occupied these spaces bore the American flag as both a shield and a statement. Numerous observers duly noted that for those who "look" West Asian or Muslim, fear of being taken for a stranger "compelled many to display the signs of 'Americanness' on their bodies to counter the color of their skins."[72] As a measure of being free, then, transnational multiculturalism acts on behalf of the individual life as well as the amalgam of the population as an instrument for calculating the costs and risks of tolerance and vulnerability.[73] But transnational multiculturalism not only seeks to determine how much of "other" cultures an ascendant white "we" can tolerate in the enlightened West (through logics of commodity, exchange) but also acts to review and regulate how well strangers and new friends comply with liberalism.[74] Tolerance, as Wendy Brown tells us, is a civilizing discourse.[75] Indeed, Melamed argues it is Muslims' perceived monoculturalism, a slavish adherence to so-called traditional, doctrinal beliefs, that marks them as illiberal.[76] The striking analogy made earlier between the heritage and freedom flag and the rainbow flag, both invoked as testaments to a global humanity best cultivated under liberalism, further admits into this already complicated picture what Puar calls "homonationalism," an assemblage distinguishing between good gay patriots and bad "monster terrorist fags," that here operates to authenticate the refugee patriot's multicultural credentials.[77]

It is impossible to predict the path of the vanquished flag prior to our contemporary wars, but it is nonetheless incriminated in them and the new American century. This flag, especially because of these ongoing wars, is recruited to a transnational multiculturalism that systematizes the racial knowledges and powers that calibrate between friends and enemies, and further describes the epistemic violence of their normalization as breathing new life into freedom.[78] Roused by such dreams of sovereignty and virtue, the old new friend seizes ownership of his or her body, interiority, and life direction ("this is my heritage") so to exhibit his or her adherence to the idealist principles though which the United States claims global providence. (As the gift of freedom would have it, interviews with Vietnamese in the U.S. armed forces bespeak their indebtedness. Captain Carlos Thanh Do, for instance, says: "We have freedom because we came here. If we don't contribute, then that's very selfish of us. We must sacrifice to protect the freedom for our children's future."[79]) In doing so, transnational multiculturalism and the refugee patriot it conjures—equated not just with the protection of a tolerant collectivity but also the racial differentiation of capacities (such as waving the proper flag) that determines a relationship to governance—become part of Didier Fassin and Mariella Pandolfi's "military and humanitarian government" of the world.[80] In ways that could not have been foreseen, the forces of liberal war have brought these refugees forward to fight the future. These refugee passages stage a continuous history between righteous wars, past and present, and recompense the debt in the spirit of the gift—war.

Security and Vigilance

Concerned with what seemed to be an amnesiac act, the Asian American arts and politics magazine *Hyphen* sought some clue to the interior life of Viet D. Dinh, the Vietnamese refugee whose escape from communism presumably led to his authoring the Patriot Act and his support for subsequent war in Iraq: "While many regard him as a paragon of the American Dream, others find Dinh's shift from struggling immigrant to chief architect of what is considered the most anti-immigrant legislation in decades to be as confounding as it is amazing. . . . What baffles Dinh's critics is how radical the government's proactive measures have become, and how a man with Dinh's refugee background could be the mastermind behind them."[81] This expression of bemusement perceives Viet Dinh as a puzzle, whose racial, colonial difference—as struggling immigrant, as refugee—should confound cooptation by the security state. But the puzzle is not that he fits at all, but how he does and what he clarifies for us. Excerpts such as this one rightly point to the importance of this conversion from "struggling immigrant to chief architect," and it is this refugee passage that acquaints us once more with the disciplining intents and powers aimed at the subjection and subjectivization of the new friend of freedom, including given time and hospitality. In this vein, the gift of freedom carries a reminder of its absence, that is also a debt. Dinh's conversion is therefore no amnesia, no requirement that those who bear the trace (people of color, women, refugees, immigrants) forget so that they may inhabit the present. His conversion is precisely an homage to what was missing and what is issued in its place, including the debt that follows—he remembers the terrifying past in order to prevent its collision with our near future.

There are many other individuals whose labors fueled the securitization that led to the making of the Patriot Act. Yet what is remarkable about the Patriot Act is not merely its dramatic expansion of domestic police powers in service of a war on terror but also the manner in which Dinh was also put in service as a kind of representation whose persuasiveness for this expansion resided not in racial incongruity, but in complicity. Hailed as the author of the Patriot Act, this refugee figure not only condenses and organizes knowledge about the war in Viet Nam, and the United States as the global guarantor of freedom, but also brings into focus a particular vision of the world into being. That is, the figuration of Dinh fleshes out the rhetorics and pragmatics for liberal war as a gift of freedom, especially in his conversion from a target of imperial powers to their agent, a refugee patriot.

Here we must consider once again the coupling of freedom and security under liberalism's purview. Critics of Dinh charge him with sacrificing freedom for security, or even for nothing (that is, we are no more secure than before, they argue). Others defend the necessity of "striking a new balance between liberty and security."[82] Such a balancing act, Jeremy Waldon writes, with its "connotations of quantity and precision, as when we use it to describe the reconciliation of a set of accounts or the relative weight of two quantities of metal," seems to some a poor analogy.[83] But in some ways, this is precisely how liberal empire works: through it freedom and security are produced continuously as objectified, quantifiable, exchangeable, and therefore comparable relations and properties, in a circuit of exchange between governors and governed. In this context, freedom by necessity requires recourse to control and even coercion—or, put another way, the law of rights and freedoms itself renders new violence possible. But balance *is* a false binary. Freedom and security are not opposing things, forces, or gazes (to recall Jean-Luc Nancy[84]) but, more precisely, constitutive, mutually productive ones; as we shall see, freedom and security together generate new procedures of control and forms of rational, calculated intervention. Or, as Dinh and the former U.S. attorney general John Ashcroft offer, "Freedom is a value that is without parallel. Freedom never requires balancing. What it requires is enhancement. Freedom must be supported and safeguarded. Freedom must be secured. *Security, then, is not a counterweight to freedom, but rather a means to ensure that freedom remains intact and contributes positively to the character of humanity*. Simply put, appropriate security enables freedom, rather than competes against it."[85] Foucault theorizes security, identified as the state's continuation over time and those measures that ensure this, as correlative and commensurate with freedom as the rationale for liberal government. That is, securitization is those forms of police and regulation that permit and preside over "natural phenomena, economic processes and the intrinsic processes of population,"[86] through which the notion of freedom is not simply the right to oppose the abuses of a sovereign, but realized as the indispensable reason for governmental action. From the eighteenth century onward, "security," Colin Gordon argues, "tends increasingly to become the dominant component of modern governmental rationality."[87] A principle and a practice apart from, but nonetheless linked to, the law, sovereignty (which object is territory), and discipline (which object is the body), security is capable of combining these other principles and practices in new configurations addressed to "the ensemble of a population."[88] Indeed, as I contend in the first chapter, liberalism determines that free people's self-interest and security are best served by others having the benefit of freedom. Insofar as security is the medium of governing properly and a necessity for right living, where the ensemble of the population is expansively conceived, all the freedom-loving peoples of the world (including new friends and asylum seekers) might be incorporated into an existing interior of empire.

In this world order, freedom and security are partners in an economy of power and effects that circulate in a continuous, uninterrupted manner, individualized and organized throughout the social body as collectivity, or population. For these reasons, Foucault proposes that liberalism's other precept be: "'Live dangerously,' that is to say, individuals are constantly exposed to danger, or rather, they are conditioned to experience their situation, their life, their present, and their future as containing danger. . . . In short, everywhere you see this stimulation of the fear of danger which is, as it were, the condition, the internal psychological and cultural correlative of liberalism. *There is no liberalism without a culture of danger.*"[89] As it operates in our epoch, neoliberalism escalates the scope of security as it concerns possible and probable risks or eventualities, assesses through calculations of cost, and "prescribes not by absolute binary demarcation between the permitted and the forbidden, but by the specification of an optimal mean within a tolerable bandwidth of variation."[90] The Patriot Act is emblematic of this culture of danger, cohering legal provisos and biopolitical measures in a domestic policing operation as a piece of a broader directive of security as preemption in the war on terror. To forestall an abominable future, the September 2002 National Security Strategy of the United States of America warned:

> Traditional concepts of deterrence will not work against a terrorist enemy whose avowed tactics are wanton destruction and the targeting of innocents. . . . The United States has long maintained the option of preemptive actions to counter a sufficient threat to our national security. *The greater the threat, the greater is the risk of inaction—and the more compelling the case for taking anticipatory action to defend ourselves, even if uncertainty remains as to the time and place of the enemy's attack. To forestall or prevent such hostile acts by our adversaries, the United States will, if necessary, act preemptively.*[91]

In the age of the world as target, liberalism disciplines peoples (both distant and near) according to these newly developed dictates of time and space. We know well now that the indeterminacy of terror became the motor for the preemptive exercise of power. Because security implies continuation, the extension of life forward into time, the primary direction of security is toward the future; security as *preemptive* constitutes a category of action that understands the threat to the future as a concrete possibility in the present. Even if unsubstantial or unsubstantiated, *especially* if unsubstantial or unsubstantiated, the threat is rendered as pure potential realizable at any coming moment. (Even as the threat "passes by," as Sara Ahmed suggests, it heightens the anticipation of a time when it will not.[92]) This insecurity, the moment that might be at any time interrupted by death and disruption, produces a time-space of danger that stretches out indefinitely. Time is no longer fleeting; the precarious moment becomes a continuous state, a permanent and pervasive crisis saturating all aspects of life.[93] Thus the Patriot Act, as one of a slew of new policing measures, enacted discourses and practices of security that are future-inflected, including cost evaluations, risk assessments, and modifiable specifications for identifying terror along a spectrum of variation and indeterminacy. This indeterminacy represents the state as vulnerable and unstable, in part because of its obligations to freedom, but as we shall see, also provides it an alibi for its racial violence. The Patriot Act thus manifests Foucault's insights about the comprehensive objective of the police, defined as the rational government of human coexistence, and enfolding life's necessities and conveniences as effectively useful to the development of the state's forces.[94]

Foucault elaborates on liberalism's culture of danger as splitting into parallel, seemingly paradoxical, series of pragmatic consequences. The first consequence is "the considerable extension of procedures of control, constraint, and coercion which is something like the counterpart and counterweights of different freedoms."[95] In the Patriot Act, we discern that the machinery of preemption, and the culture of danger it fosters, produces those procedures of control, constraint, and coercion as that counterpart and counterweights to the *wrong* freedoms abused by some wayward others whose existence must be rigorously regulated, and possibly exiled. In this regard, the Patriot Act authorizes new measures for producing knowledge about the foreign or alien body, as strategic intelligence for the calculation of possible or probable danger in the service of a broader imperative of liberal war. Put another way, the Patriot Act as modern racial governmentality that here envisions the world as target is how state power is vitalized. Through new procedures of information gathering and documentation, including the fingerprinting of thousands of men traveling from designated danger zones, closer surveillance of foreign students and other immigrants both legal and otherwise, and practices of indefinite detention and secretive deportation, the foreign or alien body is registered in the national consciousness as a carrier of potential threat. The Patriot Act thus systematizes a racialized political rationality that identifies what Chow calls "target fields"—"fields of information retrieval and dissemination that were necessary for the perpetuation of the United States' political ideological hegemony."[96] These processes are both not new and new. Not new, because we easily detect a linkage with historical and still existing nonemergency laws and regulations that enact for racial, colonial others deliberate social death ("the fact of exposing someone to death, increasing the risk of death for some people, or, quite simply, political death, expulsion, rejection, and so on"[97]). Lisa Marie Cacho observes, for instance, that the Patriot Act builds upon the "ordinary" enforcement of contemporaneous immigration laws against brown bodies deemed ontologically illegal, and thus alienable.[98] Rather than differentiate between series of exceptions, then, here instead we might perceive a continuity through which the exception is not exceptional but is incorporated as foundational to the workings of this empire. But these processes are also new, because these so-called emergency powers oversaw the creation and regulation of the racial category of "Muslim looking," an ambiguous, and thus increasingly anxious, set of visual and attitudinal markers deployed to identify threats to public safety.[99] These processes of racial distinction target persons who, as Foucault might describe them, were imagined to already resemble the crimes they are believed to perpetrate—if not in the present, then in the future. Put another way, these processes identify the racial, colonial other as permeable at any moment by race as a biological threat. (We might further observe, as Sara Han does of Japanese internment as a national emergency measure, "a positive finding of need for national defense negates the presence of racial animus. However, it does not say that a positive finding of racial animus negates a finding of a need for national defense."[100]) Such security measures eliminated the legal status of these individuals and produced entities that could be neither named nor classified by the law and thus were denied the right to appeal to it. Indeed, at a public forum about the Patriot Act (and its violations), Dinh definitively declared that some are excluded from such concerns as human rights: "When you adopt a way of terror, you've excused yourself from the community of human beings."[101]

The second consequence of liberalism's culture of danger that Foucault describes is "the appearance in this new art of government of mechanisms with the function of producing, breathing life into, and increasing freedom, of introducing additional freedom through additional control and intervention."[102] Dinh's biography as the architect of the Patriot Act—or, as he describes himself, the more modest "attendant of freedom"—animates this appearance, narrating his achievement of autonomous personhood in charge of his decisions and life direction, once given time, given freedom.[103] In 1992, the New York Times published an opinion piece the then twenty-three-year-old law student composed about his harrowing escape to the United States, "drifting to freedom" on a small fishing boat that lost its engine in a storm, and about the father held in a reeducation camp and the eldest daughter left behind to care for him.[104] This piece facilitated Dinh's reunion with his sister in 1992 in a squalid Hong Kong refugee camp—a reunion filmed by the television newsmagazine *Dateline* NBC. Dinh is also the central figure in a 1993 *New York Times* reflection by the Pulitzer Prize–winning journalist Anthony Lewis, called "Abroad at Home—An American Story." Calling forth a "country of countries," or what we also know as liberal imperium, Lewis opines of this hospitable exchange: "There is no other country that has taken in so many people from so many places and cultures, and gained so much in the process." Lewis ends with a personal note sent by Dinh, word that he is newly graduated with a law degree and set to clerk for a Supreme Court judge. By the end of the twentieth century, Dinh's ascendance through the ranks (including a stint working for Kenneth Starr investigating the Clinton Whitewater scandal) to an appointment in the Department of Justice had long been publicly heralded as an exemplary "American Story."[105] But Dinh's benign story takes a turn after September 11, 2001, as an asylum seeker who, upon receiving life and liberty from empire, becomes a man of action, an agent of war who intuits increased freedom through intensified security. Under crisis conditions, it is as a warning from a traumatic past to an as-yet insecure future that this refugee patriot, as Foucault might observe, and as I argue in what follows, "turns into a mechanism continually having to arbitrate between the freedom and security of individuals by reference to [a] notion of danger."[106]

Transnational multiculturalism and race war are inextricably bound by neoliberal racial governmentality, and through that the stimulus of danger and its paranoid configuration of time and space are realizable in the wayward figure of the bogeyman, the terrorist, but also its shadow, the refugee. Found outside the purview of legitimate citizenship, the terrorist and the refugee constitute categories of the stranger and the state of emergency, conceived both as the boundary objects and as the consequences of biopower and geopolitics. On the one hand, the terrorist ranges out of the reach of any single state, and thus often demands (or justifies) strategies of radical disenfranchisement and extraterritorial murder in order to meet, and extinguish, this enemy. On the other, the refugee cannot appeal to the state from which she is fleeing, or expelled, to recognize her as legitimate life, a human being worthy of rights. On closer inspection, these seemingly obvious distinctions between the two categories, and the forms through which their unlawful status is reckoned with, are contingent and mutable. As the first chapter noted, refugees are oftentimes received (or refused) as a danger. In the absence of properties for self-possession as conditions for ethical action and feeling, the refugee condition as a disorientation in time and space might compound a latent criminality. For these reasons, sometimes the refugee is deemed a terrorist because he is imagined to threaten the law when he takes some kind of action on his own behalf. Palestinian refugee settlements, for instance, are understood by the Israeli state to be breeding grounds for terrorism, producing suicide bombers as the ultimate in both fanatical and indiscriminate murder, though these acts designated as terrorizing are necessarily lawless in the logic of recognition and sovereignty—such that the actions of the Israeli state (a staunch U.S. ally named a democratic bulwark in the region, despite what Jacques Rancière might call a "hatred of democracy"[107]), though these too inspire the affect of terror—are identified as appropriate maneuvers for the purpose of national—but also, importantly, racial, global—security. Thus do refugee and terrorist figurations often threaten to delay or disrupt the continuity of nations and empires whose own futures are often staked on their banishment or annihilation.

But liberalism's empire, in distilling and distinguishing threats, must bring some humanity to the inside. Thus, though some usefully remark that "the constant presence of an enemy and the threat of disorder are necessary in order to legitimate imperial violence,"[108] the argument of this book might paraphrase, that the constant presence of the precarious life of an *other other* is also necessary in order to legitimate liberal imperial violence. (Indeed, the multifarious campaigns to declare Israel and the Netherlands, for instance, refuges for queer persons over and against the Islamic specter, who is targeted as an obdurate stranger in conjoined figurations in law and culture, precisely manage this dual character of liberal imperial violence.[109]) It is in this regard that the refugee who comes to another's door to beg his hospitality, and who gladly submits to government, might return the self-concept of liberal empire as a generous force operating as necessity demands in a state of emergency. As aliens, as strangers, both the terrorist and the refugee coalesce fears about the disruption of lawless beings, and about unbearable states shaping what can be lived as a social formation; both are limit figures of an individual life as well as the life of the population given over to the indeterminate future. If liberalism's empire promises, "I am going to produce what you need to be free. I am going to see to it that you are free to be free," the refugee and the terrorist then become paradigmatic figurations for a contemporary culture of danger.

We can see this dynamic between terrorist and refugee at work in a lecture Dinh delivered at the University of Florida Law School in 2004, soon after he stepped down from his post as assistant attorney general. In this lecture, later published as "Nationalism in an Age of Terror," Dinh argues for nationalism through which the divide between the citizen subject and the noncitizen other is the ground for biopower's optimization of life, as well as the reiteration to the sovereign right to kill. While Dinh attests that liberalism invests in a set of freedoms against which the enemy rages ("Knowing what we know about al Qaeda, we can say that its extremist, fundamentalist ideology is offensive to our liberal democratic ideals. Al Qaeda seeks to subjugate women; we work for their liberation. Al Qaeda seeks to deny choice; we celebrate the marketplace of ideas. Al Qaeda seeks to suppress speech; we welcome open discussion."),[110] he is most insistent that the liberal state-cum-empire—and the United States in particular, as an exemplar—is best defined by its necessary and rational monopoly on violence: "The value of the nation-state as the basic unit of political organization is perhaps best, and most relevantly, illustrated by the use of force. Each sovereign has an internal monopoly on the use of force within its jurisdiction. Each nation can project force externally in order to wage war. Because preventing and limiting war is the whole point of the exercise, the law of nations as it has traditionally developed governs, first and principally, use of force."[111] For Dinh, because the terrorist untethered from the rule of a sovereign state threatens this monopoly on violence, he is not simply a wayward figure, but an unworlding disorder. Indeed, in his challenge to the state (and to empire), the terrorist is elevated by historical (or imperial) necessity to the unnatural status of a rival: "By adopting the way of terror, it [terrorism] has attacked not only our citizens in our territory, but also the very foundation of world order grounded on sovereignty."[112] Thus, "by fomenting terror among the masses, the terrorist seeks to incapacitate them from exercising the liberty to pursue their individual ends. This action is not mere criminality; it is a warlike attack on the polity."[113] In this schema, the terrorist is the inhuman other produced by the basic division of the race that underlies the premise of total war. This figure is notably a foreign or alien body, rendered in Dinh's rhetoric as a viral contagion presumably programmed to destroy: "Neither endowed with the rights nor encumbered by the responsibilities of being a person in the international community [which includes recognition of the sovereign power to monopolize violence], the terrorist attacks that community as a virus, moving from one person to the next, infecting each indiscriminately with its lethal poison."[114]

Against contagion, Dinh counterposes the refugee patriot whose love of country transcends the accidents of birth to revere a universal liberalism as a politics of life. Here he marshals transnational multiculturalism as an explicitly geopolitical instrument in a global war, citing George W. Bush's inaugural address: "America has never been united by blood or birth or soil. We are bound by ideals that move us beyond our backgrounds, lift us above our interests and teach us what it means to be citizens."[115] Dinh proposes that nationalism, and in particular American patriotism, stimulates the desire to sustain such virtuous ideals via a commitment to freedom as guaranteed by sovereignty (that is, a monopoly on violence). Our attachment to these things, he claims, induces in us a heightened sense of responsibility to others who live in distant elsewheres perhaps not as fortunate: "That we love those close to us, of course, does not mean that we cannot love those distant from us. . . . *Indeed, loving one's country allows one to love others more.* Liberal democracy requires a healthy dose of mutual commitment. Countermajoritarian norms, protection of minority rights, and redistributive justice go against parochial self-interest and take a lot of enlightenment—the empathy and commitment that national identity and unity facilitates."[116] In this account, American patriotism claims a self-love that opens up into presumably unself-interested care for others, for humanity.

Thus does the Patriot Act, together with the refugee patriot, illustrate "I am going to produce what you need to be free" and "live dangerously" as conjoined operations of liberalism's empire. Put another way, the refugee patriot is the figuration of these policing powers not as repressive, but productive, operations. In such terms does Dinh boost his patriotism through a proprietary claim to those powers that act in the name of the global race of humanity, and that produce the governance the human deserves. Again Dinh quotes Bush: "Unlike any other country, America came into the world with a message for mankind, that all are created equal, and all are meant to be free. *There is no American race. There's only an American creed: We believe in the dignity and rights of every person.*"[117] Using language that disavows an American race as an actionable imperative, an American creed operates instead as the obligation to alleviate the deprivation of others. Here lies the strategic force of a transnational multi-culturalism, "with a citizen in our ranks from every land, attached by a thousand cords to the world at large," standing for that global race and claiming thereby a supersovereignty. Carl Schmitt defines sovereignty as the right to suspend the law and abandon life to violence, which informs Giorgio Agamben's insight on the state of exception, through which law does not then punish that violence.[118] But through global race war, we can say that a supersovereignty—which here goes by the name the gift of freedom, and might also be conceived through humanitarianism—claims a more planetary purview for extralegal action. Indeed, writing of liberal-ism's colonialist destinies, Uday Mehta comments, "The declared and ostensible referent of liberal principles is quite literally a constituency with no delimiting boundary, namely, that of all mankind."[119]

Through such recourse to universality, liberal empire claims a self-concept that has no limits, even as it is itself the author of limits. This self-concept informs Bush's address before a joint session of Congress in the days following the 9/11 attacks: "This is the world's fight. This is civiliza-tion's fight. This is the fight of all who believe in progress and pluralism, tolerance and freedom."[120] Security therefore exceeds the sphere of sov-ereignty, inasmuch as the space of control is no longer a finite territory; in an empire state of mind where all humanity is threatened, those interna-tional laws that distinguish between an inside (a police concern) or outside (a military preserve) are rendered wholly irrelevant. Once again, the objec-tive to unite all the world's peoples under the signs of equivalency—human rights, universal sovereignty, and so forth—is the heart of liberal empire.

From this vantage point, the refugee patriot enables untimely compari-sons and false endings. First, if the Cold War is retroactively understood in the language of terror, the refugee patriot sutures these distinct wars into a continuous history of liberal empire as an empire of humanity, committed to producing for others rights and freedoms. That is, the refugee patriot actualizes the promise of given time as a liberalist alibi. Under the fosterage of a transnational America, his success re-places the gift of freedom as the gift of time—time to develop, time to realize one's human potential—which then becomes part of the strength of liberal imperial statecraft. Second, Dinh's story of his conversion informs those discourses that differentiate and discriminate between multiple forms of race, especially multicultural multiplicity and biopolitical necessity. Because the Patriot Act specifically targets the racial stranger for detention and deportation, Dinh's refugee story operates as a bulwark against the worry that the act might target "just anyone." If racism establishes the positive relation between the right to kill and the securitization of life, transnational multiculturalism as an account of liberalism's enlightened government disavows such racism at the same time that it is bound to it, distinguishing between *those who love the flag as we do* and *those who hate our freedoms*. It is through these routes and passages that transnational multiculturalism is absolutely key to the concept of liberal race war in the name of the optimization of life. Transnational multiculturalism undertakes the identification of dangerous entities through these moving categories of measure, and shifting thresholds of appraisal, directed at the affective and cultural (which is to say, civilizational) dispositions of racial, colonial populations and their willingness or capacity to accept the gift of freedom. This is how Dinh's refugee story (though only implied in his lecture) exerts its symbolic power: traversing the ocean in order to escape tyranny, he is that stranger whom the gift of freedom has rescued from the past and pressed into an autonomous individual, a new American, and directed toward a bold future. Or, put in the terms of this book, he figures an aporetic hospitality, as that obligation to welcome but also to discipline the stranger, lest he subvert it. He is the perfect guest, the subject of freedom who not only consents to be governed but who understands his consent to be also his obligation—a debt—to those who accorded him hospitality: "We ensure that our doors remain open to those who seek entry for the promise and opportunity America offers. A commitment to inspiring American ideals among immigrants will also help foster their dedication to the freedom and liberty for which we are fighting."[121]

Third, as futural indeterminacy became politically operational as a pragmatic affect, this refugee patriot sharply focuses our attention on the specter of state failure without preemption, without vigilance. In another venue, Dinh counterposes unfree and free states of being in an argument for the expansion of police powers under the Patriot Act: "I came to this country as a refugee from Vietnam and as such I have lived under war torn Vietnam and I have lived under communism. I have seen government that does not work either through the chaos of war or the totalitarian oppression of a communist regime. I love this country. I love this country not only because of the land and the people but because of the institutions that define us as a community and protect our rights and make government work." Of particular preoccupation here is the collocation of temporalities, the duration (and duress) of indebtedness, and the looming horizon of terror and antiprogressive time. Construed as constitutively cognizant that safety and security are provisional, because it is a defining condition of his radical dispossession after war, this refugee figure is perceived as uniquely positioned to appreciate the seriousness of homeland defense. In this substitution, the refugee becomes the horizon of possible existence for all those who might be irreparably harmed by the empire's vulnerability—first through the lived memory of his past privation, and second through the vigilance that memory, that privation, inspires. Here the refugee patriot calls to mind his incarnation as the new friend of freedom, poised precariously between horizons of possible, antipathetic times. In the first instance, Dinh is the incarnate figure of devastated personhood: the citizen undone, shorn of rights and property, made dead or dying. A reminder of the failures of the war in Southeast Asia, including its so-called syndrome of militaristic hesitancy, he highlights both the precariousness of liberal empire, because it gives so much of itself, and the mandate that its powers wage wars and regularize populations, because it is an empire of humanity. Recruited into an analogy for the dispossession of sovereignty and the destruction of security, his losses loom as forewarning about the danger of inadequate measures. But such losses are also transformative, as an investment in anticipatory futures. If the refugee refers to one whom is "not at home," whose existence is understood to encompass fear, uncertainty, and the deprivation of territory and world-historical time, who better to embody the American architect against the possibilities of more devastating loss? Who better to extend the practices of security "abroad at home" as an extension of the war "out there"? He, refashioned as a vigilant patriot, permits us to feel an intuition about a possible or probable event before we are forced to actually experience it for the first time. In doing so, his memory shapes the conditions of the preemptive present (including permanent war, and increased surveillance) in order to foreclose on an indeterminate future. His past is our future to come, unless we are vigilant *now and forever* in securing ourselves against the enemies of freedom. Thus does Dinh remind us, or more allows us an inadvertent foothold in understanding, that liberalism is always already both power *and* violence.

At this juncture are some profound analytic consequences. The repeated emphasis on his racial, colonial difference—that is, his refugee presence as enduring reference to another liberal war, another global war—suggests that Dinh is the bearer of at least two useful truths. First, under neoliberalism, security as biopower expands its field of application from a concern with life conditions within a territory to the globe, the future—more than a population, but all life. Second, war is inseparable from our everyday existence. It is as such that the refugee who receives the gift of freedom, and whose capacities for life are secured thereby, facilitates the normativization of war. The war instates insecurity as a new way of being, impacting both those deemed dangerous and detainable and also those who are provisionally recognized as legitimate persons, transforming their daily habits, their somatic systems, their emotional dispositions. (As Brian Massumi argues, "affective modulation of the populace was now an official, central function of an increasingly time-sensitive government."[122]) Violence and exception are not interruptions of our continuity, but the permanent condition of peace. Or as Chow observes: "The space and time of war are no longer segregated in the form of an other; instead, they operate from within the here and now, as the internal logic of the here and now." And more, "from being negative blockade to being normal routine, war becomes the positive mechanism, momentum, and condition of possibility of society, creating a hegemonic space of global communication through powers of visibility and control."[123]

The analytic of liberal empire, therefore, is never distant from an analytic of race war, and their intimacy—as concepts, as practices—is exercised and normalized through the promise of freedom as its regime of truth. That is, if the defining feature of the modern state is its authority to monopolize its control over the methods and meanings of violence, and to do so through the internal control of bodies and populations and the external projection of its attachments, it is the promise of freedom that defines and sustains those actions undertaken by liberal empire as literally vital. Here we find a foundational paradox. On the one hand, war as murderous intent, and violent event, is external to society and to liberal empire especially, as an agent of perpetual peace. On the other hand, war as the promise of continuity is vital to life's prolongation into the future—which is to say, *society must be defended*. It is through this very paradox, producing freedom while living dangerously, that the refugee patriot crucially models the debt that *all* peoples owe to freedom's empire, which claims that *all is given* under its direction and makes way for more war.

The Bomb Will Bring Us Together

Let us consider now the bomb, that terrible thing that so often conveys, or constitutes, the gift of freedom. The anthropologist Marcel Mauss describes the exchange of gifts, including countergifts and debts, as agonistic, while Derrida calls this madness. For Kennan Ferguson, drawing on Mauss's *The Gift* and Georges Bataille's *Accursed Share* in his own critique of the violence of war as the gift of freedom, there is no gift but its excess, its destruction: "Freedom . . . is not measured by journalistic autonomy or national self-determination or even formal balloting—it is measured, instead, by the exertion expended for it."[124] In this view, the United States and its stated commitment "to bring freedom to others"[125] is also to bring annihilation. But here madness (what would be called in a previous era a mutually assured destruction) is not quite the measure of liberal war, even or especially as it becomes neoliberal war. Instead, the technologically "sophisticated" bomb illumines for us neoliberal war as a rational-technical system that fragments race into differentiated forms of life, cutting into a biological field, which, as "life itself," is made abstract through these means and measures. And, through these rationings, these cuttings, the United States tenders the gift of freedom.

But first: how does one repay the debt of a life, after war? What constitutes the economy of equivalence and exchange for the refugee rescued from not mere injury but a living death? Encompassing rules, expectations, and social bonds between giver and receiver, as we know, the gift demands a reciprocal return of value that cannot be simply repaid in financial terms—though such terms are not *not* included in the tally.[126] The gift of freedom—especially when it takes the form of military intervention, as it so often does in the name of humanitarianism—requires in return acknowledgment of nigh unpayable debt extending endlessly into the future. It is in large part the devastation of the racial enemy and the extravagant expenditure of equipment and troops toward that end that solicits a lasting gratitude among those who continue to be free, or who are freed, by this death and destruction. (As Foucault notes, the continuous looping between freedom and security "make[s] the field of the life it manages, protects, guarantees, and cultivates in biological terms absolutely coextensive with the sovereign right to kill anyone, meaning not only other people, *but also its own people*."[127]) Thus the soldier's sacrifice, for example, is understood as the coin with which the liberal state secures its powers; and the refugee soldier's received as the squaring of old debts, for American lives gone before in another war.[128] ("When he puts his uniform on, he doesn't think about death. He just thinks about his responsibility."[129]) It should not be surprising, then, that the act of thanksgiving or repayment might take the feeling if not also the form of the gift—war, or at least its weapons.

This equivalency is at work in a striking example—the former refugee dubbed the Pentagon "bomb lady," Nguyet Anh Duong, who repays the debt she owes for her freedom with more war. In a profile that begins with her dangerous dive from a fishing boat onto a US Navy ship, hers is a predestined mandate: "The Communists were overrunning South Vietnam [in April 1975]. At that time, Osama bin Laden was 18. The arc of his life, and Anh Duong's, would intersect."[130] Here the precipitous collapse of this timeline produces a continuity between wars as well as a comparison between enemies. Her grief, her rage, her fear: these are activated in a causal sequentiality between her childhood terrors then and those terrors threatening her children now. The past haunts the near future, once again. However, her vulnerability ends with her vigilance. Under imperial aegis, she is a modern woman, a bomb maker now. Accordingly, "Duong is still angry, though no longer helpless."[131]

As the director of science and technology for the Naval Surface Warfare Center of the Department of Defense, and called by some "one of the most important weapons-developers of the modern era,"[132] Nguyet played a central role in the development of a high-impulse thermobaric weapon designed and manufactured specifically for the destruction of mountainous hideouts in the war in Afghanistan, named Operation Enduring Freedom. This bunker-busting weapon, praised for its efficient delivery of life-negating powers, earned Nguyet the 2007 Service to America National Security Award. In a *Washington Post* article recounting her speech at the award ceremony, Nguyet accents the need for more and bigger weapons: "I'm here because in Vietnam, we ran out of bullets. I don't want to ever be in that position again. By building bombs, the other guys realize they shouldn't mess with us. If you have a gun, I have a bazooka. If you have a grenade, guess what? I have a bomb."[133] In this language we discern the pernicious rhetoric of escalation and proliferation as deterrence. How can we ponder this commitment to the creation of such terrible weapons designed for mass murder? What is the nature of a concept of deterrence predicated on the presence of intensifying danger, its escalating potential?

(Consider this description of the punishing power of her weapons making: "It's a terrifying device. The thermobaric bomb crushes caves with a super-hot blast that can destroy internal organs as far as a quarter-mile away. Its explosion is designed to tunnel through convoluted caves and pulverize anyone hiding as deep as 1,100 feet inside, and then incinerate what remains."[134]) As Chow has observed elsewhere of this concept, weapons whose magnitude is such that their existence might deter war do so by escalating and intensifying violence to an unheard-of scale: "What succeeded in 'deterring' the war was an ultimate (am)munition; destruction was now outdone by destruction itself."[135] This too might be understood as a preemption that identifies foreign and alien bodies for continuous targeting. We could also ask, as Mbembe does, "Is the notion of biopower sufficient to account for the contemporary ways in which the political, under the guise of war, of resistance, or of the fight against terror, makes the murder of the enemy its primary and absolute objective? War, after all, is as much a means of achieving sovereignty as a way of exercising the right to kill."[136] Thus does necropolitics characterize weapons such as the thermobaric bomb, "deployed in the interest of the maximum destruction of persons and the creation of death-worlds."[137]

I would not here argue a contradiction, or even a tension, between necropolitics and biopower. Instead, as a politics of comparison illuminates, we see a convergence, a collusion. (We can observe, as Foucault does, that the sovereign right to take life or let live is thoroughly permeated by the newer power to make live and let die.[138]) In a series of equivocations, Nguyet enacts a metonymic fusing of one war with another, a fusing that compels linkages between the war in Viet Nam as the gift's mechanism of delivery to the wars of the present as the stage for her debt's payment, which takes the form of war as the redoubling of the gift to others. In these equivocations, life and death are necessarily entwined as conditions of possibility for each the other. Thus, the rhetorical force of Nguyet's motives casts her weapons work as the ultimate act of thanksgiving, even as the thermobaric bomb is the summation of new military inventions that seek total destruction. Of her work for the Department of Defense, and the machinery of war making, Nguyet states: "my life is payback: I'm indebted to the soldiers and to Americans."[139] She dedicated her award to the soldiers who died during the war in Viet Nam, both American and South Vietnamese, "in order for people like me to earn a second chance to [sic] freedom. May God bless all those who are willing to die for freedom—especially those who are willing to die for others."[140] These deaths (and even the willingness to die), as the cost of the gift of freedom, link her commitment to warfare as the cultivation of life through the technological capability for death, arcing from Viet Nam to Iraq as a continuous timeline. Thus an equation that measures freedom less as rights or their sustained presence, or even as the destruction exerted on its behalf, but more as a relation between governor and governed, allows us to uncoil the economy of value and exchange occurring in these patriot acts. In a *Newsweek* article about Nguyet, the conservative journalist and author George Will confirms that the gift of freedom is not without the expectation of return.[141] But, as Will informs us, Nguyet has more than paid her dues. Not only does she acknowledge the incalculable sacrifice involved in securing her freedom, but she also further honors the sacrifice with what we might call an act of mimicry—reproducing liberal war as a moral obligation, securing life through the manufacture of a devastating weapon via a concept of deterrence premised on total destruction—and through which total destruction is the only incalculable, and yet exchangeable, value for her sovereign subjectivity.

In this sense, empire regularizes a grim equivalency. Such weapons of mass destruction as those that Nguyet develops in the name of the more massive gun, the more lethal bomb, expose whole populations to death to secure another's life, to prolong it, improve it. Here, as Foucault might say, racism intervenes to harness the power of the bomb. Like Dinh, profiles and interviews with Nguyet describe her harrowing escape from Viet Nam, and her rescue to a generous America, as the grounds for her diligent labors toward more efficient weaponry. Driven by her memories of the savage and indiscriminate weaponry of the Viet Cong, she avows that the pioneering explosives she develops for the American military are instead life affirming. Once again, the liberal way of war requires a civilizational distancing to establish a positive relation between the right to kill and the securitization of life. This affirmation is operationalized via a transnational multiculturalism, as it is here in America that Nguyet is given new life to create more of it (she raises a family; she builds bombs), but also through a racial splitting that occurs along at least two fault lines. First, Nguyet distinguishes the sophisticated weaponry of liberal war making from other, cruder forms by its care to sort and kill enemies discriminately. Recounting her fears that "the next Viet Cong rocket would smash into her house," the insensible destruction of innocent human life, Nguyet implicates the Viet Cong in terms of pure terror, reducible to the desire to kill. Of her childhood fears, she observes: "Why would you want to randomly blow up civilians?"[142] Dinh makes the same distinction of the terrorist: "Civilians are no longer sacred; military installations are not necessarily the primary targets. By way of comparison, an enemy nation targets the instruments of our defense; the terrorist targets the core of society."[143] (Of course, we well know that by these standards, the United States is a vector of tremendous terror.)

Here Nguyet differentiates between weapons delivery systems in terms of intention (which can be further discerned via technical vocabularies), which is implicitly determined by the racial splitting of the human from the inhuman. It is here that an odd juxtaposition surfaces to affirm this racial distinction, contrasting the Viet Cong's indiscriminate murder of civilians with the "accidental" slaughter committed by American soldiers. When Nguyet contends, "I don't want My Lai in Iraq,"[144] this might appear at first to be an indictment—of the racisms of American soldiers who could not or would not discern one Vietnamese from another, or the routine murder of civilians.[145] But Nguyet in fact refuses to indict American soldiers as murderous; indeed, she recounts her teenaged anger ("How dare they?") at those Hollywood films depicting GIS as rapists and baby killers.[146] It instead appears that in her perspective, My Lai is not the insensible destruction wrought by a supremacist empire, but a regrettable failure to discern between the good racial subject and the bad one. War as a violent event commits deliberate injury to the bodies and properties of a named enemy; but in which liberal war claims atrocity is incidental, My Lai becomes an accident, the unfortunate symptom of soldiers' unbearable experiences. (Indeed, it is the racial, colonial other, the Viet Cong, the gook, whose irrational violence renders the United States, and its soldiers, so vulnerable to death, or to the madness whose symptom is atrocity.) Atrocity is therefore conceived not as a problem of state racism or the nature of war, even liberal war, but rather a failure in troop support or information retrieval. Or as Nguyet remarks: "The biggest difficulty in the global war on terror—just like in Vietnam—is to know who the bad guys are. How do we make sure we don't kill innocents?"[147] There is no accusation here, only the much more faultless presence of "difficulty."

Once again we find the valorization of life as an objective of liberal war giving rise to processes of differentiation between categories of life. That is, what distinguishes liberal war is the organization of biopower in the service of killing more discriminately. ("We've gotten more sophisticated compared to the old days of dumb weapons," Nguyet insists. "Now you can deliver it exactly where you want it to go."[148]) This pledge to restrain more brutal and indiscriminate measures returns us to technical vocabularies manifesting "good" intention, through which race is reconfigured as a rational-technical process for distinguishing between proliferating forms of life. Nguyet notes: "A war fighter needs to know one of three things: Do I let him go? Keep him? Or shoot him on the spot? In Vietnam, our guys didn't have this tool." She adds: "The best missile is worthless if you don't know who to shoot."[149]

But this pledge also normalizes these rational, efficient means for greater and more widespread application, committing more routine, and more intensely thorough, forms of violence. The above description of her weapons development as rational systems of racial differentiation is thus contiguous with her subsequent projects establishing biometrics systems for mobile forensics labs to use, scanning the irises and fingerprints of Iraqis in order to process and catalog persons and their gradations of possible or probable danger. Accordingly, "hundreds of Marines are learning how to process a crime scene," and the data will be "beamed to the Biometric Fusion Center [in West Virginia] to check against more than a million Iraqi fingerprints."[150] Nguyet describes this biometrics undertaking as an aid to freedom's soldier in assessing, in the field, whether or not a suspect is properly available for killing, or not. Thus facilitating and calibrating a rational ordering of the world's peoples, the technologically sophisticated weapons of liberal war making (including hers) are figured as uniquely capable of distinguishing between innocent civilians and terrorist targets in order to free the former from the tyranny of the latter. Chow notes: "Rather than straightforwardly assuming the form of a callous willingness to kill, therefore, racist genocide partakes of the organization, calculation, control, and surveillance characteristic of power—in other words, of all the 'civil' or 'civilized' procedures that are in place primarily to ensure the continuation of life."[151] In the collection and production of data, details, and descriptions, Nguyet's "lab in a box"[152] renders populations as knowable and measurable objects, converting and dividing these bodies into actionable categories for life and death. Especially because it *is* a preemptive rather than repressive measure, such data mining is conceived of as a "positive" process, though these technical systems depend upon the compliance of whole populations to knowledge's field of control and power's regime of intervention. Biopolitics and sovereign power become indistinguishable here as mechanisms for regulating collectives, as information and bodies merge seamlessly with strategies of war and more "rational" destruction.

In other words, and in addition to her successes in developing more-devastating weaponry, Nguyet also labors to generate those technologies of biopolitical knowledge that give rise to new calculative processes of improved discrimination, and more efficient extermination. Moreover, she does so in order for the diminution of "mistakes" that might otherwise traumatize "our" soldiers who do so much good in her name. (At the same time Nguyet, in response to the question of her creation's consequences, deflects: "I'm not on the operation side. We don't deal with human fatality."[153]) We discern much about the discursive construction of liberal empire and warcraft here, in which massive death in Viet Nam or Afghanistan or Iraq as a consequence of neoliberal war making is deemed a failure of a specific policy, or an unconnected succession of unfortunate, though foreseeable, accidents (a rational calculation about the value of another's life also known as collateral damage), and a liberal empire that acts murderously nonetheless evades indictment for doing so. Or, as we know from the last chapter, such an empire may yet be redeemed from such terrible "error." Here we see that liberal schema deem atrocities as natural and inherent to undemocratic regimes, impaired by perverted modernizations, failed states, or antimodern fundamentalisms, and thereby discerned as the others of liberalism. Or as A. Dirk Moses observes, "liberal theories of genocide are really theories of totalitarianism," which means that liberal states—or empires—preclude themselves from being perceived as genocidal because of their biopolitical commitment to life.[154] Furthermore, neoliberal war emphasizes the gap between full destructive capacity and actual destruction to preserve the illusion of both precision and restraint—and also retain the option of escalation, if "necessary." In this way, the neoliberalization of race war does not herald less violence, but even more violence—it is just conceived as "better" violence, normalized, accepted, legitimate violence. When liberal empire commits murder, then, it is an oversight, an accident, or a calculation. In each case, exception is normalized as part of the *cost* of the continuous government of human freedom. (Of course, critical scholars intervene here to observe that genocidal impulses, especially those that inform settler colonialisms, are in fact the currency of liberalism, and modernization.[155] As Stoler comments, "Racism was intrinsic to the nature of all modern, normalizing states and their biopolitical technologies."[156]) At the second fault line, then, as Foucault warns, a liberal way of war exists for the sake of race: the human race. Wars are now "waged on behalf of the existence of everyone; entire populations are mobilized for the purpose of wholesale slaughter in the name of life necessity."[157]

It is perhaps obvious to say that life necessity is decisively wrought through concepts of gender and sexuality, which permeate the time consciousness of anticipatory futures.[158] For instance, heritage as the reproduction of a people is both a racial moral imperative and a heterosexual one. As Lee Edelman so memorably observes, the demands of what he calls a "reproductive futurism" are very frequently murderous even while sentimentalized as the *preemptive* protection of the child.[159] In this regard, it is absolutely no small thing that Nguyet is "hardly a weaponized woman."[160] That is, she is no unnatural creature. She is described as a devoted mother, though her teenage daughter is disgusted by her use of frosted-pink nail polish. She is endearingly clumsy; her nickname in Vietnamese means "klutz." She explains the bomb-making process via domestic metaphors of life-giving sustenance: "It's like baking a cake," she says. "You start with the liquids. Add the solids."[161] (She continues, noting that after a long day mixing and casting thermobaric ingredients, she goes home and prepares dinner—"but no brownies or cakes," because she has already been baking.) In her home, she enforces a ban on toy weapons and censors her children's Disney films: "Our *Pocahontas* movie had all the fight scenes cut out," her daughter shares.[162]

This move to comprehend the activity of bomb making persistently *in the interior of a biologized imperative*—which hinges upon a notion that the United States in particular is the scene for progressive, but also natural, gender and sexual norms—suggests yet again that war is not simply the destruction of a political adversary, or an enemy race, but the regeneration of one's own race (a regeneration we might call, after the flag resolutions, "heritage and freedom").[163] A seemingly unambiguous feminine nature arouses feelings of protection and preemption in the name of an absolute, non-negotiable value—her children, our future—and thereby fuses national security to personal security in a continuous series of appropriations. We are invited, in these profiles, to consider that Nguyet might even be excessively pacific. Thus is her weapons development made analogous with her excision of the "harmful" scenes of childhood, a comparison that is then to be read with indulgence, betraying only a forgivably obsessive maternal love. As Grewal notes in her portrait of the security mom, such articulations of motherhood can and do merge with, and are enhanced by, new military technologies of surveillance and security.[164] With the work of security governmentalized through the function of the mother, and the presence of danger drawing together "space and territory in an assemblage in which gender, race, and nation become integrated," the expansion of both (that is, of security and danger) relegates her weapons work as a public duty continuous with the more ordinary security she pursues in her private life.[165] Thus Nguyet's commitments as the Pentagon's "bomb lady" are coupled with the exercise of her maternal duties, banning Harry Potter and video games (both deemed too violent) from the sphere of her domestic rule. In this regard she is the penultimate security mom—not only because, as a refugee patriot, she is especially cognizant of security as a historical necessity for freedom (that is, the legitimacy of state violence), but also because, as a mother, she engages in continuous surveillance and removal of dangers *present or possible everywhere* (the children's book, the stranger to our shores) as a way of caring for a precious future. The forms of racial death that this mother pursues are thereby obscured by seemingly natural and transparent feelings, through which maternal protection slips into militaristic preemption. Family and nation, home and homeland, as Grewal observes, are made coextensive.[166] (As one of Nguyet's colleagues, a fuse specialist on Nguyet's team, tells her four year old, "Mommy is making a bomb for Osama bin Laden."[167]) In this formula for race war, the other's death is the necessary conversion of the will to live into action—and all horror evacuated as unimportant, negligible. Nguyet protects her innocent children—and America's innocent children—from any exposure to potential violence, a continuum that describes and substitutes fictional magic duels and terrorist attacks.

For the architect of new patriot acts and the designer of more lethal bombs, the gift of freedom and its debt are one and the same. For an empire of humanity that targets a racial enemy to ensure life, the refugee patriot is liberalism's alibi for this global war. In other words, he or she performs the epistemological and ontological coordinates of the gift of freedom as subjection *and* subjectivization and also enacts the literally vital distinction between those who love freedoms and those who are imagined to despise them. This distinction is made global in absolute terms, such that the refugee patriot who might incarnate the knowledges and powers that map universal want and imperfect presence also illumines freedom as never anything more than the actual relation of an exchange between governors and governed, in which multiculturalism revitalizes sovereign power, ordinary life unfolds into war, and peace renews violence. Hence, this refugee is a limit figure of the condition of exteriority and yet enters signification (the realm of human contract and intercourse) into an existing interior of a liberal empire, through refuge, hospitality, and war—that is, the gift of freedom—as a useful remainder of a racial, colonial other, and a haunted future.

Refugee Returns

Power can be invisible, it can be fantastic, it can be dull and routine. It can be obvious, it can reach you by the baton of the police, it can speak the language of your thoughts and desires. It can feel like remote control, it can exhilarate like liberation, it can travel through time, and it can drown you in the present. It is dense and superficial, it can cause you bodily injury, and it can harm you without seeming ever to touch you. It is systematic and it is particularistic and it is often both at the same time. It causes dreams to live and dreams to die.

— AVERY GORDON, *Ghostly Matters*

It is imperative that we always look for the "something more" in order to see and bring into being what is usually neglected or made invisible or thought by most to be dead and gone — that is, to always see the living effects of what seems to be over and done with. We need to see, and then to do something with, the "endings that are not over."

— YEN LE ESPIRITU, "The Endings That Are Not Over"

Throughout this book, I have pursued a partial account, assembled from fragments of evidence, of the conditions that permit a particular discourse or discipline to arise and order worlds, that give the gift of freedom a particular form and force for the simultaneous making of hope and despair, law and exception, life and death. Indeed, it has necessarily been a partial account because a certain limitlessness is implicated in the gift of freedom, a character vested less in what it gives than in what passes in the act of giving: its diffuse effects and direct forces, coercion, discipline, and normalization, running throughout an ever-expanding social body—in short, the intensification of imperial powers. To understand the gift of freedom, then, is to heed the warring nature of the phrase—not just its seemingly paradoxical, aporetic, and impossible nature, but also the powers it authorizes through these paradoxes, aporias, and impossibilities in the name of historical necessity. Each chapter considered a troublesome story (or stories) of the refugee's passage as a movement from subjection to subjectivity through their simultaneity instead. The first chapter explored this simultaneity at a historical moment that brings forth the refugee from disciplinary power and biopolitics, sovereign power and governmentality, brought together as an assemblage of freedom, as a benefaction. Both war and refuge target the subject of freedom—the new friend who becomes the new arrival—through the concatenation of evolutionary and given times, developmental stages and universal humanity, as a temporalizing strategy. The second chapter regarded the photograph of war's atrocity, remembered as the irruption of a narration of freedom, through the archival rescue of the girl pictured there as an object whose story is unfinished, restoring her to subjectivity and thereby to continuous history. Through the affective temporality of her presence in our present, in which her forgiveness is an empire's release from the past, the gift of freedom is renewed, and liberal empire reinstated as a tolerant collectivity. The renewal of this gift was also the focus of the third chapter, which found the expansion of scenes of control and command as a historical necessity for peace. In the name of freedom's empire, the refugee patriot redeems in part the debt of his or her life by securing the future for a common humanity, in giving to others more war, and death. The gift of freedom, moreover, as a neoliberal way of war, annexes "homeland security" on a continuum of police powers and paramilitarization; and the refugee patriot, in lending to empire a living memory of failure, reminds every citizen to be grateful for freedom and realizes the conduct of war as recompense for it. In each of these scenes throughout this book, I have therefore sought to unsnarl an ongoing set of contestations and controversies that attach to the concept of the gift of freedom, and that animate the continuing life of liberal empire.

A trouble of timing besets this book and calls for further reflection on the crucial labor of thinking questions of captivity and freedom, absence and presence, through heterogeneous forms of domination. In "The Intimacies of Four Continents," Lisa Lowe examines a politics of knowledge shaping a historicist unfolding of the interdependencies between continents as the crucible for modern humanism. Fired there, structures of race and coloniality and international (gendered) divisions of labor emerged as

the material and philosophical fundamentals for Europe's colonial regimes and a received genealogy of human sovereignty. In this way, African
slave and Asian labor in the New World, Lowe observes, "were the conditions of possibility for European philosophy to think the universality of
human freedom, however much freedom for colonized peoples was precisely foreclosed within that philosophy."[1] (Reading Lowe, Jodi Byrd urges
us to further consider settler colonialism, and the conquest of the indigenous Americas, as the crucible—and not just the stage—for such named
intimacies.[2]) This script thus stretches back to the political and economic
logics of conquest and forced labor, and reaches forward to freedom's
empire, through which fresh intimacies interpolating new friends, grateful
refugees, forgiving survivors, and loving patriots envisage once again the
world as target. Illumining for us these conjunctions of sorting and saving
"the human," Lowe writes that "the affirmation of the desire for freedom
is so inhabited by the forgetting of its conditions of possibility, that every
narrative articulation of freedom is haunted by its burial, by the violence
of forgetting. What we know as 'race' and 'gender' are the traces of this
modern humanist forgetting. They reside within, and are constitutive of,
the modern narrative of freedom, but are neither fully determined by nor
exhausted by its ends. They are the remainders of the formalism of affirmation and forgetting."[3]

As I have argued throughout this book, another name for these traces is
debt. The wish to be free of history is a cornerstone of liberalism's empire
—especially where history may include indigenous genocide, African enslavement, Vietnamese napalm, and so-called enemy encampment or incarceration—but those who are obliged to accept the gifts of freedom
(sometimes to the point of death) are denied such a relation to the past. In
this regard, whether the gift comes as a blow or a caress, we cannot under-
estimate the import of debt as the conditional recognition of racial, colonial subjectivity. Describing the given time during which the consciousness of the debt, which is also the consciousness of the distance between
giver and recipient that is the rationale for the exchange, must be sustained
for the duration, Derrida notes, "There must be time, it must last, there
must be waiting—without forgetting."[4] And yet, we might conceive of the
debt as an alternate historical understanding, an impure politics of knowledge. "Without forgetting" might instead refer us to a consciousness of
both the blows and the intimacies that secure human freedom at considerable cost to *what could have been*, and its repressive relation to the pres-

ent.[5] Debt is a politics of loss and absence. Significantly, scholars working within the resonance of what is left behind urge that we receive ghosts as the empirical evidence of a dense, dark tangle of horror and history. In Avery Gordon's much-cited meditations, "the ghost or the apparition is one form by which something lost, or barely visible, or seemingly not there to our supposedly well-trained eyes, makes itself known or apparent to us, in its own way, of course."[6] In this way, Grace Cho draws our attention to the chilling transformation of secrets untold turned ghostly, a "transgenerational haunting"; Sharon Holland suggests that we "raise the dead" to bear witness to murderous structures; Bliss Cua Lim attunes us to the supernatural to share time with heterogeneous otherness; and Yen Le Espiritu movingly calls on us to become "tellers of ghost stories," to animate the dead or the living dead of wars and empires.[7] And, writing of such a politics, David Eng and David Kazanjian propose that our queries "investigate the political, economic and cultural dimensions of how loss is apprehended and history is named—how that apprehension and naming produce the phenomenon of 'what remains.'"[8]

Debt is all these things—a revenant, a ruin, a reminder of what has been lost—but debt is also a politics of what is given in its place. To be indebted is to continue to live after war and dispossession, but with these things not having ended. Indeed, the future is wrought through these events, these powers; the gift of freedom produces rule in a continuous and permanent way because it extends out along the horizon endlessly. The premise that we who are subjects of freedom are in a moment that must be lived through, that we must undergo a dangerous passage at the end of which we find freedom, is therefore fundamentally flawed. It is in this manner that the gift of freedom, as Lauren Berlant might observe, innovates an art of government through which political optimism and a dream of plentitude perceives the details of imperial failure as evidence of freedom said to be imminent in its form.[9] Or we might call for one last time on Jacques Derrida (riffing here on Walter Benjamin), who writes of our contemporary wars that the promised "democracy to come" will never be present in the present, will never come, is always to come.[10] A politics of debt thus might illumine the failure of the one who gives to give what is promised, having given instead damage and deficit but also the desires for those things we want, we cannot but want, we cannot want (to conjure Spivak here)—desires that cause more harm in the present.

In these closing notes, I am fumbling toward a politics that does not presume to know in advance the shape of freedom from what is given, that does not prescribe another narrative of freedom as relation or a property just beyond the horizon. What I have gestured toward in this book belongs to a hope of descrying the past not in terms of objects that are lost and can be found, or as separate from the time of the modern observer, but in and against the durational claim of debt—a claim that requires not thanksgiving or repayment according to unendurable equivalences and values, but a profoundly plural relation with and recognition of the received genealogies of the human that made us and—perhaps more precisely—our scars. That is, debt might structure a call to understand what remains, to sharpen our understanding of a history of the present through the continuing presence of what forces remain but are hard to call *force*, and what is emergent even long after the war that can be called the *afterlife of the gift of freedom.* Duration and deferral as the temporal forms that debt induces may then be crucial to the cognizance that only impossible futures rest within the horizon of liberal humanism and modernity's now. Or, as Fiona Ngô offers, "failure need not be overcome, rehabilitation need not be desired, subjectivity need not be recovered." Rather, "we must conceive of an ethical stance that refuses to cover over the violence that brought us to the present."[11] In this way, the trace that we might call debt animates a crucial analytic of freedom as a relation and a property, and revivifies the sundry ways its unended histories continue to cross us. How do people live with debt? How does debt disturb our sense of history or inform our critique? Indeed, can debt construe instead a conception of time that keeps the past and the future open to us? To begin to answer, let me now turn to one such refugee return.

Explosions in the Sky is one part of a multichannel video series and installation by the visual artist Hong-An Truong called *Adaptation Fever* (2006–7), which draws on found footage from the French colonial chapter in Viet Nam to unearth a history that has been partially buried by time, and shadowed by the portentous encounter with U.S. empire. This three-minute, black-and-white video features archival film of exploding ordnance belonging to the French forces at Dien Bien Phu in 1954. These moving images appear to us as a sequence of strobing flashes, illumining a nighttime sky. A particularly keen observer might glimpse the shape of a cannon, or a tree's canopy, in the afterimage. But the viewer does not hear the thunderous boom of "explosions in the sky." These bursts are edited to coincide with the synthesized beat of a bilingual (Vietnamese and English)

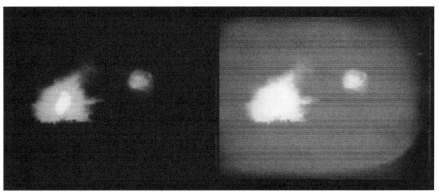

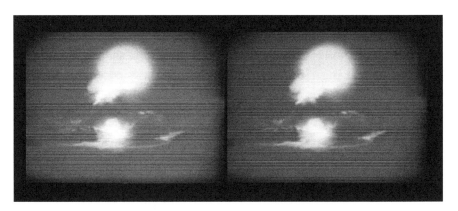

1–3. Stills from Hong-An Truong, *Explosions in the Sky* (2006).
Courtesy of the artist.

cover of the 1964 Paul Simon song "The Sound of Silence." Speeding up and slowing down the succession of blasts over these three minutes, *Explosions in the Sky* then ends in darkness ("my old friend") and captions seeming to mark the passage of time ("Dien Bien Phu 1954" and "Hong-An Truong 2006"). We might well consider this uncanny collocation a scene of imperial remains.

Truong's art practice is full of ambiguous doubles and parallel histories. Asking of her viewers a temporally nuanced consideration of production, circulation, and reception, Truong's usage of archival materials insists on the survival of the past, but in no clear, transparent fashion or direction. In this respect, her practice accentuates for us a process of selection if there is to be anything like a specific intervention into a specific economy—for history, memory. The fragmentation of time in *Explosions in the Sky* allows the viewer to reengage the narrativization of this past and its relevance, and to question how we assemble an archive, a history of an object and the peoples and places from which the object is understood to emanate. The video's coupling of image and sound is especially provocative. Editing, as a practice of establishing human actions and passions in time and space, is always a discourse about things but also *about something*—about those things as examples of a linkage between the object at hand (a reel of footage, a cover song) and a principle under review. The video thus enacts what Patricia Clough called a critical discourse that is no "mere interdisciplinarity," but a matter of "the timing and intensities of form" that move us beyond a historical, narrative account of the transition between regimes to a genealogical apperception of the forces crisscrossing them.[12] In this regard, *Explosions in the Sky* is a fractured archive, consigning filmed footage of French artillery alongside a bilingual cover of an American anthem in an unfolding of tactile and intangible powers of empire.

Inasmuch as the gift of freedom supposes a historical turn, *Explosions in the Sky* narrates coeval temporalities through which we might observe that French coloniality and American friendship are continuous and discontinuous at once. Truong's video disrupts the chronology of world-historical, homogeneous time and its central feature of progress to bind colonial violence and liberal promise together to the Enlightenment project of human consciousness. No evolutionary arc here. The coupling of found footage and cover song both distinguishes the claims of difference between these scenes of power and *also undermines them*. Remembered as a decisive battle in the comprehensive defeat of a colonial power, "Dien Bien Phu 1954"

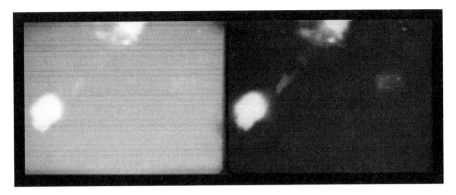

4. Still from Hong-An Truong, *Explosions in the Sky* (2006).
Courtesy of the artist.

is the image event that denotes the periodization of forms of Vietnamese
sovereignty and foreign intercession. Exploding ordnance conveys to the
viewer a conventional image of ruinous subjection, and yet in its reference
here to "Dien Bien Phu 1954," comes to light—though only briefly, as a flash
of danger, we might say (after Walter Benjamin)—as an ineffectual class of
action for establishing supremacy.

But the song cites another time, another space, in the imagination. The
American singer and songwriter Paul Simon penned "The Sound of Silence" in the aftermath of the November 22, 1963, assassination of President John F. Kennedy. Originally performed by Simon and Art Garfunkel,
"The Sound of Silence" registers a moment in which the ascendancy of
freedom's empire is interrupted—by the death of a president and a mythical Camelot, the confrontation with a century's worth of Jim Crow, the
mounting body counts of dead and injured American soldiers and Vietnamese people. The song lyrics refer to absence and alienation, suppression and frustrated connection: "People talking without speaking, people
hearing with listening, people writing songs that voices never share, and
no one dare disturb the sound of silence." No more a utopia, the United
States mourns itself. And, because of this affective dynamic, "The Sound
of Silence" also belongs to the antiwar repertoire, something of an irony
inasmuch as the song commemorates the actual but also symbolic death
of Kennedy's vision of the world. "The Sound of Silence" thereby keens the
error of a course of action too far gone to correct, the ache of impossibly
faraway futures.[13]

The uncredited cover Truong uses, alternating verses in English and Vietnamese, carries the lyrics' affective intensity into the fullness of their historical resonance in multiple ways. We might consider the "fact" of this cover as the power of American popular music as an envoy to the rest of the world, and rock 'n' roll especially with its investments in autonomous individuality as the modern sound of human freedom. In *Explosions in the Sky*, the song might function as a metonym, and a substitute, for U.S. empire. But "The Sound of Silence," as an exemplary expression of modernity's malaise, promises nothing certain about the future that might follow. Progress, it suggests, may be indistinct from paralysis. And in the video's collocations, we are moreover made aware that "The Sound of Silence" stands for another principle that operates in the name of freedom —that is, war—and which the cover invests with a particular presence as a copy. While it might be possible to perceive the cover as evidence of a historical seduction in which the copy, the new friend, follows the original after an interlude, it does not foreclose the plausible contemporaneity through which the Vietnamese cover expresses suspicion of the future promised by liberal war. Indeed, the Vietnamese lyrics that follow the first stanza are not a direct translation. Instead, these words speak to a communion between peoples, dedicating poems of love and hope to one other, even as the night sky closes overhead and the sound of rain—or perhaps bombs—rings out like a tambourine.[14] And in its pairing with the found footage of artillery fire, labeled "Dien Bien Phu 1954," the English lyric "when my eyes were stabbed by the flash of a neon light that split the night" is especially devastating, because the future promised by modernity's forces becomes inseparable from the past. The scene of freedom's giving is shadowed by the sound of silence.

The song and the footage together suggest that the passage of time, and the promise of transition, is powerful and also underwhelming. Everything changes, and nothing changes. In this regard, the viewer's contact with these objects—found footage, cover song—also renders an ephemeral and intimate experience with timeliness, or that which is inimitable: life. From this vantage point, both image and sound are retroactively charged with meanings that "cover," in the word's multiple senses of masking, but also investigating, and *repeating*, an assemblage of perceptions and fantasies about the past. The archive, the cover song: each entails techniques for ensuring something's continued presence, such as its museumizing, its mythologizing, or its miming—what we might understand as formal as well as social contracts to repeat and return to the event or the feeling (both like and unlike debt). In her interdisciplinarities and intensities, Truong's alterations of the viewer's experiences with war times stem from the force of singularity, war as a *unique* thing that is also an allegory, and a formula for seriality, war as an *enduring* thing that is also an allegory. That the French-Indochine colonial war cannot be considered in isolation from other wars that followed demands attention to forms of empire that do not stem from an exception but from precisely its seriality.

This video therefore disrupts our consumption of time, conceived multiply as periodicity, as history, as process, as duration, and as repetition. Truong furthermore conjures for us a troubled transition not between coloniality and liberal empire, but between the ghosts of these wars and their materialization before us, felt (rather than seen) here through hearing, memory, history, duration. There are no people pictured, but bodies do populate this video as implied by these objects' exchange. Someone shoots, and someone else dies, though there is no record of the dead. Someone calls out, and someone else listens—in this instance, that someone else is "Hong-An Truong 2006," who then draws the contemporaneous viewer into an intimacy between continents, to return to this past in our present. (To recall Foucault once again, "the body is the inscribed surface of events. . . . Genealogy as an analysis of descent is thus situated within the articulation of the body and history. Its task is to expose a body totally imprinted by history and the process of history's destruction of the body."[15]) Inasmuch as *Explosions in the Sky* proposes that we consider again the distance between these two times, in its drawing us closer we find that these sounds of silence, these flashes of danger, are still with us, and that we who are indebted are caught in a loop, in a cover, in a repetition, in new wars. This is a rich and resonant allegorical palimpsest through which the viewer is made to contemplate his or her connection to a social history in which the film's missing bodies are rendered meaningful in the present, and the near future—we who are life after death, future life, and future death.

As a process that does not have as its end completion, but instead continually stages postponement or deferral, the gift of freedom is a thing, force, gaze, and event that refers both to the wars that promised it and those that must follow after. In this spirit, because there is as yet no end to empire, mine is an argument that we do not forget the debt that demands of us that we remember. But in remembering, we need not for a moment consider accepting the debt in the received currency of the human, or the terms of historicism. Instead, an alternate attachment to debt troubles those received histories of anachronism and distance that are its conditions of possibility and impossibility. Against the commodity logic of race, gender, or property, can we think of debt as producing another economy of intense contact with all the multiple, heterogeneous, not-same strangers that goes into the making and remaking of the boundaries of an exclusionary collectivity of humanity? How might this conception of debt challenge those modes of knowing the past as wholly other, as assimilable into a continuous history of the present, or as the place to which freedom must come from an other, and where we are bound to wait for? Can this debt vanquish the threat of a predestined time that closes, rather than opens, before us? Clearly we cannot acquit the debt (indeed, we cannot but default),[16] but, moreover, we can refuse to be circumscribed by the horizons of significance or obligation brought to bear on us. We might insist on the untranslatability of what is owed for the shape of our lives (and others' deaths), and bespeak the disjunctures of those existential hopes to which liberal self-possession or world-historical time pledge human becoming, while acknowledging that so many of our struggles are waged through these very hopes. Debt points toward a different social order, keeping us in contact with alternate collectivities of others who bear the trace of human freedom that falls apart, or seizes hold, in its giving. Put another way, we may join an audience of all those who have heard this song of freedom and empire before, and therein lie other passages to an unknowable future.

NOTES

Preface

1. Obama, "Remarks by the President in Address to the Nation on the End of Combat Operations in Iraq."

2. Butler, *Frames of War*.

3. Karen DeYoung and Greg Jaffe, "U.S. 'Secret War' Expands Globally as Special Operations Forces Take Larger Role," *Washington Post*, June 4, 2010. For further discussion of these special operations forces, see the May 2011 PBS/*Frontline* special "Kill/Capture," and the official summary by Gretchen Gavett, "What Is the Secretive U.S. 'Kill/Capture' Campaign?" (http://www.pbs .org/wgbh/pages/frontline/kill-capture/what-is-kill-capture/).

4. The concept of the "zone of indistinction" is examined at length in Agamben, *Homo Sacer*. We might also observe that in the Obama administration, such "secret wars" and aggressive policing actions—including deportations of undocumented people—are rapidly increasing, not decreasing, from numbers posted by the previous Bush administration.

5. Said, *Orientalism*, xxi.

6. As Obama declared in his August 31, 2010, speech, "Throughout our history, America has been willing to bear the burden of promoting liberty and human dignity overseas, understanding its links to our own liberty and security" ("Remarks by the President in Address to the Nation on the End of Combat Operations in Iraq").

7. United Nations High Commission on Refugees, "UNHCR Global Report 2010" (http://www.unhcr.org/gr10/index.html#/home). Today's refugees include 4.7 million people fleeing wars—namely, the wars now being waged by the United States—and almost 5 million Palestinians.

Introduction

1. I enclose "America" in quotes in order to signal, first, that this shorthand for the United States elides the contiguous Americas, including Central and South Americas, and, second, that I hereafter mean "America" as the epistemological and ideological terrain for such erasure and U.S. exceptionalism.

2. San Chu Lim, "Vietnamese Woman Thanks America with Parade Float," *Asianweek*, January 16, 2002, 13.

3. Dan Whitcomb, "U.S. Woman Sells Home for Parade Float," *Reuters*, December 28, 2001 (http://uk.news.yahoo.com/011228/80/cmofs.html).

4. Daisy Nguyen, "Vietnamese Refugee Sells Home to Buy Rose Parade Float as Thank-You Gift to Nation," *Associated Press*, December 29, 2001.

5. Quoted in Boyd, *The Papers of Thomas Jefferson*, Vol. 1, 237–38.

6. Chomsky regularly denounced the "good impulses" of liberal empire during the course of the war in Southeast Asia, observing in an interview: "When precisely did the United States try to help the South Vietnamese choose their own form of government and social order? As soon as such questions are posed, the absurdity becomes evident. From the moment that the American-backed French effort to destroy the major nationalist movement in Vietnam collapsed, the United States was consciously and knowingly opposed to the organized political forces within South Vietnam, and resorted to increasing violence when these political forces could not be crushed. . . . The liberal press cannot question the basic doctrine that the United States is benevolent, even though often misguided in its innocence, that it labors to permit free choice, even though at times some mistakes are committed in the exuberance of its programs of international goodwill" (Chomsky and Foucault, *The Chomsky-Foucault Debate*, 112–13).

7. For an extensive examination of the liberal way of war, see Dillon and Reid, *The Liberal Way of War*. As a contemporary example of the denunciation of the gift of freedom in its multiple permutations, Vijay Prashad observes that humanitarian intervention is "the window dressing that imperialism needs to counter our wider ideas and aspirations for democracy" ("Conversations Up-town"). Other speakers at this fundraising panel for Critical Resistance and the Brecht Forum included Angela Davis, Ruth Wilson Gilmore, and Laura Flanders.

8. Stoler and Bond, "Refractions off Empire," 95.

9. Williams, *Marxism and Literature*.

10. For studies of some of these forms and logics of liberal empire, see Ahmed, "The Politics of Bad Feeling"; Povinelli, *The Empire of Love*; Stoler, "Imperial Debris;" Stoler and Bond, "Refractions off Empire."

11. See Chow, *The Age of the World Target*.

12. Katherine Nguyen, "Vietnamese Celebrate Their First Roses Parade Float: Tears and Cheers Greet the Tribute to Immigrant Heritage, Eight Years in the Making," *Orange County Register*, January 2, 2002.

13. Amy Kaplan writes: "The denial and disavowal of empire has long served as the ideological cornerstone of U.S. imperialism and a key component of American exceptionalism" ("Violent Belongings and the Question of Empire Today," 3).

14. Here I use *imperial formations* in much the way that Stoler describes them as "relations of force." For Stoler, these formations "harbor political forms that endure beyond the formal exclusions that legislate against equal opportunity, commensurate dignities, and equal rights. In working with the concept of imperial formation rather than empire, the emphasis shifts from fixed forms of sovereignty and its denials, to gradated forms of sovereignty and what has long marked the technologies of imperial rule–sliding and contested scales of differential rights" ("Imperial Debris," 193).

15. Foucault, *The Birth of Biopolitics*, 63.

16. Derrida, *Specters of Marx*, 89.

17. Foucault, "What Is Enlightenment?," 47–48.

18. A bibliography of the gift would be enormous, including anthropological, philosophical, theological, and sociological inquiry. Some key works include, Mauss, *The Gift*; Bataille, *The Accursed Share*; and Strathern, *The Gender of the Gift*.

19. Derrida, *Given Time*, 12.

20. Derrida writes: "The simple consciousness of the gift right away sends itself back the gratifying image of goodness or generosity, of the giving-being who, knowing itself to be such, recognizes itself in a circular, specular fashion, in a sort of auto-recognition, self-approval, and narcissistic gratitude" (*Given Time*, 23).

21. Ibid., 12.

22. Ibid., 147.

23. Butler, "Subjection, Resistance, Resignification," 230.

24. Derrida, *Given Time*, 41.

25. Hegel, *Hegel's Philosophy of Mind*, 239.

26. Kant, *Critique of Practical Reason*, 3; Nancy, *The Experience of Freedom*, 96.

27. Foucault, *The Birth of Biopolitics*, 63.

28. Ibid., 65.

29. Ibid., 63.

30. Ibid.

31. Here I am reminded of Gayatri Spivak's insight: "Sometimes it seems as if the very brilliance of Foucault's analysis of the centuries of European imperialism produces a miniature version of that heterogeneous phenomenon: management of space—but by doctors; developments of administration—but in asylums; considerations of the periphery—but in terms of insane, prisoners and children. The clinic, the asylum, the prison, the university—all seem to be screen allegories that foreclose a reading of the broader narratives of imperialism" (*A Critique of Postcolonial Reason*, 279).

32. Lowe, "The Intimacies of Four Continents," 200.

33. Reddy, *Freedom with Violence*, 220.

34. Foucault, *Security, Territory, Population*, 121–22.

35. Harry S. Truman, "Inaugural Address," January 20, 1949 (http://www .trumanlibrary.org/calendar/viewpapers.php?pid=1030).

36. Ibid.

37. Saldaña-Portillo, *The Revolutionary Imagination in the Americas and the Age of Development*, 25.

38. Foucault, *History of Sexuality*, 247.

39. Truman, "Inaugural Address" (my italics).

40. For brilliant studies that urge our attention toward the dead, see A. Gordon, *Ghostly Matters*; Holland, *Raising the Dead*; and Derrida, *Specters of Marx*.

41. See D. Silva, *Toward a Global Idea of Race*; Cacho, *Social Death*.

42. Agamben, *Homo Sacer*; Spillers, "Mama's Baby, Papa's Maybe."

43. Derrida, *Memoirs of the Blind*, 30.

44. See, for instance, K. Silva, "AID as Gift."

45. Abu-Lughod, "Do Muslim Women Really Need Saving?"

46. Truman, "Inaugural Address."

47. For instance, see Arendt, *The Human Condition*. For a critique of homogeneous, world-historical time, far beyond my own capacity in this book, see Bliss Cua Lim's brilliant *Translating Time*.

48. McClintock, *Imperial Leather*, 30.

49. Fabian, *Time and the Other*, 31.

50. Lim, *Translating Time*, 14.

51. Fabian cited in Chow, *The Age of the World Target*, 66. The words in brackets are hers.

52. Hartman, *Scenes of Subjection*, 115.

53. Patterson, *Slavery and Social Death*, 241.

54. "There were three kinds of claims that the patron could make on his freedman (in ancient Rome during late republican and imperial times). First, there was the *obsequium*. This basically meant the showing of proper reverence and gratitude to the patron and his kinsmen. . . . The second and more practically significant claim of the patron was the *operae*. This was the obligation of the freedman to work for the patron which 'sprang, not from the status of libertus, but from an oath which the freedman took after manumission.' . . . The third kind of claim the patron had on his freedman was the right to half, and in some cases all, of the freedman's estate on his death" (ibid., 242).

55. Derrida, *Given Time*, 41.

56. In other words, to turn to Marcel Mauss (*The Gift*), this is the twofold obligation of receiving and reciprocating the gift.

57. Lim, *Translating Time*, 12.

58. Ibid., 15.

59. Rey Chow observes in China's release of political dissidents in exchange

for Western trade agreements the commodification of human rights: "It would perhaps be more productive, in light of Foucault's notion of biopower, to view the West and China as collaborative partners in an ongoing series of biopolitical transactions in global late capitalism, transactions whereby human rights, or, more precisely, humans as such, are the commodity par excellence" (*The Protestant Ethnic and the Spirit of Capitalism*, 20).

60. Also noteworthy here is that in the gift exchange, according to Mauss, objects acquire greater moral power, animated with the spirit of the one who gives them, which ensures that the gifts return to their place of origin.

61. Quoted in Bower, *Why America Fights*, 179.

62. Foucault, *The Birth of Biopolitics*, 63.

63. Derrida, *Given Time*, 31.

64. In an essay on *Given Time*, Marcel Hénaff proposes that Derrida's concept of the gift is imprecise, and therefore "the entire reasoning runs the risk of collapsing" ("The Aporia of Pure Giving and the Aim of Reciprocity," 217). Hénaff goes on to distinguish three categories of gift-giving—ceremonial and public, gracious and unilateral (such as between loved ones), and aid pertaining to solidarity with others—which I argue are much less distinct than he imagines, especially in the context of giving freedom to an other.

65. For a brilliant analysis of the rhetorics and pragmatics of modern development in the Americas, see Saldaña-Portillo, *The Revolutionary Imagination in the Americas and the Age of Development*.

66. This is, of course, a reference to Ann Laura Stoler's edited collection, *Haunted by Empire: Geographies of Intimacy in North American History*.

67. The full text of the declaration can be found at the UN site: http://www.un.org/en/documents/udhr/.

68. Contemporary humanitarian interventions refer to so-called weak or failed states. See also, Fassin and Pandolfi, *Contemporary States of Emergency*; Jabri, *War and the Transformation of Global Politics*.

69. Ronald Reagan, "Peace: Restoring the Margin of Safety," August 18, 1980, Veterans of Foreign War Convention, Chicago, Illinois (http://www.reagan.utexas.edu/archives/reference/8.18.80.html).

70. Lê, *Slander*, 33 (my italics).

71. This doubled interpellation informs my decision to circumvent Agamben's conception of the refugee as the present-day exemplar of "bare life."

72. The "West" that rescues "the rest" might come to encompass those who themselves were once rescued, as befitting the gift of freedom. The Vietnamese American nonprofit organization Boat People SOS, formed in 1980 in San Diego, California, conducted joint missions with international organizations every spring for ten years, rescuing over three thousand Vietnamese boat people adrift in the South China Sea. In a 1986 fundraising video, titled "Rescue Mission in South China Sea," the viewer follows rescuers as they attempt to

guide wooden fishing boats to larger rescue vessels. Following these efforts, the camera focuses on the faces of children staring into the lens with their "sad, sweet eyes." The actress Kieu Chinh, whose fame as a film star began before and continued after her own refugee flight, offers the following appeal: "They are homeless, they are alone, they are drifting on the high seas with no place in the world." Parts 1, 2, and 3 are available on YouTube: http://www.youtube.com/watch?v=V8pUiZb5ups.

73. An exemplar among California-produced Vietnamese musical variety shows is *Paris by Night*, commemorating the thirtieth anniversary of the exodus with grainy documentary footage of boat people above a stage full of modern dancers in simple, monochromatic peasant costumes enacting the ordeal and the refugees' grief, set to sorrowful orchestral music. Films such as the recently released Vietnamese American *Journey from the Fall* (2007, directed by Ham Tran) and the 2005 *The Forgotten Ones*, a collection of photographs by Brian Doan published by the Southern California–based Vietnamese American Arts and Letters Association, also return to this spectacular scene. *The Forgotten Ones* is a photo project documenting the last boat people, still residing in a squalid camp in Palawan, the Philippines. These photographs are located in the humanist genre of photojournalism—stretching from Jacob Riis and his photographs of nineteenth-century U.S. urban slums, in which European immigrants were crammed into dark and dangerous tenements; Dorothea Lange and her portraits of Americans suffering from the deprivations of the Great Depression and the Dust Bowl as well as the Japanese internment camps (previously withheld from public view lest non–Japanese Americans feel pity for internees); and Sebastian Salgado and his gorgeously composed images of miners engaged in backbreaking labor in the global South —through which the gazes of saviors, both the photographer and the spectator, intersect over the bodies pictured. A reviewer of *The Forgotten Ones* highlighted on the book's website describes the photographs as "creat[ing] elegiac landscapes of individuals who maintain hope despite their bitter lives." Two Pulitzer Prize–winning photojournalists, including Associated Press photographer Huynh Cong "Nick" Ut (whose most famous photograph I discuss in chapter 2), both describe the refugees in the collection, or the images of them, as portrayed "as suspended in time and space." For a fascinating study of Vietnamese American cultural productions that reflect or reject the refugee as "our" temporal other, see Lieu, *The American Dream in Vietnamese*.

74. My project in this book does not necessarily pursue the question of what Avery Gordon calls "complex personhood" (*Ghostly Matters*, 4), and what other scholars of "Vietnamese America" argue is the reduction of the Vietnamese migrant to the tragic refugee, and of Viet Nam to a war. Isabel Pelaud observes in her survey of Vietnamese American literature: "To view Vietnamese American texts only as refugee narratives restricts the full recognition of Vietnamese

American experiences and identities." At the same time, as she next notes, "to view Vietnamese American literature outside the framework of war, in reaction to dominant representations and expectations, is also limiting" (Pelaud, *This Is All I Choose to Tell*, 59). These questions and concerns about "complex personhood" are undeniably important inquiries, but they are not quite the focus here, except where complex personhood figures the subject of freedom.

75. Espiritu, "Toward a Critical Refugee Study."

76. See Claudia Casteñeda's neat summary of "figuration": "To use figuration as a descriptive tool is to unpack the domains of practice and significance that are built into each figure. A figure, from this point of view, is the simultaneously material and semiotic effect of specific practices" (*Figurations*, 3).

77. Agamben, *Homo Sacer*, 134.

78. International, governmental, and juridical narratives; historical and political conditions; and institutional formations intersect to produce and regulate categories of migrants, including the political refugee. It is not in the scope of this book to outline these formations. However, it bears noting that in various ways—including through orientalisms and colonialisms—institutional and ideological discourses and practices gender and racialize groups of refugees to produce categories of need and solicit kinds of affect. Engaging the language of universalism while limiting potential infringement on sovereign states, human rights discourse emerged in the last century as an ideological instrument providing a vehicle for U.S. economic and foreign policy. Presidential administrations from Eisenhower's through Reagan's used the authority to grant asylum as an executive prerogative to strengthen certain foreign policies. Accordingly, the State Department initiated decisions to provide special immigration opportunities to certain populations without strong congressional opposition until the late 1970s, when fears about the impact of Southeast Asian refugees on the American landscape gained popular momentum.

Because the genealogy of Western—and particularly U.S.—human rights discourse is intimately tied to the discourse of anticommunism, its usage has always been ideological. With State Department preference granted to those individuals fleeing what were commonly called communist-totalitarian regimes, the political refugee was considered both to bear witness to and provide evidence of a national cultural fantasy of American benevolence. Over the decades, this special immigrant status was granted to Jews fleeing the Soviet Union, anti-Castro middle-class professionals from Cuba, members of the Hungarian 1957 uprising, and—with amendments to the Immigration Act of 1965 allowing for a greater number of migrants from the Eastern hemisphere, especially those fleeing communism—people from so-called Red China. Successive administrations categorized dissidents and other refugees from communist regimes as "freedom fighters," whether symbolic or literal. Other refugees from other countries were often denied entrance or asylum hearings because they did not advance the U.S. anticommunist agenda. In some instances, these refusals constituted official foreign policies appeasing right-wing authoritarian regimes that the United States counted as allies, or countries the United States had a hand in destabilizing, including El Salvador, Chile, and Haiti. Thus, despite the formal removal of the ideological litmus test for refugee status in 1980, over 90 percent of refugees granted entry into the United States from the 1950s to the present originated in communist states.

Historically, domestic and popular positions toward refugees and their resettlement were often ambivalent or hostile. Western, and particularly American, concerns with the international human rights order focused on the possible contravention of state sovereignty. In the Cold War United States, many conservatives increasingly viewed international human rights agreements and declarations as Trojan horses, within which lurked dangerous political and social forces. During the formative years of the United Nations and the international human rights regime, these conservatives argued that international human rights standards threatened states' rights to endorse and maintain segregation and antimiscegenation laws and certain racial immigration policies, and undermined state and federal sovereignty at the risk of communist interference and influence. Beginning in the late 1970s, domestic discourses (including in Congress) revived these fears in debates about immigration and infiltration, producing the Vietnamese refugee as an alien creature; a dangerous, unknown agent introduced into the national body. As increasing anti-Asian sentiments coincided with a domestic recession and efforts to contain the ascendancy of Asian-Pacific economies, the foreign policies and practices of the Reagan administration regenerated and reinvented Cold War discourses. This administration argued that there is a need for communist containment to ward against the threat of refugees overrunning the American landscape, explicitly alluding to Southeast Asian refugees. In the 1990s, the Clinton administration adopted new policies toward refugees, repatriating Cubans intercepted at sea and reclassifying thousands of Vietnamese migrants in Southeast Asian camps as economic refugees ineligible for asylum. For more on this subject, see Koshy, "From Cold War to Trade War"; Loescher and Scanlan, *Calculated Kindness*; Buff, *Immigration and the Political Economy of Home*; A. Ong, *Buddha Is Hiding*.

79. Ngô, "Sense and Subjectivity," 97.

80. Debates in the last two decades about the analytical traction of concepts such as *diaspora* and *transnationality* for ethnic studies—especially Asian American studies—are rife with these tensions about the national order of things. See, for instance, Wong, "Denationalization Reconsidered." For works that put pressure on this joint, see Campomanes, "New Formations of Asian American Studies and the Question of U.S. Imperialism"; Chuh and Shimakawa, *Orientations*.

81. Chuh, *Imagine Otherwise*, 151.

82. Lowe, "The Intimacies of Four Continents," 206.

83. See Kaplan and Grewal, "Transnational Feminist Cultural Studies."

84. Timothy Linh Bui and Tony Bui, "Note from the Filmmakers," DVD insert, *Green Dragon*, 2002. I should note that Timothy directed the film, but both brothers are credited for the story.

85. Lyndon B. Johnson, "Remarks at a Dinner Meeting of the Texas Electric Cooperatives, Inc.," May 4, 1965 (http://www.presidency.ucsb.edu/ws/?pid= 26942#axzz1gStwaqYB).

86. I am thinking here of Chuh's argument for a subjectless discourse: "I mean subjectlessness to create a conceptual space to prioritize difference by foregrounding the discursive constructedness of subjectivity. In other words, it points attention to the constraints on the liberatory potential of the achievement of subjectivity, by reminding us that a 'subject' only becomes recognizable and can act by conforming to a certain regulatory matrices. In that sense, a subject is always also an epistemological object" (*Imagine Otherwise*, 9).

87. C. Kaplan, *Questions of Travel*; Ngai, *Ugly Feelings*; Mahmood, *The Politics of Piety*; Chow, *The Age of the World Target*.

88. Arondekar, *For the Record*, 3 (my italics).

89. I first wrote about this event in 1996, not long after it passed, and returned to it continuously over the years; one version is published as M. Nguyen, "Operation Homecoming." This brief paragraph cannot possibly capture all the dimensions of this complicated event, which might also be understood as a rebuke to the Clinton administration's efforts at the time to normalize diplomatic relations with Viet Nam.

90. Indeed, there are innumerable examples of such thanksgiving to the U.S. military apparatus. The black POW flag as well as the U.S. flag often appear alongside the former South Vietnamese flag at commemorations, political rallies, and festivals. Another particularly striking example appears in Lieu, "Assimilation and Ambivalence," 2. Lieu reproduces a still image from *Paris by Night 77*, by Thúy Nga et al. This DVD-event, commemorating the thirty-year anniversary of the "fall" of Saigon, ends with a dedication "To America, Love and Gratitude," in elaborate script and superimposed on a long, perspectival shot of the wall of the Vietnam Veterans Memorial, in Washington, D.C. The wall and the profession of "love and gratitude" to U.S. forces both dead and surviving are discussed at greater length throughout this book.

91. Cacho, *Social Death*.

92. In bringing these scenes together, I also hope to illuminate Derrida's insight that amnesia shadows presence: "The concept of the archive shelters in itself, of course, this memory. . . . But it also shelters itself from this memory which it shelters: which comes down to saying also that it forgets it" (*Archive Fever*, 2).

93. As Arondekar observes so well in her study of sexuality's relationship to the colonial archive, "the break between what it desires and what it otherwise (re)covers renders its promise inevitably incomplete" (*For the Record*, 5).

1. The Refugee Condition

1. Derrida, *Given Time*, 41.

2. Benjamin, "Theses on the Philosophy of History." For a thorough and enlightening study of these temporal strategies, see Lim, *Translating Time*.

3. One article about the 2010 commemoration reports: "Nearly 900 Marines and civilians worked for six days to erect the 958 tents and 140 Quonset huts" (Jeanette Steele, "1975 Vietnamese Camp Relived at Pendleton: Tent City Exhibit Opens Today," *San Diego Union-Tribune*, April 8, 2010 [http://www.signonsandiego.com/news/2010/apr/08/1975-vietnamese-camp-relived-pendleton/]).

4. I refer here to Agent Orange, one of the herbicides and defoliants used by the U.S. military in Viet Nam from 1961 to 1971, destroying an estimated ten million hectares of agricultural land and exposing millions of Vietnamese to the toxin, resulting in nearly a half-million people killed or maimed, and another half-million children born with birth defects.

5. D. Silva, "A Tale of Two Cities," 125.

6. Truman, "Truman Doctrine," March 12, 1947 (http://millercenter.org/president/speeches/detail/3343) (my italics).

7. LaFeber, *America, Russia, and the Cold War, 1945–1992*, 52–53.

8. As an influential member of the Secretary of State George Marshall's policy planning staff, George Kennan, using the pseudonym "X," penned "The Sources of Soviet Conduct," published in July 1947. In this piece, he argued of the "thoughtful" Americans that "their entire security as a nation [is] dependent on their pulling themselves together and accepting the responsibilities of moral and political leadership that history plainly intended them to bear" (Kennan, "The Sources of Soviet Conduct," 582).

9. Lansdale, "On the Importance of the South Vietnamese Experiment," 127.

10. John F. Kennedy, Inaugural Address, January 20, 161 (http://www.americanrhetoric.com/speeches/jfkinaugural.htm).

11. The so-called innocence of the United States also underwrote its colonial dominion in Hawaii and the Philippines. See, for instance, V. González, *Securing Paradise*; Go, "Introduction." Indeed, in 1945, President Franklin Roosevelt made this genealogy clear: "The situation there [in Indochina] is a good deal like the Philippines were in 1898. It took fifty years for us to . . . educate them for self-government" (quoted in Mark Bradley, "Slouching toward Bethlehem," 23). As Oscar Campomanes observes, these imperialist excursions are subject to what he calls a "'historical unconscious' that both sanctions imperial practices within and without the American hemisphere while also claiming

exception to Old World antecedents." Even at those times when U.S. empire is acknowledged, it is also "diluted" with "qualifiers as 'insular' (the empire did not have the territorial stretch of the British or the French), 'sentimental' or 'benevolent' (the drive to imperial power was propelled by compassion for those subjected to tyrannical regimes), and 'ambiguous' or 'hesitant' (a U.S. president in 1898 reportedly sought divine sanction for the annexation of the 'Philippine Islands' and finally claimed that he was given no choice 'but to take them all')" ("New Formations of Asian American Studies and the Question of U.S. Imperialism," 537, 538). Of course, I argue in this book that these qualifiers are not just excuses for empire, but that they substantially inform the intuitive and institutional press of U.S. global hegemony.

12. Indeed, as William Pietz elaborates, the relationship between Cold War and colonial discourses is a continuous one ("The 'Post-Colonialism' of Cold War Discourse").

13. Foucault, *The Birth of Biopolitics*, 63.

14. Said, *Orientalism*, xxi.

15. Foucault, *The History of Sexuality*, 142.

16. Foucault, *The Birth of Biopolitics*, 63.

17. See, for instance, Koshy, "From Cold War to Trade War."

18. Jabri, *War and the Transformation of Global Politics*, 72.

19. Ibid., 73.

20. UN General Assembly, "The Universal Declaration of Human Rights," 1948 (http://www.un.org/en/documents/udhr/index.shtml) (my italics).

21. It bears noting that the domino theory is also an inheritance from the French empire, which borrowed a bowling metaphor—"ten pin"—to name the worry that any one part of empire that might escape its grasp would catastrophically overturn its control elsewhere. See McCormick, *America's Half-Century*, 149.

22. Jodi Kim unpacks the document's contents for its orientalist and Manichaean implications in the chapter called "Cold War Logics, Cold War Poetics," in her *Ends of Empire*, 37–62.

23. United States National Security Council, "NSC 68," 27.

24. J. Kim, *Ends of Empire*, 55.

25. Chakrabarty, *Provincializing Europe*, 7.

26. Ibid., 8.

27. Gupta, "Imagining Nations," 275.

28. Bourdieu, *Outline for a Theory of Practice*, 7.

29. D. Silva, "A Tale of Two Cities," 122.

30. United States Department of State, "Statement of U.S. Policy toward Indochina, 1948," 75.

31. Ibid., 125.

32. United States National Security Council, "NSC 68," 35.

33. National Security Council, "The Position of the United States with Respect to Asia," 240, 248, 228. Again, see J. Kim for a thorough reading of the document's orientalisms (*Ends of Empire*, 37–62).

34. Claudia Castañeda sees childhood's useful metaphorical transposition as twofold: "As the infant biography suggests, the Now of the primitive was not only placed in the time of childhood, but also in the child-body: the child was seen as a bodily theater where human history could be observed to unfold in the compressed time-span of individual development" (*Figurations*, 13). See also Steedman, *Strange Dislocations*.

35. John F. Kennedy, "America's Stake in Vietnam," August 1, 1956 (http://www.jfklibrary.org/Asset-Viewer/Archives/JFKPOF-135–015.aspx).

36. Mbembe, "Necropolitics," 24.

37. John F. Kennedy, Inaugural Address, January 20, 161 (http://www.americanrhetoric.com/speeches/jfkinaugural.htm).

38. Stoler, "Imperial Debris," 193.

39. UN General Assembly, "The Universal Declaration of Human Rights."

40. Or, as Jodi Kim observes, "it is to mark the Cold War of the second half of the twentieth century as an imperial governmentality whose dominant logics have operated (and continue to do so) through a flexible combination of nonterritorial imperial tactics that include military intervention or occupation, war, treaties, mutual security agreements, covert CIA operations, trade barriers and agreements, economic support or aid, humanitarian aid, and the work of international organizations such as the United Nations and the World Trade Organization, as well as World Bank and International Monetary Fund 'structural adjustment policies' and loans" (*Ends of Empire*, 18).

41. United States Department of State, "Statement of U.S. Policy toward Indochina, 1948," 75.

42. Foucault, *Security, Territory, Population*, 96.

43. Andrew Hammond observes: "The 'Cold War' is an erroneous term for a global conflict which, spanning several continents and a multitude of coups, civil wars, insurgencies and interventions, was characterized by ongoing armed aggression. . . . For a Western population, certainly, the military confrontations may have appeared distant phenomena. . . . Globally, however, the Western experience is a clear exception to the norm. In all, the Soviet sponsoring of left-wing regimes and the U.S. roll-back of communism resulted in over a hundred wars through the Third World and a body count of over 20 million. In Asia alone, some 11 million died fighting in Korea, Laos, Cambodia, and Vietnam" ("From Rhetoric to Rollback," 1). This is the founding premise of Jodi Kim's *Ends of Empire*, a brilliant account of its terrible consequences through an Asian American critique.

44. United States National Security Council. "NSC 68," 50.

45. It bears noting that this tactic was also deployed by the British colonial authorities in Malaya for the pacification of the rural populations.

46. Mbembe, "Necropolitics," 26.

47. Butler, *Precarious Life*, 52.

48. *The Pentagon Papers*, 2:150.

49. For a brilliant study of orientation, see Ahmed, *Queer Phenomenology*.

50. Jabri, *War and the Transformation of Global Politics*, 72.

51. In his study of Ngo Dinh Diem, the historian Seth Jacobs remarks of the American political establishment: "Frequently, they justified U.S. support of Diem's regime on the grounds that the South Vietnamese were different from other Asians, then, often within the same breath, excused Diem's trampling of civil liberties as being necessary throughout 'the Orient'" (*America's Miracle Man in Vietnam*, 14).

52. Ibid., 15.

53. H. Bhabha, *The Location of Culture*, 86.

54. "John F. Kennedy Criticizes the South Vietnamese Government, 1963," 169.

55. Richard Nixon, Address to the Nation on the War in Vietnam, November 3, 1969 (my italics) (http://watergate.info/nixon/silent-majority-speech-1969 .shtml). For more on Vietnamization, see Kimball, "The Nixon Doctrine."

56. Nixon, address to the nation on the war in Vietnam (my italics).

57. I am reminded here of Long Bui's work: "In trying to theorize this historic term Vietnamization and extend into the current moment to speak about South Vietnamese now, I employ it differently than Nixon by speaking to the never-fulfilled desires and belated struggles of former colonized groups to become 'free' modern subjects on their own terms, and their 'arrested' ability to achieve political freedom—a disability often seen as owing to their cultural 'difference' and deficiencies rather than the structures of colonialism, racism and violence" ("Suspended Futures," 7–8).

58. "Deliverance," *Washington Post*, April 30, 1975 (my italics).

59. VanDeMark, "To Avoid a Defeat," 238–39.

60. Marie Therese, "O'Reilly-Bush Interview: Transcript; Part One," News Hounds, September 28, 2004 (http://www.newshounds.us/2004/09/28/oreilly bush_interview_transcript_part_one.php).

61. The wars in Southeast Asia continue to be surmised through asymmetry, between the United States and the former South Vietnamese republic. Controversies about the historical significance of South Vietnamese and other Southeast Asian refugee soldiers, to borrow a term from Ma Vang, erupt into renewed disputes about the "fitness" of the Southeast Asian forces to stand with U.S. forces ("The Refugee Soldier"). That they would literally be standing together in numerous proposals to erect statues commemorating South Viet-

namese veterans in American veterans' memorial, as well as the debt owed to benefactors becomes more complicated. In Kansas City, for instance, a proposed plaque from Vietnamese petitioners would read, in part, "we would like to express our profound gratitude for those who fought along our side, and to the American people who have embraced us with wide open arms and provided us with new opportunities." Furthermore, the plaque would show "an American service member, in bronze, his arm resting protectively around the shoulder of a [kneeling] South Vietnamese comrade—an appreciation, they [the petitioners] said, of the Americans' alliance in a war that shaped their lives" (Monica Davey, "In Kansas, Proposed Monument to a Wartime Friendship Tests the Bond," *New York Times*, August 3, 2009). In response, the Kansas Veterans Action Committee released a statement to reiterate that the American presence in Viet Nam was an *American* sacrifice: "OUR MISSION is to preserve, honor and protect our Veterans Memorial Park for memorials that honor men and women who have served in the United States Armed Forces. America owes no debt of gratitude to the South Vietnamese Army. And while, philosophically, we can appreciate and respect what they did for their own country; they did not fight for our freedoms, our country, or our way of life" (quoted ibid.). In the wake of this furious opposition, the compromise in Kansas City walls away the South Vietnamese memorial from other monuments, and there is no causeway connecting the main park to this island. The heated brokering of degrees of nearness to other monuments recalls and restages colonial cartographies of distance and development.

62. Ngô, "Sense and Subjectivity," 97.

63. Vietnamese refugees also migrated to other first-asylum nations, including Australia, Canada, and France. See Bousquet, *Behind the Bamboo Hedge*.

64. Throughout the Cold War, multiple U.S. military operations staged dramatic rescues of children from the horrors of state socialism. Like its predecessor Operation Peter Pan, which brought thousands of Cuban children into the United States ostensibly to remove them from Soviet control, Operation Babylift began the evacuation of almost three thousand purported orphans from Saigon on April 3, 1975, to lend moral weight to a multimillion-dollar supplemental aid package for South Viet Nam hurrying through Congress (this tactic failed, though the lift is well remembered).

65. Though I do not dwell on this point here, it bears noting that immigration acts—including the 1965 Immigration and Nationality Act and most obviously those establishing emergency asylum, such as the 1975 Indochina Migration and Refugee Assistance Act, the 1980 Refugee Act, the 1982 Amerasian Immigration Act, and the 1987 Amerasian Homecoming Act—are not corrections by a liberal government but expressions of imperial governance. For instance, we might look closely at the 1965 act's anticommunist clause to understand the radical demographic (and otherwise) transformation of "Asian

America." For more on this point, see Campomanes, "New Formations of Asian American Studies and the Question of U.S. Imperialism"; Luibheid, "The 1965 Immigration and Nationality Act"; J. Kim, *Ends of Empire*.

66. *Hearts of Sorrow* is the title of a collection of oral testimonials by Vietnamese refugees (Freeman, *Hearts of Sorrow*).

67. For an analysis of refugee figurations that employs psychoanalytic concepts productively, see M. Lam, *Not Coming to Terms*.

68. Foucault, *Psychiatric Power*, 85.

69. Foucault, *Abnormal*, 312 (my italics).

70. A. Ong, *Buddha Is Hiding*, 93.

71. Stein, "The Experience of Being a Refugee," 11.

72. Ibid.

73. Kelly, *From Vietnam to America*, 81.

74. Chan and Loveridge, "Refugees in 'Transit,'" 746.

75. Foucault, *Psychiatric Power*, 313.

76. United States Department of Health and Human Services, "Mental Health Care for Asian Americans and Pacific Islanders." The study cited in this excerpt is Chung and Kagawa-Singer, "Predictors of Psychological Distress among Southeast Asian Refugees."

77. Anemona Hartocollis, "Coping; Fleeing the Killing Fields, but Not Escaping," *New York Times*, October 17, 2004.

78. Caricatures of Ho Chi Minh, demonized with fangs and glowing red eyes, are common at anticommunist protests.

79. Cold War discourses that characterized the Southeast Asian's disposition as morally unsophisticated and politically unstable also classified his or her feelings as out of sync—inhumanly unfeeling or exaggeratedly expressive. The course of the war yielded widely circulated examples of the Vietnamese absence of proper—that is to say, civilized—emotional competency. Recall the horror at Madame Nhu's response to the self-immolation of Buddhist monks protesting her brother Ngo Dinh Diem's regime—that she would "clap hands at seeing another monk barbecue show"—or the shudder that met Eddie Adam's photograph of the police chief General Nguyen Ngoc Loan executing a Vietcong suspect on a Saigon street during the opening stages of the 1968 Tet Offensive.

80. Foucault, *Abnormal*, 307.

81. We can easily discern such a script in readings of other controversial events, including the Hi-Tek protests; the protests at the Pacific Arts Gallery in Oakland, California, during an exhibition of a series of silk-screened portraits of Ho Chi Minh by a Vietnam War veteran; the premature closure of the Vietnamese American Arts and Letters Association's group exhibition called *FOB II: Art Speaks*, in response to the inclusion of photographer Brian Doan's image of a young Vietnamese woman in a red tank top and yellow star, seated

next to a small bust of Ho Chi Minh and a cellphone; the uproar after the Vietnamese-language daily newspaper *Nguoi Viet* published a photograph of a Vietnamese American artist's yellow-and-red-striped footbath to honor her mother's labor at a nail salon; and the objections to the University of Southern California's display of the Vietnamese flag alongside other international banners. We might also cite the recruitment of underground paramilitary groups to recover the homeland; the intermittent political assassinations throughout the 1980s of Vietnamese American journalists accused of sympathizing with communism; or the proto-sovereign impulse surfacing as local ordinances designating "communist free" zones, such as in Southern California's Little Saigon, part of the neighboring cities of Westminster and Garden Grove, into which no member or official of the Vietnamese state can safely enter.

82. Foucault, *Abnormal*, 312–13.

83. I hope to defamiliarize, as it were, the customary script through which refugees as a group are understood as having no referentiality apart from their condition. Such a critique might bear on the understanding of anticommunist protests more usefully. A study of these distinct events and discussions of them, however individually and collectively fascinating, is beyond the scope of this chapter. What I wish to point to instead is the troubling use of the condition as an explanation for "bad" behavior, documented through and also substantiating liberal knowledge structures.

84. Ivy, "Trauma's Two Times," 168.

85. Caruth, *Unclaimed Experience*.

86. UN High Commission for Refugees, "Convention and Protocol Relating to the Status of Refugees" (http://www.unhcr.org/3b66c2aa10.html). Jacqueline Bhabha notes that, under pressure from the Western bloc, "The definition of a refugee incorporated into the [Human Rights] Convention reflected liberal political values of nondiscrimination, individual autonomy and rationality and excluded socialist socio-economic concerns" ("Embodied Rights," 8).

87. Malkki, "National Geographic," 25.

88. Quoted in Nevzat Soguk, *States and Strangers*, 10–11.

89. For a critique of the problem specific to Vietnamese in the United States, see Espiritu, "Toward a Critical Refugee Study."

90. Soguk, *States and Strangers*, 53 (my italics).

91. Ibid., 19.

92. Lowe, "Intimacies of Four Continents," 200.

93. Furthermore, as Malkki notes of the field of refugee studies, "again and again, one finds in this literature the assumption that to become uprooted and removed from a national community is automatically to lose one's identity, traditions, and culture" ("Refugees and Exile," 508). Even with new citizenship, the refugee might still feel, and be understood as, a stranger in a strange land.

As postcolonial feminist theorists have taught us so well, there is no reason to believe that home is a place of safety.

94. Grewal and Kaplan, "Global Identities," 668.

95. Sontag, *Illness as Metaphor and AIDS and Its Metaphors*, 3.

96. Quoted in Cheah, "Crises of Money," 191. Elsewhere, Freud argues that "early trauma—defence—latency—outbreak of neurotic illness—partial return of the repressed" result in "a compulsive quality: that is to say that they have great physical intensity and at the same time exhibit a far-reaching *independence of the organization of other mental processes* . . . they are insufficiently or not at all influenced by external reality, pay no attention to it or to its psychical *representatives*, so that they may easily come into *active opposition* to both of them. They are, one might say, *a State within a State*, an inaccessible party, with which cooperation is impossible, *but which may succeed in overcoming what is known as the normal party and forcing it into its service*" ("Moses and Monotheism," 76).

97. Sontag also observes the troubling conceptualization of illness through schemas of warfare (*Illness as Metaphor and AIDS and Its Metaphors*, 64–67, 98–99).

98. Trauma also functions as a diagnosis and a metaphor to describe colonized persons. In considering how the trauma concept is deployed in political critiques of colonial violence, Pheng Cheah notes that the concept of an alien power undermining the self-control and security of an individual critically informed Frantz Fanon's influential analysis of this violence. In this commonplace critique, "(Colonial) political domination or subjugation is traumatic because it causes the erosion and loss of the colonized subject's psychical self-mastery" (Cheah, "Crises of Money," 199).

99. Arendt, *Origins of Totalitarianism*, 277.

100. C. Kaplan, *Questions of Travel*, 110.

101. To give just two most obvious examples: First, in 1954, the Central Intelligence Agency encouraged Catholics to flee from the north to the south of the line partitioning Viet Nam at the 17th Parallel. Second, U.S. efforts to disperse the refugees to discourage the establishment of ad hoc ethnic enclaves failed, as many refugees migrated soon after initial resettlement to certain cities and neighborhoods, many dubbed Little Saigons. See Aguilar-San Juan, *Little Saigons*.

102. For instance, Stein describes the Vietnamese as "the first sizable non-European or European-culture refugees to come to the U.S. and no other large refugee group has come from a land with so low a level of development" ("Occupational Adjustment of Refugees," 37). Such a statement elides the long century of both French colonial rule and U.S. occupation, and it repeats the historicist assessment of the racial, colonial other as backward or behind the times.

103. Cacho, *Social Death*. Cacho quotes D. Silva, *Toward a Global Idea of Race*, xv.

104. Malkki, *Purity and Exile*, 8.

105. Ngai, *Ugly Feelings*, 188.

106. The last two quotes are in My-Thuan Tran, "Vietnamese Art Exhibit Puts Politics on Display," *Los Angeles Times*, January 10, 2009 (http://articles.latimes.com/2009/jan/10/local/me-vietarts10).

107. Nam-Giao Do, "Censorship of Exhibit More Offensive than Art Itself: Premature Closure of Vietnamese American Gallery Stifles Valid Community Expression," UCLA *Daily Bruin*, January 29, 2009 (http://www.dailybruin.com/index.php/article/2009/01/censorship-exhibit-more-offensive-art-itself).

108. Both sympathetic and condemnatory statements about anticommunist refugee protests reproduce the now commonsensical presumption of cognitive, and therefore temporal, disorder in the refugee figure. As an OC *Weekly* editorial naming the refugees "losers" puts it: "As they paraded near Bolsa Avenue, they screamed in hatred of Ho Chi Minh, who died more than 13,000 days ago. They waved miniature flags of a nonexistent South Vietnam, dead 30 years" (R. Scott Moxley, "Losers Again: Communists, Bush Defeat Little Saigon in Human Rights War," OC *Weekly*, June 30, 2005). The argument is clear: Ho Chi Minh is long dead; the war is decades done; communism is an obsolete enemy. The reiteration of the passage of time between these old harms and the present is to argue that the interval between the violation and the compulsive repetition is stretched beyond reason. Because time's passage makes increasingly tenuous the causal temporality of the traumatic event and the distant moment of encounter with the flag or the bust, decades later, the editorial continues: "They told horrible, true stories about the war, re-education camps, property confiscation, sea escapes and communist atrocities. They also rightly demanded more religious, social and political freedom in Vietnam. *But nobody important was listening*" (my italics). Listening is what the illiberal refugee does not do, and so his incomprehensible rage is met with its mirror image: an irruption that has no meaning because it is out of sync, out of time. Unable to observe a critical or historical distance from the traumatic past, the present appears to the refugee in a mimetic relation to anterior events.

In response to regular protests at the offices of *Viet Weekly*, a local Vietnamese American newspaper, a giant vinyl banner authored by Peter Katz, a Vietnam War veteran and Little Saigon business owner, proclaimed his fatigue with anticommunist protesters: "Viet Protesters Are Communists, Communists Oppose Free Speech, Free Press, Free Enterprise, Communists Favor Censorship in All Forms." A *Los Angeles Times* article reported: "Peter Katz can't read or speak Vietnamese, but he knows a showdown between free speech and free assembly when he sees it. 'The first time they protested, it was a novelty. The second time, it got old. The third time, people started complaining,' said Katz, 60, a Vietnam War veteran who runs the Main Street Postal Center. 'They're trying to drive them out of business. . . . These people are using the same tactics as the Communists in Vietnam do to stifle the free press. That really sticks in my craw.' Weimer, *Viet Weekly*'s landlord, said he has gotten several calls from people asking if he was going to evict the Communists. 'When I tell them, "No," they say, "Why not?" ' Weimer said. 'I tell them, "You're in America. They can write anything they want." . . . They're wonderful tenants, hard-working, honest, stand-up, intelligent people. If they're Communists, they're the hardest-working Communists I've ever known' " (Mike Anton, "Stores Paying Price of Free-Press Backlash," *Los Angeles Times*, September 2, 2007). In these figurations, the illiberal refugee is a political formation who cannot participate properly in the deliberative practices of democratic governance: he distorts them according to his traumatic consciousness; she is unsophisticated in her attempts to impose her fractured will.

109. The most obvious example of this is the continuing denial to Palestinian refugees of the right to refuge, the right to have rights, under the shadow of Israeli necropolitics, including the inaugural violence of state creation. Some stateless persons are deemed terrorists, classified ontologically as lawless remainders and thus denied the moral weight of being traumatized by decades of devastation and death. We might also note the repatriation of thousands of people in refugee camps throughout Asia in the 1990s after the normalization of relations between the United States and Viet Nam and their subsequent reclassification as "merely" economic migrants, a juridical category that excluded them from consideration for asylum. The implications of reclassification are multiple, including the summary expulsion of economic peril from the realm of political malice.

110. This is an all-too-familiar diagnosis. In an essay aimed at American school administrators who hope to "reduc[e] Asian youth involvement in violent gang activities," Melissa Cowart and Ronald Cowart write: "The cycle of violence has followed Southeast Asian refugee youth for virtually their entire lives" ("Southeast Asian Refugee Youth and the Cycle of Violence," *NASSP Bulletin* 77, no. 557 [1993]: 41, 45).

111. See Kwon, *Uncivil Youth*; Cacho, *Social Death*.

112. M. Smith and Tarallo, "Who Are the 'Good Guys'?," 72.

113. Ibid., 62.

114. "Although I was on the safe side of the screen now [watching this tragedy unfold on my TV set] and judging their barbaric acts, I was not without this singular sense of foreboding: six years ago I could have been *one of them*" (A. Lam, *Perfume*, 52).

115. Ibid., 55.

116. Foucault, *Abnormal*, 315.

117. Stiker, *A History of Disability*, 123 (my italics).

118. Ibid., 122.

119. Cacho, *Social Death*.

120. Ngô, "Sense and Subjectivity," 96.

121. Foucault, *Abnormal*, 47.

122. Quoted in Norwegian Refugee Council and Refugee Policy Group, *Norwegian Government Roundtable Discussion on United Nations Human Rights Protections for Internally Displaced Persons*, 82.

123. Robert McRuer observes: "People of color, from one perspective, were not the ideal subjects for hegemonic processes of either twentieth-century rehabilitation or social engineering. . . . This does not mean, however (by any means), that people of color were not subject to discourses of rehabilitation—the ideological saturation that [David] Serlin conjures up, like any saturation, permeated everywhere. In fact, the perceived failures of the black family or of black communities more generally proved very useful to rehabilitation initiatives and helped to entrench these discourses. From another perspective, in other words, people of color were precisely the ideal subjects for hegemonic processes of rehabilitation" (*Crip Theory*, 115).

124. Ngô, "Sense and Subjectivity," 98.

125. Bui and Bui, "Note from the Filmmakers" (my italics).

126. See Cvetkovich, *Archive of Feeling*.

127. *Transition to Nowhere* is the title of a 1979 book subtitled *Vietnamese Refugees in America*, by Mary Ann Lamanna, William Thomas Liu, and Alice K. Murata.

128. For more on the refugee camp as a "standardized, generalizable technology of power in the management of mass displacement" see Malkki, "Refugees and Exile," 498.

129. It is unclear if Nam Loc was also the de facto camp manager. Others suggest instead the manager was a refugee named Tony Lam, who later became the first Vietnamese American to be elected to public office in the United States. See Pham, *A Sense of Duty*.

130. The film's subtitled translation of the Vietnamese lyrics.

131. Brooks, *The Melodramatic Imagination*, 56.

132. For others' theorization of the presence of ghosts among us, see Lim, *Translating Time*; Espiritu, "Thirty Years AfterwARd"; Holland, *Raising the Dead*; A. Gordon, *Ghostly Matters*.

133. Foucault, *"Society Must Be Defended,"* 245.

134. "Deliverance," *Washington Post*, April 30, 1975.

135. Derrida, *Of Hospitality*, 4.

136. Ibid., 5.

137. See Agamben, *Homo Sacer*.

138. McRuer observes of the "abnormal" racialized person that "rehabilitation requires [her] degradation, regardless of the fact that narration of [her] or anyone's own story would seem to depend on autonomy and subjectivity" (*Crip Theory*, 123).

139. Das, *Life and Words*, 205.

140. Foucault, *The History of Sexuality*, 145–46.

141. A. Ong, *Buddha Is Hiding*, 93.

142. Ibid., 245.

143. Tang, "Collateral Damage."

144. Buchwald et al., "Screening for Depression among Newly Arrived Vietnamese Refugees in Primary Care Settings," 341. Stein affirms this diagnosis: "Besides restoring the refugees' sense of 'self regard,' employment provides contacts with colleagues, the boss, and the company. It also offers opportunities to learn and practice the language, discover and conform to group norms, and develop social involvement and acceptance" ("Occupational Adjustment of Refugees," 26–27).

145. Quoted in Tollefson, *Alien Winds*, 58.

146. Palumbo-Liu, *Asian/American*, 242.

147. Ibid.

148. Ibid., 242–43.

149. Lam, *Perfume Dreams*, 61.

150. Palumbo-Liu further writes: "In short, the refugees' relation to the welfare state presents a litmus test of assimilation. Of most concern throughout is the identification of refugees as welfare recipients: the world of welfare is a world radically segmented off from viable sociality. It is emphasized over and over that these welfare recipients are to be distinguished from welfare's *pathological* populations. Thus, the 'American' subjectivization of Asian refugees comments not only upon their adaptability but also, by contrast, upon the failure of other populations" (*Asian/American*, 235–36).

151. Operations and Readiness Directorate Office, Deputy Chief of Staff for Operations and Plans, *Department of the Army after Action Reports, Operations New Life/New Arrivals*.

152. Foucault, *Psychiatric Power*, 187.

153. For the most extensive analysis of the "place making" of Little Saigon, see Aguilar-San Juan, *Little Saigons*.

154. Morris, "Giving Up Ghosts," 245.

155. Viet Thanh Nguyen writes: "The subject who refuses to be hailed by dominant ideology can also refuse to be hailed by resistant ideology" (*Race and Resistance*, 157). See also Lisa Marie Cacho's moving meditation "'You Just Don't Know How Much He Meant'" and Eric Tang's "Collateral Damage."

156. I am reminded here of Randy Martin, who writes: "The passage of

biological time between generations would be reinscribed as upward mobility, giving the movement of time itself a positive connotation" ("From the Race War to the War on Terror," 259).

157. In an unsubtle metaphor about roots, the general daily waters the small mound of dirt in which he tenderly nestles the seeds of a small red chili pepper native to Viet Nam. The death of the Viet Nam he knew is the impetus for his own demise; unlike other refugees, he cannot imagine rooting anew in this strange land, so far from his native soil. These scenes draw on disturbing but certainly well-entrenched arboreal metaphors of metaphysical nativism as life-affirming nationalism. Young Minh, whose roots are still shallow and vital, stands for new growth. He nurtures the seeds into a tenacious tendril, which we see him watering on the Fourth of July, an auspicious date for the rebirth of a nation and its people in a new world. For more on such arboreal metaphors, see Malkki, "National Geographic."

158. Berlant, "Cruel Optimism."

159. The so-called Provisional Government of Free Vietnam is a paramilitary political organization based in the United States and established in 1995. Operatives of this exilic organization have been arrested on terrorism charges, including acts of arson and bombings, directed at the Socialist Republic of Vietnam.

160. Cacho, "'You Just Don't Know How Much He Meant,'" 197.

2. The Gift of the Girl in the Photograph

1. Butler, *Precarious Life*, xviii.

2. There are near endless iterations of these powers and their attribution to the photograph. For instance, The History Channel, a cable television network, broadcasts a series called *Unsung Heroes* that features episodes from Western military history. One episode, "Camera Martyrs of the Vietnam War," about photojournalists in Southeast Asia, called the photograph of the na-palmed Vietnamese girl the "touchstone picture of the war" (first aired December 6, 2001).

3. The phrase used here, "the girl in the photo goes to Washington City," follows in homage to Lauren Berlant's *The Queen of American Goes to Washington City*. Marita Sturken's reflections in *Tangled Memories* about the controversy surrounding the Vietnam Veterans Memorial Wall provide a fascinating history of this "black gash of shame and sorrow"—an apt description that served both to anger conservative observers and deeply touch many veterans and their families (51).

4. The full text of her statement on November 11, 1996, at the national Veterans Day commemoration in Washington, D.C., is: "Dear Friends, I am very happy to be with you today. I thank you for giving me the opportunity to

talk and meet with you on this Veterans Day. As you know, I am the little girl who was running to escape from the napalm fire. I do not want to talk about the war because I cannot change history. I only want you to remember the tragedy of war in order to do things to stop fighting and killing around the world. I have suffered a lot from both physical and emotional pain. Sometimes I thought I could not live, but God saves me and gave me faith and hope. Even if I could talk face to face with the pilot who dropped the bombs, I would tell him we cannot change history but we should try to do good things for the present and for the future to promote peace. I did not think that I could marry nor have any children because of my burns, but now I have a wonderful husband and lovely son and a happy family. Dear friends, I just dream one day people all over the world can live in real peace—no fighting, and no hostility. We should work together to build peace and happiness for all people in all nations. Thank you so much for letting me be a part of this important day." That day's speeches can be found on the PBS website: http://www.pbs.org/ newshour/bb/military/vets_11–11.html.

5. Freund, "Vietnam's Most Harrowing Photo."

6. Mbembe, "Necropolitics," 12.

7. Adorno, *Aesthetic Theory*, 455.

8. Ricoeur, "On Narrative Time," 181.

9. Ibid.

10. Arendt, *The Human Condition*, 257.

11. Hesford and Kozol, "Introduction," 9.

12. Barthes, *Camera Lucida*, 10.

13. Foucault, "Nietzsche, Genealogy, History," 146.

14. Sifting through five hundred hours of recordings of President Richard Nixon in the Oval Office, released in 2002, reporters found Nixon and his White House chief of staff, H. R. Halderman, debating the truthfulness of the photograph. Nixon mused, "I wonder if that was fixed," and Halderman replied, "Could have been." Such suspicion might be read through declining domestic support for the war and an increasingly embattled administration, or a desire to disbelieve or dismiss the photograph's haunting resonance.

15. Quoted in Perlmutter, *Photojournalism and Foreign Policy*, 23.

16. Davis, *Hearts and Minds*.

17. See Trask, "The Indian Wars and the Vietnam War"; Bates, *The Wars We Took to Vietnam*.

18. See Jodi Byrd, *The Transit of Empire*.

19. Mbembe, "Necropolitics," 40.

20. As a historical footnote, the United States, after Truman's 1947 address, increased its military aid to the Greek government by introducing to its armed forces the uses of napalm against communist insurgents. The UN Convention on Certain Conventional Weapons (CCW) banned the usage of napalm against

civilians in 1980, with Protocol III of the CCW restricting the usage of all incendiary weapons. The United States, though a party to the CCW, did not sign Protocol III.

21. For more on which lives are grievable, see Butler, *Frames of War*.

22. Such conflations are plentiful. For instance, Philip Caputo notes: "Our mission was not to win terrain or seize positions, but simply to kill: to kill Communists and to kill as many of them as possible. Stack 'em like cordwood. Victory was a high body-count, defeat a low-kill ratio, war a matter of arithmetic. The pressure on unit commanders to produce enemy corpses was intense, and they in turn communicated it to their troops. This led to such practices as counting civilians as Viet Cong. 'If it's dead and Vietnamese, it's VC,' was a rule of thumb in the bush. It is not surprising, therefore, that some men acquired a contempt for human life and a predilection for taking it" (*A Rumor of War*, xix–xx). There is also the infamous motto of this war: "Kill them all and let God sort them out!"

23. Foucault, "*Society Must Be Defended*," 228.

24. For these reasons, the photograph is also viewed as an indictment of *all* war, circulating in campaigns for the continued disarming of land mines or against the Reagan administration's covert anticommunist war in El Salvador, the U.S. war on drugs, and military abuses at Abu Ghraib.

25. Hariman and Lucaites, *No Caption Needed*, 176.

26. Butler, *Precarious Life*, 150.

27. Warner, "What Like a Bullet Can Undeceive?," 54.

28. Mbembe, "Necropolitics," 14.

29. See Virilio, *War and Cinema*; Terry, "Killer Entertainments"; Caren Kaplan, "Precision Targets: GPS and the Militarization of US Consumer Identity;" Ngô, "Sense and Subjectivity."

30. Chow, *The Age of the World Target*, 36.

31. Barthes, *Camera Lucida*, 9.

32. This is a slight paraphrase of Barthe's question, "What does my body know of Photography?" (Barthes, *Camera Lucida*, 9).

33. Years after the event, the photograph "still transforms its viewers into witnesses; it still asks of them the same fearsome question: What have you to do with this?" Freund, "Vietnam's Most Harrowing Photo."

34. Barthes, *Camera Lucida*, 84.

35. Ibid., 81.

36. Chow, *Writing Diaspora*, 32.

37. Chong, *The Girl in the Picture*, 365.

38. Freund, "Vietnam's Most Harrowing Photo."

39. Chakrabarty, *Provincializing Europe*, 119.

40. Sontag, *Regarding the Pain of Others*, 41.

41. Razack, *Dark Threats and White Knights*, 26.

42. Hartman, *Scenes of Subjection*, 21.

43. Amy Gearan, "Two Who Created a War Image Share Their Pain," *Buffalo News*, April 13, 1997.

44. Denise Chong, "What Happened Next . . . ," *Observer* (UK), September 2, 2000 (http://www.guardian.co.uk/theobserver/2000/sep/03/featuresreview.review).

45. Chow, *Writing Diaspora*, 68.

46. Ngô, "Sense and Subjectivity," 114.

47. Chow, *Writing Diaspora*, 29.

48. Here I am thinking of Dorothy Lange's "Migrant Mother" and Steven McCurry's "Afghan Girl" as two other iconic photographs that ask the viewer to regard the pain of others. Efforts to return to those others a subjecthood beyond the photograph are not nearly as prolific, perhaps because neither subject easily fits a redemption of the indices of their suffering (liberal capitalism on the one hand, and an imperial legacy on the other). Florence Owens Thompson was unhappy with Lange's photograph of her and the publicity it received. The Associated Press published a story, "Woman Fighting Mad over Famous Depression Photo," in which Thompson is quoted as saying: "I wish she [Lange] hadn't taken my picture. I can't get a penny out of it. She didn't ask my name. She said she wouldn't sell the pictures. She said she'd send me a copy. She never did." See Wells, "Case Study." Sharbat Gula's "second" portrait is veiled and circulates much less than the first—though there is also a National Geographic documentary (narrated by Sigourney Weaver) called *The Search for the Afghan Girl*. See Edwards, "Cover to Cover."

49. Arondekar, *For the Record*, 8.

50. Foucault, *Archeology of Knowledge and the Discourse on Language*, 12 (my italics).

51. Ibid.

52. Benjamin, *Illuminations*, 257–58.

53. Judith Coburn, "The Girl in the Photograph," *Los Angeles Times Magazine*, August 20, 1989.

54. Ibid.

55. There is another "after" photograph of an adult Kim Phúc, holding her infant son up to her bared, scarred shoulder, which hangs on a wall at the Museum of Tolerance in Los Angeles alongside the original photograph. Of this photograph there is much more to say. For more insight on such maternal images, see Tapia, *American Pietas*.

56. Coburn, "The Girl in the Photograph." Consider, for instance, what might be meant by "Vietnamese Marilyn." The comparison and assessment in the most obvious sense defines *Marilyn* as an archetypal ideal, in which Marilyn Monroe incarnates the apotheosis of white feminine beauty. But those codes of cinematic beauty used in the *Los Angeles Times Magazine* article

connote not only gender and racial ideologies, but also an American ideology as a geopolitical condition for idealization.

57. Coburn, "The Girl in the Photograph." We may well observe here with Isabel Molina Guzmán that reportage "performs beyond the function of information" ("Gendering Latinidad through the Elián News Discourse about Cuban Women," 182).

58. Coburn, "The Girl in the Photograph."

59. Barthes, *Camera Lucida*, 15.

60. I refer here to Susan Sontag's *Regarding the Pain of Others* and her earlier *On Photography*. Other works in photography studies that worry at this relation of spectacle and spectator include Rosler, "in, around, and afterthoughts"; Tagg, *The Burden of Representation*; Watney, "Photography and AIDS"; Baer, *Spectral Evidence*; Reinhardt, Edwards, and Duganne, *Beautiful Suffering*.

61. Kant, *Observations on the Feeling of the Beautiful and Sublime*.

62. Burke, *A Philosophical Enquiry into the Origin of Our Ideas of the Sublime and Beautiful*, 142–43.

63. See, for instance, Cheng, "Wounded Beauty."

64. Kant, *Critique of Judgment*, 98.

65. Danto, *The Abuse of Beauty*, 160.

66. Scarry, *On Beauty and Being Just*, 81.

67. For an analysis of the biopower of beauty in the contemporary war on terror, see M. Nguyen, "The Biopower of Beauty."

68. Both deprivation and doubt, I should note, also lead to long passages in the biography about Kim Phúc's inner turmoil as she wrestles with the meaning of her life, leading eventually to her conversion to Christianity and a salvational telos.

69. Chong, *The Girl in the Picture*, 96.

70. Coburn, "The Girl in the Photograph." Such an accord might also make clearer to us the reference to Marilyn Monroe, whose enigmatic depths, beneath but also the basis of her tragic beauty, are part of an enduring fascination: that beauty *does* suffer.

71. Chong, *The Girl in the Picture*, 89.

72. Ibid., 90.

73. Ibid., 120.

74. Spelman, *Fruits of Sorrow*, 7.

75. Bal, "The Pain of Images," 95.

76. Chong, *The Girl in the Picture*, 235.

77. Ibid., 212.

78. Ibid., 201.

79. Chow, *Writing Diaspora*, 150.

80. Spillers, "Mama's Baby, Papa's Maybe."

81. Chong, *The Girl in the Picture*, 183.

82. Margaret Power observes that right-wing women in Chile, organizing against Salvador Allende who was then running for president, often appealed to their countrywomen through the existential threat posed by communism to natural femininity: "Communism desexes women and converts them into dull robots whose energies are absorbed by the tasks delegated to them by the communist authorities. As a result, they no longer spend their time loving their husbands and children and making themselves appealing to men" (*Right-Wing Women in Chile*, 82).

83. Chow, *Writing Diaspora*, 153.

84. Moallem, *Between Warrior Brother and Veiled Sister*, 161.

85. Chong, *The Girl in the Picture*, 194.

86. Ibid., 195.

87. Spivak, "Can the Subaltern Speak?," 66–111.

88. The West German photojournalist is a recurring foil to the portrayal of petty-minded government handlers who trap Kim Phúc in propaganda and poverty. He further serves as a foil to the inadequacies of his Vietnamese counterparts, including the photographer who took her photo on that terrible day. Years later, after the interview with the *Los Angeles Times* reporter included a surprise meeting with Ut, Kim Phúc wonders why he did not do more to aid her in her plight (without knowing that his attempts to dodge her government minder and slip her some dollars were unsuccessful). She muses: "*Why did Uncle Ut never come back to rescue her? If Perry Kretz could come back for me, why not Uncle Ut?*" (Chong, *The Girl in the Picture*, 309). Such a rhetorical question explicitly sets up the comparison, and reaffirms the gap, between each man's powers.

89. Quoted in Chong, *The Girl in the Picture*, 234.

90. That said, I do not wish to overemphasize beauty's significance in this biography, especially given the prominence of a Christian telos in Kim Phúc's life story (deliberately presented as a more catholic faith in contrast to the indigenous, syncretic religion *cao dai*, which her mother practices). Her conversion, recounted midway through the biography, is a transformation that strikes her as a revelation about the deepest meaning of her life and marks the start of her pursuit of the *something more* that the illiberal forms that surround her cannot imagine, let alone provide. With a fatalism attributed to her religious devotion to *cao dai*, her mother advises Kim Phúc to resign herself to a life without love or family. But while her mother insists on speaking about war's violence and about her belief in karmic cycles with their temporal premise of return and consequence, her perceived pessimism is received as an obstacle to her daughter's happiness. Thus, it is not only communism that prohibits Kim Phúc from moving on, but also the peasants' anachronistic world with its emphases on the supernatural and filial obligation. Chong presents Kim Phúc's fantasy of escape as a radical subjectivity whose dis-

tinctiveness from her family and all they are made to represent—a staid peasant tradition, a backward religious stance focused on the sins of the past, the parochial organization of human connection through kinship, and so forth—signals the acquisition of liberal, modern self-possession. Evangelical Christianity, here distinctly focused on the promise of a good life leading to a future heaven, offers Kim Phúc hope that she might yet attain those social goods—"I want to live my life, marry, have children"—as significant points along a chronological life course. The increasing tension between mother and daughter is portrayed as an appropriate and necessary (if tragic) transgression of the boundaries of the family in order to expand the possibilities for feminine and heteronormative fulfillment. In her pursuit of an individuating love, Kim Phúc becomes an unconventional daughter by desiring conventional forms of social good.

91. Aparacio and Chávez-Silverman, *Tropicalizations*.

92. Chong, *The Girl in the Picture*, 287. Cuba, in Chong's biography, is the scene for "relaxed sexual mores" (276); where "even older women, with hips like Nuria's, wore bikinis" (287). "As Cubans, the Diaz women came to [uninhibited declarations about love] naturally. . . . Nuria and Yamilen tried to impart to Kim the feminine mystique that Cubans call swing" (289). In comparison to Viet Nam, "Cuban families would throw a coming-out party for their daughters when they reached fifteen, the age when they may openly begin their sexual life without family recrimination" (294).

93. Ibid. (my italics).

94. Ibid., 289.

95. Ibid., 287.

96. Nuttall, "Introduction," 28.

97. For more on love and liberalism, see, for example, Chakrabarty, *Provincializing Europe*; Povinelli, *The Empire of Love*.

98. Povinelli, *The Empire of Love*, 191.

99. Chong, *The Girl in the Picture*, 287 (my italics).

100. Ibid., 256.

101. Ibid., 255–56.

102. I remember watching a local news report about Kim Phúc's appearance at the commemoration, and the on-the-scene reporter ending his account on this solemn, and seemingly resentful, note: "She is alive, but all those men whose names are on that Wall are not."

103. Phan Thi Kim Phúc, Veterans Day speech, transcript, November 11, 1996 (http://www.pbs.org/newshour/bb/military/vets_11–11.html).

104. Sturken, *Tangled Memories*, 44.

105. Barthes, *Camera Lucida*, 80.

106. Ibid., 81.

107. See Sherene Razack's inquiry into the Canadian intervention in Somalia for a necessary critique of the self-concept of the peacekeeper (*Dark Threats and White Knights*).

108. The full text of Col. Norm McDaniel's (U.S. Air Force, Ret.) statement on November 11, 1996, at the national Veterans' Day commemoration in Washington, D.C., is: "Those of us who went in harm's way to serve our nation and to help our friends do not want our sacrifice to be in vain or forgotten. Some of us endured and still endure mental and physical trauma. Some of us endured long, painful, torturous years as prisoners of war, and some of those who served paid the ultimate price, as represented by the thousands of names on these very walls. If those who gave their lives could speak today, I believe their words to us would be similar to those penned by the poet as referenced earlier, John McCray, when he wrote in 'Flander's Fields,' 'I can hear our fallen comrades say, "To you, from failing hands we throw the torch. Be yours to hold it high. If you break faith in us who die, shall we not sleep." So life goes on in Vietnam.' Certainly we want them to rest in peace. So let us make today and tomorrow a time of peace, a time of healing, and a time of continual rededication to the principles that made and keep our great nation free and strong. We owe no less to the men and women we honor here today. Let each of us strive to make our life meaningful by being thankful for each day we live and by truly fulfilling the purpose for which we were created. God bless each of you and God bless America." That day's speeches can be found on the PBS website: http://www.pbs.org/newshour/bb/military/vets_11–11.html.

109. As Lauren Berlant argues, the pilgrimage to Washington, D.C.—and contact with the monumental nation there—makes over the pilgrim into a national body (*The Queen of America Goes to Washington City*).

110. Caruth, *Unclaimed Experience*, 7.

111. Transcripts of all the official speeches from that November 11, 1996, event can be found on the PBS website: http://www.pbs.org/newshour/bb/military/vets_11–11.html.

112. Jeffords, *The Remasculinization of America*, 168–69.

113. Berg and Rowe, "The Vietnam War and American Memory," 2.

114. Sturken describes the wall as a "black gash" (51), a "living wound" (73), a "cut into the sloping earth" (46) (*Tangled Memories*).

115. Ibid., 54–56.

116. This hesitation also leads to the willful desire to *see no more*. Consider contemporary practices of restricting access to or publication of photographs of the warrior dead—because the war in Viet Nam daily intruded into living rooms on the evening news with wounded or slain bodies—and embedding journalists within military units to render journalists' and soldiers' fields of vision simultaneous and the same.

117. Ivy, "Trauma's Two Times," 171.

118. See W. Scott, *The Politics of Readjustment*; A. Young, *The Harmony of Illusions*; Lembcke, *The Spitting Image*; Shepard, *War of Nerves*.

119. Fassin and Rechtman, *The Empire of Trauma*, 91.

120. Ibid.

121. Ibid., 95.

122. Foucault, *Abnormal*, 312.

123. Fassin and Rechtman, *The Empire of Trauma*, 91.

124. Ibid., 93 (my italics).

125. Ibid., 92.

126. A. Young, *The Harmony of Illusions*, 125.

127. A. Young, "The Self-Traumatized Perpetrator as a 'Transient Mental Illness,'" 632.

128. In defense of those soldiers who committed atrocities during wartime, including My Lai, the psychiatrist and antiwar activist Robert Jay Lifton argued: "Atrocities are . . . the well adjusted form of behavior in Vietnam. . . . It takes the unusual man—someone who is in some way idiosyncratic or not too well adjusted—to avoid atrocities. . . . I had occasion to talk to a man who had been at My Lai, who had not shot at all, and sure enough it turned out that he was not too well adjusted in many ways. He was a kind of a loner. He was not in with his group." Quoted in Kunen, *Standard Operating Procedure*, 273–74, 281.

129. Here we might observe that Palestinian refugees, for instance, are not afforded the same claims to dignity through the diagnosis of trauma; instead, trauma is read back through the refugees as a racialized willingness to transform their bodies into bombs.

130. David Serlin examines in more detail and depth the assemblages of discourses and practices around war, disability, normative masculinity, and the modern United States in *Replaceable You*.

131. McRuer, *Crip Theory*, 111.

132. Chong, *The Girl in the Picture*, 255.

133. Ibid., 361.

134. As *The Girl in the Picture* hints, and as I will discuss below, it may be that this encounter is not "divine" but prearranged by the documentarian responsible for *Kim's Story*, Shelley Saywell. Chong notes that before Kim Phúc's appearance in Washington, "Word got to a Canadian filmmaker who was making a television documentary on Kim (entitled *Kim's Story: The Road From Vietnam*, it first aired in 1997) and thus to Kim herself: the American commander who had 'ordered' the napalm strike that injured her, now a church minister, had surfaced." Ibid., 361–62.

135. Ibid., 363.

136. Ann Gearan, "Cruelty of War Finds Peace in Forgiveness," *San Francisco Examiner*, April 13, 1997.

137. Foucault, *The History of Sexuality*, 1:60.

138. Chong writes: "On the strength of his faith, he came to accept that God had forgiven him the pain he'd caused the girl in the picture. Though he slept better at night, the burden of the remorse he carried never got lighter" (*The Girl in the Picture*, 361).

139. Ibid., 360–61.

140. In an interview, Chong reports being unable to confirm Plummer's position in the chain of command with the U.S. military. Yet, she argues, "when people like John Plummer look at that picture, they see inside themselves . . . and out comes guilt. It doesn't matter that it was South Vietnamese planes and that it wasn't a direct operation. It's guilt that they can taste. And that torments him. . . . I'll tell you another example of that guilt. I had hours of conversation with a helicopter pilot who described how he alighted on the Highway Route 1 [where the incident happened] and picked up the burn victims, and picked up Kim and took her to a field hospital. He had it in exact detail: the village, the attack, the aerial view of the village. This was hours of conversation. I saved my important question for the very end. I asked him when he served in Vietnam. And it doesn't overlap. It's guilt, you see. He's tormented. The picture provokes that . . . it doesn't have to be personal, it can be a sense of collective guilt. It doesn't matter whether it's 'your' war, or 'our' war, because it's what one human being does to another" (quoted in Steinman, "The Girl in the Photo"). It bears noting that those veterans who especially challenged Plummer did so to assert that the United States bore no responsibility at all for the napalm strike, that all responsibility lay with the South Vietnamese—a sidestepping of the U.S. role in manufacturing and supplying napalm, let alone in escalating and conducting the war.

141. Peter Pae, "Vets Challenge Minister's Account of Napalm Attack; Va. Man Says He Ordered Strike that Led to Photo," *Washington Post*, December 19, 1997.

142. Ahmed, "The Politics of Bad Feeling."

143. Gearan, "Cruelty of War Finds Peace in Forgiveness."

144. Derrida, *On Cosmopolitanism and Forgiveness*, 30.

145. Ibid., 42.

146. Ibid., 49.

147. Ibid., 31–32.

148. Chong writes: "Word got to a Canadian filmmaker who was making a television documentary on Kim (entitled *Kim's Story: The Road from Vietnam*, it first aired in early 1997) and thus to Kim herself: the American commander who had 'ordered' the napalm strike that injured her, now a church minister, had surfaced" (*The Girl in the Picture*, 361–62). Plummer and Kim Phúc both attest to the universalism of their encounter, and its strategic significance for their Christian faith. In Plummer's words: "It's a story about forgiveness and

reconciliation, and we see that as part of the ministry. Kim and I realized it could be a valuable tool for the ministry, and that's why we've become more open about sharing it" (quoted in Peter Pae, "At Long Last, a Conflict Ends for Minister; Decades after Napalm Bombing, U.S. Commander, Vietnamese Woman Make Their Peace," *Washington Post*, February 20, 1997).

149. Saywell's other films include *Rape: A Crime of War* (1996), which tracks the use of rape against women in war—presumably throughout history—up to the first persecution of rape as a crime against humanity in Bosnia; *Crimes of Honor* (1998), about radical Islamic "honor killings" of women; and *A Child's Century of War* (2000), an examination of the last century's wars from a child's perspective.

150. This tale brings to the fore a series of questions about the geography of the globe. In this telling, on Kim Phúc's "road from Vietnam," Canada is a way station but not the destination. There are scenes that unfold in Toronto, where she lives with her husband and child, but Canada cannot function as the endpoint because the plot must conclude with the confrontation and communion with the war's perpetrators. During the war, Canada was officially neutral, though it provided some aid and a small number of troops late in the war to enforce the 1973 Paris Peace Accords. Additionally, Canada was a major supplier of equipment and other supplies—including napalm—to U.S. forces. However, the war is remembered as a U.S. war.

151. As promotional copy for the documentary puts it, "In order to confront her past, Kim comes to America, where she meets many people who help fill in the holes of her story." "Reuniting" Kim Phúc with (mostly Western) benefactors is a popular plot. Perry Kretz is reunited with her again and again, and in "The Girl in the Photograph," Coburn clandestinely brought Ut, then based in Los Angeles, to Cuba. More recently, the BBC staged a meeting between Kim Phúc and the ITN correspondent Christopher Wain, who stood with other photographers and cameramen capturing images of her flight, and who poured a canteen of water over her burning body (Rebecca Lumb, "Reunited with the Vietnamese 'Girl in the Picture,'" *BBC News*, May 17, 2010 [http://news.bbc.co.uk/2/hi/asia-pacific/8678478.stm]).

152. Tellingly, throughout *The Girl in the Picture*, Kim Phúc identifies Americans and other Westerners as her "saviors." Other Vietnamese, even Ut, are unable to help her. *The Girl in the Picture* does insist, in passages that appear to be asides by the author, that some Vietnamese did also, or attempted to, aid Kim Phúc in her distress.

153. For an extended analysis of this documentary, see Miller, "The Girl in the Photograph."

154. For a brilliant analysis of the maternal and the visual, see Tapia, *American Pietas*.

155. Ricoeur, "On Narrative Time," 174.

156. For another example of this meeting, see my reading of Liz Merkn's 2006 *The Beauty Academy of Kabul* (M. Nguyen, "The Biopower of Beauty").

157. The hope that dialogue will enact some transformation is not an uncommon sentiment. For example, Pulma Gobodo-Madikizela writes: "Through dialogue, victims as well as the greater society come to recognize perpetrators as human beings who failed morally, whether through coercion, the perverted convictions of a warped mind, or fear" ("Intersubjectivity and Embodiment," 543). In this very recent statement, occasioned by the Truth and Reconciliation Commission of South Africa, we can see all the hallmarks of post-traumatic stress disorder, which presumes that no rational human being could possibly commit terrible harm and mean it.

158. A. Kaplan, *The Anarchy of Empire in the Making of U.S. Culture*, 1.

159. Chow, "'I Insist on the Christian Dimension,'" 225.

160. To greater or lesser effect, to be sure—as numerous critics observe, Japanese admissions to forcing Korean women into sexual servitude are rhetorically tortured. See H. Kim, "The Comfort Women"; Kang, "Conjuring 'Comfort Women'"; Matsui, "Women's International War Crimes Tribunal on Japan's Military Sexual Slavery"; Yang, "Revisiting the Issue of Korean 'Military Comfort Women.'"

161. See Pupavac, "International Therapeutic Peace and Justice in Bosnia"; Cobb, "The Domestication of Violence in Mediation"; Castillejo-Cuellar, "Knowledge, Experience, and South Africa's Scenarios of Forgiveness"; S. Young, "Narrative and Healing in the Hearings of the South African Truth and Reconciliation Commission"; Feldman, "Memory Theaters, Virtual Witnessing, and the Trauma-Aesthetic"; Lund, "'Healing the Nation'"; Hamber and Wilson, "Symbolic Closure through Memory, Reparation and Revenge in Post-Conflict Societies"; Yoneyama, "Traveling Memories, Contagious Justice"; Vang, "The Refugee Soldier."

162. Ahmed, "The Politics of Bad Feeling," 77.

163. This chapter is quite long enough, but I wish to observe here that some U.S. veterans are angered that their empire should express any shame at all. There are numerous online forums where veterans decry the language of shame and forgiveness as politically correct—indeed, their premise is that no wrong was ever committed, and no apology is necessary.

164. This editorial allows no time to consider these errors either, or to hold those responsible for admitted "excesses" accountable, instead noting that "not just the absence of recrimination, but also the presence of insight and honesty is required to bind up the nation's wounds" ("Deliverance," *Washington Post*, April 30, 1975).

165. Most obviously, the more spectacular forms of violence—such as the photograph of the bombing of a screaming girl—come to occlude the more ordinary forms of ontological damage. Alejandro Castillejo-Cuellar observes

of South Africa's "scenarios of forgiveness" following apartheid: "In this case, the notions of violence underlying the idea of gross violations (largely around personal and individual bodily mistreatment) and the category of human being that emerged from the infliction of this pain—the subject ironically and tragically formed out of this process of dislocation, the victim—ruled out other mechanisms through which violence . . . could have been conceptualized and understood" ("Knowledge, Experience, and South Africa's Scenarios of Forgiveness," 31).

166. Berlant, *The Female Complaint*, 34.

167. This global feeling is significantly a national feeling—barring one photograph of Princess Diana's wedding, the other images in this episode are American touchstones, including the Camelot-era Kennedys, Marilyn Monroe, Woodstock, the deaths at Kent State, and the *Challenger* explosion.

168. Though it is not a focus of this chapter, television "in public" transforms the possible meanings and affects of its broadcasts. See McCarthy, *Ambient Television*.

169. Illouz, *Oprah Winfrey and the Glamour of Misery*, 128.

170. Jonathan Yardley, "Book World," *Washington Post*, August 6, 2000.

171. Kim Phúc, "The Long Road to Forgiveness," *This I Believe*, NPR, June 30, 2008 (http://www.npr.org/templates/story/story.php?storyId=91964687) (my italics).

172. See, for example, Lears, *No Place of Grace*; Lofton, *Oprah*.

173. Foucault, *The Order of Things*, 21.

174. Robert Karen, "How Far Will an Apology Go?," Oprah.com, February 2001 (http://www.oprah.com/relationships/How-to-Apologize-Learning-to-Forgive/). It should be noted that this article is adapted from Karen's *The Forgiving Self*.

175. *Women Today*, "Phan Thi Kim Phúc," n.d. (http://www.womentoday magazine.com/lifestories/kim_phuc.html). The categories of "life stories" have since been rearranged, and the Christian orientation of the self-help suggestions is much more obvious. Her profile still ends with the question, "Do you bear scars that you think can never be healed?" These life stories are syndicated to a number of related Christian women's online magazines. For instance, the original version of this profile of Kim Phúc can be found in *Chinese Women Today* (http://www.chinesewomentoday.com/lifestories/kim_phuc.big5.html ?encoding=utf-8).

176. Amy Gearan, "Two Who Created a War Image Share Their Pain," *Buffalo News*, April 13, 1997.

177. Janice Peck, in her study of the Oprah Winfrey Book Club, characterizes Winfrey's appeal this way: "Winfrey's commitment to 'positive' thoughts and topics and her continual assertion that all social ills are the consequence of 'negative' . . . thoughts are an ascription that holds equally for every conceiv-

able problem from depression to racism" ("Literacy, Seriousness and the Oprah Winfrey Book Club," 243). See also Illouz and Wilf, "Oprah Winfrey and Civil Society."

178. *Oprah*'s "Celebrated Photos of Our Time" stages another scene of racial reconciliation, this one between Elizabeth Eckford, famously pictured as the black high-school student being escorted through a mob of angry white youths, and Hazel Brian, whose contorted, snarling face had become a touchstone for hateful expression. The tremendous violence that met the occasion of desegregation—the dramatic upheaval of the racial order of the human after a century of Jim Crow—is performed as now redressed by the intimate encounter between victim and perpetrator. Years later, as the two women recount on the show, Hazel confessed her sins and asked for forgiveness, and Elizabeth obliged—and they are now friends, which we are led to believe is the consummation of justice. This is once again the recuperation of the racial liberalism of the United States, in which a progressivist teleology insists that we have *moved on* from racial terror or genocide, and that such things are contained events rather than structuring conditions of possibility and the present.

179. Razack, *Dark Threats and White Knights*, 19.

180. Sheridan, "Journey to Forgiveness."

181. *Women Today*, "Phan Thi Kim Phúc," n.d. (http://www.womentoday magazine.com/lifestories/kim_phuc.html) (my italics).

182. Ahmed, *The Promise of Happiness*, 132.

183. Sau-ling Wong offers insight relevant to this chapter's collocation of Kim Phúc and Oprah Winfrey, with regard to their audiences: "The figure of the person of color patiently mothering white folks serves to allay racial anxieties: those who fear the erosion of their dominance and the vengeance of the oppressed can exorcise their dread in displaced forms. . . . By conceding a certain amount of spiritual or even physical dependence on people of color—as helpers, healers, guardians, mediators, educators, or advisors—without ceding actual structural privilege, the care-receiver preserves the illusion of equality and reciprocity with the caregiver" ("Diverted Mothering," 69).

184. Ngai, *Ugly Feelings*, 6.

185. Indeed, as Vanessa Pupavac observes of the Bosnian conflict, "in this therapeutic formulation, future risks to security appear to come from the population's feelings of hurt and anger" ("International Therapeutic Peace and Justice in Bosnia," 392).

186. Ahmed, *The Promise of Happiness*, 83.

187. Chong, *The Girl in the Picture*, 365.

188. Ahmed, "The Politics of Bad Feeling," 75.

189. Phan Thi Kim Phúc, Veterans Day speech, transcript, November 11, 1996 (http://www.pbs.org/newshour/bb/military/vets_11–11.html).

3. Race Wars, Patriot Acts

1. The acronym USA PATRIOT Act stands for Uniting and Strengthening America by Providing Appropriate Tools Required to Intercept and Obstruct Terrorism Act. I will hereinafter refer to it as the Patriot Act.

2. Viet Dinh, "Drifting to Freedom—A Survivor's Story," *New York Times*, January 8, 1992.

3. Liberato, "Architect of the USA PATRIOT Act."

4. Stoler and Bond, "Refractions off Empire."

5. Grewal, *Transnational America*.

6. Ibid.

7. For the full text of Bush's speech to the American Enterprise Institute on February 26, 2003, see the TeachingAmericanHistory.org website: http://teach ingamericanhistory.org/library/index.asp?document=663.

8. For more on how the Cold War differs from the war on terror, see Medovoi, "Global Society Must Be Defended"; Morris, "The War Drive."

9. William Clinton, "Remarks to the 48th United Nations General Assembly," September 27, 1993 (http://www.presidency.ucsb.edu/ws/index.php?pid=47119#axzz1h1ouqmQc).

10. Chomsky, "In a League of Its Own." Clinton actually stated, "On efforts from export control to trade agreements to peacekeeping, we will often work in partnership with others and through multilateral institutions such as the United Nations. It is in our national interest to do so. But we must not hesitate to act unilaterally when there is a threat to our core interests or to those of our allies" (Clinton, "Remarks to the 48th United Nations General Assembly"). Many critics have called the United States an exemplary rogue state—that is, a state that does not regard itself as bound by international laws. See, for example, Chomsky, *Rogue States*; Blum, *Rogue State*; Prestowitz, *Rogue Nation*.

11. Derrida, *Rogues*, 103.

12. See "Chapter VII: Action with Respect to Threats to the Peace, Breaches of the Peace, and Acts of Aggression," which includes Article 51, at the UN website: http://www.un.org/en/documents/charter/chapter7.shtml.

13. There is an entire collection, edited by Lloyd C. Gardner and Marilyn B. Young, called *Iraq and the Lessons of Vietnam, or, How Not to Learn from the Past*.

14. J. Kim, *Ends of Empire*, 4.

15. Seibers, *Cold War Criticism and the Politics of Skepticism*, 29.

16. George H. W. Bush, "Remarks to the American Legislative Exchange Council." He would repeat this trope several more times. In a radio address to the U.S. armed forces stationed in the Persian Gulf region, made the following day, he said: "Americans today are confident of our country, confident of our future and most of all, confident about you. We promised you'd be given the

means to fight. We promised not to look over your shoulder. We promised this would not be another Vietnam. And we kept that promise. The spectre of Vietnam has been buried forever in the desert sands of the Arabian Peninsula" (George H. W. Bush, "Radio Address to the United States Armed Forces Stationed in the Persian Gulf Region"). Two days later, Bush addressed these remarks to the Veterans Service Organizations: "I made a comment right here at this podium the other day about shedding the divisions that incurred from the Vietnam War. And I want to repeat and say especially to the Vietnam veterans that are here—and I just had the pleasure of meeting some in the hall—it's long overdue. It is long overdue that we kicked the Vietnam syndrome, because many veterans from that conflict came back and did not receive the proper acclaim that they deserve—that this nation was divided and we weren't as grateful as we should be. So somehow, when these troops come home, I hope that message goes out to those that served this country in the Vietnam War that we appreciate their service as well" (George H. W. Bush, "Remarks to Veterans Service Organization").

17. Cheney has also employed the domino theory to claim the Iraq war begat the Arab Spring of 2011. In a Fox News interview, he offered: "But I think that what happened in Iraq, the fact that we brought democracy, if you will, and freedom to Iraq, has had a ripple effect on some of those other countries" (Alex Seitz-Wald, "Cheney Credits Iraq War for Helping to Start Arab Spring," ThinkProgress.org, August 31, 2011 [http://thinkprogress.org/security/2011/08/31/308769/cheney-arab-spring-iraq/]). The phone company Working Assets took out the full-page ad in the *New York Times* featuring excerpts from Max Cleland ("Welcome to Vietnam, Mr. President," Salon.com, September 22, 2003 [http://www.salon.com/2003/09/22/cleland/]).

18. I first read about this name for that pose in Jasbir Puar's *Terrorist Assemblages*. For the genealogy of the name and the pose, she cites Darius Rejali, "A Long-Standing Trick of the Torturer's Art," *Seattle Times*, May 14, 2004.

19. Stoler and Bond, "Refractions off Empire," 93.

20. For more on the militarization of humanitarianism, see, for example, Mertus, *Bait and Switch*; Razack, *Dark Threats and White Knights*; Bricmont, *Humanitarianism Imperialism*; Fassin and Pandolfi, *Contemporary States of Emergency*.

21. George W. Bush, "Major Combat Operations in Iraq Have Ended," May 1, 2003 (http://georgewbush-whitehouse.archives.gov/news/releases/2003/05/20030501-15.html).

22. Thi Q. Lam, "Time to Add Vietnam to Bush's Axis of Evil," *Pacific News Service*, July 3, 2003 (http://news.newamericamedia.org/news/view_article.html?article_id=d3d4148e4138fbbcefe390b2808f06fc).

23. Of his argument to add Viet Nam to the hit list, Lam admitted that "the request may seem far-fetched because the Vietnamese communist regime,

although autocratic and repressive, has no known weapons of mass destruction (WMD) and apparently has no plans to develop them." But he observed that the lack of evidence for such weapons in Iraq was "largely irrelevant anyway." Noting that "the American public doesn't seem to care," and that there was then reasonable speculation that no concrete evidence existed for such weapons even before the war (which is now an indisputable fact), the shifting humanitarian motive applied earlier is abandoned as no more than a useful ploy. Citing the Iraqi oil reserves at the disposal of the United States and favored corporations after the war, Lam mentioned similar possible benefits to the Bush administration and the U.S. empire if it invaded Viet Nam (ibid.).

24. Ibid.

25. The open letter from the American Vietnamese Republican Assembly of Orange County was previously published on their now-defunct website: www .avra.org. The letter is also mentioned in Lam, "Time to Add Vietnam to Bush's Axis of Evil." Meanwhile, Viet Nam has urged the United States to pursue charges of terrorism against several extremist elements in the Vietnamese American diaspora, including the self-styled Government of Free Viet Nam, that purport to seek "freedom and democracy" for Viet Nam through guerrilla campaigns. Allegedly responsible for several undetonated bombs at Vietnamese embassies throughout Southeast Asia and islands in the Pacific, one member of this group was arrested in Southern California by the FBI in October 2001. The Government of Free Viet Nam had been previously indicted in 1998 for fraud; under the auspices of raising funds for a covert military and guerrilla campaign against the Vietnamese state, the organization had sold bogus bonds to Vietnamese immigrants. It also claimed to be running a training camp for so-called freedom fighters along the Vietnamese border, and its president has boasted of the group's destructive capacity.

26. Ibid.

27. Stepan, "Race and Gender," 368.

28. Indeed, here we might remark another difference. Southeast Asian refugees were the last group of wartime refugees granted asylum in the United States en masse. The refusal of the United States to accept the new refugees being made even now through these new wars of freedom and of life finds humanitarian organizations providing aid and relief to refugees instead. This difference deserves much more attention that I can give it here, but new scholarship on humanitarianism addresses it. Adi Ophir argues that humanitarian forms may serve both democratic and totalitarian regimes alike: "Regardless of their intentions, humanitarians actually help to diffuse the challenge created by the masses of refugees and to restore the local and global order of the nation-states and the global market. They depoliticize the disaster, obstruct understanding of its local and global contexts, and tend to represent its

victims as passive objects of care, devoid of political will and organizational capacities—if they do not actually make them so" ("The Sovereign, the Humanitarian, and the Terrorist," 168). See also Fassin and Pandolfi, *Contemporary States of Emergency*.

29. Puar, *Terrorist Assemblages*, 35.

30. This information comes from the now defunct website april30.org, a temporary portal for organizing around the thirtieth anniversary of the fall of Saigon by the Vietnam Freedom March Organization Committee.

31. This letter was published on the now-defunct website of the Vietnam Freedom March Organizing Committee (http://www.april30.org).

32. Jodi Melamed explains: "A language of multiculturalism consistently portrays acts of force required for neoliberal restructuring to be humanitarian: a benevolent multicultural invader (the United States, multinational troops, a multinational corporation) intervenes to save life, 'give' basic goods or jobs, and promote limited political freedoms" ("The Spirit of Neoliberalism," 1).

33. Singh, "Culture/Wars," 490.

34. Melamed usefully observes: "At racial liberalism's core was a geopolitical race narrative: African American integration within U.S. society and advancement toward equality defined through a liberal framework of legal rights and inclusive nationalism would establish the moral legitimacy of U.S. global leadership" ("The Spirit of Neoliberalism," 4). This appearance of a racially inclusive national culture would act as proof of American exceptionalism and universality. Melamed in particular targets Gunner Myrdal's midcentury *An American Dilemma* as a template for racial liberalism: "If America should follow its own deepest convictions, its well-being at home would be increased directly. At the same time America's prestige and power abroad would rise immensely. The century old dream of American patriots, that America could give the entire world its own freedoms and its own faith, would become true. . . . America saving itself becomes savior of the world" (ibid., 7).

35. Grewal, *Transnational America*, 7.

36. As late as 1989, the Westminster, California, city council denied a parade permit to Vietnamese veterans for Armed Forces Day. One member of the council reportedly reasoned: "If you want to be South Vietnamese, go back to South Vietnam" (Scott Gold and Mai Tran, "Vietnam Refugees Finally Find Home," *Los Angeles Times*, April 24, 2000 [http://articles.latimes.com/2000/apr/24/news/mn-22846]).

37. Though I do not overtly address this question at length in this chapter, it is nonetheless informed by Stoler's pointed critique of historiographies that distinguish between the racisms of the past as more overt in their reliance on "biologized, physiological and somatic" logics and the racisms of the present as more "nuanced culturally coded and complex" ("Racial Histories and Their Regimes of Truth," 185). Thus, although the reader may notice that I do not

name some forms of race discourse either "old" or "new," this is not to say that these forms do not congeal into original configurations.

38. Efforts by the U.S. State Department to discourage such resolutions and acts of recognition on state and local levels—arguing that such measures interfere with international relations, a province of the federal government—render these demands for governmental recognition that much more complicated in an already tangled field of power and discourse. State Senator Robert P. Hull, a Democrat, who introduced a heritage and freedom flag resolution to the Virginia legislature, decried what he described as federal interference in state matters. (David Lamb, "Virginians Rally to an Old Flag: South Vietnam's," *Los Angeles Times*, February 8, 2003 [http://articles.latimes.com/2003/feb/09/nation/na-flag9]). On the other hand, Matt Gonzalez, president of the San Francisco Board of Supervisors, argued: "Recognizing a country's flag or something like that gets you dangerously close to foreign policy, something that I don't think a municipal legislature should be doing" (Patrick Hoge, "Brown Vetoes Ma's Resolution on South Vietnamese Flag," *San Francisco Chronicle*, July 26, 2003 [http://articles.sfgate.com/2003-07-26/bay-area/1749 9226_1_red-flag-golden-star-yellow-flag]). What might be useful for an American geopolitical imaginary is not always congruent with the multiple needs of a nonmonolithic state. As Minoo Moallem and Iain Boal note, these conflicts take place at the junctures between "naturalization, normalization, and nationalization" (Moallem and Boal, "Multicultural Nationalism and the Poetics of Inauguration," 245).

39. Hoge, "Brown Vetoes Ma's Resolution on South Vietnamese Flag."

40. The petition can be found at the Free Republic forums: http://www.freerepublic.com/focus/f-news/953160/posts.

41. All the resolutions passed thus far were once found at the defunct Free Vietnam Alliance site, http://www.fva.org/vnflag/. The Boston resolution passed on July 30, 2003.

42. Quoted in L. A. Chung, "South Vietnam Flag Resolution Wavers in S.F.," *San Jose Mercury News*, July 25, 2003.

43. Moallem and Boal, "Multicultural Nationalism and the Poetics of Inauguration," 245.

44. Quoted in Yvonne Abraham, "A Fight for Viet Flag," *Boston Globe*, August 13, 2003.

45. Quoted ibid.

46. "Excerpts from Powell's Opening Statement to the Foreign Relations Committee," *New York Times*, January 18, 2001 (http://www.nytimes.com/2001/01/18/us/excerpts-from-powell-s-opening-statement-to-foreign-relations-committee.html).

47. Consider this statement, " 'To me, the red on that flag is the blood of our combatants,' [Dzung] Nguyen said. 'I can't look at it without that association.' "

Quoted in Oscar Avila, "Conflicting colors of Vietnam," *Chicago Tribune*, February 22, 2004 (http://articles.chicagotribune.com/2004–02–22/ news/040222 0226_1_vietnamese-americans-official-flag-vietnamese-government).

48. Foucault, *"Society Must Be Defended,"* 254.

49. Ibid., 61.

50. Nikhil Pal Singh usefully describes race as "historic repertoires and cultural, spatial, and signifying systems that stigmatize and depreciate one form of humanity for the purposes of another's health, development, safety, profit, or pleasure" (*Black Is a Country*, 223).

51. Foucault, *"Society Must Be Defended,"* 61.

52. Ibid., 257.

53. Ibid., 254.

54. Ibid., 255.

55. Chow, *The Protestant Ethnic and the Spirit of Capitalism*, 15.

56. David Roediger argues that the "broader pan-racist past of gook provides almost a short history of modern U.S. imperial aggression and particularly of the connections between racial oppression and war" ("Gook," 50).

57. Jean O. Pasco, "McCain Hailed by Crowd at Rally in Little Saigon," *Los Angeles Times*, March 2, 2000 (http://articles.latimes.com/2000/mar/02/news/ mn-4666).

58. This account of the rally, including information about the hostile acts directed at the protesters, is based on Lindsey Jang and Robert Winn's documentary, *Saigon USA*.

59. Butler, *Precarious Life*, 78.

60. Hall, "The After-Life of Frantz Fanon," 20.

61. Butler, "Endangered/Endangering," 17.

62. Stoler, "Racial Histories and Their Regimes of Truth," 187.

63. Foucault, *"Society Must Be Defended,"* 62.

64. See Puar's navigation between and within "looks like" and "feels like" with regard to the Sikh figure (*Terrorist Assemblages*, 187).

65. Bui, "Suspended Futures," 69–70.

66. Robert Lee observes that the "model minority myth" originated in the Cold War United States, though we might observe these distinctions also during the Second World War, as other Asians in America sought to distance themselves from the possibly traitorous Japanese. It should be further noted, as Lee does, that "when the Korean War broke out in 1950, Congress passed the Emergency Detention Act and vested the US Attorney General with the authority to establish camps for any who might be deemed a domestic threat in a national emergency" (*Orientals*, 152). We might therefore observe the successive encampments of racial, colonial others (or threats of such encampments) in a series of wars throughout the twentieth and twenty-first centuries: from indigenous peoples on reservations; Japanese Americans in internment camps;

Korean diasporics in this "emergency detention"; Vietnamese refugees in the aftermath of the war in Southeast Asia; Mexicans and other Latinos in immigrant detention without trial or appeal; the mass incarceration of African Americans in the war on drugs; and Muslims and other South and West Asians detained under the Patriot Act, or held as so-called enemy combatants at Guantánamo. For more on some of these encampments, see Gilmore, *Golden Gulag*; Paik, "Rightlessness"; Rodriguez, *Forced Passages*.

67. Chow, *The Protestant Ethnic and the Spirit of Capitalism*, 15.

68. Timur Yuskaev and Matt Weiner, "Secular and Religious Rights: Ban the Croissant!," *International Herald Tribune*, December 19, 2003, quoted in Puar, *Terrorist Assemblages*, 180.

69. Melamed, "The Spirit of Neoliberalism," 18.

70. Suhasini Haidar, "Arab-American Community 'Keeping Its Head Down,'" CNN.com, September 15, 2001 (http://archives.cnn.com/2001/US/09/15/arab .american.backlash).

71. "Text: Bush, Pataki, Giuliani Discuss the Aftermath of the Attacks," transcript of conference call, *Washington Post*, September 13, 2001 (http://www .washingtonpost.com/wp-srv/nation/transcripts/bushtext_091301.html).

72. Grewal, *Transnational America*, 214.

73. Multiculturalism as the management of vectors of health and vulnerability also includes those therapeutic categories of trauma and rehabilitation, as explored in chapters 1 and 2—categories that are often targeted as power's problem as well as its solution. In addition, multiculturalism as a mode of regulation and a way to maximize life can be stretched to include those nonprofit initiatives or state-sponsored programs aimed at empowering youth of color, to manage the risks to these populations and the risks they might themselves pose. See Kwon, *Uncivil Youth*.

74. For more on ascendant whiteness, see Chow, *The Protestant Ethnic and the Spirit of Capitalism*; Puar, *Terrorist Assemblages*. Perpetuating distinctions between lawful belonging and unlawful existence, integrationist discourses about Muslim immigrants in Great Britain or the European Union often deploy a civilizational dividing line against migrants' claims to citizenship or the array of rights that adheres to such status under liberalism. Instead, their disruptive presence, their perceived unwillingness to accept the gifts of freedom freely given (including multiculturalism, but also what falls in the category of sexual and gender expression), threatens the progressive time of the modern, civilized world and its commitments to freedom and liberty.

75. Brown, *Regulating Aversion*.

76. Melamed, "The Spirit of Neoliberalism." And Sara Ahmed observes about the controversies around European caricatures of Allah: "Note here that the other, especially the Muslim subject who is represented as easily offended, becomes the one who causes injury. . . . The offendible subject 'gets in the way' of our freedom" ("Liberal Multiculturalism Is the Hegemony").

77. See Puar, *Terrorist Assemblages*. Gender and sexuality are also modular categories and moving thresholds for determining the order of the human.

78. We might also invoke here Penny Von Eschen's scholarship on the internationalist projects of Cold War cultural ambassadorship as evidence of U.S. liberalism and racial harmony ("Who's the Real Ambassador?").

79. Quoted in T. D. Le, "On the Frontlines in Iraq: Vietnamese Americans in the Military," NewAmericaMedia.org, June 2, 2007 (http://news.newamericamedia .org/news/view_article.html?article_id=f3c14f84eaec202524e3b321cb721f6a). According to one report, "the military branches do not keep track of the number of Vietnamese Americans, but the U.S. Army reported out of 488,578 active army recruits, APIS [Asian Pacific Islanders] made up 4.1 percent" (T. Le, "On the Frontlines in Iraq").

80. Fassin and Pandolfi, "Introduction," 12.

81. Phan, "Phoenix Rising," 24–25.

82. Waldron, "Security and Liberty," 192.

83. Ibid., 192.

84. Nancy, *The Experience of Freedom*.

85. Viet Dinh and John Ashcroft, "Liberty, Security, and the USA Patriot Act: An Excerpt from *Confronting Terror: 9/11 and the Future of American National Security*," *National Review Online*, September 9, 2011 (my italics) (http://www .nationalreview.com/articles/276493/liberty-security-and-usa-patriot-act-joh n-ashcroft).

86. Quoted in C. Gordon, "Governmental Rationality," 20.

87. Ibid.

88. Ibid.

89. Foucault, *The Birth of Biopolitics*, 66–67.

90. C. Gordon, "Governmental Rationality," 20 (my italics).

91. White House, *The National Security Strategy*.

92. Ahmed, *The Cultural Politics of Emotion*.

93. See Massumi, "Fear (The Spectrum Said)."

94. Foucault writes: "As a form of rational intervention wielding political power over men, the role of the police is to supply them with a little extra life— and, by so doing, supply the state with a little extra strength" (Chomsky and Foucault, *The Chomsky-Foucault Debate*, 201). He expands on the objective of the police in *Security, Territory, Population*.

95. Foucault, *The Birth of Biopolitics*, 66.

96. Chow, *The Age of the World Target*, 39.

97. Though Foucault does not use the term "social death," this list of forms of indirect murder does encapsulate some of its terms (*"Society Must Be Defended,"* 256).

98. Cacho, *Social Death*.

99. For more about this new racial formation tied to national expulsion, see

the last chapter of Grewal, *Transnational America*; Volpp, "The Citizen and the Terrorist." For an ethnography of some of the Patriot Act's effects, see Rana, *Terrifying Muslims*.

100. Han, "Strict Scrutiny," 121.

101. Quoted in Daphne Eviatar, "Foreigners' Rights in the Post-9/11 Era: A Matter of Justice," *New York Times*, October 4, 2003 (http://www.nytimes.com/2003/10/04/arts/04RIGH.html).

102. Foucault, *The Birth of Biopolitics*, 67.

103. Sandip Roy, "'Freedom's Attendant': Patriot Act Drafter Defends His Vision," Pacific News Service, January 27, 2003.

104. Dinh, "Drifting to Freedom."

105. We can easily discern here a transnational multiculturalism, through which this refugee makes good on the promise made by American liberalism to the world's peoples, availing himself of the freedom of contractual labor and economic advancement. Dinh speaks glowingly of the hard work he and his family performed as field laborers and garment workers, which allowed him to achieve a post in the Bush administration and a professorship at a prestigious law school.

106. Foucault, *The Birth of Biopolitics*, 66.

107. Rancière, *Hatred of Democracy*. Consider for instance the 2011 legislation passed by the Israeli legislature criminalizing any public call for a boycott against the Israeli state or its West Bank settlements. Critics and civil rights groups have denounced the new law as antidemocratic.

108. Hardt and Negri, *Multitude*, 30.

109. See Puar, *Terrorist Assemblages*; Nadeau, "Beastly Politics."

110. Dinh, "Nationalism in the Age of Terror," 872.

111. Ibid.

112. Ibid., 874.

113. Ibid., 875.

114. Ibid.

115. Quoted ibid., 876–77.

116. Ibid., 878 (my italics).

117. Quoted ibid. (my italics).

118. Schmitt, *Political Theology*; Agamben, *Homo Sacer*.

119. Mehta, "Liberal Strategies of Exclusion," 63.

120. George W. Bush, "Address before a Joint Session of the Congress on the United States Response to the Terrorist Attacks of September 11," 1142–43.

121. Dinh, "Nationalism in the Age of Terror," 880.

122. Quoted in Massumi, "Fear," 32.

123. Chow, *The Age of the World Target*, 34.

124. K. Ferguson, "The Gift of Freedom," 44.

125. George W. Bush, "President Bush Honors Military in Fourth of July Speech."

126. That said, so-called reparations payments in the hundreds of millions of dollars are being made by Iraq to the United States and to corporations such as Pepsi, Philip Morris, and Sheraton, ostensibly for the suffering that these parties experienced as a consequence of the past two decades of conflict. See Hussain, "Iraq Foots the Bill for Its Own Destruction."

127. Foucault, *"Society Must Be Defended,"* 260 (my italics).

128. Indeed, Christian Appy observes: "Another, perhaps less noticed, connection between the wars in Iraq and Vietnam is that in both cases the United States sent a disproportionately working-class military to kill and die while asking or demanding virtually no sacrifices from more privileged Americans at home. Despite the differences between the Vietnam-era draft and the current all-volunteer force, both systems put most of the dirty work of warfare in the hands of people with significantly fewer choices and opportunities" ("Class Wars," 137).

129. Le, "On the Frontlines in Iraq."

130. George Will, "Anh Duong, out of Debt," originally published in *Newsweek*, December 8, 2007 (http://www.thedailybeast.com/newsweek/2007/12/08/anh-duong-out-of-debt.html). Other coverage of Nguyet includes a profile in *Changing Our World: True Stories of Women Engineers*, published in 2006 by the American Society of Civil Engineers; and interviews in the 2005 film *Why We Fight* and the Discovery Channel series *Future Weapons*, aired in 2006.

131. Laura Blumenfeld, "Spurred by Gratitude, 'Bomb Lady' Develops Better Weapons for U.S.," *Washington Post*, December 1, 2007.

132. Ibid.

133. Quoted ibid.

134. Andrew Lam, "Bomb Lady: Vietnamese American Makes Tools for War on Terror," *Pacific News Service*, December 8, 2003.

135. Chow, *The Age of the World Target*, 31.

136. Mbembe, "Necropolitics," 12.

137. Ibid., 40.

138. Foucault, *"Society Must Be Defended,"* 241.

139. Blumenfeld, "Spurred by Gratitude, 'Bomb Lady' Develops Better Weapons for U.S."

140. Will, "Anh Duong, out of Debt."

141. Ibid.

142. Blumenfeld, "Spurred by Gratitude, 'Bomb Lady' Develops Better Weapons for U.S."

143. Dinh, "Nationalism in the Age of Terror," 875.

144. Blumenfeld, "Spurred by Gratitude, 'Bomb Lady' Develops Better Weapons for U.S."

145. A March 5, 2010, article in the independent magazine *Truthout* is titled "Afghanistan's My Lai Massacre." Its author, Dave Lindorff, writes: "Today's

war in Afghanistan also has its My Lai massacres. It has them almost weekly, as US warplanes bomb wedding parties or homes 'suspected' of housing terrorists that turn out to house nothing but civilians. But these My Lais are all conveniently labeled accidents."

146. Quoted in Blumenfeld, "Spurred by Gratitude, 'Bomb Lady' Develops Better Weapons for U.S."

147. Blumenfeld, "Spurred by Gratitude, 'Bomb Lady' Develops Better Weapons for U.S."

148. Quoted in Lam, "Bomb Lady."

149. Quoted in Blumenfeld, "Spurred by Gratitude, 'Bomb Lady' Develops Better Weapons for U.S."

150. Ibid.

151. Chow, *The Protestant Ethnic and the Spirit of Capitalism*, 9.

152. Blumenfeld, "Spurred by Gratitude, 'Bomb Lady' Develops Better Weapons for U.S."

153. Quoted in Lam, "Bomb Lady."

154. Moses, "Conceptual Blockages and Definitional Dilemmas in the Racial Century," 21.

155. From critical ethnic studies, see, for instance, A. Smith, *Conquest*; Rodriguez, *Suspended Apocalypse*. From genocide studies, see Moses, *Colonialism and Genocide*; Levene, *Genocide in the Age of the Nation State*; Powell, *Barbaric Civilization*.

156. Stoler, *Race and the Education of Desire*, 88.

157. Foucault, *History of Sexuality*, 1:138.

158. War and counterterrorism, it should be noted, are also touted as a means to liberate women in illiberal parts of the world.

159. Edelman, *No Future*.

160. Will, "Anh Duong, out of Debt."

161. Blumenfeld, "Spurred by Gratitude, 'Bomb Lady' Develops Better Weapons for U.S."

162. Ibid.

163. This argument, that war is about these two things, comes from Foucault, *"Society Must Be Defended,"* 257.

164. Grewal, "'Security Moms' in the Early Twenty-First-Century United States." For more on the domestication of military technologies, see C. Kaplan, "Precision Targets."

165. Grewal, "'Security Moms' in the Early Twenty-First-Century United States," 30.

166. Ibid., 31.

167. Quoted in Blumenfeld, "Spurred by Gratitude, 'Bomb Lady' Develops Better Weapons for U.S."

Epilogue

1. Lowe, "The Intimacies of Four Continents," 193.

2. Byrd, *The Transit of Empire*, xxv.

3. Lowe, "The Intimacies of Four Continents," 206–7.

4. Derrida, *Given Time*, 41.

5. For a wonderful explication of the racialization of intimacy, especially through a concept of queer diaspora including transnational adoption, see Eng, *The Feeling of Kinship*.

6. A. Gordon, *Ghostly Matters*, 8.

7. Cho, *Haunting the Korean Diaspora*, 11; Holland, *Raising the Dead*; Lim, *Translating Time*; Espiritu, "Thirty Years Afterward," xxi.

8. Eng and Kazanjian, "Introduction," 6.

9. Berlant, "Uncle Sam Needs a Wife," 145.

10. Derrida, *Rogues*, 78.

11. Ngô, "Sense and Subjectivity," 101.

12. Patricia Clough, *Autoaffection*, 184.

13. The song's observance provides a critique of the normal chronology of human life, plotted along certain points—consider its use at the close of *The Graduate* (1967), for instance, as Dustin Hoffman's idealist character confronts an unknowable, but perhaps also an all too obvious, future with the woman he presumed to rescue from what would have been a loveless marriage.

14. A rough translation of the Vietnamese lyrics follows: "One by one people walked into the dark of the night / Hand in hand they walked together / One by one in the dark of the night they reached very far / Over ten years their poems resonated further / They then dedicated every poem to each other with love / They met and opened their souls to each other / In winter, day fell to darkness sooner / The night sparkled with starlight / Each drop of rain fell like the sound of the tambourine" (translated by Hiep Nguyen).

15. Foucault, "What Is Enlightenment?," 83.

16. I owe this insight into default to David Eng.

BIBLIOGRAPHY

Abu-Lughod, Lila. "Do Muslim Women Really Need Saving? Anthropological Reflections on Cultural Relativism and Its Others." *American Anthropologist* 104, no. 3 (2002): 783–90.

Adorno, Theodor W. *Aesthetic Theory.* Edited and translated by Robert Hullot-Kentor. Minneapolis: University of Minnesota Press, 1998.

Agamben, Giorgio. *Homo Sacer.* Translated by Daniel Heller-Roazen. Stanford: Stanford University Press, 1998.

Aguilar-San Juan, Karin. *Little Saigons: Staying Vietnamese in America.* Minneapolis: University of Minnesota Press, 2009.

Ahmed, Sara. *The Cultural Politics of Emotion.* New York: Routledge, 2004.

——. "'Liberal Multiculturalism Is the Hegemony—It's an Empirical Fact'—A Response to Slavoj Žižek." *Dark Matter,* February 19, 2008, http://www.darkmatter101.org.

——. "The Politics of Bad Feeling." *Australian Critical Race and Whiteness Studies Association Journal* 1 (2005): 72–85.

——. *The Promise of Happiness.* Durham: Duke University Press, 2010.

——. *Queer Phenomenology: Orientations, Objects, Others.* Durham: Duke University Press, 2006.

Alarcón, Norma. "Conjugating Subjects: The Heteroglossia of Essence and Resistance." In *An Other Tongue: Nation and Ethnicity in the Linguistic Borderlands,* edited by Alfred Arteaga, 125–39. Durham: Duke University Press, 2001.

Anderson, Benedict. *Imagined Communities: Reflections on the Origin and Spread of Nationalism.* London: Verso, 1983.

Ang, Ien. "Desperately Guarding Borders: Media Globalization, 'Cultural Imperialism,' and the Rise of 'Asia.'" In *House of Glass: Culture, Modernity, and the State in Southeast Asia,* edited by Yao Souchou, 27–45. Singapore: Institute of Southeast Asian Studies, 2001.

——. "On Not Speaking Chinese: Postmodern Ethnicity and the Politics of Diaspora." *New Formations* 24 (Winter 1994): 1–18.

Aparacio, Frances R., and Susana Chávez-Silverman, eds. *Tropicalizations: Transcultural Representations of Latinidad.* Hanover, N.H.: University Press of New England, 1997.

Appy, Christian. "Class Wars." In *Iraq and the Lessons of Vietnam, or, How Not to Learn from the Past*, edited by Lloyd C. Gardner and Marilyn B. Young, 136–49. New York: New Press, 2007.

Appy, Christian, ed. *Cold War Constructions: The Political Culture of United States Imperialism, 1945–1966*. Boston: University of Massachusetts Press, 2000.

Arendt, Hannah. "Home to Roost: A Bicentennial Address." *The New York Review of Books*, June 26, 1975.

——. *The Human Condition*. 1958. Chicago: University of Chicago Press, 1998.

——. *Origins of Totalitarianism*. New York: Schocken, 2004.

Arondekar, Anjali. *For the Record: On Sexuality and the Colonial Archive in India*. Durham: Duke University Press, 2009.

Axel, Brian. *The Nation's Tortured Body: Violence, Representation, and the Formation of a Sikh "Diaspora."* Durham: Duke University Press, 2001.

Azoulay, Ariella. *Death's Showcase: The Power of Image in Contemporary Democracy*. Translated by Ruvik Danieli. Cambridge: MIT Press, 2001.

Baer, Ulrich. *Spectral Evidence: The Photography of Trauma*. Cambridge: MIT Press, 2005.

Bal, Mieke. "The Pain of Images." In *Beautiful Suffering: Photography and the Traffic in Pain*, edited by Mark Reinhardt, Holly Edwards, and Erina Duganne, 93–115. Chicago: University of Chicago Press, 2007.

Balibar, Etienne, and Immanuel Wallerstein. *Race, Nation, Class: Ambiguous Identities*. London: Verso, 1992.

Banet-Weiser, Sarah. "Elian Gonzalez and 'The Purpose of America': Nation, Family, and the Child-Citizen." *American Quarterly* 55, no. 2 (2003): 149–78.

Barthes, Roland. *Camera Lucida: Reflections on Photography*. New York: Hill and Wang, 1981.

Bataille, Georges. *The Accursed Share*. Translated by Robert Hurley. Vol. 1. New York: Zone, 1991.

Bates, Milton J. *The Wars We Took to Vietnam: Cultural Conflict and Storytelling*. Berkeley: University of California Press, 1996.

Benjamin, Walter. *Illuminations: Essays and Reflections*. Edited and with an introduction by Hannah Arendt. New York: Schocken Books, 1968.

——. "Theses on the Philosophy of History." In *Illuminations*, edited by Walter Benjamin, 257–58. New York: Schocken Books, 1968.

Berg, Rick, and John Carlos Rowe. "The Vietnam War and American Memory." In *The Vietnam War and American Culture*, edited by John Carlos Rowe and Rick Berg, 1–17. New York: Columbia University Press, 1991.

Berger, John. *About Looking*. London: Writers and Readers Publishing Cooperative, 1980.

Berlant, Lauren. "Cruel Optimism." *differences* 17, no. 3 (2006): 20–36.

——. *Cruel Optimism*. Durham: Duke University Press, 2011.

——. *The Female Complaint: The Unfinished Business of Sentimentality in American Culture*. Durham: Duke University Press, 2008.

—— . "National Brands/National Bodies: *Imitation of Life.*" In *The Phantom Public Sphere*, edited by Bruce Robbins, 173–208. Minneapolis: University of Minnesota Press, 1993.

—— . *The Queen of America Goes to Washington City: Essays on Sex and Citizenship.* Durham: Duke University Press, 1997.

—— . "The Subject of True Feeling: Pain, Privacy, and Politics." In *Cultural Studies and Political Theory*, edited by Jodi Dean, 42–62. Ithaca: Cornell University Press, 2000.

—— . "Uncle Sam Needs a Wife: Citizenship and Denegation." In *Materializing Democracy*, edited by Russ Castronovo and Dana D. Nelson, 144–74. Durham: Duke University Press, 2002.

Berlant, Lauren, and Michael Warner, "What Does Queer Theory Teach Us about x?" *PMLA* 110, no. 3 (1995): 343–49.

Bhabha, Homi. *The Location of Culture.* New York: Routledge, 1994.

Bhabha, Jacqueline. "Embodied Rights: Gender Persecution, State Sovereignty, and Refugees." *Public Culture* 9, no. 1 (1996): 3–32.

Blum, William. *Rogue State: A Guide to the World's Only Superpower.* Monroe, Maine: Common Courage, 2000.

Bolton, Richard, ed. *The Contest of Meaning: Critical Histories of Photography.* Cambridge: MIT Press, 1989.

Boose, Linda. "Techno-Muscularity and the 'Boy Eternal': From the Quagmire to the Gulf." In *Cultures of United States Imperialism*, edited by Amy Kaplan and Donald E. Pease, 581–616. Durham: Duke University Press, 1993.

Bourdieu, Pierre. *Distinction.* Cambridge: Harvard University Press, 1984.

—— . *Outline for a Theory of Practice.* Translated by Richard Nice. New York: Cambridge University Press, 1977.

Bousquet, Gisele L. *Behind the Bamboo Hedge: The Impact of Homeland Politics in the Parisian Vietnamese Community.* Ann Arbor: University of Michigan Press, 1991.

Bower, Susan Ann. *Why America Fights: Patriotism and War Propaganda from the Philippines to Iraq.* New York: Oxford University Press, 2009.

Boyd, Julian P., Charles T. Cullen, John Catanzariti, Barbara B. Oberg, et al., eds. *The Papers of Thomas Jefferson.* Princeton: Princeton University Press, 1950–.

Bradley, Mark. "Slouching toward Bethlehem: Culture, Diplomacy, and the Origins of the Cold War in Vietnam." In *Cold War Constructions: The Political Culture of United States Imperialism, 1945–1966*, edited by Christian Appy, 11–34. Boston: University of Massachusetts Press, 2000.

Breckenridge, Carol, and Arjun Appadurai. "Editors' Comment: On Moving Targets." *Public Culture* 2, no. 1 (1989): i–iv.

Bricmont, Jean. *Humanitarianism Imperialism: Using Human Rights to Sell War.* New York: Monthly Review, 2006.

Brooks, Peter. *The Melodramatic Imagination: Balzac, Henry James, Melo-drama, and the Mode.* New Haven: Yale University Press, 1995.

Brown, David J., and Robert Merrill, eds. *Violent Persuasions: The Politics and Imagery of Terrorism.* Seattle: Bay Press, 1993.

Brown, Wendy. *Regulating Aversion: Tolerance in the Age of Identity and Empire.* Princeton: Princeton University Press, 2008.

Buchwald, Dedra, et al. "Screening for Depression among Newly Arrived Vietnamese Refugees in Primary Care Settings." *Western Journal of Medicine* 163, no. 4 (1995): 341–45.

Buff, Rachel. *Immigration and the Political Economy of Home: West Indian Brooklyn and American Indian Minneapolis, 1945–1992.* Berkeley: University of California Press, 2001.

Bui, Long Thanh. "Suspended Futures: The Vietnamization of South Vietnamese History and Memory." PhD diss., University of California, San Diego, 2011.

Bui, Timothy Linh, and Tony Bui. "Note from the Filmmakers." Insert in *Green Dragon*, DVD. Directed by Timothy Linh Bui. Culver City, CA: Columbia TriStar Home Entertainment, 2002.

Burke, Edmund. *A Philosophical Enquiry into the Origin of Our Ideas of the Sublime and Beautiful.* 1761. Edited by James T. Boulton. New York: Routledge, 2008.

Bush, George H. W. "Radio Address to the United States Armed Forces Stationed in the Persian Gulf Region." In *Public Papers of the Presidents of the United States, 1991.* Book I: January 1 to June 30, 1991, 207. Washington, D.C.: Government Printing Office, 1992.

——. "Remarks to the American Legislative Exchange Council." *Public Papers of the Presidents of the United States, 1991.* Book I: January 1 to June 30, 1991, 197. Washington, D.C.: Government Printing Office, 1992.

——. "Remarks to Veterans Service Organization." *Public Papers of the Presidents of the United States, 1991.* Book I: January 1 to June 30, 1991, 209. Washington, D.C.: Government Printing Office, 1992.

Bush, George W. "Address before a Joint Session of the Congress on the United States Response to the Terrorist Attacks of September 11." The White House, Office of the Press Secretary, September 20, 2001. http://www.presidency.ucsb.edu/ws/?pid=64731.

——. "President Bush Honors Military in Fourth of July Speech." The White House, Office of the Press Secretary, July 4, 2003. http://georgewbush-whitehouse.archives.gov/news/releases/2003/07/20030704-1.html.

Butler, Judith. *Frames of War: When Is Life Grievable?* New York: Verso, 2009.

——. *Gender Trouble.* New York: Routledge, 1990.

——. *Precarious Life: The Powers of Mourning and Violence.* New York: Verso, 2004.

——. "Subjection, Resistance, Resignification: Between Freud and Foucault." In *The Identity in Question*, edited by John Rajchman, 229–50. New York: Routledge, 1995.

Butler, Judith, and Joan W. Scott, eds. *Feminists Theorize the Political*. New York: Routledge, 1992.

Byrd, Jodi A. *The Transit of Empire: Indigenous Critiques of Colonialism*. Minneapolis: University of Minnesota Press, 2011.

Cacho, Lisa Marie. *Social Death: Racialized Rightslessness and the Criminalization of the Unprotected*. New York: New York University Press, 2012.

——. "'You Just Don't Know How Much He Meant': Deviancy, Death, and Devaluation." *Latino Studies* 5 (2007): 182–208.

Campomanes, Oscar V. "New Formations of Asian American Studies and the Question of U.S. Imperialism." *positions* 5, no. 2 (1997): 523–50.

Caputo, Philip. *A Rumor of War*. 2nd ed. New York: Henry Holt and Co., 1996.

Carr, Robert. "Crossing the First World/Third World Divides: Testimonial, Transnational Feminisms, and the Postmodern Condition." In *Scattered Hegemonies: Postmodernity and Transnational Feminist Practices*, edited by Inderpal Grewal and Caren Kaplan, 153–72. Minneapolis: University of Minnesota Press, 1994.

Carruthers, Ashley. "National Identity, Diasporic Anxiety, and Music Video Culture in Vietnam." In *House of Glass: Culture, Modernity, and the State in Southeast Asia*, edited by Yao Souchou, 119–49. Singapore: Institute of Southeast Asian Studies, 2001.

Caruth, Cathy. *Unclaimed Experience: Trauma, Narrative and Memory*. Baltimore: Johns Hopkins University Press, 1996.

Castañeda, Claudia. *Figurations: Child, Bodies, Worlds*. Durham: Duke University Press, 2002.

Castillejo-Cuellar, Alejandro. "Knowledge, Experience, and South Africa's Scenarios of Forgiveness." *Radical History Review* 97, no. 1 (2007): 11–42.

Castronovo, Russ, and Dana D. Nelson, eds. *Materializing Democracy: Toward a Revitalized Cultural Politics*. Durham: Duke University Press, 2002.

Césaire, Aimé. *Discourse on Colonialism*. 1955. Translated by Joan Pinkham. New York: Monthly Review, 2000.

Chakrabarty, Dipesh. *Provincializing Europe: Postcolonial Thought and Historical Difference*. Princeton: Princeton University Press, 2007.

Chan, Kwok Bun, and David Loveridge. "Refugees in 'Transit': Vietnamese in a Refugee Camp in Hong Kong." *International Migration Review* 21, no. 3 (1987): 745–59.

Charlton, Roger, Lawrence T. Farley, and Ronald Kaye. "Identifying the Mainsprings of US Refugee and Asylum Policy: A Contextual Interpretation." *Journal of Refugee Studies* 1, no. 3/4 (1988): 237–59.

Cheah, Pheng. "Crises of Money." *positions* 16, no. 1 (2008): 189–219.

Cheah, Pheng, and Suzanne Guerlac, eds. *Derrida and the Time of the Political.* Durham: Duke University Press, 2009.

Cheng, Anne Anlin. "Wounded Beauty: An Exploratory Essay on Race, Feminism, and the Aesthetic Question." *Tulsa Studies in Women's Literature* 19, no. 2 (2000): 191–21.

Cho, Grace M. *Haunting the Korean Diaspora: Shame, Secrecy, and the Forgotten War.* Minneapolis: University of Minnesota Press, 2008.

Chomsky, Noam. "In a League of Its Own: Assessing US Rogue Behavior." *Harvard International Review* 22, no. 2 (Summer 2000): 69–70.

——. *Rogue States: The Rule of Force in World Affairs.* Cambridge, MA: South End, 2000.

Chomsky, Noam, and Michel Foucault. *The Chomsky-Foucault Debate: On Human Nature.* New York: New Press, 2006.

Chong, Denise. *The Girl in the Picture: The Story of Kim Phuc and the Photograph That Changed the Course of the Vietnam War.* New York: Viking, 2000.

Chow, Rey. *The Age of the World Target: Self-Referentiality in War, Theory, and Comparative Work.* Durham: Duke University Press, 2006.

——. *Ethics after Idealism: Theory-Culture-Ethnicity-Reading.* Bloomington: Indiana University Press, 1998.

——. " 'I Insist on the Christian Dimension': On Forgiveness . . . and the Outside of the Human." *differences* 20, nos. 2–3 (2009): 224–49.

——. *Primitive Passions: Visuality, Sexuality, Ethnography, and Contemporary Chinese Cinema.* New York: Columbia University Press, 1995.

——. *The Protestant Ethnic and the Spirit of Capitalism.* New York: Columbia University Press, 2002.

——. "Violence in the Other Country: China as Crisis, Spectacle, and Woman." In *Third World Women and the Politics of Feminism*, edited by Chandra Talpade Mohanty, Ann Russo, and Lourdes Torres, 81–100. Bloomington: Indiana University Press, 1991.

——. *Woman and Chinese Modernity: The Politics of Reading between West and East.* Minneapolis: University of Minnesota Press, 1991.

——. *Writing Diaspora: Tactics of Intervention in Contemporary Cultural Studies.* Bloomington: Indiana University Press, 1993.

Chuh, Kandice. *Imagine Otherwise: On Asian Americanist Critique.* Durham: Duke University Press, 2003.

Chuh, Kandice, and Karen Shimakawa, eds. *Orientations: Mapping Studies in the Asian Diaspora.* Durham: Duke University Press, 2001.

Chung, Rita Chi-Ying, and Marjorie Kagawa-Singer. "Predictors of Psychological Distress among Southeast Asian Refugees." *Social Science and Medicine* 36, no. 5 (1993): 631–39.

Clough, Patricia Ticineto. *Autoaffection: Unconscious Thought in the Age of Teletechnology.* Minneapolis: University of Minnesota Press, 2000.

Cobb, Sara. "The Domestication of Violence in Mediation." *Law and Society Review* 31, no. 3 (1997): 397–440.

Cohen, Colleen Ballerino, Richard Wilk, and Beverly Stoeltje, eds. *Beauty Queens on the Global Stage: Gender, Contests, and Power*. New York: Routledge, 1996.

Cowart, Melissa T., and Ronald E. Cowart. "Southeast Asian Refugee Youth and the Cycle of Violence." *NASSP Bulletin* 77, no. 557 (1993): 41–45.

Craik, Jennifer. *The Face of Fashion: Cultural Studies in Fashion*. London: Routledge, 1994.

Crawford, Ann Caddell. *Customs and Culture of Vietnam*. Rutland, Vt.: Charles E. Tuttle Company, 1966.

Cruikshank, Barbara. *The Will to Empower: Democratic Citizens and Other Subjects*. Ithaca: Cornell University Press, 1999.

Cunningham, Stuart, and John Sinclair, eds. *Floating Lives: The Media and Asian Diasporas*. Brisbane: University of Queensland Press, 2000.

Cunningham, Stuart, and Tina Nguyen. "Popular Media of the Vietnamese Diaspora." In *Floating Lives: The Media and Asian Diasporas*, edited by Stuart Cunningham and John Sinclair, 91–135. Brisbane: University of Queensland Press, 2000.

Cvetkovich, Ann. *Archive of Feeling: Trauma, Sexuality, and Lesbian Public Cultures*. Durham: Duke University Press, 2003.

Daniel, E. Valentine, and John Chr. Knudsen, eds. *Mistrusting Refugees*. Berkeley: University of California Press, 1995.

Danto, Arthur. *The Abuse of Beauty: Aesthetics and the Concept of Art*. Chicago: Open Court Publishing Company, 2003.

Das, Veena. *Life and Words: Violence and the Descent into the Ordinary*. Berkeley: University of California Press, 2007.

Davis, Peter. *Hearts and Minds*. DVD. Directed by Peter Davis. Criterion Collection, 1974.

Dean, Jodi, ed. *Cultural Studies and Political Theory*. Ithaca: Cornell University Press, 2000.

Derrida, Jacques. *Archive Fever: A Freudian Impression*. Translated by Eric Prenowitz. Chicago: University of Chicago Press, 1982.

——. *Given Time: I. Counterfeit Money*. Translated by Peggy Kamuf. Chicago: University of Chicago Press, 1994.

——. *Memoirs of the Blind: The Self-Portrait and Other Ruins*. Translated by Pascale-Anne Brault and Michael Naas. Chicago: University of Chicago, 1993.

——. *Of Hospitality: Anne Dufourmantelle Invites Jacques Derrida to Respond*. Translated by Rachel Bowlby. Stanford: Stanford University Press, 2000.

——. *On Cosmopolitanism and Forgiveness*. Translated by Mark Dooley and Michael Hughes. New York: Routledge, 2001.

———. *Rogues: Two Essays on Reason*. Translated by Pascale-Anne Brault and Michael Naas. Stanford: Stanford University Press, 2005.

———. *Specters of Marx: The State of the Debt, the Work of Mourning, and the New International*. Translated by Peggy Kamuf. New York: Routledge, 1994.

Devereaux, Leslie. "An Introductory Essay." In *Fields of Vision: Essays in Film Studies, Visual Anthropology, and Photography*, edited by Leslie Devereaux and Roger Hillman, 1–20. Berkeley: University of California Press, 1995.

Devereaux, Leslie, and Roger Hillman, eds. *Fields of Vision: Essays in Film Studies, Visual Anthropology, and Photography*. Berkeley: University of California Press, 1995.

Dillon, Michael, and Julian Reid. *The Liberal Way of War: Killing to Make Life Live*. New York: Routledge, 2009.

Dinh, Viet D. "Nationalism in the Age of Terror." *Florida Law Review* 4 (September 2004): 867–82.

Doan, Brian. *The Forgotten Ones: A Photographic Documentation of the Last Vietnamese Boat People in the Philippines*. Westminster, Calif.: VAALA, 2004.

Dorais, Louis-Jacques. "Defining the Overseas Vietnamese." *Diaspora* 10, no. 1 (2001): 3–27.

Doyle, Jennifer. "Tricks of the Trade: Pop Art/Pop Sex." In *Pop Out: Queer Warhol*, edited by Jennifer Doyle, Jonathan Flatley, and José Esteban Muñoz, 191–209. Durham: Duke University Press, 1996.

Doyle, Jennifer, Jonathan Flatley, and José Esteban Muñoz, eds. *Pop Out: Queer Warhol*. Durham: Duke University Press, 1996.

DuBois, Thomas A. "Constructions Construed: The Representation of Southeast Asian Refugees in Academic, Popular, and Adolescent Discourse." *Amerasia Journal* 19, no. 3 (1993): 1–25.

Duggan, Lisa. *The Twilight of Equality? Neoliberalism, Cultural Politics, and the Attack on Democracy*. Boston: Beacon Press, 2004.

Edelman, Lee. *No Future: Queer Theory and the Death Drive*. Durham: Duke University Press, 2004.

Edwards, Holly. "Cover to Cover: The Life Cycle of an Image in Contemporary Visual Culture." In *Beautiful Suffering: Photography and the Traffic in Pain*, edited by Mark Reinhardt, Holly Edwards, and Erina Duganne, 75–92. Chicago: University of Chicago Press, 2007.

Eng, David L. *The Feeling of Kinship: Queer Liberalism and the Racialization of Intimacy*. Durham: Duke University Press, 2010.

Eng, David L., and David Kazanjian. "Introduction: Mourning Remains." In *Loss: The Politics of Mourning*, edited by David L. Eng and David Kazanjian, 1–25. Berkeley: University of California Press, 2002.

Espiritu, Yen Lê. "Thirty Years AfterwaRd: The Endings That Are Not Over." *Amerasia Journal* 31, no. 2 (2005): xiii–xxiii.

———. "Toward a Critical Refugee Study: The Vietnamese Refugee Subject in US Scholarship." *Journal of Vietnamese Studies* 1, nos. 1–2 (2006): 410–33.

Fabian, Johannes. *Time and the Other: How Anthropology Makes Its Objects*. New York: Columbia University Press, 1983.

Fassin, Didier. "Another Politics of Life Is Possible." *Theory, Culture and Society* 26, no. 5 (2009): 44–60.

Fassin, Didier, and Mariella Pandolfi, eds. *Contemporary States of Emergency: The Politics of Military and Humanitarian Interventions*. New York: Zone, 2010.

———. "Introduction: Military and Humanitarian Government in the Age of Intervention." In *Contemporary States of Emergency: The Politics of Military and Humanitarian Interventions*, edited by Didier Fassin and Mariella Pandolfi, 9–25. New York: Zone, 2010.

Fassin, Didier, and Richard Rechtman. *The Empire of Trauma*. Princeton: Princeton University Press, 2009.

Feher, Michel, with Gaëlle Krikorian and Yates McKee, eds. *Nongovernmental Politics*. New York: Zone, 2007.

Feldman, Allan. "Memory Theaters, Virtual Witnessing, and the Trauma-Aesthetic." *Biography* 27, no. 1 (2004): 163–202.

Felski, Rita. *The Gender of Modernity*. Cambridge: Harvard University Press, 1995.

Ferguson, Kennan. "The Gift of Freedom." *Social Text* 25, no. 2 (2007): 39–52.

Ferguson, Roderick. *Aberrations in Black: Toward a Queer of Color Critique*. Minneapolis: University of Minnesota Press, 2003.

Flatley, Jonathan. "Warhol Gives Good Face: Publicity and the Politics of Prosopopoeia." In *Pop Out: Queer Warhol*, edited by Jennifer Doyle, Jonathan Flatley, and José Esteban Muñoz, 101–33. Durham: Duke University Press, 1996.

Foucault, Michel. *Abnormal: Lectures at the Collège de France, 1974–1975*. Edited by Valerio Marchetti and Antonella Salomoni. Translated by Graham Burchell. New York: Picador, 2003.

———. *Archeology of Knowledge and the Discourse on Language*. Translated by A. M. Sheridan Smith. New York: Routledge, 1972.

———. *The Birth of Biopolitics: Lectures at the Collège de France, 1978–1979*. Translated by Graham Burchell. New York: Palgrave Macmillan, 2008.

———. *The History of Sexuality*. Vol. 1: *An Introduction* Translated by Robert Hurley. New York: Vintage, 1990.

———. *The Order of Things: An Archaeology of Human Sciences*. New York: Routledge, 2001.

———. *Psychiatric Power: Lectures at the Collège de France, 1973–74*. Edited by Jacques Lagrange. Translated by Graham Burchell. New York: Palgrave Macmillan, 2006.

———. *Security, Territory, Population: Lectures at the Collège de France, 1977–1979*. Translated by Graham Burchell. New York: Palgrave Macmillan, 2007.

———. *"Society Must Be Defended": Lectures at the Collège de France, 1975–1976.* Edited by Mauro Bertani and Alessandro Fontana. Translated by David Macey. New York: Picador, 2003.

———. "Technologies of the Self." In *Technologies of the Self: A Seminar with Michel Foucault,* edited by Luther H. Martin, Huck Gutman, and Patrick H. Hutton, 16–49. Amherst: University of Massachusetts Press, 1988.

———. "What Is Enlightenment?" In *The Foucault Reader,* edited by Paul Rabinow, 32–50. New York: Pantheon Books, 1984.

Freeman, James M., ed. *Hearts of Sorrow: Vietnamese-American Lives.* Stanford: Stanford University Press, 1991.

Freud, Sigmund. "Moses and Monotheism." In *The Standard Edition of the Complete Psychological Works of Sigmund Freud,* translated and edited by James Strachey with Anna Freud, 23:3–137. London: Hogarth, 1953.

Freund, Charles Paul. "Vietnam's Most Harrowing Photo: From Guilt to Grace." Slate.com, November 22, 1996.

Ganguly, Keya. "Migrant Identities: Personal Memory and the Construction of Selfhood." *Cultural Studies* 6, no. 1 (1992): 27–50.

Gardner, Lloyd C., and Marilyn B. Young, eds. *Iraq and the Lessons of Vietnam, or, How Not to Learn from the Past.* New York: New Press, 2007.

Gearan, Amy. "Two Who Created A War Image Share Their Pain." *Los Angeles Times,* April 20, 1997.

Gilmore, Ruth Wilson. *Golden Gulag: Prisons, Surplus, Crisis, and Opposition in Globalizing California.* Berkeley: University of California Press, 2007.

Go, Julian. "Introduction: Global Perspectives on the U.S. Colonial State in the Philippines." In *The American Colonial State in the Philippines: Global Perspectives,* edited by Julian Go and Anne L. Foster, 1–42. Durham: Duke University Press, 2003.

Gobodo-Madikizela, Pulma. "Intersubjectivity and Embodiment: Exploring the Role of the Maternal in the Language of Forgiveness and Reconciliation." *Signs* 36, no. 3 (2011): 541–51.

Gold, Steven J. *Refugee Communities: A Comparative Field Study.* London: Sage, 1992.

Goldberg, Vicki. *Power of Photography: How Photographs Changed Our Lives.* New York: Abbeville, 1981.

González, Jennifer A. *Subject to Display: Reframing Race in Contemporary Installation Art.* Cambridge: MIT Press, 2011.

González, Vernadette Vicuña. *Securing Paradise: Tourism and Militarism in Hawaii and the Philippines.* Durham: Duke University Press, forthcoming.

Gordon, Avery. *Ghostly Matters: Haunting and the Sociological Imagination.* Minneapolis: University of Minnesota Press, 1997.

Gordon, Colin. "Governmental Rationality: An Introduction." In *The Foucault Effect: Studies in Governmentality,* edited by Graham Burchell, Colin Gordon, and Peter Miller, 1–52. Chicago: University of Chicago Press, 1991.

Grewal, Inderpal. "Autobiographical Subjects and Diasporic Locations: Meatless Days and Borderlands." In *Scattered Hegemonies: Postmodernity and Transnational Feminist Practices*, edited by Inderpal Grewal and Caren Kaplan, 231–54. Minneapolis: University of Minnesota Press, 1994.

———. "On the New Global Feminism and the Family of Nations: Dilemmas of Transnational Feminist Practice." In *Talking Visions: Multicultural Feminism in a Transnational Age*, edited by Ella Shohat, 501–32. New York: New Museum of Contemporary Art, 1998.

———. " 'Security Moms' in the Early Twenty-First-Century United States: The Gender of Security in Neoliberalism." *Women's Studies Quarterly* 34, nos. 2–3 (2006): 25–39.

———. *Transnational America: Feminisms, Diasporas, Neoliberalisms*. Durham: Duke University Press, 2005.

———. "Traveling Barbie: Indian Transnationality and New Consumer Subjects." *positions* 7, no. 3 (1999): 799–826.

Grewal, Inderpal, Akhil Gupta, and Aihwa Ong. "Guest Editors' Introduction." *positions* 7, no. 3 (1999): 653–66.

Grewal, Inderpal, and Caren Kaplan. "Global Identities: Theorizing Transnational Studies of Gender." GLQ 7, no. 4 (2001): 663–79.

———. *Scattered Hegemonies: Postmodernity and Transnational Feminist Practices*. Minneapolis: University of Minnesota Press, 1994.

———. "Warrior Marks: Global Womanisms' Neo-Colonial Discourse in a Multicultural Context." *Camera Obscura* 39 (1996): 5–34.

Gupta, Akhil. "Imagining Nations." In *A Companion to the Anthropology of Politics*, edited by David Nugent and Joan Vincent, 267–81. Malden, Mass.: Blackwell, 2004.

Guzmán, Isabel Molina. "Gendering Latinidad through the Elián News Discourse about Cuban Women." *Latino Studies* 3 (July 2005): 179–204.

Haines, David W., ed. *Refugees as Immigrants: Cambodians, Laotians, and Vietnamese in America*. Totowa, N.J.: Rowman and Littlefield, 1989.

Hall, Stuart. "The After-Life of Frantz Fanon: Why Fanon? Why Now? Why *Black Skins/White Masks*?" In *The Fact of Blackness: Frantz Fanon and Visual Representation*, edited by Alan Read, 12–37. London: Institute of Contemporary Art, 1996.

———. "Cultural Identity and Diaspora." In *Colonial Discourse and Post-Colonial Theory: A Reader*, edited by Patrick Williams and Laura Chrisman, 392–403. New York: Columbia University Press, 1994.

Hamamoto, Darrell Y., and Sandra Liu, eds. *Countervisions: Asian American Film Criticism*. Philadelphia: Temple University Press, 2000.

Hamber, Brandon, and Richard A. Wilson. "Symbolic Closure through Memory, Reparation and Revenge in Post-Conflict Societies." *Journal of Human Rights* 1, no. 1 (2002): 35–53.

Hammond, Andrew. "From Rhetoric to Rollback: Introductory Thoughts on Cold War Writing." In *Cold War Literature: Writing the Global Conflict*, edited by Andrew Hammond, 1–14. New York: Routledge, 2009.

Han, Sora. "Strict Scrutiny: The Tragedy of Constitutional Law." In *Beyond Biopolitics: State Racism and the Politics of Life and Death*, edited by Patricia T. Clough and Craig Willse, 106–38. Durham: Duke University Press, 2011.

Harasym, Sara, ed. *The Postcolonial Critic: Interviews, Strategies, Dialogues (Gayatri Chakravorty Spivak)*. New York: Routledge, 1990.

Hardt, Michael, and Antonio Negri. *Multitude: War and Democracy in the Age of Empire*. New York: Penguin, 2005.

Hariman, Robert, and John Louis Lucaites. *No Caption Needed: Iconic Photographs, Public Culture, and Liberal Democracy*. Chicago: University of Chicago Press, 2007.

Hartman, Saidiya V. *Scenes of Subjection: Terror, Slavery, and Self-Making in Nineteenth-Century America*. New York: Oxford University Press, 1997.

Hayslip, Le Ly, and Jay Wurt. *When Heaven and Earth Changed Places: A Vietnamese Woman's Journey from War to Peace*. New York: Plume Books, 1989.

Heartney, Eleanor. "Jerry Kearns at the Alternative Museum." *Art in America* 84, no 12 (December 1996): 103.

Hegel, Georg Wilhelm Friedrich. *Hegel's Philosophy of Mind*. 1894. Translated by A. V. Miller. Oxford: Clarendon Press of Oxford University Press, 1971.

Hénaff, Marcel. "The Aporia of Pure Giving and the Aim of Reciprocity: On Derrida's *Given Time*." In *Derrida and the Time of the Political*, edited by Pheng Cheah and Suzanne Guerlac, 215–34. Durham: Duke University Press, 2009.

Hesford, Wendy S., and Wendy Kozol. "Introduction: Is There a 'Real' Crisis?" In *Haunting Violations: Feminist Criticism and the Crisis of the "Real,"* edited by Wendy S. Hesford and Wendy Kozol, 1–12. Urbana: University of Illinois Press, 2001.

Holland, Sharon. *Raising the Dead: Readings of Death and (Black) Subjectivity*. Durham: Duke University Press, 2000.

Honig, Bonnie. "Immigrant America? How Foreignness 'Solves' Democracy's Problems." *Social Text* 16 (Autumn 1998): 1–27.

Huppauf, Bernd. "Modernism and the Photographic Representation of War and Destruction." In *Fields of Vision: Essays in Film Studies, Visual Anthropology, and Photography*, edited by Leslie Devereaux and Roger Hillman, 94–126. Berkeley: University of California Press, 1995.

Hussain, Murtaza. "Iraq Foots the Bill for Its Own Destruction." Salon.com, August 12, 2011.

Huyysen, Andreas. *Twilight Memories: Marking Time in a Culture of Amnesia*. New York: Routledge, 1994.

Hyndman, Jennifer. *Managing Displacement: Refugees and the Politics of Humanitarianism*. Minneapolis: University of Minnesota Press, 2000.

Illouz, Eva. *Oprah Winfrey and the Glamour of Misery*. New York: Columbia University Press, 2003.

Illouz, Eva, and Eitan Wilf, eds. "Oprah Winfrey and Civil Society." *Women and Performance* 18, no. 1 (2008): 1–7.

Ivy, Marilyn. "Trauma's Two Times: Japanese Wars and Postwars." *positions* 16, no. 1 (2008): 165–88.

Jabri, Vivienne. *War and the Transformation of Global Politics*. New York: Palgrave Macmillan, 2007.

———. "War, Security and the Liberal State." *Security Dialogue* 37, no. 1 (2006): 47–64.

Jacobs, Seth. *America's Miracle Man in Vietnam: Ngo Dinh Diem, Religion, Race, and U.S. Intervention in Southeast Asia*. Durham: Duke University Press, 2005.

Jang, Lindsey, and Robert Winn. *Saigon USA*. DVD. Garden Grove, Calif.: KOCE-TV and Corporation for Public Broadcasting, 2004.

Jeffords, Susan. *The Remasculinization of America*. Bloomington: Indiana University Press, 1989.

Jones, Mary Paumier. "Behind the Glass, within the Frame." *Georgia Review* 48, no. 1 (1994): 67–77.

Joseph, May. "Transatlantic Inscriptions: Desire, Diaspora, and Cultural Citizenship." In *Talking Visions: Multicultural Feminism in a Transnational Age*, edited by Ella Shohat, 357–68. New York: New Museum of Contemporary Art, 1998.

Kandiyoti, Deniz. "Identity and Its Discontents: Women and the Nation." In *Colonial Discourse and Post-Colonial Theory*, edited by Patrick Williams and Laura Chrisman, 376–91. New York: Columbia University Press, 1994.

Kang, Laura Hyun Yi. *Compositional Subjects: Enfiguring Asian/American Women*. Durham: Duke University Press, 2002.

———. "Conjuring 'Comfort Women': Mediated Affiliations and Disciplined Subjects in Korean/American Transnationality." *Journal of Asian American Studies* 6, no. 1 (2003): 25–55.

Kant, Immanuel. *Critique of Judgment*. 1790. Translated by Werner S. Pluhar. Indianapolis: Hackett, 1987.

———. *Critique of Practical Reason*. 1788. Edited by Mary J. Gregor. Cambridge: Cambridge University Press. 1997.

———. *Observations on the Feeling of the Beautiful and Sublime*. 1764. Translated by John T. Goldthwait. Berkeley: University of California Press, 1991.

Kaplan, Amy. *The Anarchy of Empire in the Making of U.S. Culture*. Cambridge: Harvard University Press, 2005.

———. "Violent Belongings and the Question of Empire Today: Presidential Address to the American Studies Association, October 17, 2003." *American Quarterly* 56, no. 1 (2004): 1–18.

Kaplan, Amy, and Donald E. Pease, eds. *Cultures of United States Imperialism*. Durham: Duke University Press, 1993.

Kaplan, Caren. "Hilary Rodham Clinton's Orient: Cosmopolitan Travel and Global Feminist Subjects." *Meridians: Feminism, Race, Transnationalism* 2, no. 1 (2001): 219–40.

——. "Precision Targets: GPS and the Militarization of US Consumer Identity." *American Quarterly* 58, no. 3 (2006): 767–89.

——. *Questions of Travel: Postmodern Discourses of Displacement.* Durham: Duke University Press, 1996.

Kaplan, Caren, Norma Alarcón, and Minoo Moallem, eds. *Between Woman and Nation: Nationalisms, Transnational Feminisms, and the State.* Durham: Duke University Press, 1999.

Kaplan, Caren, and Inderpal Grewal, "Transnational Feminist Cultural Studies: Beyond the Marxism/Poststructuralism/Feminism Divides." In *Between Woman and Nation: Nationalisms, Transnational Feminisms, and the State*, edited by Caren Kaplan, Norma Alarcón, and Minoo Moallem, 349–63. Durham: Duke University Press, 1999.

——. "Transnational Practices and Interdisciplinary Feminist Scholarship: Refiguring Women's and Gender Studies." In *Women's Studies on Its Own*, edited by Robyn Weigman, 66–81. Durham: Duke University Press, 2002.

Kelly, Gail Paradise. *From Vietnam to America: A Chronicle of the Vietnamese Immigration to the United States.* Boulder: Westview, 1977.

Kennan, George F. [X, pseud.]. "The Sources of Soviet Conduct." *Foreign Affairs* 25, no. 4 (1947): 566–82.

Kennedy, John F. "John F. Kennedy Criticizes the South Vietnamese Government, 1963." In *Major Problems in the History of the Vietnam War: Documents and Essays*, edited by Robert J. McMahon, 169–170. 2d ed. Lexington, Mass.: D. C. Heath and Company, 1995.

Kim, Hyun Sook. "The Comfort Women: Colonialism, War and Sex." *positions* 5 (Spring 1997): 73–108.

Kim, Jodi. *Ends of Empire: Asian American Critique and the Cold War.* Minneapolis: University of Minnesota Press, 2010.

Kimball, Jeffrey. "The Nixon Doctrine: A Saga of Misunderstanding." *Presidential Studies Quarterly* 36, no. 1 (March 2006): 59–74.

Kim's Story: The Road from Vietnam. DVD. Directed by Shelley Saywell. Brooklyn: Icarus Films, 1996.

Kipnis, Laura. "The Stepdaughter's Story: Scandals National and Transnational." *Social Text* 17 (Spring 1999): 59–73.

Klingsporn, Geoffrey. "Icon of Real War: A Harvest of Death and American War Photography." *The Velvet Light Trap* 45 (2000): 4–19.

Knudsen, John Chr. "When Trust Is on Trial: Negotiating Refugee Narratives." In *Mistrusting Refugees*, edited by E. Valentine Daniel and John Chr. Knudsen, 13–35. Berkeley: University of California Press, 1995.

Ko, Dorothy. "Jazzing into Modernity: High Heels, Platforms, and Lotus

Shoes." In *China Chic: East Meets West*, edited by Valerie Steele and John S. Major, 141–53. New Haven: Yale University Press, 1999.

Kondo, Dorrine. *About Face: Performing Race in Fashion and Theater*. New York: Routledge, 1997.

Koshy, Susan. "From Cold War to Trade War: Neocolonialism and Human Rights." *Social Text* 17 (Spring 1999): 1–32.

Kunen, James S. *Standard Operating Procedure: Notes of a Draft-Age American*. New York: Avon, 1971.

Kwon, Soo Ah. *Uncivil Youth: Activism, Neoliberalism, and Affirmative Governmentality*. Durham: Duke University Press, forthcoming.

LaFeber, Walter. *America, Russia, and the Cold War, 1945–1992*. 8th ed. New York: McGraw-Hill, 1997.

Lam, Andrew. *Perfume Dreams: Reflections on the Vietnamese Diaspora*. Berkeley, Calif.: Heyday, 2005.

Lam, Mariam B. *Not Coming to Terms: Viet Nam, Post-Trauma and Cultural Politics*. Durham: Duke University Press, forthcoming.

Lam, Truong Buu, ed. *Borrowings and Adaptations in Vietnamese Culture* (Southeast Asian Paper No. 25). Honolulu: University of Hawai'i at Manoa, Center for Asian and Pacific Studies, 1987.

Lamanna, Mary Ann, William Thomas Liu, and Alice K. Murata. *Transition to Nowhere: Vietnamese Refugees in America*. Nashville: Charter House, 1979.

Lansdale, Edward G. "On the Importance of the South Vietnamese Experiment, 1955." In *Major Problems in the History of the Vietnam War: Documents and Essays*, edited by Robert J. McMahon, 126–27. 4th ed. Boston: Houghton Mifflin, 2007.

Lê, Linda. *Slander*. Translated by Esther Allen. Lincoln: University of Nebraska Press, 1996.

Le, T. D. "Vietnamese Americans in the Military." *Wire Tap*, July 13, 2007, http://www.wiretapmag.org.

Lears, T. J. Jackson. *No Place of Grace: Antimodernism and the Transformation of American Culture, 1880–1920*. Chicago: University of Chicago Press, 1994.

Lee, Robert G. *Orientals: Asian Americans in Popular Culture*. Philadelphia: Temple University Press 1999.

Lembcke, Jerry. *The Spitting Image: Myth, Memory, and the Legacy of Vietnam*. New York: New York University Press, 1998.

Levene, Mark. *Genocide in the Age of the Nation State*. 2 vols. London: I. B. Tauris, 2005.

Liberato, Maricar. "Architect of the USA PATRIOT Act: Law Traced to Dinh's Communist Experience." *Asianweek*, April 25, 2003, http://www.asianweek .com.

Lieu, Nhi. *The American Dream in Vietnamese*. Minneapolis: University of Minnesota Press, 2011.

———. "Performing Culture in Diaspora: Assimilation and Hybridity in *Paris by*

Night Videos and Vietnamese American Niche Media." In *Alien Encounters: Popular Culture in Asian America*, edited by Mimi Nguyen and Thuy Linh Tu, 194–220. Durham: Duke University Press, 2007.

——. "Remembering 'the Nation' through Pageantry: Femininity and the Politics of Vietnamese Womanhood in the Hoa Hau Ao Dai Pageant." *Frontiers* 21 (2000): 127–51.

Lim, Bliss Cua. *Translating Time: Cinema, the Fantastic, and Temporal Critique.* Durham: Duke University Press, 2009.

——. "True Fictions: Women's Narratives and Historical Trauma." *The Velvet Light Trap* 45 (Spring 2000): 62–75.

Lim, Sam Chu. "Vietnamese Woman Thanks America with Parade Float." *Asianweek*, January 11–17, 2002, 13.

Lindorff, Dave. "Afghanistan's My Lai Massacre." *Truthout*, March 5, 2010.

Lippard, Lucy. *A Different War: Vietnam in Art.* Seattle: Real Comet Press, 1990.

——. *Risky Business: A Solo Exhibit by Jerry Kearns.* New York: Kent Fine Art Gallery, 1986.

Liu, Lydia. "The Female Body and Nationalist Discourse." In *Scattered Hegemonies: Postmodernity and Transnational Feminist Practices*, edited by Inderpal Grewal and Caren Kaplan, 37–62. Minneapolis: University of Minnesota Press, 1994.

Loescher, Gil, and John A. Scanlan. *Calculated Kindness: Refugees and America's Half-Open Door, 1945 to the Present.* New York: Free Press, 1986.

Loewen, James W. *Lies My Teacher Told Me: Everything Your American History Textbook Got Wrong.* New York: Simon & Schuster, 1995.

Lofton, Kathryn. *Oprah: The Gospel of an Icon.* Berkeley: University of California Press, 2011.

Lowe, Lisa. *Immigrant Acts: Asian American Cultural Politics.* Durham: Duke University Press, 1996.

——. "The Intimacies of Four Continents." In *Haunted by Empire: Geographies of Intimacy in North American History*, edited by Ann Laura Stoler, 191–212. Durham: Duke University Press, 2006.

Lubiano, Wahneema. "Talking about the State and Imagining Alliances." In *Talking Visions: Multicultural Feminism in a Transnational Age*, edited by Ella Shohat, 441–50. New York: New Museum of Contemporary Art, 1998.

Luibheid, Eithne. "The 1965 Immigration and Nationality Act: An 'End' to Exclusion?" *positions* 5, no. 2 (1997): 501–22.

Lund, Guiliana. "'Healing the Nation': Medicolonial Discourse and the State of Emergency from Apartheid to Truth and Reconciliation." *Cultural Critique* 54 (Spring 2003): 88–119.

Lutz, Catherine, and Jane Collins. *Reading National Geographic.* Chicago: University of Chicago Press, 1993.

Mahmood, Saba. *The Politics of Piety: The Islamic Revival and the Feminist Subject.* Princeton: Princeton University Press, 2005.

Malkki, Liisa. "Citizens of Humanity: Internationalism and the Imagined Community of Nations." *Diaspora* 3, no. 1 (1994): 41–68.

——. "National Geographic: The Rooting of Peoples and the Territorialization of National Identity among Scholars and Refugees." *Cultural Anthropology* 7, no. 1 (1992): 24–44.

——. *Purity and Exile: Violence, Memory, and National Cosmology among Hutu Refugees in Tanzania*. Chicago: University of Chicago Press, 1995.

——. "Refugees and Exile: From 'Refugee Studies' to the National Order of Things." *Annual Review of Anthropology* 24 (1995): 495–523.

——. "Speechless Emissaries: Refugees, Humanitarianism, and Dehistoricization." *Cultural Anthropology* 11, no. 3 (1996): 377–404.

Marr, David G. *Vietnamese Tradition on Trial: 1920–1945*. Berkeley: University of California, 1981.

Martin, Randy. "From the Race War to the War on Terror." In *Beyond Biopolitics: Essays on the Governance of Life and Death*, edited by Patricia Ticineto Clough and Craig Willse, 258–74. Durham: Duke University Press, 2011.

Massumi, Brian. "Fear (the Spectrum Said)." *positions* 13, no. 1 (2005): 31–48.

Matsui, Yayori. "Women's International War Crimes Tribunal on Japan's Military Sexual Slavery: Memory, Identity, and Society." *East Asia* 19 (Winter 2001): 119–43.

Mauss, Marcel. *The Gift: The Form and Reason for Exchange in Archaic Societies*. 1954. Translated by W. D. Halls. New York: W. W. Norton and Company, 2000.

May, Ernest R., ed. *American Cold War Strategy: Interpreting NSC 68*. Boston: Bedford Books of St. Martin's Press, 1993.

Mbembe, Achille. "Necropolitics." Translated by Libby Meintjes. *Public Culture* 15, no. 1 (2003): 11–40.

McCarthy, Anna. *Ambient Television: Visual Culture and Public Space*. Durham: Duke University Press, 2001.

McClintock, Ann. *Imperial Leather: Race, Gender and Sexuality in the Colonial Contest*. New York: Routledge, 1995.

McCormick, Thomas J. *America's Half-Century: United States Foreign Policy in the Cold War and After*. 2nd ed. Baltimore: John Hopkins University Press, 1995.

McMahon, Robert J., ed. *Major Problems in the History of the Vietnam War: Documents and Essays*. 2nd ed. Lexington, Mass.: D. C. Heath, 1995.

McRuer, Robert. *Crip Theory: Cultural Signs of Queerness and Disability*. New York: New York University Press, 2006.

Medovoi, Leeron. 2007. "Global Society Must Be Defended: Biopolitics without Boundaries." *Social Text* 25, no. 2, 53–79.

Mehta, Uday S. "Liberal Strategies of Exclusion." In *Tensions of Empire: Colonial Cultures in a Bourgeois World*, edited by Frederick Cooper and Ann Laura Stoler, 59–86. Berkeley: University of California Press, 1997.

Melamed, Jodi. "The Spirit of Neoliberalism: From Radical Liberalism to Neo-liberal Multiculturalism." *Social Text* 24, no. 4 (2006): 1–24.

Merish, Lori. "Cuteness and Commodity Aesthetics: Tom Thumb and Shirley Temple." In *Freakery: Cultural Spectacles of the Extraordinary Body*, edited by Rosemarie Garland Thomson, 185–203. New York: New York University Press, 1996.

Mertus, Julie A. *Bait and Switch: Human Rights and U.S. Foreign Policy*. New York: Routledge, 2004.

Metz, Christian. "Photography and Fetish." In *The Critical Image: Essays on Contemporary Photography*, edited by Carol Squiers, 155–64. Seattle: Bay Press, 1990.

Miller, Nancy K. "The Girl in the Photograph: The Vietnam War and the Making of National Memory." *JAC* 24, no. 2 (2004): 261–90.

Mitchell, William J. *The Reconfigured Eye: Visual Truth in the Post-Photographic Era*. Cambridge: MIT Press, 1992.

Moallem, Minoo. *Between Warrior Brother and Veiled Sister: Islamic Fundamentalism and the Politics of Patriarchy in Iran*. Berkeley: University of California Press, 2005.

Moallem, Minoo, and Iain A. Boal. "Multicultural Nationalism and the Poetics of Inauguration." In *Between Woman and Nation: Nationalisms, Transnational Feminisms, and the State*, edited by Caren Kaplan, Norma Alarcón, and Minoo Moallem, 243–63. Durham: Duke University Press, 1999.

Moeller, Susan D. *Shooting War: Photography and the American Experience of Combat*. New York: Basic Books, 1989.

Mohanty, Chandra Talpade, Ann Russo, and Lourdes Torres, eds. *Third World Women and the Politics of Feminism*. Bloomington: Indiana University Press, 1991.

Moon, Michael. "Screen Memories, or, Pop Comes from the Outside: Warhol and Queer Childhood." In *Pop Out: Queer Warhol*, edited by Jennifer Doyle, Jonathan Flatley, and José Esteban Muñoz, 78–100. Durham: Duke University Press, 1996.

Morris, Rosalind C. "Giving Up Ghosts: Notes on Trauma and the Possibility of the Political from Southeast Asia." *positions* 16, no. 1 (2008): 229–58.

——. "Theses on the Questions of War: History, Media, Terror." *Social Text* 20 (Fall 2002): 149–76.

——. "The War Drive: Image Files Corrupted." Special Issue on War, edited by Patrick Deer. *Social Text* 25, no. 2 (2007): 103–42.

Moses, A. Dirk. *Colonialism and Genocide*. New York: Routledge, 2006.

——. "Conceptual Blockages and Definitional Dilemmas in the Racial Century: Genocide of Indigenous Peoples and the Holocaust." *Patterns of Prejudice* 37, no. 2 (2002): 7–36.

Nadeau, Chantal. "Beastly Politics: Queer(s) and Nationalisms." Lecture at the University of Illinois, Urbana-Champaign, November 29, 2007.

Nakanishi, Don, and J. D. Hokoyama, eds. *The State of Asian Pacific America: Policy Issues to the Year 2020*. Los Angeles: Leadership Education for Asian Pacifics (LEAP) and UCLA Asian American Studies Center, 1993.

Nancy, Jean-Luc. *The Experience of Freedom*. Translated by Bridget McDonald. Stanford: Stanford University Press, 1993.

Natajaran, Nalini, ed. *Writers of the Indian Diaspora*. Westport, Conn.: Greenwood Publishers, 1993.

Nealon, Jeffrey T. *Alterity Politics: Ethics and Performative Subjectivity*. Durham: Duke University Press, 1998.

Ngai, Sianne. *Ugly Feelings*. Cambridge: Harvard University Press, 2007.

Ngô, Fiona I. B. "Sense and Subjectivity." *Camera Obscura* 26, no. 1 (2011): 94–129.

Nguyen, Mimi Thi. "The Biopower of Beauty: Humanitarian Imperialisms and Global Feminisms in an Age of Terror." *Signs* 36, no. 2 (2011): 359–83.

——. "Operation Homecoming: Memory, History, and the Production of the Vietnamese Refugee in U.S. National and Transnational Imaginaries." In "Topographies of Race and Gender: Mapping Cultural Representations, Part 2," special issue edited by Patricia Penn Hilden, Shari Huhndorf, and Timothy J. Reiss. *Annals of Scholarship* 18, nos. 2–3 (2009): 115–49.

Nguyễn, Ngạc, and Văn Luân Nguyễn. *Un Siecle d'Histoire de la Robe des Vietnamiennes*. Saigon: Direction des Affaires Culturelles, Ministere de la Culture, de l'Education et de la Jeunesse, [1974?].

Nguyen, Viet Thanh. *Race and Resistance: Literature and Politics in Asian America*. New York: Oxford University Press, 2002.

——. "Representing Reconciliation: Le Ly Hayslip and the Victimized Body." *positions* 5, no. 2 (1997): 605–42.

Norwegian Refugee Council and Refugee Policy Group. *Norwegian Government Roundtable Discussion on United Nations Human Rights Protections for Internally Displaced Persons*. Nyon, Switzerland: Refugee Policy Group, 1993.

Nuttall, Sarah. "Introduction: Rethinking Beauty." In *Beautiful/Ugly: African and Diaspora Aesthetics*, edited by Sarah Nuttall, 6–29. Durham: Duke University Press, 2006.

Obama, Barack. "Remarks by the President in Address to the Nation on the End of Combat Operations in Iraq." Washington, D.C.: The White House, Office of the Press Secretary, August 31, 2010, http://www.whitehouse.gov.

Oishi, Eve. "Bad Asians: New Film and Video by Queer Asian American Artists." In *Countervisions: Asian American Film Criticism*, edited by Darrell Y. Hamamoto and Sandra Liu, 221–44. Philadelphia: Temple University Press, 2000.

Ong, Aiwha. *Buddha Is Hiding: Refugees, Citizenship, and the New America*. Berkeley: University of California Press, 2003.

Ong, Paul, and Suzanne J. Hee. "Work Issues Facing Asian Pacific Americans: Labor Policy." In *The State of Asian Pacific America: Policy Issues to the Year*

2020, edited by Don Nakanishi, 141–52. Los Angeles: Leadership Education for Asian Pacifics (LEAP) and UCLA Asian American Studies Center, 1993.

Operations and Readiness Directorate Office, Deputy Chief of Staff for Operations and Plans, *Department of the Army after Action Reports, Operations New Life/New Arrivals, US Army Support to the Indochinese Refugee Program, 1 April 1975–1 June 1976*. Washington, D.C.: U.S. State Department, 1976.

Ophir, Adi. "The Sovereign, the Humanitarian, and the Terrorist." In *Nongovernmental Politics*, edited by Michel Feher with Gaëlle Krikorian and Yates McKee, 161–81. New York: Zone, 2007.

Paik, Naomi. "Rightlessness: Testimonies from the Camp in Narratives of U.S. Culture and Law." PhD diss., Yale University, 2009.

Palumbo-Liu, David. *Asian/American: Historical Crossings of a Racial Frontier*. Stanford: Stanford University Press, 1999.

———. "Los Angeles, Asians, and Perverse Ventriloquisms: On the Functions of Asian America in the Recent American Imaginary." *Public Culture* 6 (1994): 365–81.

Patterson, Orlando. *Slavery and Social Death: A Comparative Study*. Cambridge: Harvard University Press, 1985.

Peck, Janice. "Literacy, Seriousness and the Oprah Winfrey Book Club." In *Tabloid Tales: Global Debates over Media Standards*, edited by Colin Sparks and John Tulloch, 229–50. Lanham, Md.: Rowman and Littlefield, 2000.

Pelaud, Isabel. *This Is All I Choose to Tell: History and Hybridity in Vietnamese American Literature*. Philadelphia: Temple University Press, 2011.

The Pentagon Papers: The Defense Department History of United States Decisionmaking on Vietnam. 5 vols. Boston: Beacon Press, 1971–72.

Perkins, Maureen. *The Reform of Time: Magic and Modernity*. London: Pluto Press, 2001.

Perlmutter, David D. *Photojournalism and Foreign Policy: Icons of Outrage in International Crises*. Westport, Conn.: Praeger, 1998.

Pham, Quang X. *A Sense of Duty: Our Journey from Vietnam to America*. New York: Presidio, 2005.

Phan, Pamela. "Phoenix Rising: USA Patriot Act Author Viet Dinh's Journey from Vietnam War Refugee to Rising Star of the Republican Party." *Hyphen*, Fall 2003, 24–25.

Pietz, William. "The 'Post-Colonialism' of Cold War Discourse." *Social Text* 7, nos. 19–20 (1988): 55–75.

Povinelli, Elizabeth. *The Empire of Love: Toward a Theory of Intimacy, Genealogy, and Carnality*. Durham: Duke University Press, 2006.

Powell, Christopher John. *Barbaric Civilization: A Critical Sociology of Genocide*. Montreal: McGill-Queens University Press, 2011.

Power, Margaret. *Right-Wing Women in Chile: The Struggle against Allende, 1964–1973*. University Park: Pennsylvania State University Press, 2002.

Prashad, Vijay. "Conversations Uptown: The World We Want Is the World We Need." Talk given at a panel and fundraiser for Critical Resistance and the Brecht Forum in New York City, May 20, 2011. Comments available at http://www.counterpunch.org/2011/05/23/the-world-we-want-is-the-world-we-need/.

Prestowitz, Clyde. *Rogue Nation: American Unilateralism and the Failure of Good Intentions.* New York: Basic, 2003.

Puar, Jasbir K. "Citation and Censorship: The Politics of Talking about the Sexual Politics of Israel." *Feminist Legal Studies* 19 (July 2011): 133–42.

——. *Terrorist Assemblages: Homonationalism in Queer Times.* Durham: Duke University Press, 2007.

Puar, Jasbir K., and Amit S. Rai. "Monster, Terrorist, Fag: The War on Terrorism and the Production of Docile Patriots." *Social Text* 20 (Fall 2002): 117–48.

Pupavac, Vanessa. "International Therapeutic Peace and Justice in Bosnia." *Social Legal Studies* 13, no. 3 (2004): 377–401.

Rabinow, Paul, ed. *The Foucault Reader.* New York: Pantheon Books, 1984.

Rabinowitz, Paula. *They Must Be Represented: The Politics of Documentary.* London: Verso, 1994.

Rambo, Terry A. "Black Flight Suits and White Ao Dais: Borrowing and Adaptation of Symbols of Vietnamese Cultural Identity." In *Borrowings and Adaptations,* edited by Truong Buu Lam, 115–23. Honolulu: University of Hawai'i, Manoa, Center for Asian and Pacific Studies, 1987.

Rana, Junaid. *Terrifying Muslims: Race and Labor in the South Asian Diaspora.* Durham: Duke University Press, 2011.

Rancière, Jacques. *Hatred of Democracy.* Translated by Steve Corcoran. London: Verso, 2009.

Razack, Sherene. *Dark Threats and White Knights: The Somalia Affair, Peacekeeping, and the New Imperialism.* Toronto: University of Toronto Press, 2004.

Reddy, Chandan. *Freedom with Violence: Race, Sexuality, and the US State.* Durham: Duke University Press, 2011.

Reinhardt, Mark, Holly Edwards, and Erina Duganne, eds. *Beautiful Suffering: Photography and the Traffic in Pain.* Chicago: University of Chicago Press, 2007.

Reyes, Adelaida. *Songs of the Caged, Songs of the Free: Music and the Vietnamese Refugee Experience.* Philadelphia: Temple University Press, 1999.

Ricoeur, Paul. "On Narrative Time." *Critical Inquiry* 7, no. 1 (1980): 169–90.

Rimke, Heidi Marie. "Governing Citizens through Self-Help Literature." *Cultural Studies* 14, no. 1 (2000): 61–78.

Ritchin, Fred. "The Photography of Conflict." *Aperture* 97 (1984): 22–27.

Robbins, Bruce, ed. *The Phantom Public Sphere.* Minneapolis: University of Minnesota Press, 1993.

Robbins, Kevin. *Into the Image: Culture and Politics in the Field of Vision.* London: Routledge, 1996.

Rodriguez, Dylan. *Forced Passages: Imprisoned Radical Intellectuals and the U.S. Prison Regime.* Minneapolis: University of Minnesota Press, 2006.

——. *Suspended Apocalypse: White Supremacy, Genocide, and the Filipino Condition.* Minneapolis: University of Minnesota Press, 2009.

Roediger, David. "Gook: The Short History of an Americanism." *Monthly Review*, March 1992, 50.

Rosler, Martha. "in, around, and afterthoughts (on documentary photography)." In *The Contest of Meaning: Critical Histories of Photography*, edited by Richard Bolton, 303–42. Cambridge: MIT Press, 1989.

Ross, Kristin. *Fast Cars, Clean Bodies: Decolonization and the Reordering of French Culture.* Cambridge: MIT Press, 1996.

Rouse, Roger. "Thinking through Transnationalism: Notes of the Cultural Politics of Class Relations in the Contemporary United States." *Public Culture* 7, no. 2 (Winter 1995): 353–402.

Rowe, John Carlos, and Rick Berg, eds. *The Vietnam War and American Culture.* New York: Columbia University Press, 1991.

Rubin, Cyma, and Eric Newton, eds. *Capture the Moment: The Pulitzer Prize Photographs.* New York: W. W. Norton and Newseum, 2001.

Rumbaut, Rubén G. "Portraits, Patterns, and Predictors of the Refugee Adaptation Process: Results and Reflections from the IHARP Panel Study." In *Refugees as Immigrants: Cambodians, Laotians, and Vietnamese in America*, edited by David W. Haines, 138–82. Totowa, N.J.: Rowman and Littlefield, 1989.

Said, Edward. *Orientalism.* New York: Vintage, 1979.

Saldaña-Portillo, Maria Josefina. *The Revolutionary Imagination in the Americas and the Age of Development.* Durham: Duke University Press, 2003.

Scarry, Elaine. *On Beauty and Being Just.* Princeton: Princeton University Press, 1999.

Schein, Louisa. "Diaspora Politics, Homeland Erotics, and the Materializing of Memory." *positions* 7, no. 3 (1999): 697–731.

Schlegel, Amy. "My Lai: 'We Lie, They Die' or, a Small History of an 'Atrocious' Photograph." *Third Text* 31 (Summer 1995): 47–66.

Schmitt, Carl. *Political Theology: Four Chapters on the Concept of Sovereignty.* Translated by George Schwab. Cambridge: MIT Press, 1985.

Scott, Joan W. "Universalism and the History of Feminism." *differences* 7, no. 1 (1995): 1–14.

Scott, Wilbur J. *The Politics of Readjustment: Vietnam Veterans since the War.* New York: Aldine Transaction, 1993.

Serlin, David. *Replaceable You: Engineering the Body in Postwar America.* Chicago: University of Chicago Press, 2004.

Shepard, Ben. *War of Nerves: Soldiers and Psychiatrists in the Twentieth Century.* Cambridge: Harvard University Press, 2000.

Sheridan, Cathy. "Journey to Forgiveness." *The Plain Truth Online*, March/April 2000, http://www.ptm.org.

Shohat, Ella, ed. *Talking Visions: Multicultural Feminism in a Transnational Age*. New York: New Museum of Contemporary Art, 1998.

Siebers, Tobin. *Cold War Criticism and the Politics of Skepticism*. New York: Oxford University Press, 1993.

Silva, Denise Ferreira da. "A Tale of Two Cities: Saigon, Fallujah, and the Ethical Boundaries of Empire." *Amerasia Journal* 31, no. 2 (2005): 121–34.

———. *Toward a Global Idea of Race*. Minneapolis: University of Minnesota Press, 2007.

Silva, Kelly Cristiane da. "AID as Gift: An Initial Approach." *Mana* 4, no. 1 (2008): 141–71.

Singh, Nikhil Pal. *Black Is a Country: Race and the Unfinished Struggle for Democracy*. Cambridge: Harvard University Press, 2005.

———. "Culture/Wars: Recoding Empire in an Age of Democracy." *American Quarterly* 50, no. 3 (1998): 471–522.

Smith, Andrea. *Conquest: Sexual Violence and American Indian Genocide*. Cambridge, Mass.: South End Press, 2005.

Smith, Michael Peter, and Joe R. Feagin, eds. *The Bubbling Cauldron: Race, Ethnicity, and the Urban Crisis*. Minneapolis: University of Minnesota Press, 1995.

Smith, Michael Peter, and Bernadette Tarallo. "Who Are the 'Good Guys'? The Social Construction of the Vietnamese Other." In *The Bubbling Cauldron: Race, Ethnicity, and the Urban Crisis*, edited by Michael Peter Smith and Joe R. Feagin, 50–76. Minneapolis: University of Minnesota Press, 1995.

Soguk, Nevzat. *States and Strangers: Refugees and Displacements of Statecraft*. Minneapolis: University of Minnesota Press, 1999.

Sontag, Susan. *Illness as Metaphor and AIDS and Its Metaphors*. New York: Picador, 2001.

———. *On Photography*. New York: Delta, 1973.

———. *On Regarding the Pain of Others*. New York: Picador, 2004.

Souchou, Yao, ed. *House of Glass: Culture, Modernity, and the State in Southeast Asia*. Singapore: Institute for Southeast Asian Studies, 2001.

Spelman, Elizabeth V. *Fruits of Sorrow: Framing Our Attention to Suffering*. Boston: Beacon, 1997.

Spillers, Hortense. "Mama's Baby, Papa's Maybe: An American Grammar Book." *Diacritics* 17, no. 2 (1987): 65–81.

Spivak, Gayatri Chakravorty. "Acting Bits/Identity Talk." *Critical Inquiry* 18, no. 4 (Summer 1992): 770–803.

———. "Bonding in Difference: Interview with Alfred Arteaga." In *The Spivak Reader: Selected Works of Gayatri Chakravorty Spivak*, edited by Donna Landry and Gerald McLean, 15–28. New York: Routledge, 1996.

———. "Can the Subaltern Speak?" In *Colonial Discourse and Post-Colonial The-*

ory: *A Reader*, edited by Patrick Williams and Laura Chrisman, 66–111. New York: Columbia University Press, 1994.

———. *A Critique of Postcolonial Reason: Toward a History of the Vanishing Present*. Cambridge: Harvard University Press, 1999.

———. *Outside in the Teaching Machine*. New York: Routledge, 1993.

Spurr, David. *The Rhetoric of Empire: Colonial Discourse in Journalism, Travel Writing, and Imperial Administration*. Durham: Duke University Press, 1996.

Squiers, Carol, ed. *The Critical Image: Essays on Contemporary Photography*. Seattle: Bay Press, 1990.

Steedman, Carolyn. *Strange Dislocations: Childhood and the Idea of Human Interiority, 1780–1930*. Cambridge: Harvard University Press, 1995.

Steele, Valerie, and John S. Major, eds. *China Chic: East Meets West*. New Haven: Yale University Press, 1999.

Stein, Barry. "The Experience of Being a Refugee: Insights from the Research Literature." In *Refugee Mental Health in Resettlement Countries*, edited by Carolyn L. Williams and Joseph Westermeyer, 5–23. Washington, D.C.: Hemisphere, 1986.

———. "Occupational Adjustment of Refugees: The Vietnamese in the United States." *International Migration Review* 13, no. 1 (1979): 25–45.

Steinman, Louise. "The Girl in the Photo." Salon.com, August 3, 2000.

Stepan, Nancy Leys. "Race and Gender: The Role of Analogy of Science." In *The "Racial" Economy of Science: Toward a Democratic Future*, edited by Sandra Harding, 359–76. Bloomington: Indiana University Press, 1993.

Stepan, Peter, ed. *Photos That Changed the World*. New York: Prestel, 2000.

Stewart, Susan. *On Longing: Narratives of the Miniature, the Gigantic, the Souvenir, the Collection*. Durham: Duke University Press, 1993.

Stiker, Henry-Jacques. *A History of Disability*. Translated by William Sayers. Ann Arbor: University of Michigan Press, 2000.

Stoler, Ann Laura, ed. *Haunted by Empire: Geographies of Intimacy in North American History*. Durham: Duke University Press, 2006.

———. "Imperial Debris: Reflections on Ruins and Ruination." *Cultural Anthropology* 23, no. 2 (2008): 191–219.

———. *Race and the Education of Desire: Foucault's History of Sexuality and the Colonial Order of Things*. Durham: Duke University Press, 1995.

———. "Racial Histories and Their Regimes of Truth." *Political Power and Social Theory* 11, no. 1 (1997): 183–206.

Stoler, Ann Laura, and David Bond. "Refractions off Empire: Untimely Comparisons in Harsh Times." *Radical History Review* 95 (Spring 2006): 93–107.

Strathern, Marilyn. *The Gender of the Gift: Problems with Women and Problems with Society in Melanesia*. Berkeley: University of California Press, 1990.

Sturken, Marita. *Tangled Memories: The Vietnam War, the AIDS Epidemic, and the Politics of Remembering*. Berkeley: University of California Press, 1997.

Tabia, Ruby C. *American Pietas: Visions of Race, Death, and the Maternal*. Minneapolis: University of Minnesota Press, 2011.

Tagg, John. *The Burden of Representation: Essays on Photographies and Histories*. Minneapolis: University of Minnesota Press, 1993.

Tai, Hue-Tam Ho, ed. *The Country of Memory: Remaking the Past in Late Socialist Vietnam*. Berkeley: University of California Press, 2001.

———. "Faces of Remembrance and Forgetting." In *The Country of Memory: Remaking the Past in Late Socialist Vietnam*, edited by Hue-Tam Ho Tai, 167–95. Berkeley: University of California Press, 2001.

———. *Radicalism and the Origins of the Vietnamese Revolution*. Cambridge: Harvard University Press, 1992.

Tang, Eric. "Collateral Damage: Southeast Asian Poverty in the United States." *Social Text* 18, no. 1 (2000): 55–79.

Terry, Jennifer. "Killer Entertainments: Author's Statement." *Vectors* 3, no. 1 (2007), http://vectors.usc.edu/.

Thomson, Rosemarie Garland. *Freakery: Cultural Spectacles of the Extraordinary Body*. New York: New York University Press, 1996.

Thúy Nga. *Paris by Night 77, 30 năm viễn xú, 1975–2005*. DVD. Directed by Michael Watt. Westminster, Calif.: Thúy Nga, 2005.

Tollefson, James W. *Alien Winds: The Reeducation of America's Indochinese Refugees*. New York: Praeger, 1989.

Tölölyan, Khaching. "The Nation-State and Its Others: In Lieu of a Preface." *Diaspora* 1, no. 1 (Spring 1991): 3–7.

Tran, Ham. *Journey from the Fall*. DVD. Directed by Ham Tran. United States: ImaginAsian Pictures and Lam Nguyen Productions, 2007.

Trask, David. "The Indian Wars and the Vietnam War." In *America's Wars in Asia: A Cultural Approach to History and Memory*, edited by Phillip West, Steven Levine, and Jackie Hiltz, 254–62. Armonk, N.Y.: Sharpe, 1998.

Trinh, T. Minh-ha. *When the Moon Waxes Red: Representation, Gender and Cultural Politics*. New York: Routledge, 1991.

———. *Woman, Native, Other: Writing Postcoloniality and Feminism*. Bloomington: Indiana University Press, 1989.

Turim, Maureen. *Flashbacks in Film: Memory and History*. New York: Routledge, 1989.

United Nations General Assembly. "Universal Declaration of Human Rights." 1948. http://www.un.org/en/documents/udhr/.

United Nations High Commission on Refugees. "UNHCR Global Report 2010." Geneva: United Nations High Commission on Refugees, 2010, http://www.unhcr.org/gr10/index.html#/home.

United States. Department of Health and Human Services. "Mental Health Care for Asian Americans and Pacific Islanders." In *Mental Health: Culture, Race, and Ethnicity: A Supplement to Mental Health: A Report of the Surgeon*

General*, chapter 5. Rockville, Md.: Substance Abuse and Mental Health Services Administration, 2001, http://www.ncbi.nlm.nih.gov/books/NBK 44245/.

United States. Department of State. "The Position of the United States with Respect to Asia, NC-48/2," December 30, 1949. In *United States Department of State, Foreign Relations of the United States, 1949*, 1215–20. Washington, D.C.: Government Printing Office, 1983.

———. "Statement of U.S. Policy toward Indochina, 1948." In *Major Problems in the History of the Vietnam War: Documents and Essays*, edited by Robert J. McMahon, 75–78. 2nd ed. Lexington, Mass.: D.C. Heath and Company, 1995.

United States National Security Council. "NSC 68: United States Objectives and Programs for National Security." 1950. Reprinted in *American Cold War Strategy: Interpreting NSC 68*, edited by Ernest R. May, 23–82. Boston: Bedford Books of St. Martin's Press, 1993.

VanDeMark, Brian. "To Avoid a Defeat." In *Major Problems in the History of the Vietnam War: Documents and Essays*, edited by Robert J. McMahon, 231–42. 2nd ed. Lexington, Mass.: D. C. Heath and Company, 1995.

Vang, Ma. "The Refugee Soldier: A Critique of Recognition and Citizenship in the Hmong Veterans' Naturalization Act of 1997." In "Southeast Asians in the Diaspora," edited by Fiona I. B. Ngô, Mimi Thi Nguyen, and Mariam Beevi Lam, special issue. *positions* 20, no. 3 (Winter 2012).

Virilio, Paul. *War and Cinema: The Logistics of Perception*. New York: Verso, 2009.

Volpp, Leti. "Blaming Culture for Bad Behavior." *Yale Journal of Law and the Humanities* 12, no. 1 (2000): 86–116.

———. "The Citizen and the Terrorist." *UCLA Law Review* 49 (June 2002): 1575–600.

Von Eschen, Penny M. "Who's the Real Ambassador? Exploding the Cold War Racial Ideology." In *Cold War Constructions: The Political Culture of United States Imperialism, 1945–1966*, edited by Christian G. Appy, 110–32. Amherst: University of Massachusetts Press 2000.

Waldron, Jeremy. "Security and Liberty: The Image of Balance." *Journal of Political Philosophy* 11, no. 2 (2003): 191–210.

Wark, McKenzie. "Fresh Maimed Babies: The Uses of Innocence." *Transition* 65 (1995): 36–47.

Warner, Michael, ed. *Fear of a Queer Planet: Queer Politics and Social Theory*. Minneapolis: University of Minnesota Press, 1993.

———. "What Like a Bullet Can Undeceive?" *Public Culture* 15, no. 1 (2003): 41–54.

Watney, Simon. "Photography and AIDS." In *The Critical Image: Essays on Contemporary Photography*, edited by Carol Squiers, 173–92. Seattle: Bay Press, 1990.

Weizman, Eyal. "Thanato-tactics." In *Beyond Biopolitics: Essays on the Governance of Life and Death*, edited by Patricia Ticineto Clough and Craig Willse, 177–212. Durham: Duke University Press, 2011.

Wells, Liz. "Case Study: Image Analysis; The Example of the Migrant Mother." In *Photography: A Critical Introduction*, edited by Liz Wells, 37–48. New York: Routledge, 1996.

Weston, Kath. "Do Clothes Make the Woman? Gender, Performance Theory, and Lesbian Eroticism." *Genders* 17 (1993): 1–21.

White House. *The National Security Strategy*. Washington, D.C.: White House, September 2002, http://georgewbush-whitehouse.archives.gov/nsc/nss/2002/index.html.

Wiegman, Robyn, ed. *Women's Studies on Its Own*. Durham: Duke University Press, 2002.

Will, George. "Anh Duong, Out of Debt." *Newsweek*, December 17, 2007, 84.

Williams, Patrick, and Laura Chrisman, eds. *Colonial Discourse and Postcolonial Theory: A Reader*. New York: Columbia University Press, 1994.

Williams, Raymond. *Marxism and Literature*. Oxford: Oxford University Press, 1977.

Wong, Sau-Ling Cynthia. "Denationalization Reconsidered: Asian American Cultural Criticism at a Theoretical Crossroads." *Amerasia Journal* 21, nos. 1–2 (1995): 1–27.

——. "Diverted Mothering: Representations of Caregivers of Color in the Age of Multiculturalism." In *Mothering: Ideology, Experience, Agency*, edited by Evelyn Nakano Glenn, Grace Chang, and Linda Rennie Forcey, 67–93. New York: Routledge, 1994.

Yang, Hyunah. "Revisiting the Issue of Korean 'Military Comfort Women': The Question of Truth and Positionality." *positions* 5 (Spring 1997): 51–72.

Yoneyama, Lisa. "Traveling Memories, Contagious Justice: Americanization of Japanese War Crimes at the End of the Post-Cold War." *Journal of Asian American Studies* 6, no. 1 (2003): 57–93.

Yoshihara, Mari. *Embracing the East: White Women and American Orientalism*. New York: Oxford University Press, 2003.

Young, Allan. *The Harmony of Illusions: Inventing Post-Traumatic Stress Disorder*. Princeton: Princeton University Press, 1995.

——. "The Self-Traumatized Perpetrator as a 'Transient Mental Illness.'" *L'Evolution Psychiatrique* 67, no. 4 (2002): 630–50.

Young, Sandra. "Narrative and Healing in the Hearings of the South African Truth and Reconciliation Commission." *Biography* 27, no. 1 (2004): 145–62.

Yuval-Davis, Nira, and Floya Anthias, eds. *Woman-Nation-State*. London: Macmillan, 1989.

INDEX

abnormality, of refugee, 54–55, 57–58
Abnormal lecture collection (Foucault), 54
Abu Ghraib, 138–39, 227 n. 18
Abu-Lughod, Lila, 15
accident, violence of war as, 88–89
affectability, 62–63
Afghanistan: bunker-busting weapon use in, 170; invasion of, 136; refugees of, xii; Southeast Asian wars, comparison to, 29, 137, 235–36 n. 145
Agamben, Giorgio: on bare life, 14, 195 n. 71; on indistinction between liberal war and liberal peace, xi, 191 n. 4; on refugee, 25; on state of exception, 165
Agent Orange. *See* napalm bombing
Ahmed, Sara: on adjustment, 129; on caricatures of Allah, 232 n. 76; on confessional performances, 122; on giving and taking of empire, 131; on insecurity of threat, 158; on virtue of suffering, 118
Amerasian Homecoming Act (1987), 204–5 n. 65
Amerasian Immigration Act (1982), 204–5 n. 65
American exceptionalism, 229 n. 34
American flags: as post-9/11 statement of allegiance, 154; POW flag, 199 n. 90

American Vietnamese Republican Assembly of Orange County, 228 n. 25
Anh Duong, Nguyet: on biometrics systems use; 174–75; on categorization of life; 172–73; media features of, 235 n. 130; motherhood and weapons production and, 176–77; on motive of thanksgiving, 171–72; on support of weapons escalation and proliferation, 170–71
Archeology of Knowledge (Foucault), 95
archive: continuous history and, 31–32, 95–96; critique of, 31–32, 124–30; and forgetting, 199 n. 92; as salvage, 94
Asia: child as metaphor for, 44; position of, in global conflict of communism, 37
asylum: global laws, 58–59; U.S. policies, 197–98 n. 78, 209 n. 109, 228–29 n. 28. *See also* hospitality; refugee
Authorization for Use of Military Force Against Terrorists Act, x
Axis of Evil, proposed inclusion of Viet Nam, 139, 227–28 n. 23

beauty: biopower of, 97, 216 n. 63; conceptions of, 99, 105–6, 109; femininity and, 100; in relation to pain, 98–99; as social good, 217–18 n. 90; as subjectivization, 96–98; as transformative power, 107–8

crime against humanity, 118

Crimes of Honor (Saywell film), 222 n. 149

Crip Theory (McRuer), 210 n. 123

Critique of Postcolonial Reason, A (Spivak), 193 n. 31

Cuba: depiction of femininity in, 218 n. 92; tropicalization of, 107; U.S. refugee policy and, 198 n. 78

cycle of violence, 63–64

diaspora, 198 n. 80

debt: freedom, as value of, 19, 20; in Indochina policy, 49; as modern humanist forgetting, 181–82

democracy: as colonial discourse, 50–51; compared to communism, 2, 40–41; "democracy to come," 182; as developmental discourse, 12–13; freedom and, 19–21; institutional structures for, 45, 47–50; Iraq and, 136–37, 227 n. 17; Islam as other to, 136, 162; Kantian view of, 39; supplement to, 49–50; time of democracy as, 33–34; universal premise of, xi, 11, 229 n. 34; Viet Nam and, 36–37, 47, 146; war and, xi–xii, 36–37. *See also* transition

deportation agreements, 63, 159

Derrida, Jacques: on archival amnesia, 199 n. 92; on forgiveness, 118–19; gift of freedom definition and, 6, 7–8, 193 n. 20, 195 n. 64; on hospitality, 36, 70–71

detention camps: under National Defense Authorization Act (2012), 10; during World War II and Korean War, 231–32 n. 66

Diagnostic and Statistical Manual of Mental Disorders, 113

Diem, Ngo Dinh, 37, 49, 203 n. 51; Buddhist monks' protest against, 205 n. 79

Dinh, Viet D.: on exclusion from human rights, 160; *Hyphen* critique of, 155–56; "Nationalism in an Age of Terror" lecture, 163–65; as successful "American Story," 160–61, 234 n. 105

disability theory, 64. *See also* rehabilitation

domino theory, 40, 201 n. 21; in Arab Spring explanation, 227 n. 17

empire, freedom as consequence of, 3–4

Explosions in the Sky (Truong), 183–88

femininity: androgyny and, 107; among anticommunist Chilean women, 217 n. 82; beauty and, 100; in communist Viet Nam, 105–6

forgiveness: Arendt on forgiveness as moral obligation, 86–87, 117–18; historical finality and, 118–19; as impossible, 71, 118–19; intersubjectivity and, 118; state reconciliation and, 84, 118–19, 121–22; uses of, 121–23, 126

Foucault, Michel: on abnormal individual, 54; on biopower, 38–39, 72, 89, 133, 134, 141, 148–49; *Birth of Biopolitics* lectures, 9–10, 20; on the condition of the refugee, 55, 56–57; on freedom, 6–7, 9–10, 18, 38; on governmentality, 11, 47, 48; on liberal humanism, 95; on liberalism, 9–10, 20–21, 159, 160; on race war, 30, 128, 151; on racism, 148–49; on security and sovereignty, 157–58, 169; theories of power, 3; 233 n. 94

four-point program (of Truman), 12–13

freedom: conceptual complexity of, 9–12; dual character of, 5, 6–7, 26–27; heritage and, 144–47, 154–55;

freedom (*cont.*)
injurious properties of, 15–16; as property or self-possession, 10–11, 59; and security, 156–59; time consciousness of, 33–34; Universal Declaration of Human Rights codification and, 39–40. *See also* gift of freedom

French empire: American support of, 192 n. 6; defeat of, 36–37; Dien Bien Phu ordinance explosion, 183–85; domino theory to explain, 40, 201 n. 21

Freud, Sigmund, 60, 207

gang violence, 63, 209 n. 109

Geneva Agreements (1954), 36–37, 48

Ghostly Matters (Gordon), 179

gift: aporia of giving, 7–8, 195 n. 64; exchange, economy, and, 6, 7–8; gesture of giving, 8, 29–30; giver and recipient, 7–8, 88, 181; gracious gift-giving, 195 n. 64; the impossible, giving as, 71, 118–19; reciprocity and, 7, 135–36, 169; of time, 8, 9, 181–82

gift of freedom: calculation and the incalculable, 171–72; critique of, 3–4; debt and, 19–21; definition of, 6–8, 12, 193 n. 20, 195 n. 64; exchange and expenditure for, 21, 112, 169–70; the impossibility or imposition of, 71, 118–19; manumission as, 18; modes of functioning and, 8–9; reciprocity for, 135; responsibility for, 20–21, 22, 141–42, 146–47; subject in, 51–52; temporality of, 33–34, 45; time of, 19–20, 50–51, 166–68; war as, 141–42, 169–70

girl in the photograph, the. *See* Kim Phúc, Phan Thi

Girl in the Picture, The (Chong), 92; alienations of Kim Phúc in, 101–2;

Cuban femininity depicted in, 107, 218 n. 92; reunion with benefactors, 222 nn. 151–52; Ut and Kretz compared, 217 n. 88

gook, 149–53, 231 n. 56

governmentality, 47; security as component of, 157; in vitalizing sovereign power, 48

grace. *See* gift

Greece, U.S. support of, during Cold War, 36–37

Green Dragon (Bui and Bui), 27, 34–35, 199 n. 84; as camp commemoration, 79–80; death, interpretation of, 80–82; freedom abstracted in, 77–79; referential claims, 66; refugee condition in, 67–70; rehabilitation structures in, 72–73, 75–77

guilt: confession of, 116–18; as expression of trauma, 221 n. 140; and forgiveness, 4, 116–19; and reconciliation, 84, 225 n. 178; and responsibility, 221 n. 140

Gulf War. *See* Iraq War

historical time and historicism, 41–42

history, continuous, 31–32, 95–96

Hi-Tek protests, 56, 205–6 n. 81

Hmong refugees, 121–22

Ho Chi Minh: racial caricature of, 151, 205 n. 78; refugee protests against, 208–9 n. 108

homeland security, xi, 167, 180

homonationalism, 154

hospitality: aporia of, 7–8, 70–71; host and, 70–71; refugee camp as, 27, 70–72; the stranger and, 135–36, 165–66

hostage situation, in Sacramento Good Guys store, 63–64

human freedom, 42–43

humanism: through the archive, 93; and continuous history, 31–32, 95–96 human rights: commodification of, 194–95 n. 59; vs. communism, 146; and democracy, 13–14; in U.S. economic and foreign policy, 197–98 n. 78. *See also* Universal Declaration of Human Rights (1948)

Hyphen critique, of Viet D. Dinh, 155–56

Immigration and Nationality Act (1965), 204–5 n. 65
imperial formation, 5, 193 n. 14
In America: The Vietnamese Story, 146–47
Indian country, Viet Nam as, 89
Indochina: sovereignty of, 36–37; U.S. policy toward, 46–47, 49, 53
Indochina Migration and Refugee Assistance Act (1975), 23–24, 74, 204–5 n. 65
Indochinese Hopkins Symptom Checklist Depression Subscale, 74
Indochinese Refugee Program, 75
International Catholic Migration Commission, 74
interrogation techniques, 138–39, 227 n. 18
Iraq War: Arab Spring and, 138, 227 n. 17; avowed purpose of invasion, 136; presidential speeches and, ix–x, 51, 133, 136–37; refugee soldier support of, 141–42; reparation payments by Iraq, 235 n. 126; Viet Nam War analogies to, 138–40, 235 n. 128. *See also* Operation Iraqi Freedom
Israeli state: criminalizing of boycott calls, 234 n. 107; on Palestinian refugee settlements, 162

Japanese Americans: apologies to, 121–22; in internment camps, 160, 196, 231–32 n. 66
Japanese military, use of Korean comfort women, 223 n. 160

Kansas Veterans Memorial Park, 203–4 n. 61
Kennedy, John F.: commitment to freedom, 44; pledge to decolonizing world, 37
Kim Phúc, Phan Thi, 83–84; femininity of, 107, 215–16 nn. 55–56, 216 n. 70; *Life* magazine story on, 101; *Los Angeles Times Magazine* feature, 96–97; moral power of, 118, 120, 127, 216 n. 68; *The Oprah Winfrey Show* appearance, 123, 124–25; religiosity of, 217–18 n. 90, 224 n. 175; Veterans Day speech and, 84, 110–11, 212–13 n. 4, 218 n. 102
Kim's Story: The Road from Vietnam (Saywell), 119–21
Korean War, 231–32 n. 66
Kretz, Perry: anticommunist charges by, 105–6; comparison to Ut, 21

Lai, Madalenna, 1–2, 5
liberal empire: biopolitical commitment of, to life, 175–76; debate on benevolence of, 3, 192 n. 6, 200–201 n. 11; exceptionalism of, xi–xii; privileging of transition, 38–39; rationale for governance, 14–15
liberalism: colonialism vs., 37–38; culture of danger in, 159–61; freedom as political reference in, 9–11; observer and observed vulnerability, 92–93
liberalist alibi, of multiculturalism, 153
liberal war: biopower in, 173–74; gift of freedom as, xi–xii, 3–4, 192 n. 7; under neoliberalism, 29–30; as regeneration of race, 177–78; as shared ordeal between perpetrator and victim, 110–20; as tactic, 48–49
Little Saigon ethnic neighborhoods, 207 n. 101

Loc, Nam, 68, 210 n. 12

Patriot Act (2001), 134; acronym, 226 n. 1; expansion of police powers under, 166–67; preamble, 153; preemptive practices, 159

patriotism and nationalism, 164–65; performance of, after 9/11, 154. *See also* refugee patriot

peace: Kant and "perpetual peace," 39, 49; Universal Declaration of Human Rights codification of, 39

Personal Responsibility and Work Opportunity Reconciliation Act (1966), 73

the Philippines, Indochina comparison to, 200 n. 11

photography: gaze of the other through, 29, 91–92, 196 n. 73; intersubjectivity and recognition, 94; "shudder" in, 85, 91, 93; subjectification and, 94; in world as target, 98–99

photojournalism: documentation of war, 84–85; humanist genre of, 196 n. 73; iconic images, 215 n. 47; as racial death depiction, 89–90. *See also* Kim Phúc, Phan Thi

Plummer, John, 116–18, 127, 131, 221 n. 140; faith of, 220 n. 134, 221 n. 138, 221–22 n. 148

Position of the United States with Respect to Asia Report, The, 44

post-traumatic stress disorder, 57; desubjectifying experience of, 117; diagnostic category of, 113; political usefulness of, 114–16

Powell, Colin, 147

POW flag, 199 n. 90

property: hospitality dependent on, 70–71; human freedom as, 9–11, 39, 59; refugees' lack of, 59, 206–7 n. 93; as secret to success, 77–78; and self-possession, 3, 10–11, 18–19

Provincializing Europe (Chakrabarty), 41–42

Provisional Government of Free Viet Nam, 212 n. 159, 228 n. 25

psychometric measures, 73–74

race: description of, 231 n. 50; Foucault on, 128, 148–49, 151; legitimate violence and, 175–76; multiculturalism and, 135, 142–43, 149; racial typology and racial difference, 89, 115, 149–53, 231 n. 56; and subrace, 148; as visual, 151–52

race war, 30, 128, 151

racial antipathy, 99

racial death, 14; in war imagery, 89

racial liberalism, 142–43, 153; as American exceptionalism, 229 n. 34; reconciliation as indicator of, 225 n. 178

racism: as biopolitics of disposability, 89; Foucauldian view of, 148–49; gook epithet and, 149–53; state racism, 119, 173

Rape: A Crime of War (Saywell film), 222 n. 149

reason, sovereign: irrationality and, 54–57; as self-possession, 10–11, 59

recognition: of gift, 7–8, 193 n. 20; intersubjectivity and, 94, 124; reciprocal, 92–93

refugee: affectability, 62–63; asylum-granting policies, 197–98 n. 78; dynamic between terrorist and, 161–64; evacuation of, 23–24, 204 n. 64; historicist assessment of, 61, 207 n. 102; occupation as adjustment tool, 21 n. 144; psychological health of, as threat, 63, 162; UN definition of, 58, 206 n. 86; as welfare recipient, 211 n. 150; as without property, 59, 206–7 n. 93. *See* refugee illness

state: failed states, 175; liberal states, 163, 175; rogue states, 138, 139–40; sovereignty and, 163–65; totalitarian states, 40, 45, 197–98 n. 78

statelessness, 58, 60; medical/psychopathological analogies, 64–65

state power, modern forms of, 46

Stoler, Ann Laura: critique of historiographies of racism and, 229 n. 37; on imperial formations, 193 n. 14; on racial thinking, 151; transition requirements and, 45; on untimely comparison of wars, 135, 139

Strategic Hamlet Program, 48

subject, modern, 93; individuality of, 18; self-possession as, 59

subjection, gift's power of, 8–9

subjectivity, 27

subjectivization: beauty as, 96–98, 100, 108–9; giving as, 7–8; receiving as, 17–18

subjectlessness, 57–58, 199 n. 86

Task Force New Arrivals, 75

terrorist: dynamic between refugee and, 161–62; pathology of, 162–63; as racial other, 163–64

Tet Offensive, 205 n. 79

Thao, Bui Thanh, 141–42

time: anachronism and, 16–17; denial of coevalness, 16, 42, 64; and futurity, 19, 20, 159, 173–75; gift of, 6, 7–8, 41–42, 43–45, 77–79; gift giving and, 7–8; liberal concepts of, 9; metaphysics of presence and passage through, 23–25; reason, irrationality, and, 54–57

time-as-space, trope of colonialism, 16

totalitarianism: as communism, 40; compared to liberal democracy, 45–46, 175–76; danger of, 40; genocide

and, 175; political refugees and, 197–98 n. 79

trace, 18–19; of modern humanist forgetting, 181. *See also* debt; photography

transition: distinctiveness of, 43, 45; and gift of freedom, 43–45; as interval, 35, 39, 45; occupation, x–xii; timing of, xi–xii, 35, 38–39, 43; Vietnamization, 49–50

transnational America, 135

transnationality concept, 198 n. 80

transnational multiculturalism, 24; as geopolitical instrument, 164, 229 n. 32; as liberalist alibi, 153; multidimensionality of race in, 149; overview of, 142–43; as security measure, 154

trauma, 57, 207 n. 96; analogies for, 60; of colonized persons, 207 n. 98; critique of diagnosis, 114–16; invention of diagnosis, 113–14; of Palestinian refugees, 220 n. 129; witnessing and perpetrating as, 111–18. *See also* refugee illness

Truman, Harry: four-point program, 12–13; Truman Doctrine, 21, 36

Truong, Hong-An, 183–88

Turkey, U.S. support during Cold War, 36–37

United Nations Charter (Article 51), 138

United Nations Convention and Protocol Relating to the Status of Refugees (1951), 58, 206 n. 86

United Nations Convention on Certain Conventional Weapons (1980), 213–14 n, 20

United States Objectives and Programs for National Security. *See* National Security Council Report (NSC) 68

Universal Declaration of Human Rights (1948), 22–23, 39–40; crime against humanity concept, 118; early opposition to, 198 n. 78

USA Patriot Act (2001). *See* Patriot Act (2001)

U.S. troop withdrawal, from Iraq, x

Ut, Huynh Cong Nick: comparison to Perry Kretz, 217 n. 88; Phan Thi Kim Phúc photograph, 83; refugee photography description by, 196 n. 73

Veterans Day commemoration (1996): Norm McDaniel statement, 219 n. 108; Phan Thi Kim Phuc at, 84, 110–11, 212–13 n. 4, 218 n. 102

Veterans' memorials: opposition to South Vietnamese veterans in, 203–4 n. 61; Vietnam Veterans Memorial in Washington, D.C., 112, 199 n. 90, 212 n. 3

Viet Cong: civilian deaths counted as, 214 n. 22; indiscriminate killing by, 172–73

Viet Nam (South): as anachronistic, 63–64, 217–18 n. 90; nation building in, 49; as "new friend of freedom," 44, 45, 48–51; as potential rogue nation, 139; as undemocratic, 62–63

"Vietnam, the" (interrogation pose), 138–39, 227 n. 18

Vietnam Center and Archive, 152

Vietnamese American eXposure (vax), 56

Vietnamese American literature, 196–97 n. 74

Vietnamese American Public Affairs Committee, 144

Vietnamese Depression Scale, 74

Vietnamese flag resolutions, 144–48

Vietnam Freedom March, 142

Vietnamization, 49–50, 203 n. 57

Vietnam syndrome, 57, 112

Vietnam veterans: collective guilt, 221 n. 140; as discriminated against, 112; and posttraumatic stress disorder, 113–14, 117; War Memorial in Washington, D.C., 112, 199 n. 90, 212 n. 3; as war victims, 113–14

Viet Nam War: Mai Lai massacre, 173; refugee arrival in the U.S., 23–24, 195–96 n. 72; refugee stories, 1–2, 4–5, 152; South Vietnamese experiment, 37; Strategic Hamlet Program, 48; Tet Offensive, 205 n. 79

Viet Weekly, protests against, 208–9 n. 108

violence: cycle of, 63, 209 n. 110; epistemic, 65, 154–55; and freedom, 2–4, 20–21; of giving, 7–8; indiscriminate, 161–62, 172–74; race war and, 30; rational, 173–75

visual imagery of war. *See* photojournalism; napalm bombing

Wain, Christopher, 222 n. 151

war. *See* liberal war

Washington Post, editorial on Viet Nam War, 51, 122

weapons: escalation and proliferation as deterrence, 170–73; racial differentiation systems, 173–74; thermobaric weaponry, 170. *See also* napalm bombing

Westmoreland, William, 89

whiteness, ascendance of, 149

witnessing: liberal subjectivity and, 94, 121–22; pain of, 111–13; photography as, 92–94; "shudder" in, 29, 85, 86–87, 91–92, 99, 205 n. 79

World War II, detention camps, 231–32 n. 66

zone of indistinction, xi, 191 n. 4

MIMI THI NGUYEN is an assistant professor of
gender and women's studies and Asian American
studies at the University of Illinois, Urbana-
Champaign. She is the editor (with Thuy Linh
Nguyen Tu) of *Alien Encounters: Popular Culture
in Asian America* (Duke, 2007).

Library of Congress Cataloging-in-Publication Data
Nguyen, Mimi Thi
The gift of freedom : war, debt, and other refugee pas-
sages / Mimi Thi Nguyen.
p. cm. — (Next wave: new directions in women's studies)
Includes bibliographical references and index.
ISBN 978-0-8223-5222-8 (cloth : alk. paper)
ISBN 978-0-8223-5239-6 (pbk. : alk. paper)
1. Refugees—United States. 2. Ideology—United States.
3. United States—Foreign relations. 4. Liberty.
I. Title. II. Series: Next wave.
HV640.4.U54N48 2012
323.0973—dc23
2011053304

.